State Sponsored Cyber Surveillance

*To my daughter, Elizka Jadwiga Watt*

# State Sponsored Cyber Surveillance

## The Right to Privacy of Communications and International Law

Eliza Watt

*Lecturer in Law, School of Law, Middlesex University, London, UK*

Edward Elgar
PUBLISHING

Cheltenham, UK • Northampton, MA, USA

Published by
Edward Elgar Publishing Limited
The Lypiatts
15 Lansdown Road
Cheltenham
Glos GL50 2JA
UK

Edward Elgar Publishing, Inc.
William Pratt House
9 Dewey Court
Northampton
Massachusetts 01060
USA

A catalogue record for this book
is available from the British Library

Library of Congress Control Number: 2021932266

This book is available electronically in the **Elgar**online
Law subject collection
http://dx.doi.org/10.4337/9781789900101

ISBN 978 1 78990 009 5 (cased)
ISBN 978 1 78990 010 1 (eBook)

Printed and bound in Great Britain by TJ Books Limited, Padstow, Cornwall

# Contents

# Acknowledgements

It is my great pleasure to thank Professor Marco Roscini for his support and sharing of his expertise, which helped to bring this book to fruition. I am also grateful to him for reviewing and providing invaluable comments and guidance on a number of the chapters. Equally, I am immensely indebted to Dr Russell Buchan, who offered critical insights and guidance on numerous aspects of the manuscript and supported the project from the outset.

I am thankful to Ben Booth, senior commissioning editor at Edward Elgar Publishing, for his kindness, professionalism and understanding throughout the entire undertaking. My gratitude also goes to the editorial and production staff, including Carolyn Boyle, Natasha Rozenberg and Stephanie Mills.

On a personal level, my deepest regards and gratitude go to my husband, Dr John H Watt, for his commitment and unwavering support throughout my education and during the process of this project's completion. I would also like to thank a dear friend, Professor Aftab Khan of Leicester University, for being most extraordinary in relation to a whole host of personal matters. Last but not least, my mother Jadwiga, sister Agnieszka and two brothers, Rafał and Bogumił, have provided much-needed encouragement and have been pillars of strength during the completion of this book, for which I shall be always grateful. Finally, I dedicate this book to my daughter Elizka, for the love and happiness that she has brought to my life.

# Abbreviations

| | |
|---|---|
| ACHR | American Convention on Human Rights |
| ACLU | American Civil Liberties Union |
| ADHR | American Declaration of the Rights and Duties of Man |
| AG | Attorney General |
| AI | Artificial intelligence |
| ASR | Articles on State Responsibility |
| BCD | Bulk Communication Datasets |
| BND | Federal Intelligence Service Act |
| BPD | Bulk personal datasets |
| CCDCOE | NATO Cooperative Cyber Defence Centre of Excellence |
| CCPA | California Consumer Privacy Act |
| CJEU | Court of Justice of the European Union |
| CoE | Council of Europe |
| Covid-19 | Coronavirus |
| CSP | Communication Service Providers |
| CVA | Coronavirus Act |
| DNI | Director of National Intelligence |
| DoD | Department of Defense |
| DRD | Data Retention Directive |
| DRIPA | Data Retention and Investigatory Powers Act |
| DSL | Data Security Law |
| ECHR | European Convention on Human Rights |
| ECtHR | European Court of Human Rights |
| EEA | Economic Espionage Act |
| EFF | Electronic Frontier Foundation |
| EO | Executive Order |

| EU | European Union |
|---|---|
| FBI | Federal Bureau of Investigation |
| FISA/FAA | Foreign Intelligence Surveillance Act/FISA Amendment Act |
| FISA ARA | FISA Reauthorization Act |
| FISC | Foreign Intelligence Surveillance Court |
| FSB | Federal Security Service |
| GC | Grand Chamber |
| GCHQ | Government Communications Headquarters |
| GDPR | General Data Protection Regulation |
| GGE | UN Group of Government Experts |
| GRU | General Staff Main Intelligence Directorate |
| HRA | Human Rights Act |
| HRC | Human Rights Committee |
| HUMINT | Human intelligence |
| IACHR | Inter-American Commission on Human Rights |
| IACtHR | Inter-American Court of Human Rights |
| ICANN | Internet Corporation for Assigned Names and Numbers |
| ICCPR | International Covenant on Civil and Political Rights |
| ICESCR | International Covenant on Economic Social and Cultural Rights |
| ICJ | International Court of Justice |
| ICT | Information and communications technologies |
| IDAA | International Data Access Authority |
| IDAW | International Data Access Warrant |
| ILC | International Law Commission |
| IoT | Internet of Things |
| IPA | Investigatory Powers Act |
| IPT | Investigatory Powers Tribunal |
| ISP | Internet service provider |
| MI5 | Military Intelligence Section 5 |
| MLAT | Mutual Legal Assistance Treaty |
| NGO | Non-governmental organization |

| NPO | New Policy Opinion |
| NSA | National Security Agency |
| OAS | Organization of American States |
| ODNI | Office of the Director of National Intelligence |
| OEWG | UN Open-Ended Working Group on Developments in ICTs in the Context of International Security |
| OHCHR | Office of the High Commissioner for Human Rights |
| OSA | Official Secrets Act |
| PA | Patriot Act |
| PCIJ | Permanent Court of International Justice |
| RIPA | Regulation of Investigatory Powers Act |
| SC | Supreme Court |
| SCA | Stored Communications Act |
| SCO | Shanghai Cooperation Organization |
| SIA | Swedish Intelligence Act |
| SICJ | Statute of the International Court of Justice |
| SIGINT | Signals intelligence |
| UDHR | Universal Declaration of Human Rights |
| UN | United Nations |
| UNGA | United Nations General Assembly |
| UNODA | United Nations Office for Disarmament Affairs |
| VCLT | Vienna Convention on the Law of Treaties |

# 1. Introduction: the surveillance, security and privacy paradox

## 1. INTRODUCTION

In his dystopian novel *Nineteen Eighty-Four*,[1] published in 1949, George Orwell predicted a world in which the ruling class was in almost complete control of information and expression. The book epitomized political oppression and influenced millions, with phrases such as 'Big Brother' and 'doublethink' becoming synonymous with totalitarianism, the surveillance state and the power of mass media to manipulate public opinion, to rewrite history and even the truth.[2] Seven decades later, the world of fiction so vividly portrayed by Orwell seems to have become an all-pervasive reality in most societies, including liberal democracies, dominated by cyber technologies exploited by government and non-government actors alike. This to a large extent is the result of the 'digital revolution' of the late twentieth and early twenty-first centuries, which has profoundly affected almost every aspect of human activity, allowing for information exchange, access and sharing at heretofore unprecedented scale and speed. The birth of the Internet in particular has altered practically beyond recognition the manner in which individuals around the globe conduct their work-related, social and consumer activities, together with how they interact with public services and institutions. These seemingly irreversible changes in communications have been accompanied by significant advances in states' intelligence-gathering[3] activities.

---

[1]   George Orwell, *Nineteen Eighty-Four* (Penguin Books, 1949).
[2]   Jonathan Freeland, '1984 by George Orwell, Book of a Lifetime: An Absorbing, Deeply Affecting Political Thriller', *The Independent* (2 July 2015).
[3]   US Department of Defense (DoD), *Dictionary of Military and Associated Terms* (as of June 2020) 107 ('US DoD *Dictionary*'). The US DoD defines 'intelligence' as: '(1) the product resulting from the collection, processing, integration evaluation, analysis, and interception of available information concerning foreign nations, hostile or potentially hostile forces or elements or areas of actual or potential operations; (2) the activities that result in the product; (3) the organizations engaged in such activities.'

The origins of collecting signals intelligence (SIGINT)[4] can be traced to the advent of the telegraph. Developed in the 1830s and 1840s by Samuel Morse, among others, the telegraph revolutionized long-distance communications by transmitting electronic signals over a wire laid between stations.[5] Telegraphic transmissions became recognized as public property and thus, once they entered the public domain, were perceived as open and available for anyone to detect and collect.[6] Today, SIGINT forms a vital part of states' foreign policy decision making. Indeed, as acknowledged by the United States' (US) Central Intelligence Agency (CIA): 'world leaders communicate with their people in a variety of ways. All of these forms of communication emit a signal that can be collected. The information gathered from these intercepted signals is of vital importance to national security.'[7]

In recent decades, intelligence agencies[8] around the globe have developed sophisticated methods of accumulating vast amounts of data transmitted over the Internet, the analysis of which became possible by technological advancements in algorithmic and related computer analysis. Equally, the increased capacity to store information, coupled with the decreased costs of such retention, transformed methods of data acquisition, examination and

---

[4]    'SIGINT' is 'intelligence derived from electronic signals and systems used by foreign targets, such as communication systems, radars, and weapons systems. SIGINT provides a vital window for our nation into foreign adversaries' capabilities, actions, and intentions' – see National Security Agency/Central Security Service, 'Signals Intelligence', www.nsa.gov/what-we-do/signals-intelligence.

[5]    History, 'Morse Code and the Telegraph' (6 June 2019), www.history.com/topics/inventions/telegraph.

[6]    For example, the British Government Code and Cypher School was established in 1919 and played a major role during the Second World War, when it was based at Bletchley Park. The 'ultra-intelligence' produced at Bletchley Park through regular breaking of the secret communications of the Axis Powers, especially through its Enigma and Lorenz cipher machines, possibly reduced the length of the Second World War by four years. The name of the organization was changed to Government Communications Headquarters in 1946 and it is now based in Cheltenham, Gloucestershire – see John Ferris, *Behind the Enigma: The Authorized History of GCHQ, Britain's Secret Cyber-Intelligence Agency* (Bloomsbury Publishing Plc, 2020); see also Glenn Sulmasy and John Yoo, 'Counterintuitive: Intelligence Operations and International Law' (2007) 28(3) *Michigan Journal of International Law* 625–38, 631.

[7]    US CIA, 'News and Information. INTelligence: Signals Intelligence' (30 April 2013), www.cia.gov/news-information/featured-story-archive/2010-featured-story-archive/intelligence-signals-intelligence-1.html.

[8]    US DoD *Dictionary* (n 3) 107. There is no universal definition of 'intelligence agencies'; however, the US DoD *Dictionary* refers to 'intelligence community' and defines it as '[a]ll departments or agencies of a government that are concerned with intelligence activity, either in an oversight, managerial, support, or participatory role'.

sharing. These activities became collectively known as 'mass surveillance', the ubiquity of which is usually justified by the need of states to protect themselves from internal and external threats emanating from complex forms of terrorism and serious crime. However, the indiscriminate collection and retention of enormous volumes of digital communications, foreign and domestic alike – as first exposed in 2013 by Edward Snowden – present a paradox. This is because such information may be of value to security agencies while concurrently posing a serious risk to individuals' rights – in particular, by eroding and undermining the right to privacy of communications. At the heart of this conundrum is the conviction, evidenced by the policy stance of many governments, that greater surveillance and bulk collection of communications lead to greater security.[9] However, the weakness of this argument is the danger that if there are any benefits to societies – and by extension, to the international community – in terms of safeguarding peace and security, these are inevitably outstripped by the sacrificing of individuals' fundamental rights and freedoms to achieve these goals. This creates a tension between proponents of greater securitization on the one hand and civil liberties advocates on the other.

This chapter explores this traction. It consists of eight sections. Section 2 engages with some aspects of global and national security, outlining their respective goals and identifies contemporary threats. Section 3 defines mass surveillance of communications and highlights some of the means and methods that governments deploy to assist in achieving their security goals, including the programs used and intelligence-sharing agreements among state agencies. Section 4 considers a number of challenges that this presents to the protection of human rights, focusing on the right to privacy in the digital age and discusses numerous responses to the problem in the years that followed the Snowden disclosures from the United Nations (UN) and outside of its institutions. Section 5 reviews current trends in state led mass surveillance. This is then followed by a discussion of the security, privacy and surveillance paradox in section 6. Section 7 circumscribes the books' aims, while its scope is outlined in section 8.

---

[9]    This is indicated in, for example, the statement of former UK Home Secretary Theresa May when introducing the Investigatory Powers Bill to the House of Commons in 2015 – see Matt Burgess, 'Investigatory Powers Bill: What Is It and What Does It Mean', *Wired* (4 November 2015), www.wired.co.uk/article/surveillance-bill -government-internet-history.

## 2.        SECURITY

'Security' means 'the state of being secure, especially from danger or attack'.[10] This term encompasses a plethora of meanings, including global, national, human, environmental, economic and, most recently, cyber security.[11] There is no single agreed definition, but two useful descriptions of this term are those of the Council of the European Union (EU) and the UN. Thus, according to the former, 'security' denotes 'protecting people and the values of freedom and democracy, so that everyone can enjoy the daily lives without fear';[12] while the latter sees this concept as 'the preservation of the norms, rules, institutions and values of society'.[13] Accordingly, all institutions, principles and structures associated with a society – including its people – are to be protected from 'military and non-military threats'.[14] While national security is the ability of a state to cater for the protection and defence of its citizenry,[15] global security:

> evolved from the necessity that nature and many other activities, particularly globalization, have placed on States. These are demands that no national security apparatus has the capacity to handle on its own and, as such, call for the cooperation of States.[16]

It has been suggested that the nature of the challenges to the international community is such that nations' security concerns are deeply interconnected, to the extent that one state's safety needs cannot realistically be evaluated without taking into consideration those of other countries.[17] This in turn breeds rivalry among states, which can be remedied only through their cooperation in global

---

[10]    Bryan A Garner, *Black's Law Dictionary* (West Group, 1999) 1358.

[11]    The UK National Cyber Security Centre (NCSC) states that 'cyber security' is 'how individuals and organizations reduce the risk of cyberattack. Cyber security's main function it to protect the devices we all use (smartphones, laptops, tablets and computers) and the services we access -both online and at work- from theft or damage. It's about preventing unauthorised access to the vast amounts of personal information on these devices and online' – see UK NCSC, 'What is Cyber Security?', www.ncsc.gov.uk/section/about-ncsc/what-is-cyber-security.

[12]    Council of the European Union, *Internal Security Strategy for the EU, Towards a European Security Model* (March 2010) 12.

[13]    See Samuel M Makinda, 'Sovereignty and Global Security' (1998) 29(3) *Security Dialogue* 281–92 in Segun Osisanya, 'National Security Versus Global Security', *UN Chronicle* (October 2014), https://unchronicle.un.org/article/national-security-versus-global-security.

[14]    *Ibid.*

[15]    *Ibid.*

[16]    *Ibid.*

[17]    *Ibid.*

security initiatives.[18] In short, the global character of the various security challenges requires international responses and cooperation.

States must not only identify current and future threats to national security, but also construct effective strategies to deal with them, as they are many and varied. Some of the issues that decision makers must deal with on a national level are counter-terrorism, together with serious and organized crime (such as child sexual exploitation; fraud; money laundering and other economic crimes; bribery; modern slavery and cyber crime). For example, the United Kingdom (UK) government set out in its 2010 National Security Strategy[19] 15 main security risks, of which four have been and continue to be classed as of highest priority: (1) international terrorism, including through the use of chemical, biological, radiological and nuclear materials, together with terrorism relating to Northern Ireland; (2) cyber attacks, including by other states, organized crime and terrorists; (3) international military crises between states; and (4) major accidents or natural hazards.[20] The nation's safety is a government's primary responsibility, and the potential for large-scale harm caused by hostile actions is often neither tangible nor immediate. In the UK, for example, in 2019 the terrorist threat level was described as 'large and multi-faceted' – a classification which took into account (among other acts of criminality) the 2017 London and Manchester attacks, which claimed the lives of 36 innocent people.[21] However, although the menaces to national defence are becoming more complex, unpredictable and alarming, they must be viewed in perspective. Thus, as observed by the independent reviewer of terrorist legislation, David Anderson QC, in his 2015 report *A Question of Trust*,[22] it would be a mistake to describe the current danger level as 'unprecedented', as events capable of taking life on a massive scale (eg, the Black Death)[23] are a feature of every age, while some threats will simply not be realized.[24] Therefore, although the challenges to national security must not be ignored, 'claims of

---

[18]   *Ibid.*

[19]   HM Government, *A Strong Britain in an Age of Uncertainty: The National Security Strategy* (October 2010) Cm 7953. The Strategy is updated and reviewed annually.

[20]   *Ibid* 28–31. See also HM Government, *National Security Strategy and Strategic Defence and Security Review 2015: Third Annual Review* (July 2019) para 1.8.

[21]   *Ibid* 12.

[22]   David Anderson, *A Question of Trust. Report of the Investigatory Powers Review* (June 2015) ('Anderson').

[23]   *Ibid* 39. It is estimated that the Black Death may have killed at least one-third of Europe's population in the years after 1346.

[24]   *Ibid.*

exceptional or unprecedented threat level – particularly for the purposes of curbing well-established liberties – should be approached with scepticism'.[25]

Governments respond to national security concerns through, among other means, the use of covert investigatory methods, of which the routine monitoring of electronic communications is a central and growing part.[26] These powers encompass a range of methods, such as direct and intrusive surveillance (tailing, bugging); property interference; the use of covert human intelligence; surveillance cameras; and DNA databases.[27] This spectrum of practices involves 'communications surveillance', defined as 'the monitoring, intercepting, collecting, obtaining, analysing, using, preserving, retaining, interfering with, accessing or similar actions taken with regard to information that includes, reflects, arises from or is about a person's communications in the past, present or future'.[28]

That states' investigatory powers are now routinely exercised on a previously unprecedented scale was exposed in 2013 by Edward Snowden, with the publication of documents removed from the US National Security Agency (NSA). These revealed an array of activities, including: (1) bulk interception of communications and collection of Internet and international communications data; (2) tools for advanced searching and analysis of intercepted data; (3) cooperative relationships between governments and telecommunications service providers; and (4) intelligence sharing.[29] This mass collection, retention and examination of communications contents and metadata has been the leading source of controversy ever since the Snowden disclosures and is outlined next.

## 3.    MASS SURVEILLANCE

'Mass surveillance' can be defined as the indiscriminate monitoring of the population or a significant component of a group of persons.[30] In recent decades, it has become one of the preponderant methods of intelligence col-

---

[25]   *Ibid* 40.
[26]   Office of the UN High Commissioner for Human Rights (OHCHR), 'The Right to Privacy in the Digital Age. Report of the United Nations High Commissioner for Human Rights' (30 June 2014) UN Doc A/HRC/27/37 47 ('A/HRC/27/37').
[27]   Anderson (n 22) 19.
[28]   International Principles on the Application of Human Rights to Communications Surveillance, *Necessary and Proportionate* (10 July 2013) 13 ('*Necessary and Proportionate*').
[29]   Anderson (n 22) 125.
[30]   Privacy International, *Mass Surveillance*, https://privacyinternational.org/learn/mass-surveillance#:~:text=Mass%20surveillance%20involves%20the%20acquisition,they%20are%20suspected%20of%20wrongdoing ('*Mass Surveillance*').

lection. This type of information gathering takes place without prior suspicion or a specific query and can be distinguished from targeted surveillance, which is directed towards individuals or organizations of interest.[31] In essence, mass interception of communications has a proactive element, aimed at identifying future dangers, rather than investigating known threats.[32]

As discussed in Chapter 2, there are a number of designations adopted by various UN bodies, regional institutions and courts to describe these practices, such as 'online surveillance', 'bulk interception' and 'strategic surveillance'. This book adopts the term 'mass surveillance' as an umbrella expression that encompasses general, large-scale interception and collection of communications through technical means in cyberspace.

### 3.1    Mass Surveillance: Means and Methods

The tools for conducting mass surveillance are many and varied. With advancements in digital science, they can be developed and deployed relatively quickly. This at least to some extent explains why the law (domestic and international) lags behind the rapidly developing technologies of surveillance and does not always allow for an adequate response to the resultant changes.

Broadly speaking 'digital surveillance' comprises: (1) bulk data interception – that is, the interception, collection and storage of content and metadata contained in packets that travel through several Internet exchange points (a well-known example discussed in this book is the tapping of undersea fibre-optic cables); (2) Internet communication technology monitoring, which focuses on human activity on social media platforms such as Twitter, Facebook and Instagram and peer-to-peer communications tools such as WhatsApp, analysing content (the text of the message), metadata (its time, location, duration) and network responses ('follow', 'friends', 'retweet' and 'like' patterns); (3) geolocation and remote sensing, which relate to closed-circuit television monitoring, mobile device signals and global positioning systems data; (4) biometrics, which involves the tracking of unique biometric identifiers such as facial/retinal recognition, voice recognition, skin reflection and thermograms; (5) and Internet of Things (IoT), a term that describes consumer devices that are controlled through Internet-enabled applications and allows for the collection

---

[31]    EU Agency for Fundamental Rights, 'Surveillance by Intelligence Services. Fundamental Rights Safeguards and Remedies in the EU. Volume II: Field Perspectives and Legal Update' (Luxembourg Publications Office of the EU, 2017).

[32]    Council of Europe Thematic Factsheet, *Mass Surveillance* (August 2017), https://rm.coe.int/factsheet-on-mass-surveillance-corrected-and-final-rev2august2017/1680736031.

of data on individuals' behavioural indicators, such as time spent at home or at work, speech detection, together with purchasing and consumption patterns.[33]

### 3.1.1   Bulk data interception

This book is predominantly focused on the first of the aforementioned methods of mass surveillance – that is, bulk data interception. Some of the best-known computer systems that this book makes frequent references to are PRISM[34] and Tempora,[35] the use of which was first revealed on 6 June 2013 by British newspaper *The Guardian*.[36] The allegations pertaining to the US and UK security services' use of these interception methods came to the fore following Edward Snowden's exposure of the global clandestine interception and gathering of communications conducted by the NSA and its Five Eyes partner agencies: the UK Government Communications Headquarters (GCHQ); Canada's Communications Security Establishment Canada (CSEC); Australia's Australian Signals Directorate; and New Zealand's Government Communications Security Bureau.[37] The subsequent inquiry into the extent of these practices by, among others, the Council of Europe (CoE) – published in 2015 report titled *Mass Surveillance*[38] – confirmed a 'stunning array' of means and methods of collecting, storing and sharing data by intelligence and law enforcement agencies around the globe.[39]

The report confirmed the existence in several countries of 'surveillance-industrial complex … fostered by the culture of secrecy sur-

---

[33]   Akin Üner, *Politics of Digital Surveillance, National Security and Privacy* (Centre for Economic and Foreign Policy Studies, 2018) 5–6.

[34]   Anderson (n 22) 330. Under the PRISM program, first authorized by the then US President Bush following the attacks of 11 September 2001, the NSA can collect private data such as emails, chats, videos, photos, stored date and online social networking details from servers of nine US Internet companies (the so-called 'PRISM providers'): Microsoft, Yahoo, Google, Facebook, PalTalk, AOL, Skype, YouTube and Apple.

[35]   *Ibid*. Tempora has been allegedly operated since 2011 by UK GCHQ and involves the attachment of intercept probes to transatlantic fibre-optic cables located on British soil, which carry data to Western Europe from telephone exchanges and Internet servers in North America. This provides analysts with data from all email, web and social chats.

[36]   Glen Greenwald, 'NSA Collecting Phone Records of Millions of Verizon Customers Daily', *The Guardian* (6 June 2013).

[37]   Privacy International, *Eyes Wide Open. Special Report* (26 November 2013) ('*Eyes Wide Open*').

[38]   CoE, Committee on Legal Affairs and Human Rights, 'Mass Surveillance. Explanatory Memorandum by Mr Pieter Omtzigt, Rapporteur' (26 January 2015) ('CoE Mass Surveillance Memorandum').

[39]   *Ibid*.

rounding surveillance operations [and] their highly technical character'.[40] The methods of surveillance listed by the CoE include the acquisition of internet companies' customer data by the 'front door' – as is the case with PRISM, which enables direct access to data from nine Internet firms, including Google, Microsoft and Yahoo.[41] The program is said to be the biggest single contributor to the NSA's current intelligence collection efforts. In addition, the agencies have 'back-door access', whereby data from these companies is intercepted without their knowledge via systems such as MUSCULAR.[42] Furthermore, the UK and the US have tapped into fibre-optic cables carrying global communications, made possible since the relevant physical infrastructure (switches, routers, servers and cables) is located in their territories.[43] Reportedly, in this way GCHQ:

> has been able to access at least 200 fibre optic cables, giving the agency a capability to monitor up to 600 million communications every day [with the ability to allegedly store] internet and phone use data up to 30 days in order for it to be sifted and analysed.[44]

The intelligence agencies are also said to be involved in the collection of metadata (often referred to as 'communications data') – that is, 'information about the time and location of a phone call or email, as opposed to the content of these conversations or messages'[45] – thus allowing them to compile a more accurate and detailed profile of a person than through accessing the content of these communications alone.[46] For example, in March 2013, the NSA allegedly amassed up to 97 billion pieces of metadata from computer networks worldwide.[47]

In addition, the security services have been able to access phone text messages and phone calls through such programs as DISHFIRE, which in April 2011 was shown to collect on average 194 million text messages a day, enabling the NSA to gain information on people's travel plans, contact lists and financial transactions, including from individuals not suspected of any illegal activities.[48] The NSA has also developed MYSTIC, a voice inter-

---

[40]  CoE, Committee on Legal Affairs and Human Rights, 'Mass Surveillance. Draft Resolution' (2015) AS/Jur 2 ('CoE Mass Surveillance Resolution').
[41]  CoE Mass Surveillance Memorandum (n 38) para 10.
[42]  *Ibid.*
[43]  *Ibid* para 11.
[44]  *Ibid.*
[45]  *Ibid* para 12.
[46]  *Ibid.*
[47]  *Ibid* para 13.
[48]  *Ibid* para 15.

ception program designed 'to gather mobile calls placed in countries with a combined population of more than 250 million people'.[49] It has enabled the US to record every single phone call in the Bahamas (on the basis of an operation codenamed SOMALGET) without the knowledge or consent of that country's government, processing approximately 100 million calls per day.[50] Additionally, the NSA can retrospectively listen to previously recorded phone calls in order to 'figure out what targets said during calls that occurred even before the targets were identified as such', using, among others, the RETRO program.[51] This array of surveillance techniques is further enhanced by the intelligence agencies' ability to amass millions of facial images, fingerprints and other identifiers from emails and other communications. Reportedly, one of the boldest efforts of the NSA to obtain facial images is through its WELLSPRING program, which collects them from the Internet and uses them to track suspected terrorists and other intelligence targets.[52] These investigatory techniques are supported by both the US government and the private sector investing heavily in facial recognition research and development.

### 3.1.2    Intelligence-sharing arrangements

In conjunction with these methods of gathering information, intelligence sharing has become one of the main methods of cooperation in the effort to combat international terrorism and organized crime. It occurs in various ways and includes accessing 'raw' (unanalysed) information, such as Internet traffic intercepted in bulk from fibre-optic cables by other security organs; obtaining data stored in databases held by other governments or jointly managed with other countries; and receiving already analysed information, usually in the form of an intelligence report.[53] It also consists of operational cooperation, facilities and equipment hosting, training and capacity building, together with technical and financial support.[54]

These practices have significantly intensified since the 11 September 2001 attacks on the US ('9/11 attacks'). Indeed, such intergovernmental bodies as the North Atlantic Treaty Organization (NATO) have made every effort to increase consultation on terrorism and related issues among their member and

---

[49]   *Ibid* para 16.
[50]   *Ibid*.
[51]   *Ibid* para 17.
[52]   *Ibid* para 19.
[53]   Privacy International, *Secret Global Surveillance Networks: Intelligence Sharing Between Governments and the Need for Safeguards* (April 2018) 5 ('*Secret Surveillance Networks*').
[54]   *Ibid*.

non-member countries.[55] This global collaboration has been underpinned by the UN's explicit recognition of the need for a common strategic and operational approach of the international community on security and related matters. It has thus recommended that practical steps be taken to individually and collectively prevent and combat the terrorist threat. As a result of this policy stance, in 2006 the UN adopted the Global Counter Terrorism Strategy,[56] a unique instrument to enhance national, regional and international efforts to counter terrorism.[57] The Strategy comprises a resolution[58] and an action plan consisting of four pillars, one of which propagates 'measures to build States' capacity to prevent and combat terrorism and to strengthen the role of the United Nations system in this regard'.[59] The document thus recognizes that such capacity building in all states is a core element of the global counterterrorism effort and consequently encourages states and relevant international, regional and sub-regional organizations to work closely together, 'including by sharing information, with all bilateral and multilateral technical assistance providers'.[60] At the same time, it recognizes and stresses the need for states 'to ensure respect for human rights for all and the rule of law as the fundamental basis of the fight against terrorism'.[61]

Intelligence sharing usually occurs pursuant to intelligence-sharing agreements. Although it is impossible to provide a complete account, one of the best-known co-operations is the Five Eyes alliance pursuant to the UKUSA Signals Intelligence Agreement,[62] first entered into by the UK and the US in 1946 and later extended to Australia, New Zealand and Canada. However, very little is known outside the intelligence community regarding what exactly it presently comprises. It has purportedly given the Five Eyes partners much

---

[55]   NATO Multimedia Library, 'Intelligence/Information Sharing in Combating Terrorism' (16 May 2019), www.natolibguides.info/intelligence.

[56]   UN Office of Counter Terrorism, *UN Global Counter Terrorism Strategy* (2006) ('UN Counter Terrorism Strategy'). The Sixth Review of the UN Global Anti-Terrorism Strategy took place on 26 June 2018, followed by UNGA Resolution, 'The UN Global Counter Terrorism Review' (2 July 2018) UN Doc A/Res/72/284.

[57]   *Ibid.*

[58]   UNGA Resolution, 'The United Nations Global Counter-Terrorism Strategy' (20 September 2006) UN Doc A /Res/60/288 ('A/Res/60/288').

[59]   UN Counter Terrorism Strategy (n 56). The other three pillars are: (1) 'measures to address the conditions conducive to the spread of terrorism'; (2) 'measures to prevent and combat terrorism'; and (3) 'measures to ensure respect for human rights for all and the rule of law as the fundamental basis of the fight against terrorism'.

[60]   *Ibid* part III para 6.

[61]   *Ibid* part IV.

[62]   British-US Communications Intelligence Agreement (5 March 1946), www.nsa .gov/Portals/70/documents/news-features/declassified-documents/ukusa/agreement _outline_5mar46.pdf.

wider scope of operations besides sharing primary signals intelligence and enables their security services to intercept, collect, analyse and decrypt intelligence information.[63] An example of this collaboration is ECHELON, a global network operated with the primary aim of intercepting private and commercial (rather than military) communications and purportedly capable of intercepting any 'telephone, fax, internet, or email message sent by any individual'.[64]

The UKUSA Agreement is said to assign the responsibility for surveillance to various partners by allocating them the 'interception rights' in specific parts of the globe.[65] Thus, the UK zone of operations includes Africa and Europe, together with the region east of the Ural Mountains;[66] Canada's covers the north latitudes and the Polar regions; while Australia's and New Zealand's extends to Oceania and the South Pacific respectively.[67] Since 1946, the web of intelligence sharing has unsurprisingly evolved beyond the original UKUSA Agreement and now includes the Five Eyes acting in collaboration with other intelligence agencies on the basis of a variety of arrangements, such as SIGINT Seniors Europe (the Five Eyes plus Belgium, Denmark, France, Germany, Italy, the Netherlands, Norway, Spain and Sweden);[68] SIGINT Seniors Pacific (the Five Eyes plus India, Singapore, South Korea and Thailand);[69] the Nine Eyes (the Five Eyes plus Denmark, France, the Netherlands and Norway);[70] the Fourteen Eyes (the Nine Eyes plus Belgium, Germany, Italy, Spain and Sweden);[71] and the Forty Three Eyes (the Fourteen Eyes plus the 2010 members of the International Security Assistance Forces to Afghanistan).[72] Apart from these methods of cooperation, there are a number of equally secretive bilateral and multilateral agreements in other regions of the globe – such as the Club of Berne (an intelligence-sharing arrangement among the EU intelligence services) and the Shanghai Cooperation Organizations (an affiliation among the People's Republic of China ('China'), India, Kazakhstan, Kyrgyzstan, Pakistan, the Russian Federation ('Russia'), Tajikistan and Uzbekistan) – together with intelligence exchange arrangements within a group of states comprising Russia, Iraq, Iran and Syria to facilitate the fight against the Islamic State.[73]

---

[63]   *Eyes Wide Open* (n 37) 6–7.
[64]   CoE Mass Surveillance Memorandum (n 38) 9.
[65]   *Ibid.*
[66]   *Eyes Wide Open* (n 37) 8.
[67]   *Ibid.*
[68]   *Secret Surveillance Networks* (n 53) 8.
[69]   *Ibid.*
[70]   *Ibid.*
[71]   *Ibid.*
[72]   *Ibid.*
[73]   *Ibid* 9.

Intelligence sharing has thus become one of the most pervasive, yet least regulated surveillance practices in the modern world.[74] At least one report based on an international collaborative investigation carried out in 2018 by 40 non-governmental organizations (NGOs) in 42 countries found 'alarming weaknesses in the oversight arrangements that are supposed to govern the sharing of intelligence between State intelligence agencies'.[75] The UN Human Rights Committee (HRC) – a body of independent experts that monitors the implementation of the International Covenant on Civil and Political Rights 1966 (ICCPR)[76] by its states parties[77] – has recognized that intelligence sharing *prima facie* constitutes an interference with the right to privacy, and expressed concerns about insufficient safeguards against arbitrary interference with that right with regard to the sharing of raw data.[78] Particularly problematic in this context is the intelligence services' ability to 'outsource' surveillance to other agencies, thus bypassing domestic restrictions on intelligence gathering by relying on allied services to obtain and then share information on their own nationals.[79] Such practices have been termed 'collusion for circumvention'.[80] This entails using relationships with foreign partners to access information that the agency either could not lawfully gain or would find it difficult to obtain due to domestic legal constraints regarding, for example, the types of techniques used to conduct the surveillance, or generally its ability to perform such activities on its own citizens.[81] Thus, it has been confirmed that GCHQ and the NSA 'may exploit their relationship to acquire information that would be more difficult to obtain lawfully themselves within their own jurisdictions'.[82]

---

[74]   *Ibid* 3.

[75]   *Ibid.*

[76]   UNGA, International Covenant on Civil and Political Rights (adopted 16 December 1966, entered into force 23 March 1976) 999 UNTS 999, 171 ('ICCPR').

[77]   OHCHR, 'Human Rights Committee. Monitoring Civil and Political Rights', www.ohchr.org/en/hrbodies/ccpr/pages/ccprindex.aspx.

[78]   See UNHRC, 'Concluding Observations on the Seventh Periodic Report of Sweden' (28 April 2016) UN Doc CCPR/C/SWE/CO/7 paras 36-37; UNHRC, 'Concluding Observations on the Initial Report of Pakistan' (23 August 2017) UN Doc CCPR/C/PAK/CO/1 para 35; UNHRC, 'Concluding Observations on the Seventh Periodic Report of the United Kingdom of Great Britain and Northern Ireland' (17 August 2015) UN Doc CCPR/C/GBR/CO/7 para 24 ('Concluding Observations, UK').

[79]   See Hans Born, Ian Leigh and Aidan Wills, 'Making International Intelligence Cooperation Accountable' (21 May 2015) Norwegian Parliamentary Oversight Committee 48–50 ('Born *et al*').

[80]   CoE Mass Surveillance Memorandum (n 38) paras 30–31.

[81]   Born *et al* (n 79). See also CoE Mass Surveillance Memorandum (n 38).

[82]   UK Hansard, 10 June 2013, Cols 34, 35 and 39.

Commenting on this issue, the UN High Commissioner for Human Rights (OHCHR), in her 2014 report, observed that there is:

> credible information to suggest that some Governments systematically have routed data collection and analytical tasks through jurisdictions with weaker safeguards for privacy. Reportedly some Governments have operated a transnational network of intelligence agencies through interlocking legal loopholes, involving the coordination of surveillance practices to outflank the protection provided by domestic legal regimes.[83]

Indeed, in the aftermath of the Snowden exposés and partly as a result of them, both the UN General Assembly (UNGA) and the UN human rights treaty bodies have begun to pay very close attention to this and various other forms of state surveillance, and how these implicate international law. Particular emphasis has been placed on their impact on the right to privacy of communications, thrusting this right firmly into the limelight in various international forums.

## 4.    PRIVACY

Privacy is a complex and multifaceted concept, difficult to encapsulate in a neat definition. However, in essence, it is 'the presumption that individuals should have an area of autonomous development, interaction and liberty free from State intervention and excessive unsolicited intrusion by other uninvited individuals'.[84] International human rights law[85] expressly recognizes privacy as a fundamental right. It is thus enshrined in a number of international instruments, including in Article 12 of the Universal Declaration of Human Rights 1948 (UDHR)[86] and Article 17 of the International Covenant on Civil and Political Rights 1966.[87] It is also stipulated in numerous regional treaties

---

[83]    A/HRC/27/37 (n 26) para 30.

[84]    UNGA, 'Report of the Special Rapporteur on the Promotion and Protection of Human Rights and Fundamental Freedoms While Countering Terrorism, Ben Emmerson' (23 September 2014) UN Doc A/69/397 para 28 ('A/69/397').

[85]    Yuval Shany, 'Cyberspace: The Final Frontier of Extra-Territoriality in Human Rights Law' (26 September 2017) HUJI Cyber Security Research Blog, https://csrcl.huji.ac.il/people/cyberspace-final-frontier-extra-territoriality-human-rights-law. Writing in the context of states' extra-territorial obligations in cyberspace, Shany describes international human rights law as a 'legal hybrid' – that is, 'a system of norms and institutions that channels universal norms through the apparatus of the state system'.

[86]    Universal Declaration of Human Rights (adopted 10 December 1948) UNGA Res 217 A(III) Art 12 ('UDHR').

[87]    ICCPR (n 76) Art 17.

– in particular, Article 8 of the European Convention on Human Rights 1950 (ECHR)[88] and Article 11 of the American Convention on Human Rights 1969 (ACHR).[89] This normative framework is enhanced by a large body of jurisprudence that has contributed to the interpretation of this right by the HRC, various UN human rights mandate holders and regional human rights courts – in particular, the European Court of Human Rights (ECtHR), where a sizeable body of case law pertaining to privacy protection in the context of state surveillance has been amassed. The post-Snowden years have seen a number of important developments in this regard, both within and outside the UN.

### 4.1    The Right to Privacy in the Digital Age at the UN

Since 2013, the UNGA and the Human Rights Council – an inter-governmental organization made up of 47 UN member states responsible for strengthening the protection of human rights around the globe and for addressing and making recommendations in relation to their violations[90] – have paid particular attention to the right to privacy in the digital age. Previously, however, privacy rights seem to have been given scant attention by the UN human rights institutions. Some commentators even contend that the topic was neglected between the period of the publication by the HRC of the General Comment 16[91] in 1988 (a document providing interpretative guidance on Article 17 of the ICCPR) and the issue of two seminal Special Rapporteurs' reports in 2009 and 2013.[92] The first of these – by the Special Rapporteur on the promotion and protection of human rights and fundamental freedoms while countering terrorism, Martin Scheinin[93] – discussed a number of legal and policy aspects arising from states' communication interception activities. The second – authored by the Special

---

[88]    CoE, European Convention for the Protection of Human Rights and Fundamental Freedoms amended by Protocols Nos 11 and 14 (4 November 1950) (European Convention on Human Rights) Art 8 ('ECHR').
[89]    Organization of American States, The American Convention on Human Rights (The Pact of San José, Costa Rica) (entered into force 18 July 1978) Art 11 ('ACHR').
[90]    UNHRC, 'Welcome to Human Rights Council', www.ohchr.org/en/hrbodies/hrc/pages/aboutcouncil.aspx.
[91]    UNHRC, 'CCPR General Comment No. 16: Article 17 (Right to Privacy). The Right to Respect of Privacy, Family, Home and Correspondence, and Protection of Honour and Reputation' (8 April 1988) UN Doc HRI/Gen/1/Rev.9 (Vol 1) ('General Comment 16').
[92]    Carly Nyst and Tomaso Falchetta, 'The Right to Privacy in the Digital Age' (2017) *Journal of Human Rights Practice* 104–18 ('Nyst and Falchetta').
[93]    UNHRC, 'Report of the Special Rapporteur on the Promotion and Protection of Human Rights and Fundamental Freedoms while Countering Terrorism, Martin Scheinin' (28 December 2009) UN Doc A/HRC/13/37.

Rapporteur on the promotion and protection of the right to freedom of opinion and expression, Frank La Rue – brought into sharp focus the effects of counterterrorism policies on the right to privacy and the impact of mass surveillance technologies on this and related rights (including the freedom of expression).[94]

In the years that followed and largely as a result of the 2013 Snowden exposures, the right to privacy in the digital age was pushed to the top of the policy agenda and became the focus of a number of UNGA and Human Rights Council Resolutions.[95] On 18 December 2013, the UNGA adopted by consensus a Resolution on the right to privacy in the digital age (Resolution 68/167),[96] expressing deep concerns over the negative impact of surveillance and communications interception on human rights. Crucially, the UNGA affirmed that the same rights that people have offline must also be protected online and called upon all states to respect and protect the right to privacy of digital communications.[97] In addition, the Resolution requested the OHCHR to:

> submit a report on the protection and promotion of the right to privacy in the context of domestic and extraterritorial surveillance and/or the interception of digital communications and the collection of personal data including on the mass scale to the Human Rights Council.[98]

The resultant 2014 OHCHR report, titled 'The Right to Privacy in the Digital Age',[99] made a significant contribution and impact, as it not only confirmed that government mass surveillance is 'emerging as a dangerous habit rather than an exceptional measure', but also pointed out some alarming gaps in the implementation of the international legal framework governing these issues.[100] It is thus widely regarded as 'the yardstick against which to assess States' compliance with their human rights obligations in the context of surveillance'.[101] These developments have been further enhanced by the Human Rights

---

[94]    UNHRC, 'Report of the Special Rapporteur on the Promotion and Protection of the Right to Freedom of Opinion and Expression, Frank La Rue' (17 April 2013) UN Doc A/HRC/23/40.

[95]    UNGA Resolution, 'The Right to Privacy in the Digital Age' (21 January 2014) UN Doc A/Res/68/167 ('A/Res/68/167'); see also UNGA Resolution, 'The Right to Privacy in the Digital Age' (10 February 2015) A/Res/69/166 ('A/Res/69/166'); UNGA Resolution, 'The Right to Privacy in the Digital Age' (19 December 2016) UN Doc A/Res/71/199 ('A/Res/71/199'); UNHRC Resolution, 'The Right to Privacy in the Digital Age' (26 March 2015) UN Doc A/HRC/Res/28/16 ('A/HRC/Res/28/16').

[96]    A/Res/68/167 *ibid.*

[97]    A/Res/68/167 *ibid*; see also A/Res/69/166 and A/Res/71/199 (n 95).

[98]    A/Res/68/167 *ibid* para 5.

[99]    A/HRC/27/37 (n 26).

[100]   *Ibid.*

[101]   Nyst and Falchetta (n 92) 108.

Council's adoption of Resolution 28/16[102] establishing a dedicated UN special procedures mandate on the right to privacy – that is, the office of the Special Rapporteur on the right to privacy.[103] The mandate holder is appointed for three years and tasked, among other responsibilities, with reporting on alleged violations on the right to privacy, including in connection with the challenges arising from new technologies.[104]

The HRC has also been closely scrutinizing governments' compliance with the right to privacy under Article 17 of the ICCPR. In concluding observations on Canada,[105] France,[106] Namibia,[107] New Zealand,[108] Rwanda,[109] South Africa,[110] Sweden,[111] the US[112] and the UK,[113] among others, the HRC emphasized its concerns in relation to states' legal regimes allowing for mass interception of communication and the lack of sufficient safeguards against arbitrary interference with the right to privacy.[114]

Also worthy of note are the efforts of the international community in the field of information and communications technology (ICT) in the context of cyber security. Developments in ICT have been on the UN agenda since Russia's introduction in 1998 of a draft resolution on this subject in the First Committee of the UNGA, adopted without a vote as Resolution 53/70.[115] On

---

[102]   A/HRC/Res/28/16 (n 95).

[103]   UNHRC, 'Special Rapporteur on the Right to Privacy', www.ohchr.org/en/issues/privacy/sr/pages/srprivacyindex.aspx.The current mandate holder is Professor Joseph Cannataci of Malta.

[104]   *Ibid.*

[105]   UNHRC, 'Concluding Observations on the Sixth Periodic Report of Canada' (20 July 2015) UN Doc CCPR/C/CAN/CO/6.

[106]   UNHRC, 'Concluding Observations on the Fifth Periodic Report of France' (17 August 2015) UN Doc CCPR/C/FRA/CO/5.

[107]   UNHRC, 'Concluding Observations on the Second Report of Namibia' (23 August 2016) UN Doc CCPR/C/NAM/CO/2.

[108]   UNHRC, 'Concluding Observations on the Sixth Periodic Report of New Zealand' (28 April 2016) UN Doc CCCPR/C/NZL/CO/6.

[109]   UNHRC, 'Concluding Observations on the Fourth Periodic Report of Rwanda' (2 May 2016) UN Doc CCPR/C/RWA/CO/4.

[110]   UNHRC, 'Concluding Observations on the Initial Report of South Africa' (27 April 2016) UN Doc CCPR/C/ZAF/CO/1.

[111]   Concluding Observations, Sweden (n 78).

[112]   UNHRC, 'Concluding Observations on the Fourth Periodic Report of the United States of America' (23 April 2014) UN Doc CCPR/C/USA/CO/4 ('Concluding Observations, US').

[113]   Concluding Observations, United Kingdom (n 78).

[114]   See, for example, Concluding Observations, UK *ibid* para 24 and Concluding Observations, US (n 112) para 22.

[115]   UNGA Resolution, 'Developments in the Field of Information and Telecommunications in the Context of International Security' (4 December 1998) UN Doc A/RES/53/70.

this basis, five UN Groups of Governmental Experts (GGEs) have been convened to examine existing and potential threats in the cyber sphere and possible cooperative measures to address them.[116] One of the main achievements of this collaboration was a broad agreement reached by the 2013 GGE that international law – and in particular, the Charter of the United Nations[117] – applies in cyberspace.[118] This was followed by the 2015 GGE consensus report,[119] stipulating numerous non-legally binding norms along with confidence-building measures.[120] Framed as 11 recommendations (Recommendations 13(a)–(k)), these voluntary non-legally binding rules and principles of responsible state behaviour are aimed at promoting an open secure, stable, accessible and peaceful ICT environment.[121] In particular, in Recommendation 13(e), the GGE agreed that states, in ensuring the secure use of ICT, should respect human rights and guarantee their full protection, including the right to privacy and freedom of expression.[122]

### 4.2    The Right to Privacy in the Digital Age outside of the UN

Numerous efforts have also been made outside of the UN, which have contributed to the global discussion on the relationship between states' use of ICT and human rights protection. These include a number of initiatives at the multi-stakeholder level, involving intergovernmental organizations, private industry and civil society, together with a valuable contribution from academia.

Thus, at the multi-stakeholder level, the 2014 Statement from the Global Multistakeholder Meeting on the Future of Internet Governance

---

[116] UN Office for Disarmament Affairs, 'Fact Sheet. Developments in the Field of Information and Telecommunications in the Context of International Security' (January 2019), www.un.org/disarmament/ict-security/.

[117] UN, Charter of the United Nations (24 October 1945) 1 UNTS XVI ('UN Charter').

[118] UNGA, Group of Government Experts on Developments in the Field of Information and Telecommunications in the Context of International Security (24 June 2013) UN Doc A/68/98*.

[119] UNGA, 'Group of Governmental Experts on Developments in the Field of Information and Telecommunications in the Context of International Security' (22 July 2015) UN Doc A/70/174.

[120] For more details in relation to the UN GGE process, see Chapter 7, section 4.

[121] A/70/174 (n 119) paras 13 (a)–(k).

[122] *Ibid.* For the interpretation of the GGE Recommendations 13(a)–(k), see UN Office for Disarmament Affairs, *Voluntary, Non-binding Norms for Responsible State Behaviour in the Use of Information and Communications Technology. A Commentary* (UN Office for Disarmament Affairs, 2017).

('NETmundial')[123] expressly acknowledged the need for human rights to underpin Internet governance,[124] including the right to privacy. According to the NETmundial Statement:

> The right to privacy must be protected. This includes not being subject to arbitrary or unlawful surveillance, collection, treatment and use of personal data. The right to the protection of the law against such interference should be ensured. Procedures, practices and legislation regarding the surveillance of communications, their interception and collection of personal data, including mass surveillance, interception and collection, should be reviewed, with a view to upholding the right to privacy by ensuring the full and effective implementation of all obligations under international human rights law.[125]

Intergovernmental cooperation saw the introduction in 2013 of a set of guidelines governing the protection of privacy and transborder data flows by the Organization for Economic Co-operation and Development.[126] The contribution from civil society groups, industry and international experts in communications surveillance has helped to further explore and define how the right to privacy applies to digital interception and collection of communications. Of particular note in this regard are the International Principles on the Application of Human Rights to Communications Surveillance,[127] which articulate a number of guiding principles to facilitate the protection of this right in the digital age in the context of increased state surveillance.

In tandem with the diplomatic processes at the UN and the range of voluntary norms and recommendations made outside that organization, a group of legal scholars embarked on a project to elaborate how international law applies in cyberspace. The work commenced under the auspices of NATO's Cooperative Cyber Defence Centre of Excellence initially resulted in the *Tallinn Manual*

---

[123] Global Multistakeholder Meeting on the Future of Internet Governance, 'NETmundial Multistakeholder Statement' (24 April 2014) ('NETmundial Statement').

[124] The term 'Internet governance' was first introduced in the 1980s and is defined by the UN Working Group on Internet Governance as '[t]he development and application by governments, the private sector and civil society, in their respective roles, of shared principles, norms, rules, decision making procedures and programmes that shape the evolution and use of the internet' – see UN Report of the Working Group on Internet Governance (2005), www.wgig.org/docs/WGIGREPORT.pdf.

[125] NETmundial Statement (n 123) para 1 'Internet Governance Principles'.

[126] Organization for Economic Co-operation and Development, *Guidelines Governing the Protection of Privacy and Transborder Flows of Personal Data, Recommendation of the Council Concerning Guidelines Governing the Protection of Transborder Flows of Personal Data*, C(80)58/FINAL as amended on 11 July 2013 by C(2013)79; see 'Annex. Guidelines Governing the Protection of Privacy and Transborder Flow of Personal Data. Part II' paras 7–14.

[127] *Necessary and Proportionate* (n 28).

*on the International Law Applicable to Cyber Warfare*,[128] published in 2013, which focused on the application of *jus ad bellum* and *jus in bello* to cyber conflict. This volume was then superseded by the *Tallinn Manual 2.0 on the International Law Applicable to Cyber Operations*,[129] which, in addition, analysed the applicability of international law to cyber operations that fall below the 'use of force' threshold. To date, the Manuals are the most comprehensive articulation of how international law – including human rights law[130] – applies to cyberspace and cyber operations.

## 5.    MASS SURVEILLANCE AS CONTINUING STATE PRACTICE

Mass surveillance and privacy issues were the subject of fierce debate in the aftermath of the Snowden disclosures. However, seven years on, these concerns have almost disappeared from open public debate and reporting, despite an overwhelming majority of states around the globe continuing to routinely engage in various methods of unrestrained interception and collection of communications. Thus, according to *Boundaries of Law*[131] – a study conducted under the auspices of the University of Cambridge – mass generalized surveillance is an exponential and indiscriminate practice, which goes beyond the Five Eyes' intelligence gathering operations. The survey, carried out between 2013–17, considered a diverse selection of 14 countries across five continents to attest to this ongoing and widespread state practice. The document reported on a number of issues, including mass surveillance being undertaken either without any legal basis or on the premise of secret and opaque laws,[132] allowing 'governments to interfere arbitrarily with the right to confidentiality of communications of hundreds of millions of people worldwide by collecting data in bulk without proven cause for suspicion'[133] – meaning that

---

[128]  Michael N Schmitt (ed), *Tallinn Manual on the International Law Applicable to Cyber Warfare* (Cambridge University Press, 2013).

[129]  Michael N Schmitt (ed), *Tallinn Manual 2.0 on the International Law Applicable to Cyber Operations* (Cambridge University Press, 2017) ('*Tallinn Manual 2.0*').

[130]  See *ibid* Chapter 6.

[131]  Douwe Korff, Ben Wagner, Julia Powles, Renata Avila and Ulf Buermeyer, *Boundaries of Law: Exploring Transparency, Accountability and Oversight of Government Surveillance Regimes* (University of Cambridge Faculty of Law, 2013). The study surveyed the United Kingdom, the United States, Colombia, the Democratic Republic of the Congo, Egypt, France, Germany, India, Kenya, Myanmar, Pakistan, Russia, South Africa and Turkey.

[132]  *Ibid.*

[133]  *Ibid* 8.

the surveillance is mostly conducted illegally.[134] Furthermore, in most of the countries surveyed, the intelligence community can demand direct access to telecommunications infrastructure through a 'back door'[135] and thus intercept both content and metadata.[136] In addition, the most commonly invoked ground for the interference with privacy – that is, 'national security' – is so broadly defined in most domestic legal instruments that it is meaningless.[137] Furthermore, the document reported that such intelligence collection rarely requires judicial authorization, instead being approved in many countries by the prime minister, a minister, a senior official, the police, the military and intelligence services, or any authorized agency;[138] while oversight systems are often non-existent or ineffective because they are not independent.[139] There is also a trend towards countries conducting surveillance under semi-permanent states of quasi-emergency.[140] The report's overall tenor is therefore that the right to privacy is guaranteed in principle, but not respected in practice.[141]

That mass surveillance is now a permanent feature of everyday life has also been confirmed by the 2019 report of the Special Rapporteur on the promotion and protection of the right to freedom of opinion and expression referred to other types of surveillance enabled by a wider range of technologies to gain surreptitious access to digital communications, work product, browsing data, research and location history, together with individuals' online and offline activities.[142] These include affect recognition (a technology that seeks to infer a person's feelings, emotions or intentions from facial expression); deep packet inspection (this enables the monitoring, analysis and redirection of traffic passing through communications and Internet networks, which may lead users to sites infected with malware and block them from accessing certain websites); and social engineering practices (ie, strategies to lure a target into unwittingly downloading malware on their devices, to spy on their communications).

---

[134]  *Ibid.*
[135]  *Ibid.*
[136]  *Ibid.*
[137]  *Ibid.*
[138]  *Ibid.*
[139]  *Ibid.*
[140]  *Ibid.*
[141]  *Ibid.*
[142]  UNHRC, 'Surveillance and Human Rights. Report of the Special Rapporteur on the Promotion and Protection of the Right to Freedom of Opinion and Expression' (28 May 2019) UN Doc A/HRC/41/35.

## 6.    THE SURVEILLANCE, SECURITY AND PRIVACY PARADOX

Drawing on this thumbnail sketch, it can be said that surveillance, security and privacy present a difficult paradox – perhaps best illustrated by the seemingly competing policy strands at both the UN and domestic levels, which ostensibly pull in opposite directions.

Thus, for a number of decades the UN has expressed a 'strong condemnation of terrorism in all its forms and manifestations … as it constitutes one of the most serious threats to international peace and security'.[143] To this end, the UN has urged states to take action to prevent and combat terrorism, including by 'intensifying cooperation, as appropriate, in exchanging timely and accurate information concerning the prevention and combating of terrorism'.[144] Concurrently, however, it has also recognized that international cooperation must comply with international human rights law.[145] This has been emphasized on numerous occasions, including in the UNGA Resolution on the right to privacy in the digital age (Resolution 68/167), which noted that:

> the rapid pace of technological development … enhances the capacity of governments, companies and individuals to undertake surveillance, interception and data collection, which may violate or abuse human rights, in particular the right to privacy, as set out in article 12 of the Universal Declaration of Human Rights and article 17 of the International Covenant on Civil and Political Rights.[146]

Domestically, a small group of countries have begun to 'modernize' or 'overhaul' their surveillance laws by putting their bulk powers of interception and data collection on a statutory footing. The impetus for this seems to have derived from the intensity of the terrorist attacks that ensued in quick succession between 2015–19, including those in Paris,[147] Brussels,[148] Orlando,

---

[143]   A/Res/60/288 (n 58) para 2.
[144]   *Ibid* Plan of Action point 4.
[145]   *Ibid* Plan of Action point 3.
[146]   A/Res/68/167 (n 95) para 4.
[147]   *International Business Times*, 'Europe Terrorist Attacks 2016: Timeline of Bombings and Terror Threats Before Brussels' (24 April 2016). Paris was subject to two terrorist attacks that year, in January and November.
[148]   *Ibid.*

Florida,[149] London[150] and Sri Lanka.[151] A number of nations have responded by adopting more draconian surveillance legislation justifying the enactment of these measures on national security grounds. Examples include the UK Investigatory Powers Act 2016;[152] the US Cybersecurity Sharing Act 2015;[153] the French Intelligence Act 2015;[154] and the German Act on the Federal Intelligence Service 2016.[155] The introduction of these statutes was accompanied by heated public debate centred on the need to reconcile two purportedly opposing paradigms: that is, individuals' entitlement to privacy[156] and the state's right to restrict it on the grounds of national security in order to provide the police and intelligence agencies with access to information necessary to conduct their investigations.[157] In the context of this dichotomy, achieving a balance between the need for security and the protection of the privacy of individuals is seen as essential to a free society, yet these values are often presented and perceived as opposites. As a result, any attempt to accommodate the need for these seemingly competing rights is highly challenging in an era of digitalization and continued threats to collective security, at both the domestic and global levels. This complexity seems to be magnified by the view that security can be achieved only if individuals and societies resign themselves to the fact that states must conduct mass surveillance in order to discharge their obligations to keep their citizens safe and in that sense, trade off their fundamental rights, ultimately achieving greater safety. This is the stance adopted by some government officials – including the former UK Foreign Secretary William Hague, who insisted, in his 2013 response to the growing concerns

---

[149] *The Guardian*, 'Orlando: Obama Condemns "Acts of Terror" After Worst Mass Shooting in US History' (13 June 2016). The June 2016 shooting in Orlando, Florida was described by the then US President Barak Obama as 'the most deadly shooting in American history'.

[150] *BBC News*, 'London Attack: Seven Killed in Vehicle and Stabbing Incidents' (2 June 2017).

[151] *BBC News*, 'Sri Lanka Attacks: The Family Networks Behind the Bombings' (11 May 2019).

[152] Investigatory Powers Act 2016 c 25.

[153] CISA S.2588 [113th Congress], S 754 [114th Congress].

[154] French Intelligence Act 2015 (Law 2015-912).

[155] German Act on the Federal Intelligence Service 2016 ('BND Act').

[156] *The Guardian*, 'Extreme Surveillance Becomes UK Law with Barely a Whimper' (19 November 2016). In that article, *The Guardian* quoted the statement made by Edward Snowden, who on 19 November 2016 tweeted that 'the UK has just legitimised the most extreme surveillance in the history of western democracy. It goes further than many autocracies'.

[157] Paul Bernal, 'Data Gathering, Surveillance and Human Rights: Recasting the Debate' (2016) *Journal of Cyber Policy* 243–64.

over the US PRISM program, that 'if you have nothing to hide you have nothing to fear',[158] reiterating a phrase first popularized by Joseph Goebbels.

There can be no doubt that at the domestic level, a decisive trend can be discerned towards achieving greater security by means of mass surveillance of both foreign and domestic communication. This pronounced shift towards greater securitization[159] adopted by many states in the second decade of the twenty-first century indicates that there is little prospect of these practices being abandoned. They are thus of concern to international law. To this end, following the Snowden disclosures, the UN institutions and mandate holders have begun to recognize that the cost to civil liberties might ultimately far outstrip the gains realized by the policy of achieving relative freedom from dangers or threats to security. This is because unrestrained surveillance abrogates the rule of law and thus poses a serious challenge to core human rights, including the right to privacy.[160] On these bases, therefore, the 'surveillance, security and privacy paradox' can be framed in terms of a cost-benefit analysis – that is, a process of estimating the costs involved in attaining global and domestic security through mass surveillance and the possible benefits to be derived from this for individual nations and for the international community.

## 7.    THE AIMS OF THIS BOOK

As already observed, the cyber surveillance, security and privacy paradox is replete with competing interests and thereby represents a challenge not only to individual states, but also to the international community as a whole – and by extension, to international law. Therefore, it must be addressed as a global problem. Accordingly, the primary purpose of this book is to show that there is a need to establish common international law standards to address state sponsored cyber surveillance. Such a legal framework, regulating the working methods of intelligence and law enforcement agencies, should be put into place in order, among other things, to impose minimum benchmarks for transparency, accountability and oversight in relation to both intelligence gathering and sharing. At present, there are no specific rules of international law – in the form of either an international treaty or customary international law – that directly address this problem.

---

[158] *The Telegraph,* 'William Hague: British Public 'Have Nothing to Fear' From US Spies' (9 June 2013).

[159] Bary Buzan *et al, Security: A New Framework* (Lynne Rienner Publishers, 1998) 24. In the context of international relations, an issue is 'securitized' when it 'is presented as an existential threat, requiring emergency measures and justifying actions outside the normal bounds of political procedures'.

[160] See, for example, A/HRC/27/37 (n 26).

To this end, the aim of this book is threefold. First, it ascertains how existing international human rights law applies to state sponsored cyber surveillance, focusing on the right to privacy of communications. To this end, it identifies the sources of this right and examines whether online privacy has attained customary international law status. Second, it engages with the question of whether existing treaty rules that aim to protect it are adequate to meet the challenges posed by ubiquitous mass surveillance, or whether there is a need for a specific international legal framework regulating these activities. In this context, the book proposes a legal taxonomy that reflects various state intelligence operations that have emerged in recent years, which can be broadly divided into three categories: (1) cyber espionage; (2) cyber surveillance; and (3) cyber electoral interference. Based on this differentiation, the book's third and final aim is to evaluate the prospects of a multilateral surveillance treaty being adopted at an international and/or regional level, acknowledging the fact that any success in this regard is dependent on states' vested interests and political will. With this in mind, the book considers other methods of controlling mass surveillance – in particular, states being guided by cyber-specific non-legally binding norms for responsible behaviour in the digital domain.

This book predominantly scrutinizes the relationship between the individual's right to privacy of communications and state cyber surveillance. It assesses how the existing rules laid down in Article 17 of the ICCPR, Article 8 of the ECHR and Article 11 of the ACHR apply to these activities. The book's focus on these legal instruments stems from the fact that most countries, including the Five Eyes partners, are signatories to these treaties, although, as will be discussed later, the US does not regard itself as being bound by the ICCPR in relation to acts conducted outside of its territory. Nevertheless, most governments are under a legal duty both to protect and to respect individuals' right to privacy as stipulated and interpreted by the relevant judicial organs. Related to this right is a body of rules pertaining to the protection of personal data.[161] However, a detailed analysis of this area of law is beyond the scope of this book. This is because data protection law has grown exponentially and is increasingly recognized as a distinct human right,[162] thus warranting detailed and separate analysis. Notwithstanding, frequent references are made to the

---

[161] See Kriangsak Kittichaisaree, *Public International Law in Cyberspace* (Springer, 2017) 59. Data protection and the right to privacy may be distinguished because '[t]he former regulates the processing of an individual's personal data – be it private or non-private, whereas the latter protects an individual against intrusions into his private sphere'.

[162] See, for example, Monika Zalnieriute, 'An International Constitutional Moment for Data Privacy in the Times of Mass-Surveillance' (2015) 23 *International Journal of Law and Information Technology* 99–133.

EU data protection regime and to a number of landmark decisions of the Court of Justice of the European Union (CJEU) relating to the issues of data retention, cross-border transfers and mass interception of communications.

The book is concerned with states, as against non-state actors, examining their obligations for human rights protection in cyberspace, since under international law the former are the main parties to be considered responsible for wrongful acts or omissions, including violations of human rights.[163] A consideration of the role played by the latter – principally the private sector, comprising powerful Internet companies – has been deliberately omitted from its scope, since their involvement in surveillance and the responsibilities that this creates warrant a discrete legal analysis.

The Snowden exposures concentrated attention on the Five Eyes. Although global digital surveillance goes far beyond these states' involvement, the book makes frequent references to that alliance, with particular regard paid to US and UK laws and practice. This is because these countries are not only considered to be among the most technologically advanced in the world, giving them a dominant position in the cyber domain,[164] but also due to their unparalleled surveillance capabilities, together with the domination of US corporations of the provision of Internet services globally.

## 8.    THE SCOPE OF THIS BOOK

To achieve its stated aims, this book takes as its starting point the positioning of mass surveillance within the security-privacy trade-off, according to which greater security can be achieved only by sacrificing some fundamental freedoms, including privacy. This issue has been addressed in this introductory chapter, which conceives of the problem in terms of 'cost-benefit' analysis and contends that it is misleading to suggest that security can be achieved only at the cost of forfeiting fundamental rights.

The book then situates state cyber surveillance within international law discourse pertaining to peacetime cyber espionage, to explore how these activities are similar and how they differ. The rationale for such delineation is based on the emerging state practice, which dictates a need for the adoption of a more granular distinction that recognizes different types of intelligence-gathering

---

[163]   See International Law Commission, 'Draft Articles on Responsibility of States for Internationally Wrongful Acts with Commentary' (2001) *Yearbook of the International Law Commission, General Commentary* para 1.

[164]   See Tony Morbin, 'UK and US Sign Military Cyber Accord to Dominate Cyber Domain-With Help From Business', *Cyber Security Source* (23 October 2018), www .scmagazineuk.com/uk-us-sign-military-cyber-accord-dominate-cyber-domain-help -business/article/1496952.

operations in cyberspace. This is the subject for consideration in Chapter 2, which separates these activities into three distinct categories, namely, cyber espionage, cyber surveillance and cyber electoral interference, to gain an understanding of how international law applies to each of them.

Chapter 3 outlines the value of privacy both as a social norm and as an international human right. To this end, it discusses whether the right to online privacy – as proclaimed by the UNGA and the Human Rights Council Resolutions[165] – can be considered as a customary international law rule, thus constituting a separate source of rights. Having concluded that this cannot yet be said with any certainty, the chapter concludes that international treaties are the main basis of states' obligations to protect the privacy of communications.

Chapter 4 proceeds to analyse the scope of states' obligations under the ICCPR, the ECHR and the ACHR. Since current practice confirms that nations habitually undertake mass surveillance outside their territories – often either without a specific legal basis or pursuant to legislation that differentiates on the grounds of nationality (or the nature of communications) – this chapter argues that such laws breach the right to equal treatment and non-discrimination. Furthermore, it asserts that states' human rights obligations in the context of extraterritorial surveillance of foreign communications are engaged when effective control over an individual's rights is being exercised.

Chapter 5 then delineates the ambit of the right to privacy stipulated in the ICCPR, the ECHR and the ACHR, and discusses what constitutes an interference with this right in the context of mass surveillance.

Chapter 6 engages with the principal legal grounds upon which states legitimize interference with the right to privacy, with particular attention paid to the ostensible fragmentation of approaches between the UN human rights bodies, the inter-American human rights organs on the one hand, and the ECtHR on the other.

Chapter 7 considers the feasibility of regulating the working methods of state intelligence and security agencies through a legally binding treaty, positioning this discussion within the broader context of cyber security discourse. Having outlined a number of failed efforts to agree legally binding rules for this domain, including for state surveillance, it examines non-legally binding cyber norms as a means of guiding responsible states' behaviour when engaged in mass surveillance.

---

[165] A/Res/68/167 (n 95); A/Res /69/166 (n 95); A/Res/71/199 (n 95); UNHRC, 'The Promotion, Protection and Enjoyment of Human Rights on the Internet' (16 July 2012) UN Doc A/HRC/Res/20/8; UNHRC, 'The Promotion, Protection and Enjoyment of Human Rights on the Internet' (14 July 2014) UN Doc A/HRC/Res/26/13.

Chapter 8 offers a summary of findings and considers the future of the right to privacy in the light of developing technologies. It concludes that any process aimed at curtailing the practice of mass cyber surveillance is likely to be incremental at best.

# 2. Cyber espionage, cyber surveillance, foreign electoral interference and international law

## 1. INTRODUCTION

International law is a key legal order that aims to regulate states' conduct of activities in cyberspace, thereby obliging them to observe such principles as state sovereignty, sovereign equality and non-intervention in other nations' internal affairs. It is generally agreed that there are numerous aspects of international law that may be engaged by a state's cyber operations conducted on another's territory. However, it remains uncertain how these rules and principles should be applied in this domain. An important aspect of the disagreements and conflicts among states is the application of the rules of *lex lata* to cyber activities that fall below the use of force threshold, including those broadly termed as 'cyber espionage'.

This preponderant state practice is not directly regulated, although general principles of international law and specialist regimes pertain to these activities. Nevertheless, to date there is no universal consensus as to which rules should play a role to deter and/or mitigate these pernicious and growing states' exploits. Doubts as to how international law should regulate states' behaviour in this context are further exacerbated by the fact that all cyber intelligence operations, such as mass surveillance[1] and a relatively new phenomenon – cyber electoral interference – seem to be subsumed within the broad category of cyber espionage.

This chapter aims to demonstrate that espionage, mass surveillance and electoral interference by cyber means are different in terms of their aims, scope and scale. While it may have been justifiable for international law to categorize signals intelligence (SIGINT) operations as espionage when the Internet was

---

[1] For example, the *Tallinn Manual 2.0* collates the bulk collection of Internet traffic and cyber surveillance within the broader category of cyber espionage – see Michael N Schmitt (ed), *Tallinn Manual 2.0 on the International Law Applicable to Cyber Operations* (Cambridge University Press, 2017) Rule 32 para 7, 170 ('*Tallinn Manual 2.0*').

in its infancy, this no longer seems appropriate in light of new and evolving technologies. Simply put, conflating all of the above activities as cyber espionage does not take account of their *sui generis* characteristics, thus making it unclear how the existing international law framework applies to these practices and how any normative gaps should be filled in, if needs be.

This chapter supports the need for establishing of specialist regimes to regulate each of these activities through separate set of rules and in particular the necessity to develop an internationally binding treaty specifically addressing indiscriminate and large-scale data interception and collection.[2] To this end, it is divided into the following sections. Section 2 outlines the practice of peacetime espionage and positions cyber espionage therein. It also delineates two broad categories into which it may be divided: politically and economically motivated cyber spying. It discusses cyber electoral interference in the latter context and argues that only operations known as 'doxing' fit within the category of political cyber espionage. Section 3 then analyses the nature of surveillance and highlights some of the features of targeted and mass cyber surveillance, including the legal bases upon which they are conducted, taking as an example the UK and US surveillance legislation. It shows that mass cyber surveillance possesses a unique character based on the volume, the type of intercepted data and the targets involved. Section 4 proceeds to explore some of the uncertainties relating to the application of international law rules to cyber espionage, illustrating this with the principles of territorial sovereignty and non-intervention. It concludes that the features comprising mass cyber surveillance warrant a separate legal classification, thus strengthening the case for a bespoke legal framework underpinned by states' obligations to conduct these activities in line with their human rights obligations.

---

[2]    See, for example, Statement by HE Dilma Rousseff, President of the Federative Republic of Brazil at the Opening of the General Debate of the 68th Session of the United Nations General Assembly (24 September 2013), proposing the creation of a 'multilateral mechanisms for the worldwide network that are capable of ensuring principles such as freedom of expression, privacy of individuals and respect for human rights' ('Dilma Rousseff's Statement'); see also Council of Europe (CoE), Committee on Legal Affairs and Human Rights, 'Mass Surveillance. Draft Resolution' (2015) AS/Jur 2, putting forward the Intelligence Codex discussed in Chapter 7, section 3.2 ('CoE Mass Surveillance Resolution'); Office of the High Commissioner for Human Rights, UN Special Rapporteur on the Right to Privacy, 'Draft Legal Instrument on Government-led Surveillance and Privacy' (10 January 2018), discussed in Chapter 7, section 3.3; Russell Buchan, *Cyber Espionage and International Law* (Hart Publishing, 2019) 195 ('Buchan'); Eliza Watt, 'The Right to Privacy and the Future of Mass Surveillance' (2017) 21(7) *The International Journal of Human Rights* 773–99 ('Watt').

## 2.    PEACETIME ESPIONAGE

Espionage (informally referred to as 'spying') is often described as the oldest intelligence-gathering activity for political and military purposes known in history.[3] In the context of international relations, its roots can be traced to ancient Egypt, Greece, Rome and China.[4] Accounts of spying appear in some of the world's earliest documents, including those dating from the times of Pharaoh Ramses (ca 1274 BC)[5] and the Chinese military treaties of the fifth century BC.[6] Today, it is also widely regarded by states as 'a necessary tool for pursuing their foreign policy and security interests and for maintaining the balance of power at the inter-[S]tate level'.[7]

Espionage involves the gathering of information related to closely protected secrets, often considered as a matter of national security or of military importance. It is thus regarded as an activity that is associated with nation states, since it is generally conducted by states against other states. Indeed, in the words of one commentator:

> the revolution in intelligence gathering is felt most strongly in nation State intelligence gathering. Disposing of a high degree of political control within their territories and capable of marshalling vast resources for the collection of intelligence, the contemporary nation State has always been one of the foremost gatherers and processors of constitutive intelligence.[8]

Although to date there is no agreed definition in international law, 'espionage' is often defined as 'a consciously deceitful collection of information, ordered by a government or organization hostile to, or suspicious of those the information concerns, accomplished by humans unauthorised by the target to do the collecting'.[9]

As a method of acquiring information that would otherwise be unobtainable, espionage has traditionally been sub-divided into two broad catego-

---

[3]   Allen Dulles, *The Craft of Espionage* (David West Group Co, 1963).

[4]   *Ibid.*

[5]   *Gale Encyclopedia of Espionage and Intelligence*, 'Espionage and Intelligence, Early   Historical   Foundations',   www.faqs.org/espionage/Ep-Fo/Espionage-and -Intelligence-Early-Historical-Foundations.html.

[6]   Sun Tzu, *The Art of War* (Pax Librorum, 2009).

[7]   *Max Planck Encyclopedia of Public International Law*, 'Spies' (September 2015).

[8]   Myres S McDougal, Harold D Lasswell, W Michael Reisman, 'The Intelligence Function and World Public Order' (1973) 46(3) *Temple Law Quarterly* 335–448, 379.

[9]   Geoffrey B Demarest, 'Espionage in International Law' (1996) *Denver Journal of International Law and Policy* 321, 325–26 ('Demarest').

ries: the collection of information from human sources (HUMINT)[10] and SIGINT. The latter denotes data obtained from the gathering and analysis of electronic signals[11] and comprises communication intercepts and other electronic intelligence.[12] SIGINT is further split into communications intelligence (COMMINT) and electronic intelligence (ELINT).[13] The former is information derived from intercepted communications, also described as 'technical information and intelligence derived from foreign communications by other than intended recipients'.[14] Furthermore, COMMINT entails the acquisition of 'foreign communications passed by radio, wire, or other electromagnetic means'.[15] In other words, COMMINT is the collection of electronic signals, including those emanating from foreign sources, that comprise the written and spoken imparting of information.

One of the features that characterizes states' intelligence gathering is its secretive nature. Most governments engage in the collection of confidential information and do so covertly – that is, without the consent of the state that controls it.[16] Secret intelligence is therefore the gathering of information from closed, publicly unavailable sources,[17] usually clandestinely and for the benefit

---

[10]     'HUMINT' is '[the] collection of information by a trained HUMINT collector … from people and their associated documents and media sources to identify elements, intentions, composition, strength, disposition, tactics, equipment, personnel and capabilities. It uses human sources as a tool and a variety of collection methods, both passively and actively, to gather information'; see UN Department of the Army, *Human Intelligence Collector Operations FM 2-22.3* (2006) in Buchan (n 2) 15.
[11]     National Security Agency (NSA)/Central Security Service (CSS), 'Signals Intelligence', www.nsa.gov/what-we-do/signals-intelligence.
[12]     Simon Chesterman, 'Secret Intelligence', *Max Plank Encyclopedia of Public International Law* (January 2009) ('Chesterman').
[13]     'ELINT' is 'information derived primarily from electronic signals that do not contain speech or text' and is subdivided into three major branches: technical ELINT (TechELINT), operational ELINT (OpELINT) and telementry intelligence (TELINT) – see US National Security Agency (NSA), Centre for Cryptographic History, 'Electronic Intelligence (ELINT) at NSA' (2009), https://permanent.access.gpo.gov/gpo7719/elint .pdf.
[14]     US Department of Defense (DoD), *Dictionary of Military and Associated Terms* (as of June 2020) 107, 46 ('US DoD *Dictionary*').
[15]     National Security Council Intelligence Directive No 6 (17 February 1972) in Buchan (n 2) 15.
[16]     Chesterman (n 12) para 1.
[17]     This can be distinguished from 'acquiring information from open sources, that is information, which is publicly available and comprises that contained in *inter alia* speeches, official documents, newspaper reports, technical and professional journals, company websites and online databases. This is a separate activity and as such does not raise legal concerns' – see Simon Chesterman, 'The Spy Who Came in from the Cold: Intelligence and International Law' (2006) 27 *Michigan Journal of International*

of the foreign state, often endangering the national interest of the state that is spied upon.[18] Most domestic legal systems recognize that such operations are deleterious and seek to prohibit them by imposing criminal sanctions, while protecting their own capacity to engage in espionage abroad.[19] For example, in the UK, the legal safeguards against espionage are set out in the Official Secrets Acts 1911–89,[20] which together comprise the main legal framework protecting against espionage. The 1989 Act provides that information relating to security or intelligence must not be subject to unauthorized disclosure.[21] Section 1 of the 1911 Official Secrets Act (as amended by the 1920 and 1939 Official Secrets Acts) criminalizes numerous activities that are prejudicial to the state; while Section 8(1) of the 1920 Act imposes a term of minimum three and maximum 14 years' imprisonment, although longer sentences are permissible for a series of offences.[22] It has been recognized that some parts of this legal framework are now outdated, having been drafted in the Edwardian era and implemented over 100 years ago; whereas others have been subject to very little independent scrutiny. Consequently, as a result of the 2015 Cabinet Office's request, the Law Commission was tasked with reviewing its effectiveness and acknowledged that the law in this area must be improved – both to ensure that it protects state information more effectively and to update the treason laws, bearing in mind the impact of technology.[23] The calls for modern rules relating to spying on English soil have intensified following the publication in July 2020 of the so-called Russia Report[24] – the

---

*Law* 1071, 1073; and Darien Pun, 'Rethinking Espionage in the Modern Era' (2017) 18 *Chicago Journal of International Law* 353, 358.

[18] UK Law Commission, *Protection of Official Data. Consultation Paper No 230* (2017) para 2.3 ('LC Consultation Paper').

[19] Chesterman (n 12) para 4.

[20] Official Secrets Act 1911 (1 & 2 Geo 5 c 28) ('OSA 1911'); Official Secrets Act 1920 (10 & 11 Geo 5 c 75); Official Secrets Act 1939 (2 & 3 Geo 6 c 121); Official Secrets Act 1989 c 6 ('OSA 1989').

[21] OSA 1989 *ibid* s 1(1); OSA 1911 *ibid* s 1.

[22] OSA 1911 *ibid* s 1(a)-(c); OSA 1920 (20) s 8(1).

[23] LC Consultation Paper (n 18) para 1.8. This also relates to the involvement of Huawei Technologies in the building of the UK's future 5G network. Further to concerns raised by, *inter alia*, the UK National Cyber Security Centre, the UK announced a ban on the procurement of the company's products and the withdrawal of its equipment from the 5G network by 2027 – see Department of Digital, Culture, Media and Sport and the Rt Hon Oliver Dowden, Oral Statement to Parliament, 'Digital, Culture, Media and Sport Secretary's Statement on Telecoms' (14 July 2020), www .gov.uk/government/speeches/digital-culture-media-and-sport-secretarys-statement-on -telecoms.

[24] Intelligence and Security Committee of Parliament, 'Russia. Presented to Parliament Pursuant to Section 3 of the Justice and Security Act 2013' (21 July 2020) ('Russia Report').

result of an investigation into that country's activities in the UK. The Report examined the threat that the Kremlin represents to Great Britain, recommending that greater powers be granted to handle Russia's espionage in view of its involvement in the 'Salisbury incident'[25] and the alleged interference with the 2016 referendum concerning the UK leaving European Union (the Brexit referendum). These concerns have reinforced the need to update UK law in this area and as a result legislative changes are afoot whereby the Official Secrets Acts will soon be replaced with a modernized Espionage Act, more attuned to dealing with present-day tactics of influence, big data manipulation and cyber espionage.[26]

Crucial to understanding why states conduct espionage against other nations is their motivation. In this context, two forms of spying can be distinguished: (1) political/military espionage; and (2) economic espionage.

## 2.1    Political and Military Espionage

This type of spying gathers information relating to the political and military affairs of rival states.[27]

Historically, for kings and other heads of state, 'intelligence in all its aspects was part of statecraft, inseparable from exercise of power'.[28] For example, England's Queen Elizabeth I had a sophisticated network of spies and informers, her secret service, supervised by spymaster Francis Walsingham, whose role was to intercept letters, crack codes and capture those involved in various plots to overthrow her.[29] These methods of intelligence collection,

---

[25]   The attack concerned the poisoning of Sergei Skripal (a former officer of Russia's military intelligence agency) and his daughter Yulia in 2018 with the Novichok nerve agent, as a result of which the then Prime Minister Theresa May called for greater powers to punish and prevent Russian agents from performing espionage operations, including in the UK – see Prime Minister's Office and the Rt Hon Theresa May MP, Oral Statement to Parliament, 'PM Statement on Salisbury Investigation: 5 September 2018' (5 September 2018), www.gov.uk/government/speeches/pm-statement-on-the-salisbury-investigation-5-september-2018.

[26]   See UK Home Office, 'Home Secretary: Keeping Our Country Safe' (20 May 2019), www.gov.uk/government/news/home-secretary-keeping-our-country-safe. In his speech, Home Secretary Rt Hon Sajid Javid supported the Espionage Bill, stating that post-Brexit, it is the UK government's priority to have the right powers and resources in place for countering hostile states.

[27]   Buchan (n 2) 21.

[28]   Michael Herman, *Intelligence Power in Peace and War* (Cambridge University Press, 1996) 13.

[29]   Alexandra Briscoe, 'Elizabeth's Spy Network', *BBC History* (2011), www.bbc.co.uk/history/british/tudors/spying_01.shtml. For a detailed historical account of the evolution in secret intelligence, see *ibid.*

together with the coding and decoding of messages, have evolved significantly since then. However, states' rationale for conducting political espionage seems to have remained unchanged: this form of spying is undertaken primarily to gather 'confidential information on political and security affairs, negotiating positions, sensitive economic information and details of policy developments'.[30]

Military espionage involves the collection of intelligence pertaining to:

> technical information about weapons, details of where troops are located, information on defences … especially useful to an enemy country in wartime. It can help an enemy to find weak points or launch a surprise attack. It can also be useful to terrorists, as it can help them to pick out targets and weak points.[31]

In a nutshell, political and military espionage is conducted by states both to gain an advantage and to inform the decision-making process, especially in the area of international relations.

## 2.2     Economic Espionage

This category of peacetime spying involves states covertly acquiring trade and/ or industrial secrets held by a foreign private enterprise[32] located in another country, which includes information on that company's technology, products and plans. Governments engage in these practices in order to promote their economic growth and thus to strengthen their own national security, as the maintenance of the latter is increasingly seen as contingent upon a prosperous national economy.[33] To this end, the UK security service, MI5, has explicitly acknowledged the dangers of economic espionage, stating that:

> spies are especially interested in details of new inventions that may be of military or commercial use. Examples include communications technology, computers, genetics, aviation, lasers, optics and electronics. Such secrets may also help to give some countries an economic or military advantage.[34]

---

[30]   Security Service MI5, 'Targets of Espionage', www.mi5.gov.uk/targets-of -espionage ('MI5').
[31]   *Ibid.*
[32]   David P Fidler, 'Economic Cyber Espionage and International Law: Controversies Involving Government Acquisition of Trade Secretes Through Cyber Technology' (2013) 17 *American Society of International Law Insights.*
[33]   Buchan (n 2) 23.
[34]   MI5 (n 30).

Most governments appreciate the perils associated with the theft of industrial secretes and take protective measures. For these reasons, acts of economic espionage are criminalized in many jurisdictions. One example is the US Economic Espionage Act 1996[35] – the result of the US Congress recognizing the importance of the nation's economic health and security and thus the need to protect intellectual property and trade secrets.[36] The Act addresses the growing problem of the theft of trade secrets by, among other things, imposing penal sanctions in relation to foreign economic espionage when such appropriation benefits a 'foreign government, agent or instrumentality'.[37] In the UK, the ongoing radical overhaul of the Official Secrets Acts 1911–89 has confirmed a number of deficiencies of the 1989 Official Secrets Act in relation to economic espionage, including the lack of protection of sensitive economic information by that legislation. Consequently, it has been recommended that the ambit of the forthcoming Espionage Act must include sensitive information relating to the economy insofar as it pertains to national security, in effect making its unauthorized disclosure for the benefit of a foreign power a criminal offence.[38]

In summary, peacetime espionage involves: (1) the clandestine gathering of confidential, non-publicly available information contained in closed sources; (2) pertaining to a state's secrets; (3) performed by one state against another; (4) to obtain information from human (HUMINT) or non-human sources (SIGINT); (5) for political, military and economic gains; (6) without the consent of the entity that controls that information; (7) considered as endangering the target state's interests; and therefore (8) subject to national laws imposing criminal sanctions upon conviction.

## 2.3    Cyber Espionage

While it could be said that espionage has existed since the dawn of human history, peacetime cyber espionage is a relatively new, but rapidly growing phenomenon, considered by most nations as an extension of traditional spying.[39] This method of obtaining intelligence 'allows a hostile actor to steal

---

[35]   Economic Espionage Act 1996, Pub L 104-294, 110 Stat 3489 (11 November 1996) ('EEA'96').

[36]   US Department of Justice, 'Introduction to the Economic Espionage Act' (June 2015)    www.justice.gov/jm/criminal-resource-manual-1122-introduction-economic -espionage-act.

[37]   EEA'96 (n 35) 18 USC §1831. The Act also criminalizes the theft of trade secrets regardless of who benefits – see 18 USC §1832.

[38]   LC Consultation Paper (n 18) para 3.45.

[39]   UK Security Service MI5, 'Cyber', www.mi5.gov.uk/cyber.

information remotely, cheaply and on industrial scale. It can be done with relatively little risk to a hostile actor's intelligence officers or agents overseas'.[40] The propensity for this activity is such that, according to some commentators, cyber espionage is currently enjoying a 'golden age'.[41] There are numerous reasons for this, including that it reduces risks to state agencies; allows for the large-scale outsourcing of intelligence collecting; and offers possibilities hitherto unheard of in terms of the ease, swiftness and cost-effectiveness of collecting high volumes of information.[42]

### 2.3.1   Copying of confidential data

In much the same vein as classic spying, 'cyber espionage' lacks a definition in international law, but according to the *Tallinn Manual 2.0*, it can be understood as 'the use of cyber capabilities to surveil, monitor, capture or exfiltrate electronically transmitted or stored communications, data, or other information'.[43] Thus, cyber espionage denotes the use of exploitation operations[44] to copy confidential data that is resident in or transmitted through cyberspace, even if it is not read or analysed.[45]

Although a uniform definition of 'cyber espionage' is elusive, it is possible to identify certain common features among the existing typology adopted

---

[40]   *Ibid.*

[41]   See, for example, Katharina Ziólkowski, 'Peacetime Cyber Espionage – New Tendencies in Public International Law' in *Peacetime Regime for State Activities in Cyberspace. International Law, International Relations and Diplomacy* (NATO CCDCOE Publications, 2013) 425.

[42]   *Ibid.*

[43]   *Tallinn Manual 2.0* (n 1) Rule 32, 168.

[44]   'Cyber operations' are 'the deployment of cyber capabilities to achieve objectives in or through cyberspace' – see *Tallinn Manual 2.0* (n 1) Glossary. They include 'cyber attacks' and 'cyber exploitations'. 'Cyber attacks' are operations 'reasonably expected to cause injury or death to persons or damage or destruction to objects'- see *Tallinn Manual 2.0* Rule 92, 415. 'Cyber exploitation' is 'unauthorised access to computers, computer systems, or networks, in order to exfiltrate information, but without affecting the functionality of the accessed system or amending/deleting the data resident therein' – see Marco Roscini, *Cyber Operations and the Use of Force in International Law* (Oxford University Press, 2014) 16 ('Roscini').

[45]   Buchan (n 2) 17.

by a number of governments[46] and within the academic community.[47] The first of these is the clandestine nature of the act in question. It means that the information is obtained without the awareness or consent of the entity being spied upon,[48] and that the information is not publicly available. This signifies both that the data is resident in a closed source[49] and that it is considered as confidential because the party that controls it has a 'reasonable expectation of privacy',[50] as it is protected by a password, a firewall and/or encryption.

---

[46]   The UK definition equates cyber espionage with computer network exploitation, stating that it is 'the use of a computer network to infiltrate a target computer network and gather information' – see UK HM Government, *National Cyber Security Strategy 2016-2021* Annex 2: Glossary. The US Cyber Operations Policy terms 'cyber espionage' as 'cyber collection' and defines it as 'operations and related programs or activities conducted … in or through cyberspace, for the primary purpose of collecting intelligence … from computers, information or communication systems, or networks with the intent to remain undetected' – see US Presidential Policy Directive 'PPD-20', US Cyber Operations Policy (October 2012).

[47]   See, for example, Buchan (n 2) 27, who defines 'cyber espionage' as 'the non-consensual use of cyber operations to penetrate computer networks and systems with the objective of copying confidential data that is under the control of another actor'. See also Kilovaty, who defines 'cyber espionage' as 'the science of covertly capturing e-mail traffic, text messages, other electronic communications, and corporate data for the purpose of gathering national security or commercial intelligence'- Ido Kilovaty, 'World Wide Web of Exploitations – The Case of Peacetime Cyber Espionage Operations Under International Law: Towards a Contextual Approach' (2016) 17 *The Columbia Science and Technology Law Review* 42–77, 47 ('Kilovaty').

[48]   See Kilovaty *ibid*; Buchan (n 2) 20. See also Herbert Lin, 'Offensive Cyber Operations and the Use of Force' (2010) *Journal of National Security, Law and Policy* 63–86, 63, defining 'cyber espionage' as 'cyber exploitation', stating that it is 'the use of actions and operations – perhaps over an extended period of time – to obtain information that would otherwise be kept confidential and is resident on or transmitting through an adversary's computer systems or networks. Cyber exploitations are usually clandestine and conducted with the smallest possible intervention that sill allows extraction of the information sought'.

[49]   The European Commission explains that information is contained in a closed source when it is not publicly available – that is, when it is not open data. 'Open data' is 'data that anyone can access, use and share' – see European Commission, 'What is Open Data?', www.europeandataportal.eu/elearning/en/module1/#/id/co-01.

[50]   Simon Chesterman, 'One Nation under Surveillance: A New Social Contract to Defend Freedom Without Sacrificing Liberty' (2011) New York School of Law, Public Research Paper 11–14.

Obtaining such information lawfully can therefore occur only on the basis of consent, which is understood as:

> any freely given, specific, informed and unambiguous indication of the data subject's[51] wishes, by which he or she, by a statement or by a clear affirmative action, signifies agreement to the processing of personal data relating to him or her.[52]

The second common aspect defining 'cyber espionage' is the copying, capture or collection of information. This involves covert action without the express and freely given agreement of the person, institution or organization that is spied upon. The copying of data pertains to emails, text messages and other details transmitted through computer systems. It follows that merely breaking into a system without copying, capturing or collecting closed source information resident therein will most likely not amount to espionage.

In addition to these main facets describing cyber espionage (ie, the copying of confidential data without consent), there are a number of discernible supplementary features that characterize these practices. They include the possibility of it being conducted remotely, meaning that it does not require a physical presence of spies on the target country's soil, which is usually the case with traditional peacetime espionage.[53] Furthermore, cyber espionage can be performed either to target specific information or to obtain it in bulk and on a long-term basis.[54] Importantly, however, it must be conducted by or attributed to a state; and this requirement is addressed next.

### 2.3.2   Attribution

The ability to attribute cyber espionage to a given state[55] is vital in order to hold that state legally accountable for breach of international obligations and attribution is always based on government decision.

---

[51]   For a definition of 'data subject', see Article 4(1) of the European Parliament and the Council of the European Union, General Data Protection Regulation (4 May 2016) L119 ('GDPR').

[52]   *Ibid* Art 4(11).

[53]   Craig Forcese, 'Spies Without Borders: International Law and Intelligence Collection' (2011) 5 *Journal of National Security Law and Policy* 179–210, 183.

[54]   *Tallinn Manual 2.0* (n 1) Rule 32, 170.

[55]   This is commonly accepted by states – see, for example, US DoD Speech, 'DoD General Counsel Remarks at U.S. Cyber Command Legal Conference' (2 March 2020) ('US DoD Views on International and Domestic Law in Cyberspace'); Attorney General's Office and the Rt Hon Jeremy Wright QC MP, speech, 'Cyber and International Law in the 21 Century' (23 May 2018) ('Cyber and International Law – UK'); Government of the Netherlands, 'Letter of 5 July 2019 from the Minster of Foreign Affairs to the President of the House of Representatives on the International Legal Order in Cyberspace. Annex: International Law in Cyberspace' (5 July 2019)

State responsibility – a basic principle of international law – provides that whenever one states commits an internationally wrongful act against another, international responsibility is established between them.[56] The customary nature of this concept has been confirmed on many occasions by, *inter alia*, the International Court of Justice (ICJ), in such cases as *Corfu Channel*,[57] *Nicaragua*[58] and *Gabčíkovo–Nagymaros Project*.[59] It is also set out by the International Law Commission (ILC) in the 2001 Articles on State Responsibility,[60] an authoritative – albeit non-legally binding – document that substantially reflects customary international law. Thus, according to Article 2 of the Articles on State Responsibility, an internationally wrongful act is an act and/or omission that: (1) constitutes a breach of an international legal obligation applicable to the state in question; and (2) is attributable to the state under international law.[61] Both of these elements must be established to trigger responsibility in law. Thus, an act or omission will be internationally wrongful if it both breaches an obligation under international law and is attributable to

---

6 ('International Law in Cyberspace – The Netherlands'); France, *Ministère des Armées*, '*Droit International Appliqué Aux Opérations Dans Le Cyberspace*' (2019) ('International Law Applicable to Operations in Cyberspace-France'); Australia's International Cyber Engagement Strategy, '2019 International Law Supplement. Annex A: Supplement to Australia's Position on the Application of International Law to State Conduct in Cyberspace' (2019) ('Application of International Law to State Conduct in Cyberspace – Australia'); New Zealand, *The Application of International Law to State Activity in Cyberspace,* (1 December 2020) para 19, 4 ('Application of International Law in Cyberspace – New Zealand'); Roy Schöndorf, 'Israel's Perspective on Key Legal and Practical Issues Concerning the Application of International Law to Cyber Operations', transcript of the Keynote Speech Delivered by Israeli Deputy Attorney General (International Law) Dr Roy Schöndorf on 8 December 2020 at the US Naval War College's Event on 'Disruptive Technologies and International Law' (9 December 2020) 7 ('Israel's Perspective on the Application of International Law to Cyber Operations'); see also the commentary to Rule 32 of the *Tallinn Manual 2.0,* which explains that the Rule 'is limited to cyber espionage by or otherwise attributable to States (Rules 15–18)' – *Tallinn Manual 2.0* (n 1) Rule 32, Commentary para 3, 168.

56 International Law Commission, 'Draft Articles on Responsibility of States for Internationally Wrongful Acts with Commentary' (2001) *Yearbook of the International Law Commission* Art 1 ('ILC Draft Articles on State Responsibility').

57 *Corfu Channel (UK v Albania)* (Merits) [1949] ICJ Rep 4, 23.

58 *Military and Paramilitary Activities in and Against Nicaragua (Nicaragua v United States of America)* (Merits) [1986] ICJ Rep 14, paras 283 and 292 ('*Nicaragua*').

59 *Gabčíkovo–Nagymaros Project* (Hungary/Slovakia) (Merits) [1997] ICJ Reports 7 ('*Gabčíkovo–Nagymaros Project*').

60 ILC Draft Articles on State Responsibility (n 56) Vol 2, part 2.

61 *Ibid* Art 2.

a state. Such an obligation may derive from treaty, customary international law or general principles of law, 'regardless of [their] origin or character'.[62]

The 2013 UN GGE agreed that the principle of state responsibility applies in the context of information and communications technology (ICT) activities, confirming that 'States must meet their international obligations regarding internationally wrongful acts attributable to them under international law'[63] and 'must not use proxies to commit internationally wrongful acts'.[64] Similarly, according to the *Tallinn Manual 2.0*, 'a State bears international responsibility for a cyber-related act that is attributable to the State and that constitutes a breach of an international legal obligation'.[65] It follows that acts of cyber espionage may in principle be regarded as internationally wrongful acts; but whether a state can be held responsible for breaching its international law obligations depends on whether those wrongful acts can be attributed to that state. Needless to say, the assignment of cyber activity to a particular author has long been recognized as challenging,[66] for at least three reasons: (1) the ease with which the perpetrator can hide its identity (the so-called 'anonymity problem'); (2) the possibility of launching a multi-stage cyber operation using computers operated by several individuals located in different jurisdictions; and (3) the speed of such operations.[67] Consequently, what 'is critical is not only to trace back the [cyber operation] to its source, for example a computer, but to identify the person who operated the computer and more importantly to identify the "real mastermind" behind [the operation]'.[68] Attribution must therefore be both timely and accurate, which is a complex process, comprising factual (fact finding) and legal attribution.[69]

---

[62]    *Ibid* Art 2 and Art 12.

[63]    UNGA, Group of Government Experts on Developments in the Field of Information and Telecommunications in the Context of International Security (24 June 2013) UN Doc A/68/98* para 23 ('GGE 2013').

[64]    *Ibid.*

[65]    *Tallinn Manual 2.0* (n 1) Rule 14, 84.

[66]    See for example, Roscini (n 44) discussing the attribution problem in the context of cyber operations, 33–40.

[67]    Nicholas Tsagourias, 'Cyber Attacks, Self-Defence and the Problem of Attribution' (2012) 17 *Journal of Conflict and Security Law* 233.

[68]    *Ibid.*

[69]    Michael N Schmitt, '"Virtual" Disenfranchisement: Cyber Election Meddling in the Grey Zone of International Law' (2018) 19(1) *Chicago Journal of International Law* 30–67, 58 ('Schmitt'). The government of the Netherlands states that there are three forms of attribution: technical, legal and political, with the latter defined as 'a policy consideration whereby the decision is made to attribute (publicly or otherwise) a specific cyber operation to an actor without necessarily attaching legal consequences to the decision (such as taking countermeasures). The attribution need not

### 2.3.2.1    Factual attribution

Factual attribution constitutes a 'level of certainty that a cyber operation was conducted by a particular individual, group, organization or State'.[70] The enquiry in this context focuses on whether a cyber operation can be traced to a particular computer system, and more specifically to a particular person, group or organization. When faced with *ex ante* uncertainty as to the attribution of a cyber operation, states must act as reasonable states would in similar circumstances when considering their responses.[71] Reasonableness is context dependent and numerous factors must be taken into account such as 'reliability, quantum, directness, nature (eg, technical data, human intelligence) and specificity of the relevant available information when considered in light of the attendant circumstances and the importance of the right involved'.[72] Any deficiencies in technical intelligence may be compensated by, for example, highly reliable human intelligence.[73]

### 2.3.2.2    Legal attribution

The main principle regarding legal attribution is set out in Article 4(1) of the Articles on State Responsibility, which provides that the conduct of a state's organ is attributable to that state.[74] The provision identifies entities that exercise legislative, executive or any other functions, notwithstanding their position within the state's hierarchy,[75] and covers all of the individual and collective bodies that make up its organization and act on its behalf.[76] It has been recognized that cyber operations conducted by a state institution, or by persons and organizations empowered by domestic law to exercise elements of government authority, are attributable to the state.[77] Thus, for example, all cyber activities of the US Cyber Command, China's People's Liberation Army Cyber Unit 61398 or Israel's Unit 8200 are fully attributable to the respective states.[78] Similarly, National Security Agency (NSA) and Government Communications Headquarters (GCHQ) data collection through the use of

---

necessarily relate to a state; it may also concern a private actor' – see International Law in Cyberspace – The Netherlands (n 55).

[70]    Schmitt, *ibid.*
[71]    *Tallinn Manual 2.0* (n 1) 81–82.
[72]    *Ibid* 81–82.
[73]    *Ibid.*
[74]    ILC Draft Articles on State Responsibility (n 56) Art 4(1) and the Commentary.
[75]    *Ibid.*
[76]    *Ibid.*
[77]    *Tallinn Manual 2.0* (n 1) Rule 15.
[78]    *Ibid* Rule 15, 87. See also International Law in Cyberspace – The Netherlands (n 55), confirming that 'an act by a government body in its official capacity (for example the National Cyber Security Centre) is always attributable to the state'.

such programs as PRISM and Tempora can be said to be attributable to the US and the UK respectively, not least because their existence has been to some degree officially acknowledged by these states. Furthermore, according to the *Tallinn Manual 2.0*, 'any cyber activity undertaken by the intelligence, military, internal security, customs, or other State agency engages State responsibility if it violates an international legal obligation binding on that State'.[79] It follows that if such an entity acting in an official capacity breaches international obligations, the state will bear responsibility even if the conduct in question is *ultra vires* – that is, it exceeds the authority granted by the state or contravenes its instructions.[80]

More problematic are cyber operations conducted by non-state organs. As a general rule, the conduct of a private person or entity is not attributable to the state, unless there is a factual nexus between that person or entity and the state.[81] This is addressed in Article 8 of the Articles on State Responsibility, which states that:

> the conduct of a person or group of persons shall be considered as an act of a State under international law if the person or group of persons is in fact acting on the instructions of, or under the direction or control of, that State in carrying out the conduct.[82]

When the act in question is in fact authorized by the state, attribution can be readily established.[83] If, however, a private person acts under the state's instructions, direction or control, the issue of attribution becomes more complex. The ICJ in *Nicaragua*[84] and subsequently in *Bosnian Genocide*[85] interpreted the degree of control that a state must exert over a non-state actor's operations as 'effective control'. The ICJ explained that it is necessary to prove that 'the effective control was exercised, or that the State's instructions were given in respect of each operation, in which the alleged violation occurred, not generally in respect of the overall actions taken by the persons, or groups

---

[79]  *Tallinn Manual 2.0, ibid.*

[80]  *Ibid* para 6, 89. This is in conformity with the view expressed in the Commentary to Rule 4 of the ILC Draft Articles of State Responsibility, according to which an act of a state organ acting in an official capacity, but *ultra vires*, is attributable to the state, whereas an act of such an entity acting in private capacity is not; see ILC Draft Articles on State Responsibility (n 56) para 13.

[81]  *Ibid* Commentary to Art 8.

[82]  *Ibid* Art 8.

[83]  *Ibid* Commentary to Art 8, para 1.

[84]  *Nicaragua* (n 58).

[85]  *Case Concerning the Application of the Convention on the Prevention and Punishment of the Crime of Genocide* (*Bosnia and Herzegovina v Serbia and Montenegro*) (2007) ICJ Rep 43.

of persons having committed the violation'.[86] Reflecting these principles, the *Tallinn Manual 2.0* in Rule 17 comments that cyber operations undertaken by non-state actors are attributable to the state where: (1) they are engaged in pursuant to its instructions or under its direction or control; or (2) the state acknowledges and adopts the operations as its own.[87] The rule encompasses actions of non-state actors functioning as a state's auxiliary, such as private individuals and groups instructed by the state and acting on its behalf as its instrument.[88] As for the 'effective control' standard, the Manual adopts the interpretation of the ICJ in the abovementioned cases and clarifies that:

> a State is in "effective control" of a particular cyber operation by a non-State actor whenever it is the State that determines the execution and the course of the specific operation and the cyber activity engaged by the non-State actor is an "integral part of that operation".[89]

### 2.3.2.3   *Evidentiary issues*

Needless to say, establishing the factual basis for a claim if legal proceedings are instituted is riddled with difficulties, in particular in relation to substantiating that the alleged perpetrator state had effective control over the non-state actor's cyber operations.[90] This raises evidentiary questions, such as which party bears the burden of proof and what the applicable standard of proof is where a state alleges breach of an international obligation. Answering these questions determines the victim state's legal grounds for potential responses, such as the right to resort to countermeasures[91] when the adverse cyber oper-

---

[86]    *Ibid* paras 211–15.

[87]    *Tallinn Manual 2.0* (n 1) Rule 17, 94.

[88]    *Ibid* para 4, 95. The ILC Draft Articles on State Responsibility also state that 'instruction' refers to situation whereby a non-state actor functions as the state auxiliary – see ILC Draft Article on State Responsibility (n 56) Art 8 Commentary.

[89]    *Tallinn Manual 2.0* (n 1) Rule 17 para 6, 96.

[90]    Examples of problems with identifying who is behind a cyber operation include the well-documented incidents in Estonia (2007), Georgia (2008) and the Stuxnet worm (2012) – see Marco Roscini, 'Evidentiary Issues in International Disputes Related to State Responsibility for Cyber Operations' (2015) 50(2) *Texas International Law Journal* 233–73 ('Roscini').

[91]    ILC Draft Articles on State Responsibility (n 56) Art 22. Countermeasures are legally permissible responses to most breaches of international obligations and may deviate from almost any international obligation. In *Gabčíkovo–Nagymaros Project* (n 59) the International Court of Justice accepted that countermeasures might justify otherwise wrongful conduct 'taken in response to a previous international wrongful act of another State and ... directed against that State', para 83, 55.

ations fall below the use of force,[92] or avail itself of the right to self-defence where they meet the criteria of an armed attack.

The 'burden of proof' is a party's duty to prove a disputed assertion or charge, and includes both the burden of persuasion and the burden of production (*onus probandi*). As a general rule, the party that relies on certain facts must produce evidence establishing those facts. Thus, the Permanent Court of International Justice expressly applied the rule that a party asserting a fact bore the burden of proving it;[93] while the ICJ has held that 'as a general rule it is for the party which alleges a fact in support of its claims to prove the existence of that fact'.[94] In the cyber context, where the response is in the form of counter-measures, it may suffice for the injured state to provide evidence that the cyber operation originated from a certain state and that that state did not exercise due diligence in terminating it, without having to prove attribution of the attack itself to the state.[95] Furthermore, the burden of proof does not shift and rests on the party that alleges another state's responsibility for cyber operations.[96]

The 'standard of proof' is the degree or level of proof demanded in a specific case, defined as 'the quantum of evidence necessary to substantiate the factual claims by the parties'.[97] It thus denotes the degree of probability that must be achieved for the trier of facts to determine that the factual allegations are correct.[98] On the domestic level in the context of criminal proceedings, this standard is usually high, requiring proof 'beyond reasonable doubt' (ie, indisputable evidence). In civil matters, it is lower and may be based on: 'clear and convincing evidence' (ie, more than probable, but short of indisputable); the 'preponderance of evidence' or the 'balance of probabilities' (where the existence of the fact to be proved must be more likely than not); together with a '*prima facie*' case (ie, furnishing merely an indicative proof of the correct-

---

[92]   Roscini (n 90) 235.

[93]   *The Mavrommatis Jerusalem Concessions (Greece v Britain)* [1925] PCIJ Ser A no 5; *Legal Status of Costal Greenland (Norway v Denmark)* [1933] PCIJ Ser A/B nos 52 and 53.

[94]   *Ahmadou Sado Biallo (Guinea v DRC)* (Merits) [2010] ICJ Rep 639 para 54.

[95]   However, if a state invokes self-defence against cyber attacks, 'it will have to produce evidence that demonstrates (a) the cyberattack actually occurred, that it was directed against it, and that its scale and effects reached the threshold of an "armed attack" and (b) that it was attributable to a certain [S]tate' – see Roscini (n 90) 239.

[96]   *Ibid* 248.

[97]   James A Green, 'Fluctuating Evidentiary Standards for Self-Defence in the International Court of Justice' (2009) 58(1) *International and Comparative Law Quarterly* 163–79, 165.

[98]   Markus Bensing, *The Law of Evidence Before International Courts and Arbitral Tribunals in Inter-State Disputes* (Veröffentlichungen des Max-Planck-Instituts für ausländisches öffentliches Recht und Völkerrecht, 2010) 506.

ness of the contention made).[99] In civil law jurisdictions, the standard of proof is generally limited to a single rule – that is, the judge must be convinced, or fully convinced that the disputed fact is true; while common law systems use all three variables – 'beyond reasonable doubt', 'balance of probabilities' and a *'prima facie'* threshold.[100] Although international criminal courts adhere to the standard of proof based on 'beyond reasonable doubt',[101] other international courts, tribunals and dispute settlement bodies employ different criteria. ICJ inter-state litigation is best compared with other types of civil litigation, rather than criminal trials.[102] However, neither the ICJ's Statutes nor the Rules of Court set out specific rules pertaining to the standard of proof or indicate the requisite method of proof.[103] To date, the ICJ has not specifically articulated a general standard of proof to be applied in cases brought before it, preferring to consider the issues at hand on a case-by-case basis or as they arise. This makes it difficult to identify a uniform benchmark generally applicable in inter-state litigation.[104] In the context of *jus ad bellum*, where a state resorts to self-defence as an exception to the use of force, the indication from the ICJ is that the standard required is high, being based on clear and convincing evidence,[105] to limit invocation of this exception and thus avoid abuse.[106] There is no case law pertaining to claims arising from inter-state cyber operations and therefore no pronouncements on the applicable test. However, the issue has been subject to scholarly debate. Thus, Professor Roscini has suggested that the same standard as applies to kinetic operations – that is, one based on clear and convincing evidence – seems appropriate where a state exercises the right of self-defence against cyber operations.[107] This is because the *'prima facie'* and 'preponderance of evidence' thresholds may lead to 'specious claims and false or erroneous attribution'; while the 'beyond reasonable doubt' standard

---

[99]   Roscini (n 90) 248.

[100]  *Ibid.*

[101]  Colleen M Rohan, 'Reasonable Doubt Standard of Proof in International Criminal Trials' in Karim AA Khan *et al* (eds), *Principles of Evidence in International Criminal Justice* (Oxford University Press, 2010) 650.

[102]  Roscini (n 90) 248; see also Matthew C Waxman, 'The Use of Force Against States that Might Have Weapons of Mass Destruction' (2009) 31(1) *Michigan Journal of International Law* 1–77, 59.

[103]  Roscini *ibid.*

[104]  *Ibid* 248.

[105]  See *Nicaragua* (n 58) para 29, 109; *Oil Platforms (Islamic Republic of Iran v Unites States of America)* Merits [2003] ICJ Rep para 71, 61; *Armed Activities on the Territory of the Congo (Democratic Republic of Congo v Uganda)* [2005] ICJ Rep, para 72/ 91 in *ibid.*

[106]  *Ibid* 228.

[107]  *Ibid* 253–53.

may be unrealistic.[108] However, cyber espionage does not fall within the ambit of 'cyber attack', but rather 'cyber exploitation' operations.[109] It follows that applying the same evidentiary standard as that required in case of self-defence seems quite high, as the gravity or seriousness of such activities is different. In addition, these types of operations allow states to resort only to counter-measures[110] and not to self-defence – the latter being a legally impermissible response. For these reasons, the standard of proof in cases of cyber espionage where a state resorts to countermeasures should be high or intermediate and in any case lower than that applied to self-defence – namely, based either on convincing evidence or the preponderance of evidence. This seems to be in conformity with the view taken by some governments, including that of the Netherlands, according to which 'international law does not have hard rules on the level of proof required but practice and case law require *sufficient certainty* on the origin of the attack and the identity of [its] author before action can be taken'.[111]

In summary, cyber espionage must be either conducted by or attributed to the state. It will engage its international legal responsibility if the act in question is considered as internationally wrongful – that is, if it breaches a treaty or non-treaty obligation – and if it is attributable to the state both in fact (factual attribution) and in law (legal attribution). Factual attribution considers whether a cyber operation can be traced to a particular computer, system, person, group or organization. In terms of legal attribution, a state's cyber operations are principally attributable to it if they are conducted by an organ exercising state

---

[108]  *Ibid.*

[109]  For a definition of 'cyber exploitation', see Roscini (n 44).

[110]  Some states suggest that an appropriate countermeasure in cyberspace would be, for example, 'a cyber operation... launched to shut down networks or systems that another state is using for a cyberattack', provided that strict conditions are met, such as: the requirement that the injured state invokes the other state's responsibility; the duty to notify of the intention to resort to countermeasures; together with counter-measures being temporary, proportionate, not used in violation of human rights and not amounting to the threat or use of force – see International Law in Cyberspace – The Netherlands (n 55) 7. For discussion in relation to other countermeasures against adverse cyber operations, such as 'active cyber defence', also referred to as a 'hack back' – an 'in kind response against attacker systems' – see Hans-Georg Dederer and Tassila Singer, 'Adverse Cyber Operations: Causality, Attribution, Evidence, and Due Diligence' (2019) 95 *International Law Studies* 430–66, 435; the *Tallinn Manual 2.0* defines 'active cyber defence' as 'the taking of proactive defensive measures outside the defended cyber infrastructure. A "hack-back" ... is a type of active cyber defence' – see *Tallinn Manual 2.0* (n 1) Glossary, 563.

[111]  International Law in Cyberspace – The Netherlands (n 55) 7. For a detailed dis-cussion in relation to states responding to adverse cyber operation through the use of countermeasures, see Dederer and Singer, *ibid.*

functions. However, a state may also be held responsible for the internationally wrongful act of a non-state actor if it is shown that it has: (1) given instructions pursuant to which the violation occurred; (2) exercised effective, as against overall, control over such entity; and/or (3) acknowledged or adopted the operation as its own.

Attribution poses a number of evidentiary questions, including which party bears the burden of proof and what the applicable standard of proof is. In the context of cyber exploitation operations, the victim state bears the burden of proving its allegations. The standard of proof is either high or intermediate – that is, based on convincing evidence or its preponderance, giving that state the right to resort to countermeasures. Based on current practice, at least two broad forms of cyber espionage can be distinguished: (1) politically; and (2) economically motivated cyber spying.

## 2.4    Political Cyber Espionage

Cyber espionage for political ends is based on the same rationale as its traditional counterpart: it is conducted by a state to obtain information relating to another nation's political and military secrets in order to gain an advantage, inform the decision-making process in international relations and/or protect its own national security interests from external threats. This type of espionage may be undertaken by intelligence agencies (eg, the US NSA or UK GCHQ); on the state's behalf by individual hackers; or by groups (eg, the APT1 unit believed to be linked to China's People's Liberation Army).[112]

Political cyber espionage is now almost commonplace and affords undeniable benefits, since it 'enables States to access sensitive information relating to their (actual or potential) enemies and ultimately to better understand their intentions and capabilities'.[113] Cyberspace is particularly well suited to pursue these ends, as intelligence collection is fast, inexpensive and practically unconstrained. Indeed, the former US President Barack Obama, commenting on that country's intelligence-gathering capacity, proclaimed that: 'America's capabilities are unique and the power of new technologies means that there are fewer and fewer technical constraints on what we can do.'[114]

---

[112] Mandiant, 'AP1. Exposing One of China's Cyber Espionage Units' (Mandiant, 2013) ('Mandiant Report'). Described as one of the 'most persistent China's threat actors', APT1 is said to have the capacity to wage extensive and long-running cyber espionage campaigns, enabled by direct government support.

[113] Buchan (n 2) 29.

[114] US President Barak Obama, 'Remarks by the President on Review of Signals Intelligence' (17 January 2014) ('Remarks on Review of Signals Intelligence').

Among the most publicized instances of political spying reportedly under-taken by or on behalf of a variety of governments are GhostNet;[115] Shady Rat;[116] Flame;[117] Red October;[118] the targeted spying revealed in the 2013 Snowden files;[119] and the DNC Hack (discussed below).[120]

In recent years, another form of political cyber activity – cyber electoral interference – attracted a considerable glare of publicity worldwide.[121] The following section examines these practices within the context of cyber espio-nage and demonstrates that not all cyber electoral tampering operations can be classified as espionage, but only those known as 'doxing'.

### 2.4.1 Foreign cyber electoral interference – general

Foreign electoral interference (also known as intervention, tampering or, in common parlance, 'election meddling')[122] is an attempt by a government in one state to covertly or overtly influence elections to a public office in another by various means, such as propaganda campaigns or misinformation.

---

[115] Information Warfare Monitor, 'Tracking GhostNet: Investigating a Cyber Espionage Network', www.nartv.org/mirror/ghostnet.pdf.

[116] Dimitri Alperovitch, 'Revealed: Operation Shady Rat. An Investigation of Targeted Intrusions into More Than 70 Global Companies, Governments and Non-Profit Organizations During the Last Five Years' (2011), www.mcafee.com/us/resources/white-papers/wp-operation-shady-rat.pdf.

[117] *The Daily Telegraph*, 'Flame: World's Most Complex Computer Virus Exposed' (28 May 2012).

[118] Kaspersky, 'Red October. Diplomatic Cyber Attacks Investigation. Report' (2013).

[119] CoE, Committee on Legal Affairs and Human Rights, 'Mass Surveillance. Explanatory Memorandum by Mr Pieter Omtzigt, Rapporteur' (26 January 2015) paras 54–57 ('CoE Mass Surveillance Memorandum'). Targeted spying for political ends includes GCHQ's 'Royal Concierge' operation, which 'involved monitoring at least 350 upscale hotels around the world for more than three years to target, search and analyse [hotel] reservations to detect diplomats and government officials'. Similarly, the NSA engaged in the targeted surveillance of, *inter alia*, the UN, the European Union and other international organizations through such operations as 'Blackfoot', 'Perdido' and 'Powell'.

[120] Ellen Nakashima and Shane Harris, 'How the Russians Hacked the DNC and Posted Its Emails to WikiLeaks', *The Washington Post* (14 July 2018).

[121] See Barrie Sander, 'Democracy Under the Influence: Paradigm of State Responsibility for Cyber Influence Operations on Elections' (2019) 18(1) *Chinese Journal of International Law*, 1–56 ('Sander'); Schmitt (n 69) 66.

[122] The term was popularized in the US media in July 2016 at the time of Russia's alleged release of the US Democratic National Committee's emails. In this context, the term 'election meddling' was used to suggest that Russia was supporting one US presidential candidate over the other – see Victor Clark, 'What is Election Meddling and When Did Everyone Start Using That Term?', *Lawfare* (30 July 2018), www.lawfareblog.com/what-election-meddling-and-when-did-everyone-start-using-term.

Exerting influence over democratic processes in a foreign state in nothing new. For example, in 1794, France attempted to intervene in US politics by having an agent release private information to the public to influence the presidential election in favour of Thomas Jefferson, causing one commentator to exclaim that 'there never was so barefaced and disgraceful an interference of a foreign power in any free country'.[123] The US has also historically exhibited tendencies to aggressively engage in covert operations to influence elections. Well-documented instances from the 1950s onwards include involvement in Guatemala, Iran, Chile, Nicaragua and most recently Russia, with the US intervening to support Boris Yeltsin during his 1996 re-election campaign.[124]

In July 2016, however, election tampering was thrust from relative obscurity in the minds of the general public into the media spotlight. This was the result of allegations pertaining to the involvement of the Kremlin in the US presidential elections that year. In mid-2016 claims began to emerge that Russia's General Staff Main Intelligence Directorate (GRU) had compromised the US Democratic National Committee's (DNC) computer networks, resulting in a release via WikiLeaks of a cache of emails, which contributed to damaging presidential candidate's Secretary Hilary Clinton election prospects. The interference – referred to as the 'DNC Hack' – led to suggestions that Russia was behind the operation 'for the purposes of helping Donald Trump'.[125] Shortly afterwards, an investigation conducted by the Central Intelligence Agency, the Federal Bureau of Investigation and the NSA under the auspices of the Office of the Director of National Intelligence (ODNI) was commenced into whether individuals associated with the Trump campaign were coordinating with Moscow in its interference activities.[126] The ODNI report concluded with a 'high degree of confidence' that:

> Russian President Vladimir Putin ordered an influence campaign in 2016 aimed at the US presidential elections. Russia's goals were to undermine public faith in the US democratic process, denigrate Secretary Clinton, and harm her electability and potential presidency. We further assess Putin and the Russian Government developed a clear preference for President-elect Trump.[127]

---

[123] Alden Fletcher, 'Foreign Election Interference in the Founding Era', *Lawfare* (25 October 2018), www.lawfareblog.com/foreign-election-interference-founding-era.
[124] Schmitt (n 69) 38.
[125] *Ibid.*
[126] *Ibid.*
[127] Office of the Director of National Intelligence, ICA 2017-01D, 'Assessing Russia Activities and Intentions in Recent US Elections' (6 January 2017).

As a result, in late December 2016, the Obama administration expelled 35 Russian diplomats and seized two diplomatic properties.[128] Two years later, the Trump government issued further sanctions against five entities and 19 individuals, publicly acknowledging for the first time that 'the Administration is confronting and countering malign Russian cyber activity, including their attempted interference in the US elections'.[129] In May 2017, Special Counsel Robert Muller was appointed to investigate 'the Russian government's efforts to interfere in the 2016 presidential elections, including any links or coordination between the Russian government and individuals associated with the Trump Campaign',[130] primarily focusing on whether this constituted a criminal offence under US federal law, rather than any breach of international law. The investigation's findings unequivocally confirmed Russia's involvement and were published in the March 2019 Muller Report,[131] which stated, among other things, that:

> the investigation established that Russia interfered in the 2016 elections principally through two operations. First, a Russian entity carried out a social media campaign that favoured presidential candidate Donald J. Trump and disparaged presidential candidate Hillary Clinton. Second, a Russian intelligence service conducted computer-intrusion operations against entities, employees, and volunteers working on the Clinton Campaign and then released stolen documents. The investigation also identified numerous links between the Russian government and the Trump Campaign.[132]

However, Muller found no criminal conspiracy between the president's team and the Kremlin, concluding that:

> although the investigation established that the Russian government perceived it would benefit from a Trump presidency and worked to secure that outcome … the investigation did not establish that members of the Trump Campaign conspired or coordinated with the Russian government in its election interference activities.[133]

---

[128] Peter Baker, 'White House Penalises Russian's Over Election Meddling and Cyberattacks', *The New York Times* (15 March 2018).

[129] US Department of the Treasury, Press Release, 'Treasury Sanctions Russian Cyber Actors for Interference with the 2016 US Elections and Malicious Cyber Attacks' (15 March 2018).

[130] *Ibid.*

[131] US Department of Justice, 'Report on the Investigation into Russian Interference in the 2016 Presidential Elections' (March 2019) ('Muller Report').

[132] *Ibid.*

[133] *Ibid* 2.

Another official acknowledgement of Russia's targeting Western democracies through malicious cyber activities in an attempt to interfere with their electoral processes was made by the UK government in its 2020 Russia Report.[134] The document confirmed the Kremlin's electoral interference to broaden its political influence overseas[135] and acknowledged that the UK was clearly Russia's target for both disinformation campaigns and influence operations,[136] thus potentially interfering in the UK democratic process. Having considered the widespread allegations that Russia had sought to influence the 2016 Brexit referendum, the Report recognized the possibility of Russian interference in that process. It concluded, however, that in the absence of a post-referendum assessment by the intelligence community, it was not possible to assert this with sufficient degree of certainty.[137] This, the document noted, is in contrast to the prompt assessment of Russia's interference in the 2016 US elections and is somewhat disappointing in light of credible suggestions that Russia undertook an 'influence campaign' in relation to the 2014 Scottish independence referendum. However, similarly to the Muller Report, it is inward looking, focusing on domestic responses to the Russian threat rather than employing the language of international law – although it did call for international actions in relation to 'offensive cyber'.[138]

There is no doubt that foreign electoral tampering through a variety of cyber operations is spreading fast, with a credible potential to undermine Western countries' voting systems. Indeed, as noted by Professor Michael Schmitt, the general editor of the *Tallinn 2.0 Manual*, 'such cyber operations signal their growing appeal to States wishing to manipulate foreign elections'.[139] Given

---

[134] The Report states that '[t]he security threat posed by Russia is difficult for the West to manage as … it appears fundamentally nihilistic. Russia seems to see foreign policy as a zero-sum game: any activities it can take, which damage the West are fundamentally good for Russia …' – see Russia Report (n 24) para 1.

[135] *Ibid* para 13 and para 28. Other instances include presidential election campaigns in France in 2017 and in Ukraine in 2014; see also see Constanze Stelzenmüller, Testimony before the US Senate Select Committee on Intelligence, 'The Impact of Russian Influence on Germany's 2017 Elections' (28 June 2017), referring to the 2017 German federal elections allegedly involving Russia's campaign to discredit Chancellor Angela Merkel.

[136] For a definition of 'disinformation campaign' and 'influence operations', see section 2.4.2.

[137] Russia Report (n 24) paras 39–48, 12–14.

[138] *Ibid* paras 25–26.

[139] Schmitt (n 69) 36. See also 2020 Global Inventory of Organized Social Media Manipulation, a study conducted under the auspices of the Oxford Internet Institute, which highlights recent trends of 'computational propaganda' by, *inter alia*, governments and political parties across 81 countries and the evolving tools, capacities, strategies and resources used to manipulate public opinion around the globe. These tactics

the increased prevalence of such operations and the fact that cyberspace constitutes an enabling global environment for such activities, there is a need for
international cooperation to respond to these challenges. To this end, a number
of questions arise – not least of which is how the international community is
to combat this hostile phenomenon and defend electoral processes the world
over. In this context at least, two preliminary queries require attention: (1)
how to define 'cyber election meddling' in legal terms and (2) whether these
exploits can be said to fall within the category of political cyber espionage.

### 2.4.2    Foreign cyber electoral interference defined

An election is the formal choosing of a person for an office or position, usually
by a vote.[140] The right to periodic, genuine and free elections held on the
basis of a secret ballot forms the nucleus of the right to citizens' democratic
governance and as such is prescribed in international human rights treaties
and customary international law. In particular, Article 25 of the International
Covenant on Civil and Political Rights (ICCPR) states that:

> every citizen shall have the right … to vote and to be elected at genuine periodic
> elections, which shall be by universal and equal suffrage and shall be held by secret
> ballot, guaranteeing free expression of the will of the electorate.[141]

A fundamental facet to ensuring the process of democratic governance is the
requirement that elections be unencumbered both at the time of balloting and
prior to the vote taking place, as the electorate must be able to form their opinions independently and without compulsion or manipulative influence by the
state or by private parties.[142] It follows that electoral interference is a process
undertaken by a variety of state and non-state actors (including foreign governments and their proxies) in order to manipulate the outcome of an election
and therefore deny voters the freedom of choice. 'Cyber electoral interference'
(or 'cyber electoral meddling') can therefore be defined as cyber operations
undertaken by or on behalf of a foreign state aimed at causing an impediment
to the target state's ability to hold free and fair elections.

---

comprise disinformation activities using social media to spread 'computational prop-
aganda' and disinformation about politics – Samantha Bradshaw, Hannah Bailey and
Philip N. Howard, 'Industrialized Disinformation. 2020 Global Inventory of Organized
Social Media Manipulation' (Oxford Internet Institute, 13 January 2021).

[140]  *Shorter Oxford English Dictionary* (Oxford University Press, 2007) 806.

[141]  UNGA, International Covenant on Civil and Political Rights (adopted 16
December 1966, entered into force 23 March 1976) 999 UNTS 999, 171 Art 25(1)
('ICCPR').

[142]  Niels Peterson, 'Elections, Right to Participate in, International Protection' *Max
Plank Encyclopedia of Public International Law* (October 2012) para 7.

Cyber electoral interference operations comprise a number of techniques, a typology of which has been mapped out by a number of legal scholars, including Barrie Sander.[143] Sander divides the means and methods employed by foreign state actors into two broad categories: (1) cyber tampering with a state's election infrastructure;[144] and (2) 'influence operations', also referred to as 'weaponization of information'.[145] The latter involve the 'deployment of resources for cognitive ends that foster or change a targeted audience's behaviour'.[146] Simply put, influence operations are performed to 'take advantage of human cognitive and emotional biases'.[147] They can be further subdivided into practices known as 'doxing' and 'information operations'.[148] 'Doxing' is 'the hacking or leaking of non-public information into the public domain for the purpose of harming an individual, organization or State'.[149] A good example of this is the GRU hack of the US DNC in order to undermine Secretary Clinton prior to the 2016 US presidential elections, discussed above. Information operations are a 'deliberate use of newly-created or publicly available information to threaten, confuse, or mislead a target audience'[150] and comprise malicious information (or 'malinformation', also known as 'trolling') and 'disinformation'. Trolling involves 'threatening, abusive, discriminatory, harassing or disruptive online behaviour that aims to cause harm to a person, organization or a State'.[151] Disinformation operations entail 'the spread of verifiably false or misleading information that is created, presented and disseminated for economic gain or to intentionally deceive the public and may cause public harm … [including] threats to democratic, political and policy making processes'.[152]

---

[143] Sander (n 121) 5–15; see also Duncan Hollis, 'The Influence of War; The War for Influence' (2018) 32(1) *Temple Journal of International and Comparative Law* 33–46 ('Hollis').

[144] Sander (n 121) 6. This includes tampering with voting machines in order, *inter alia,* to alter the vote tallies; and tampering with voter registration databases to block voters for casting their votes.

[145] *Ibid* 7.

[146] Hollis (n 143) 36.

[147] Sander (n 121) 7.

[148] *Ibid* 8–9.

[149] *Ibid* 8. Doxing operations comprise three other categories: (1) a 'public interest hack' – that is, a type of whistleblowing that exposes wrongdoing to promote public good; (2) a 'strategic hack' – that is, leaking material that is of interest to the public, but which may be pursued to advance the interests of the leaker and not necessarily those of the public; and (3) a 'tainted hack' – that is, the deliberate inclusion of false information within a large set of genuine confidential data that is leaked to the public.

[150] *Ibid.*

[151] *Ibid* 11.

[152] European Commission, 'Commission-Tackling Online Disinformation: A European Approach' (26 April 2018) COM(2018) 236 Final 26, 3–4 in *ibid.*

This may entail the dissemination of blended content – that is, a mixture of factual and false information.[153]

### 2.4.3     Foreign cyber electoral interference as political cyber espionage

The above taxonomy represents a complex tapestry of activities conducted by foreign actors in the context of elections. In practice, they are frequently combined in a coordinated campaign to influence voters; and the boundaries between them are not clear cut, making it difficult to pigeonhole them in a particular legal category. Doctrinally, not all cyber meddling operations fit neatly within the bracket of political cyber espionage. Cyber spying principally entails the copying of non-publicly available, confidential data without the owner's consent. It follows that foreign cyber meddling in the form of 'information operations' involving both malinformation and disinformation campaigns cannot be categorized as political cyber espionage, because these methods involve the use of publicly available information that usually derives from open sources to threaten or mislead the target audience. As noted by Sander, information operations are characterized by the 'weaponization of information' which is already in the public domain or which is newly created based on publicly available data, where the author usually operates covertly by hiding his or her identity and declines to acknowledge his or her involvement in such campaigns.[154] Furthermore, information operations do not involve any form of cyber attack[155] or require any type of cyber exploitation – that is, unauthorized access to other computers, computer systems or networks for the purpose of exfiltrating information without affecting the functionality of the accessed system, or of corrupting, amending or delating the data resident in that system.[156] For these reasons, they cannot be said to constitute acts of cyber espionage.

The same cannot be said of doxing operations, however. This type of electoral tampering involves the practice of cyber exploitation and as such can be regarded as political cyber espionage. This is because doxing involves the use of non-publicly available information gained through unauthorized access to a computer system (eg, social media or an email account) for the purpose of exfiltrating confidential data and placing it in the public domain in order to influence the political outcome (usually by causing harm through publicly discrediting or damaging the target of the exposure – be it a specific

---

[153] Sander notes that the term 'disinformation operations' has become known as 'fake news', but points out that in this context it is inadequate and misleading – see Sander (n 121) 12.

[154]   *Ibid* 15.

[155]   For a definition of 'cyber attack' see Roscini (n 44) 17.

[156]   *Ibid* 65.

candidate or a political party). A case in point is Russia's GRU exfiltration of email traffic – which, according to Professor Schmitt, clearly constituted espionage.[157] Similarly, collection operations targeting US primary campaigns, think tanks and lobbying groups that are viewed as likely to shape future US policies qualify as espionage.[158]

In summary, cyber electoral interference can be carried out through: (1) cyber espionage operations involving doxing (ie, capturing and leaking into the public domain information that is harmful to one of the candidates or a political party); and/or (2) through other means which are not cyber espionage operations *per se*, such as malinformation (trolling) or disinformation.

## 2.5    Economic Cyber Espionage

This form of cyber spying is conducted for economic gain and has become increasingly prevalent, being now widely practised by most states.

It involves the theft through cyberspace by a state of trade and other industrial secrets held by a private enterprise located in a foreign jurisdiction. The digital environment has quickly become a domain for a wide range of industrial espionage threat actors, including adversarial nation states, commercial enterprises operating under state influence and proxy hacker groups.[159]

Some countries – in particular, the US – have long recognized the detrimental nature of economic cyber espionage. It has been publicly acknowledged that they represent a significant challenge to the country's prosperity, security and competitive advantage. This is because the US has been and continues to be the target of persistent threats posed by foreign state and non-state actors with regard to its research, development and manufacturing sector, including in such areas as energy, biotechnology, defence and ICT.[160] The damage associated with these practices has been officially admitted by the US government on numerous occasions – not least in its seminal 2011 US International Strategy for Cyberspace, according to which:

> the persistent theft of intellectual property, whether by criminals, foreign firms, or State actors working on their behalf, can erode competitiveness in the global economy, and business opportunities to innovate. The United States will take measures to identify and respond to such actions to help build an international

---

[157] Schmitt (n 69) 57.
[158] *Ibid.*
[159] US National Counterintelligence and Security Centre, *Foreign Economic Espionage in Cyberspace* (26 July 2018) ('*Foreign Economic Espionage*').
[160] *Ibid* 11.

environment that recognizes such acts as unlawful and impermissible, and hold such actors accountable.[161]

Foreign intelligence services and actors working on their behalf are said to represent the most persistent and pervasive cyber intelligence threat to the US.[162] In particular, China, Russia, North Korea and Iran have been singled out as 'the most capable and active cyber actors tied to economic espionage and the potential theft of US trade secrets and proprietary information'.[163] The dangers that these countries' cyber espionage activities pose both to the US and generally to the global economy were acknowledged in the 2018 National Cyber Strategy of the United States of America, which stated that:

> Russia, Iran and North Korea conducted reckless cyber-attacks that harmed American international business and our allies and partners without paying costs likely to deter future cyber aggression. China engaged in cyber-enabled economic espionage and trillions of dollars of intellectual property theft.[164]

Chinese involvement in the theft of US trade secrets is particularly acute and was made publicly known with the release of the 2013 Mandiant Report,[165] which confirmed that China has used and 'continue[s] to use cyber espionage to support its strategic development goals-science and technology advancements, military modernization and economic policy objectives'.[166] The scale and propensity of economic cyber espionage against the US are such that it is now recognized as representing a serious threat to that country's national security. To this end, General Keith Alexander – the former director of the NSA – remarked that economic cyber espionage constitutes 'the greatest transfer of wealth in history', with US companies losing about $250 billion per year through intellectual property theft.[167]

However, the US is not entirely blameless of engaging in economically motivated cyber espionage itself. The leaked Edward Snowden documents revealed that the NSA endeavoured to exploit the technology of Chinese

---

[161] The White House, *International Strategy for Cyberspace: Prosperity, Security and Openness in a Networked World* (2011) 18.

[162] *Foreign Economic Espionage* (n 159) 1.

[163] *Ibid.*

[164] The White House, *National Cyber Strategy of the United States of America* (September 2018).

[165] Mandiant Report (n 112).

[166] *Foreign Economic Espionage* (n 159) 5.

[167] Josh Rogin, 'NSA Chief: Cybercrime Constitutes the Greatest Transfer of Wealth in History', *The Cable* (9 July 2012), https://foreignpolicy.com/2012/07/09/nsa -chief-cybercrime-constitutes-the-greatest-transfer-of-wealth-in-history/.

telecommunications giant Huawei by creating 'back doors' directly into its networks.[168] Code-named 'Shotgiant',[169] the operation's main aim was to determine whether Huawei is truly an independent company or whether it has any links to the People's Liberation Army, since Washington has long considered the company as an arm of the Chinese state and therefore a security threat.[170] In addition, as Huawei invested in new technology and laid down undersea cables to connect its $40 billion a year 'networking empire', the NSA saw an opportunity to gain access to key Chinese customers in countries such as Iran, Afghanistan, Pakistan, Kenya and Cuba.[171] Robustly rebutting the allegations of economic cyber espionage, the Obama administration was adamant that the operation was conducted for legitimate national security purposes.[172] In so doing, the US officials distinguished between the hacking conducted by the US intelligence operations against China and the corporate theft that the Chinese undertake against US companies.[173]

Most states regard acts of economic cyber espionage as a criminal offence and have adopted legislation to protect against these activities by imposing penal sanctions. For example, the US invoked the Economic Espionage Act 1996 in the 2014 Department of Justice's indictment of five members of the Chinese People's Liberation Army for the alleged economic cyber espionage activities of Unit 61398.[174] Furthermore, in 2017, four Russians – including two officers of the Russian Federal Security Service – were accused of[175] computer hacking, economic espionage and other criminal offences in relation

---

[168] According to the documents released by Edward Snowden, the NSA accessed servers and 'obtained information about the workings of the giant routers and complex digital switches that Huawei boasts connect a third of the world's population and monitored communications of the company's top executives' – see David E Sanger and Nicole Perlroth, 'NSA Breached Chinese Servers as Security Threat', *New York Times* (22 March 2014), www.nytimes.com/2014/03/23/world/asia/nsa-breached-chinese -servers-seen-as-spy-peril.html?_r=0.

[169] *Ibid.*

[170] *Ibid.*

[171] *Ibid.*

[172] *Ibid.* Caitlin M Hayden, the White House Spokesman, stated that: 'we do not give intelligence we collect to US companies to enhance their international competitiveness or increase their bottom line. Many countries cannot say the same.'

[173] *Ibid.*

[174] The US Department of Justice, Office of Public Affairs, 'US Charges Five Chinese Military Hackers for Cyber Espionage Against US Corporations and a Labour Organization for Commercial Advantages' (19 May 2014), www.justice.gov/opa/pr/us -charges-five-chinese-military-hackers-cyber-espionage-against-us-corporations-and -labor.

[175] The charges were based on numerous breaches of the computer fraud law, 18 USC §1030.

to the accessing of Yahoo's network and the contents of webmail accounts. Allegedly, they stole information from at least 500 million Yahoo accounts in order to obtain unauthorized access to other webmail providers, such as Google.[176] The purported offences were said to constitute 'one of the largest data breaches in history, [which] the United States [pledged to] vigorously investigate and prosecute the people behind such attacks to the fullest extent of the law.'[177] In 2018, the US charged nine Iranian hackers with stealing intellectual property from more than 144 US universities, allegedly at the behest of Iran's Islamic Revolutionary Guard Corps. The information was subsequently used to 'benefit the government of Iran and other Iranian customers, including Iranian universities'.[178]

Economic cyber espionage will continue to evolve with technological advancements in artificial intelligence (AI)[179] and the Internet of Things (IoT).[180] It is feared that these technologies are set to introduce new vulnerabilities to computer networks the world over.

In brief, based on the above analysis, cyber espionage comprises the following key characteristics: (1) the non-consensual, remote accessing, copying, collection and/or storage of confidential information; (2) either specific or in bulk; (3) resident in computers or computer systems; (4) conducted by or attributed to a state; (5) considered to endanger the target state's political and/ or economic interests; (6) therefore subject to national laws imposing criminal sanctions upon conviction; and (7) not directly regulated by international law, but subject to numerous rules that indirectly apply to this practice (discussed in more detail below). Cyber espionage falls into two main categories: (1) political cyber espionage, which also includes certain types of cyber-enabled

---

[176] US Department of Justice, Office of Public Affairs, 'US Charges Russian FSB Officers and Their Criminal Conspirators for Hacking Yahoo and Millions of Email Accounts' (15 March 2017).

[177] *Ibid.* Attorney General Jess Sessions of the US Department of Justice.

[178] *Foreign Economic Espionage* (n 159) 10.

[179] BJ Copeland, 'Artificial Intelligence' (11 August 2020) *Encyclopaedia Britannica.* 'Artificial intelligence' is 'the ability of a digital computer or computer-controlled robot to perform tasks commonly associated with intelligent beings. The term is frequently applied to the project of developing systems endowed with the intellectual processes characteristic of humans, such as the ability to reason, discover meaning, generalize, or learn from past experience'.

[180] See, for example, National Cyber Security Centre, 'The Cyber Threat to UK Business. 2016/2017 Report' (National Crime Agency, 2017) 4. In relation to the ecosystem created by the IoT, the Report warned that: 'the rise of Internet connected devices gives attackers more opportunity. Consumer goods and industrial systems combined with the ever increasing commercial footprint online provides threat actors with more attack vectors than ever before.'

electoral interference – that is, 'doxing' operations; and (2) economic cyber espionage – which involves the theft of trade and other industrial secrets.

## 3.     SURVEILLANCE

### 3.1     General

The word 'surveillance' derives from the French verb '*surveiller*', which means to 'oversee, watch' and came to the English language during the French Revolution of 1789–99, when in 1792 the first *Comite de Surveillance* was set up to keep watch over suspicious strangers and recommend suspects for arrest.[181]

Surveillance involves closely observing or listening in to a person or place in the hope of gathering information. It has been described as 'the focused, systematic and routine attention to personal details for purposes of influence, management, protection or direction'.[182] This scrutiny of an individual or a group is deliberate and sustained, rather than random, occasional or spontaneous. It is by no means a new practice.[183] It has been shown in a number of ethnographic studies to have existed in one form or another in even the most primitive societies.[184] It can therefore be said that surveillance has always had a role and a presence in social life. However, it has grown in importance with the rise of the modern state, becoming part of the ordinary administrative apparatus that characterizes it.[185] Performed by government organs, it plays a vital role in maintaining social order, as it facilitates crime detection and prevention, among other things. However, when unconstrained, it impairs individuals' autonomy and stifles fundamental rights, which form the bedrock of free society.

The dangers of secret and unabated state surveillance essentially comprise two facets.[186] First, surveillance is harmful because it can inhibit the exercise of civil liberties. In this sense, the close scrutiny of activities such as thinking, reading and communicating with others impedes political and social develop-

---

[181]    *BBC News*, 'The Very French History of the Word 'Surveillance'' (14 July 2015). Subsequently, local surveillance committees were established in every French municipality to monitor the actions and movements of all foreigners, dissidents and suspected persons and to deliver certificates of citizenship.
[182]    David Lyon, *Surveillance Studies* (Polity Press, 2007) 14.
[183]    *Ibid.*
[184]    Ivana Manokha, 'Surveillance, Panopticism, and Self-Discipline in the Digital Age' (2018) *Surveillance and Society* 219, 227.
[185]    *Lyon* (n 182) 14.
[186]    Neil M Richards, 'The Dangers of Surveillance' (2013) *Harvard Law Review* 1934–65, 1935.

ment, as it makes individuals reluctant to experiment with new, controversial or deviant ideas.[187] The second threat that secret surveillance creates results from the power dynamic between the watcher and the watched, which may lead to a variety of harms, such as discrimination, coercion, prosecution and blackmail.[188] This latter phenomenon and its effects on individual and social liberties were discussed and analysed in depth in the writings of Jeremy Bentham,[189] an eighteenth-century English philosopher and social theorist. Bentham devised an architectural model of a prison, called the Panopticon, which enabled the guards stationed within a single, central, concealed watchtower to keep all inmates under constant observation without them being able to ascertain whether they were being watched. The system, based on a constant state of agitation and fear, became a model of external surveillance.[190] Bentham argued that as this caused the prisoners to assume that they were always observed, it encouraged them to be self-disciplined and well-behaved. The Panopticon also served as a deterrent to those who visited the prison, as ultimately they would be disinclined to commit crimes, having witnessed the prospects of life in such circumstances. Therefore, the prison served as a disincentive not only to the inmates from misbehaving or committing future crimes, but also to general public from criminal activity and incarceration. A valuable contribution to Bentham's concept was subsequently made by the writings of French intellectual and publicist Michael Foucault, who expanded the notion of the Panopticon as a metaphor for social control applicable not only in the context of the prison system, but also for all citizens.[191] His concept – which became known as 'panopticism' – encapsulates internal rather than external surveillance, whereby the gaze of the watcher is internalized to such an extent that the individual becomes his or her own guard. Consequently, 'the power of the gaze' causes him or her, without coercion, to exercise self-discipline and self-restraint to conform to the perceived expectations of the 'watchers',[192] thus creating a power mechanism and a culture control characteristic of authoritarian states.

Subsequently, the scope of the enquiry into the practice of surveillance has significantly expanded with advances in technology, resulting in an interdisciplinary field of study that amalgamates the work of sociologists, jurists, political scientists and philosophers to engage with questions centred on the values

---

[187]   *Ibid.*
[188]   *Ibid.*
[189]   Jeremy Bentham, *The Works of Jeremy Bentham* (William Trait, 1838–43).
[190]   *Ibid.*
[191]   Michael Foucault, *Discipline and Punish: The Birth of the Prison* (Vintage Books, 1979) 195–228.
[192]   *Ibid* 202–03.

and harms of surveillance. This has inevitably led to the development of the contemporary surveillance discourse, which is much broader than that pertaining to the panoptic state. This burgeoning field comprises, among other things, an analysis of the impact of closed-circuit television; big data;[193] the IoT; the online storage of medical, banking and other personal data; the increased commodification of personal information by websites and social media; and state sponsored mass cyber surveillance. However, whether it is conceived in terms of Bentham's Panopticon or Orwell's fictitious 'Big Brother', the inescapable conclusion must be that the fear of being watched causes the watched to act and think differently from how they might normally do if they were not subject to such ubiquitous observation.

That said, an articulation of surveillance as inherently dangerous omits the counterargument usually deployed by governments, according to which it serves the intelligence and law enforcement agencies as a means of investigating crime and preventing potentially violent offences, such as acts of terrorism. In this context, three broad variables may help to determine whether surveillance is deleterious or problematic: (1) the cause for undertaking it, including (2) its proportionality; and (3) compliance with human rights obligations.

### 3.1.1    The cause for undertaking state surveillance
The purpose of state surveillance is fundamentally the safeguarding of security *sensu lato*. It is entrusted to the dedicated government agencies. For example, in the UK the security service MI5 is tasked with, among other things, the protection of 'national security against threats from espionage, terrorism and sabotage, from the activities of agents of foreign powers and from nations intended to overthrow or undermine parliamentary democracy by political, industrial or violent means'.[194] At the heart of MI5's work is the collection of intelligence to build up detailed knowledge of threats to the country.[195] The emphasis is placed on the gathering of secret as opposed to publicly available information. The principal techniques include: direct surveillance; the interception of communications (eg, monitoring emails or phone calls); communications data (including the use of bulk communications data) and

---

[193] See, for example, Omer Tene and Jules Polonetsky, 'Big Data for All: Privacy and User Control in the Age of Analytics' (2013) 11 *Northwestern Journal of Technology and Intellectual Property* 239–73.

[194] UK Security Service MI5, 'Law and Governance', www.mi5.gov.uk/law-and-governance.

[195] UK Security Service MI5, 'Gathering Intelligence', www.mi5.gov.uk/gathering-intelligence ('MI5 Gathering Intelligence').

bulk personal data sets (BPDs);[196] intrusive surveillance (eg, installing eaves-dropping devices in someone's home or car); and equipment interference (eg, covertly accessing computers, smartphones, tablets etc.).[197] Similarly, the UK GCHQ is a public body described as 'foreign focused signals intelligence agency'[198] and 'a world leading intelligence, cyber and security agency with the mission to keep the UK safe'.[199] It operates in five broadly defined mission areas: counter terrorism; cybersecurity; strategic advantage; serious and organized crime; and support to defence.[200] GCHQ's 'licence to operate' derives from the Investigatory Powers Act 2016 (IPA),[201] which supersedes the earlier Regulation of Investigatory Powers Act 2000 (RIPA).[202]

### 3.1.1.1 Proportionality

The benefits of state surveillance are recognized in most domestic legal systems, which generally allow these practices to take place, but on specific legal grounds that prescribe the circumstances in which surveillance may be lawfully conducted. At the heart of surveillance is the covert collection of closed source information, which in itself may enable the state to influence and control its population, as evidenced by a number of historical examples, where pervasive and intrusive observation was deployed to help minimize the risk of political dissent. An illustration of one of the most invasive types of surveillance apparatus is the former German Democratic Republic's[203] Ministry of State Security, known as the Stasi. Widely regarded as a symbol of repression during its period of operation, this secret police force amassed archives containing files on an estimated 6 million people.[204] The degree of intrusion was profound and encapsulated every aspect of daily life, facilitated by an army of informants acting for the government who operated in every sphere of society,

---

[196] BPDs are data sets containing information about a large number of people which can be accessed in a targeted way to identify or find information about subjects of interest.

[197] MI5 Gathering Intelligence (n 195).

[198] GCHQ, 'Legal Framework', www.gchq.gov.uk/section/governance/legal-framework ('GCHQ Legal Framework').

[199] GCHQ, 'Mission. Overview', www.gchq.gov.uk/section/mission/overview.

[200] *Ibid.*

[201] Investigatory Powers Act 2016 c 25 ('IPA').

[202] Regulation of Investigatory Powers Act 2000 c 23 ('RIPA'). Part 1 Chapter 2 of the act remained in force until its repeal at the end of 2019; the Investigatory Powers Act 2016 (Commencement No 11) Regulation 2019 No 147 c 7.

[203] The German Democratic Republic existed between 1949–90 as part of the so-called Eastern Bloc during the Cold War.

[204] Amnesty International, 'Lessons for the Stasi-A Cautionary Tale on Mass Surveillance' (31 March 2015).

using sinister spying techniques and tools to record individuals in their homes, at work and at cultural, social and sporting events.[205] As a result, the state possessed deep knowledge of what members of the public said or did, which in turn was used to manipulate and control the population.[206]

Consequently, Stasi Germany came to symbolize unrestrained surveillance through an unprecedented intrusion into private lives. It demonstrates that such a disproportionate, all-pervasive scrutiny undoubtedly has a detrimental effect not only upon individual privacy, but also has a 'chilling effect' on a wider range of other human rights, from freedom of expression, association and assembly to protection from discrimination.[207] The Stasi example is a reminder that the protection of privacy is pivotal, not only because it safeguards personal autonomy, but also because it acts as a gateway or guardian to other rights. It follows that its deprivation affects not just individuals, but also whole communities. Decades later, this was officially acknowledged by the former US President Obama in the context of NSA cyber surveillance, who conceded the need for a balance to be struck between sustained intelligence gathering and civil liberties.[208] In the 2014 Remarks on the Review of Signals Intelligence, alluding to the infamous 1972 'Watergate scandal',[209] the President stated that:

> given the unique powers of the State, it is not enough for leaders to say: trust us, we won't abuse the data we collect. For history has too many examples when that trust has been breached. Our system of government is built on the premise that our liberty cannot depend on the good intentions of those in power; it depends on the law to constrain those powers.[210]

### 3.1.1.2   Compliance with human rights obligations

Viewed from the human rights perspective and as illustrated by past examples, unbridled, covert state surveillance can potentially cause serious harm to privacy. Therefore, the need to safeguard citizens from constant observation and intrusion has long been recognized in international human rights

---

[205]   *Ibid.*

[206]   *Ibid.*

[207]   See, for example, Dilma Rousseff's Statement (n 2) to the UNGA in the aftermath of the NSA mass surveillance exposures, stating that 'in the absence of the right to privacy, there can be no true freedom of expression and opinion and therefore no effective democracy'.

[208]   *Remarks on Review of Signals Intelligence* (n 114).

[209]   'Watergate' was a political scandal that began in 1972, involving President Richard Nixon's tactics in his attempts to secure re-election to presidential office, including illegal surveillance; it ultimately resulted in his impeachment and subsequent resignation in 1974 – see *History*, 'Watergate Scandal' (29 October 2009), www .history.com/topics/1970s/watergate.

[210]   *Remarks on Review of Signals Intelligence* (n 114).

frameworks – most notably in Article 17 of the ICCPR and Article 8 of the European Convention on Human Rights (ECHR).[211] Both of these provisions assert the right to privacy of communications and protect against unlawful state interference; although they recognize that it is a qualified rather than an absolute right. To this end, in specific circumstances, privacy infringements are permissible, but only if certain conditions are met.[212] Thus, in *Leander v Sweden*[213] the European Court of Human Rights (ECtHR) held that a state can pursue its designated functions through a security service that has clear legal grounds. In principle, therefore, the jurisprudence of the ECtHR recognizes the need for the intelligence and law enforcement agencies to have powers of covert surveillance. However, the means employed must have a legitimate legal basis and be shown to be necessary to protect democratic institutions, while any interference with the right to privacy must be supported by relevant and sufficient reason and be proportionate to the aims pursued.[214] It follows that surveillance techniques must comply with the legal requirements set out in the domestic legislation authorizing the use of these powers, and with human rights laws.[215]

In the UK, following the reform of the surveillance legislation, the powers for interception of communications are laid down in the Investigatory Powers Act 2016 and its Codes of Practice (replacing the RIPA and its Codes of Practice), together with the Human Rights Act 1998,[216] and pertain to the working methods of GCHQ. Thus, in order to comply with the human rights obligations set out therein, the IPA provides that the gathering of information conducted by GCHQ must be based on interception warrants issued for the purposes of national security, the economic wellbeing of the UK and the prevention and detection of serious crime.[217]

The NSA is the official security organization in the US and is one of the most technologically advanced world agencies. It was constituted under the National Security Council Intelligence Directive (NSCID 9), issued by

---

[211]  For a full discussion on the right to privacy of communications under treaty law, see Chapters 5 and 6.

[212]  For a detailed discussion pertaining to justifications, see Chapter 6.

[213]  *Leander v Sweden* App no 9248/81 (26 March 1967).

[214]  *Segerstedt-Wiberg and Others v Sweden* App no 62332/00 (6 June 2006).

[215]  MI5 Gathering Intelligence (n 195). In the case of MI5, these are the Security Service Act 1989, the Intelligence Service Act 1994, RIPA and the associated Codes of Practice.

[216]  Human Rights Act 1998 c 42. The Act incorporates into the UK legal system the rights contained in the ECHR.

[217]  GCHQ Legal Framework (n 198).

President Harry Truman and the National Security Council in 1952.[218] The organization is a 'key member of the intelligence community, [with the main function of] collect[ing], process[ing] and disseminat[ing] intelligence information from foreign electronic signals for national foreign intelligence and counterintelligence purposes and to support military operations'.[219] Its activities are governed by the US Constitution,[220] federal law, Executive Order 12333 (as amended by Executive Order 13284, Executive Order 13555 and Executive Order 13470) and regulations of the executive branch. Thus, its tasks are primarily authorized by the Foreign Intelligence Surveillance Act 1978 (FISA) (as amended by the FISA Amendment Act 2008 (FAA)).[221] FISA is subject to periodic appraisal and in January 2019 its Title VII was reauthorized by Section 139 of the FISA Amendment Reauthorization Act 2017 (FISA ARA), which sets out the current legal framework for foreign intelligence surveillance activities.[222]

## 3.2    Cyber Surveillance

Since the 9/11 attacks against the US, cyberspace has become the prime environment for the interception of communications on an unprecedented scale. This practice is known as 'communications surveillance', defined as 'the monitoring, interception, collection, preservation and retention of information that has been communicated, relying or generated over communications networks'.[223] Reflecting current state practice, communications surveillance can be divided into two broad categories: targeted and mass cyber surveillance.

### 3.2.1    Targeted cyber surveillance

Targeted surveillance is the covert collection of conversations, telecommunications and metadata by technical means based on a suspicion against

---

[218]    Michael X Heiligenstein, 'A Brief History of the NSA: From 1917 to 2014', *The Saturday Evening Post* (17 April 2014).

[219]    NSA/Central Security Service (CSS), 'Frequently Asked Questions About Signals Intelligence (SIGINT)', www.nsa.gov/about/faqs/ ('NSA/CSS FAQs').

[220]    US Constitution (17 April 1787).

[221]    Foreign Intelligence Surveillance Act of 1978 Amendment Act of 2008 (10 July 2008) ('FISA/FAA').

[222]    FISA Amendments Reauthorization Act of 2017, s 139 Public Law No: 115-118 (01/19/2018). US Office of the Director of National Intelligence, 'The FISA Amendment Act: Q&A' (17 April 2017), www.dni.gov/files/icotr/FISA%20Amendments%20Act %20QA%20for%20Publication.pdf ('FISA AA: Q&A').

[223]    UNHRC, 'Report of the Special Rapporteur on the Promotion and Protection of the Right to Freedom of Opinion and Expression, Frank La Rue' (17 April 2013) UN Doc A/HRC/23/40, 3 ('A/HRC/23/40').

a particular target. Where it is conducted in cyberspace, it is known as targeted cyber surveillance. States conduct these activities on the basis of complex legal frameworks, which often provide disparate regimes depending on the nationality and/or location of the target. Two such statutes are outlined below: the first relating to US cyber surveillance under FISA (as amended), and the second contained in the UK IPA, which replaced the RIPA.

### 3.2.1.1   US legal regime for targeted surveillance

Intended to curtail the NSA's ability to exercise its capabilities against US citizens, FISA was a response to the backlash against the controversial surveillance of the US political, trade union and civil rights leaders at that time and consequently authorized surveillance against 'agents of foreign power'.[224] Thus, the provisions contained in Title I (known as 'traditional FISA') apply to the conduct of electronic surveillance for foreign intelligence purposes of persons, facilities or property inside the US. Under this title, any state agency must obtain a warrant from the Foreign Intelligence Surveillance Court (FISC) if it seeks to conduct electronic surveillance for foreign intelligence purposes inside the US. FISC was established to hear applications submitted by US government for the approval of electronic surveillance, physical searches and other investigative actions for foreign intelligence purposes.[225] To obtain a 'traditional FISA warrant', a detailed application must be made to authorize the electronic surveillance of a facility (eg, a telephone or an email account) or place based on a 'probable cause' that both: (1) the proposed target is a foreign power or its agent; and (2) the facility or place is being or is about to be used by that target.[226] If FISC is satisfied that there is a probable cause and that the proposed collection techniques, together with the minimization procedures, will adequately protect the information of US persons which may be acquired in the process, it will grant authority to conduct the surveillance.[227] The use of minimization procedures is a legal requirement under FISA to protect the privacy rights of individuals who are not themselves targets of surveillance, but whose conversations or personal information may be incidentally included during the interception of legitimate targets under the Act.[228] It must be stressed that the requirement for a judicial order based on a probable cause is intended to protect the constitutional rights of US persons and those inside the

---

[224]  50 USC §1801(b).

[225]  US Foreign Intelligence Surveillance Court, 'About Foreign Intelligence Surveillance Court', www.fisc.uscourts.gov/about-foreign-intelligence-surveillance -court.

[226]  FISA AA: Q&A (n 222).

[227]  *Ibid.*

[228]  50 USC § 1801(h).

US against unreasonable searches and seizures. It does not extend to foreign individuals located abroad.[229]

### 3.2.1.2    UK legal regime for targeted surveillance

Until 27 June 2018, the RIPA constituted the main legal framework for the UK security and law enforcement agencies, including GCHQ, enabling the carrying out of surveillance and the accessing of electronic, postal and digital communications of individuals.[230] Since then, the interception of communications has become the subject of regulation under the IPA,[231] although certain parts of the RIPA will continue to operate until expressly repealed. However, the old regime should be briefly outlined – not least because a number of its provisions have been reiterated in the IPA. Furthermore, it is the basis for the challenge of the legality of NSA/GCHQ cyber surveillance operations in the three joined ECtHR decisions in *Big Brother Watch v UK, Bureau of Investigative Journalism* and *Alice Ross v UK and 10 Human Rights Organisations v UK (Big Brother Watch)*,[232] referred to throughout this book. Thus, Section 1(1) of the RIPA makes it unlawful for anyone who is not authorized under that Act to carry out surveillance and monitoring of communications unless this is conducted on the basis of a warrant under Section 5 (an 'intercept warrant'). Section 5(2) allows the Secretary of State to authorize such a warrant if he or she believes that for the reasons stipulated in Section 5(3) it is necessary in the interests of national security, to prevent or detect serious crime or to safeguard the economic wellbeing of the UK. Any surveillance authorized by the warrant must also be proportionate to the purpose to be achieved. When assessing necessity and proportionality, account must be taken of whether the information sought under it could reasonably be obtained by other means. The RIPA provides for two separate intercept warrants: (1) targeted warrants, which relate to the interception of 'internal' communications under Section 8(1); and (2) untargeted warrants, pertaining to 'external communications' under Section 8(4) (dealt with in more detail below). Section 20 of the RIPA defines 'external communications' as 'communication sent or received outside

---

[229]  *Ibid.*

[230]  GCHQ, 'Investigatory Powers Act' (18 March 2019), www.gchq.gov.uk/ information/investigatory-powers-act.

[231]  Targeted interception warrants are now grated pursuant to s 15(1) and s 15(2) of the IPA.

[232]  *Big Brother Watch and Others v the United Kingdom* App no 58170/13; *Bureau of Investigative Journalism and Alice Ross v the United Kingdom* App no 62322/14; *10 Human Rights Organizations and Others v the United Kingdom* App no 24960/15 (12 October 2018) ('*Big Brother Watch*').

of the British Islands'.[233] 'Internal communications' are not defined in the Act, but refer to information that is neither sent nor received outside the British Islands. Interception of this type of communications may be conducted only if the warrant describes one person as the 'interception subject'[234] or identifies a 'single set of premises for which the interception is to take place'.[235] Furthermore, it requires that 'the addresses, numbers, apparatus or other factors, or combination of factors, that are to be used for identifying the communications that may be or are to be intercepted' be provided.[236]

The statute that replaced the RIPA, the IPA, also makes it a criminal offence to intercept communications of a person in the UK without a lawful authority.[237] Interception is thus lawful only where it is conducted on the basis of a warrant issued by the Secretary of State and, following the enactment of additional safeguards, which is also approved by the Judicial Commissioner.[238] Issued where necessary and proportionate, a targeted warrant[239] is primarily described as an investigative tool that enables the interception of communications in relation to specific subject matter, such as an individual person or persons carrying out a particular activity or common purpose (eg, organized crime).[240] Examples of targeted surveillance authorized under the IPA include interception of communications and equipment interference, briefly outlined next.

Thus, 'interception' is defined as obtaining the content of communications, such as telephone calls, emails or social media messages, while in transit or when stored on a telecommunications system.[241] In the UK, the interception of communications is conducted lawfully when it takes place pursuant to a warrant issued under Part 2 of the IPA. This provides for three types of warrants: targeted interception warrants,[242] targeted examination warrants[243] and

---

[233] RIPA (n 202) s 20. IPA s 136(3)(a)–(b) replaced RIPA s 20 and refers to 'overseas-related communications' rather than 'external communications'. It stipulates that overseas-related communications are communications sent or received by individuals who are outside of the British Islands.

[234] *Ibid* s 8(1)(a).

[235] *Ibid* s 8(1)(b).

[236] *Ibid* s 8(2).

[237] IPA (n 201) s 3.

[238] This comprises the new 'double lock' safeguard introduced by the IPA 2016; see section 3.2.2.

[239] IPA (n 201) Part 2 Chapter 1.

[240] UK Home Office, 'Revised Explanatory Memorandum to the Investigatory Powers (Codes of Practice) Regulations 2018' (2018).

[241] UK Home Office, 'Safeguards Governing Investigatory Powers Come into Effect' (28 November 2018).

[242] IPA (n 201) s 15(2).

[243] *Ibid* s 15(3).

mutual assistance warrants.[244] The first two authorize the interception together with the selection for examination of the intercepted content obtained under a bulk warrant only in relation to the communications described therein.

Equipment interference (colloquially known as 'hacking') is used to obtain communications, equipment data and other information from such devices as desktop computers, laptops, tablets, smartphones and other Internet-enabled or networked devices.[245] It encompasses a range of techniques which vary in complexity, such as covertly downloading data from a subject's mobile device when left unattended or using someone's login details to gain access to data held on a computer.[246] More complex hacking may involve the exploitation of existing vulnerabilities in software to gain control of devices or networks to remotely extract material or monitor the user. Equipment interference is lawful if it is conducted on the basis of a warrant. Part 5 of the IPA provides for two types of targeted warrants: targeted equipment interference warrants and targeted examination warrants. The former[247] approve the hacking of any equipment to obtain communications, equipment data or other communication. The latter[248] authorize the selection for examination of protected material obtained under a bulk equipment interference warrant and must be sought in all cases where such material relates to an individual known to be in the British Islands at the time it is selected for examination.

### 3.2.2  Mass surveillance

In contrast to targeted surveillance, mass surveillance is the indiscriminate monitoring of the population or a significant component of a group of persons, and involves 'the acquisition, processing, generation, analysis, use, retention or storage of information about large numbers of people without any regard to whether they are suspected of wrondoing'.[249] It generally does not start with a suspicion against a particular person or persons, but has a proactive element.[250] Thus, 'mass cyber surveillance' can, in a nutshell, be defined as

---

[244]  *Ibid* s 14(4).

[245]  UK Home Office 'Equipment Interference, Code of Practice. Pursuant to Schedule 7 to the Investigatory Powers Act 2016' (March 2018) para 2.2, 6 ('IPA Equipment Interference Code of Practice').

[246]  *Ibid* para 3.3, 10.

[247]  IPA (n 201) s 99(2).

[248]  *Ibid* s 99(9).

[249]  Privacy International, *Mass Surveillance*, https://privacyinternational.org/learn/ mass-surveillance#:~:text=Mass%20surveillance%20involves%20the%20acquisition ,they%20are%20suspected%20of%20wrongdoing ('*Mass Surveillance*').

[250]  CoE, 'Mass Surveillance. Thematic Factsheet' (August 2017), https://rm.coe.int/ factsheet-on-mass-surveillance-corrected-and-final%20rev2august2017/1680736031.

a state's indiscriminate monitoring and capture of personal data aimed at identifying future rather than investigating known threats to national interests.

A variety of terms have been adopted by numerous institutions and commentators when referring to this large-scale technical collection of intelligence.[251] Thus, the UN human rights mandate holders refer to 'mass digital surveillance',[252] 'online surveillance',[253] 'bulk interception'[254] and 'bulk telephone metadata collection'.[255] The Parliamentary Assembly of the CoE speaks of 'mass surveillance' and describes it as 'massive surveillance industrial complex' in its report and resolution on the topic.[256] The ECtHR describes these practices variably as 'exploratory or generalised surveillance',[257] 'bulk interception of communications'[258] and 'strategic monitoring' to identify unknown risks (as against individual monitoring of specific persons based on suspicion).[259] The term 'strategic surveillance', also used by the European Commission for Democracy Through Law (Venice Commission), is defined as 'the process of filtering out relevant information from a bulk of data that has been collected without particular suspicion'.[260]

The phrase 'bulk', featured in the IPA, denotes the collection of vast quantities of data to identify threats to national security. The use of bulk powers is stipulated in Part 7 of that Act[261] and relates to the acquisition of

---

[251] EU Agency for Fundamental Rights, 'Surveillance by Intelligence Services. Fundamental Rights Safeguards and Remedies in the EU. Volume II: Field Perspectives and Legal Update' (Luxembourg Publications Office of the EU, 2017) 29.

[252] Office of the UN High Commissioner for Human Rights (OHCHR), 'The Right to Privacy in the Digital Age. Report of the United Nations High Commissioner for Human Rights' (30 June 2014) UN Doc A/HRC/27/37 para 3 ('A/HRC/27/37'); UNHRC, 'Report on the Special Rapporteur on the Promotion and Protection of Human Rights and Fundamental Freedoms while Countering Terrorism' (21 February 2017) UN Doc A/HRC/34/61 10.

[253] *Ibid.*

[254] *Ibid.*

[255] *Ibid* 11.

[256] See CoE Mass Surveillance Memorandum (n 119) and CoE Mass Surveillance Resolution (n 2).

[257] *Klass and Others v Germany* App no 5029/71 (6 September 1978) para 51.

[258] See, for example, *Weber and Saravia v Germany* App no 54934/00 (29 June 2006) para 4; *Big Brother Watch* (n 232) para 314.

[259] *Weber ibid.*

[260] CoE, European Commission for Democracy Through Law, 'Report on the Democratic Oversight of Signals Intelligence Agencies' Study no 719/2013 (Venice Commission, 2015).

[261] There is no statutory definition of this phrase, but the Bulk Personal Datasets Factsheet, explaining certain provisions contained in the Investigatory Powers Bill, describes 'bulk powers' as involving the availability of 'information about a wide range of people, most of whom are not of interest to the security and intelligence agencies'

overseas-related communications. Bulk surveillance of foreign communications has been a standard intelligence practice for decades and comprises the interception, collection, management and transfer of vast troves of communications (content and metadata) that are transmitted via different telecommunications networks (eg, fixed telephone lines, mobile and satellite networks and the Internet).[262] However, the use of bulk powers is controversial, as it may have serious adverse human rights implications. To this end, David Anderson QC observed that:

> this involve[s] potential access by the State to the data of large number of people whom there is not a slightest reason to suspect of threatening national security or engaging in serious crime ... any abuse of those powers could thus have particularly wide ranging effects on the innocent ... even the perception that abuse is possible, and that it could go undetected, can generate corrosive mistrust.[263]

Despite widespread practice, states are generally reluctant to enact legal regimes for foreign untargeted communications surveillance. In Europe, for example, it was reported in 2015 that almost all EU member states (except for Cyprus and Portugal) have passed laws on targeted surveillance; while only five countries (France, Germany, the Netherlands, Sweden and the UK) have also introduced legislation pertaining to untargeted surveillance activities.[264] According to the CoE Commissioner for Human Rights, this means that untargeted bulk surveillance is 'either not regulated by any publicly available law, or regulated in such a nebulous way that the law provides few restraints

---

– see UK Home Office, 'Bulk Personal Datasets Factsheet. Investigatory Powers Bill' (2016) ('BPDs Factsheet'); see also David Anderson QC, 'Report of the Bulk Powers Review' (2016) explaining at para 1.6 that: 'in the context of the powers contained in the [IP] Bill – *"the interception of communications, equipment interference and the acquisition and retention of communications data, bulk personal datasets and other information"* – the exercise of bulk powers implies the collection and retention of large quantities of data which can subsequently be accessed by the authorities.' However, at para 1.9 Anderson points out that collection and retention of data in bulk does not equate to so-called 'mass surveillance' ('Anderson'); see also US National Academy of Science, 'Bulk Collection of Signals Intelligence: Technical Options' (Washington DC, 2015), which defines 'bulk powers' as allowing public authorities to have access for specific purposes to large quantities of data, 'a significant proportion of which is not associated with current targets'.

[262] Thorsten Wetzling and Kilian Vieth, *Upping the Ante on Bulk Surveillance. An International Compendium of Good Legal Safeguards and Oversight Innovations* (Heirich Böll Stiflung Publicaiton Series on Democracy, 2018) 12–13.

[263] Anderson (n 261) para 9.6.

[264] EU Agency for Fundamental Rights, 'Surveillance by Intelligence Agencies: Fundamental Rights Safeguards and Remedies in the EU-Mapping Member States' Legal Frameworks' (European Union Agency for Fundamental Rights, 2015), 18–26.

and little clarity on these measures'.[265] Consequently, bulk surveillance of foreign communications – mostly conducted secretly and outside legislative frameworks – is rarely officially acknowledged. However, increased public interest in the wake of the Snowden revelations has led to greater scrutiny of these practices and forced some governments to publicly admit the use of surveillance programs. Thus, the US acknowledged the existence of the PRISM and Upstream collection in June 2013, when the then US Director of National Intelligence, James Clapper, confirmed the use of these systems authorized pursuant to Section 702 of the FISA (discussed in more detail below).[266] Similarly, the UK government acknowledged that it has received data from PRISM via its intelligence-sharing relationship with the US.[267] However, at the time of the Snowden disclosures, the UK officials adopted a 'neither confirm nor deny' policy towards its use of Tempora. Nevertheless, the former Director General of the UK Office for Security and Counter Terrorism Charles Farr recognized that UK individuals' Google search queries, Facebook and Twitter accounts may all be intercepted without state agencies having to specify the target of their surveillance.[268]

The UK government – partly because of the Snowden leaks revealing the scale of bulk interception conducted by GCHQ and partially due to the subsequent reviews of investigatory powers conducted by the Parliamentary Intelligence and Security Committee,[269] by David Anderson QC[270] and by the Royal United Services Institute[271] – undertook to overhaul the ways in which investigatory powers are authorized and overseen. As a result, in November 2016, the UK government introduced the IPA, which represents one of the world's foremost surveillance laws, legitimizing the UK's global bulk surveillance of foreign and domestic communications. It consolidates and updates the existing powers that are available to law enforcement, security and intelligence agencies in the UK. Furthermore, it creates additional competence, allowing access to Internet connection records; establishes new safeguards, known

---

[265] CoE Commissioner for Human Rights, 'Democratic and Effective Oversight of National Security Services' (2015) 23.

[266] *Privacy International v GCHQ*, Witness Statement of Charles Blandford Farr on Behalf of the Respondent (16 May 2014) IPT/13/92/CH paras 36-37 ('Farr').

[267] Watt (n 2) 774.

[268] Farr (n 266).

[269] Intelligence and Security Committee of Parliament, 'Statement on GCHQ's Alleged Interception of Communications under the PRISM Programme' (July 2013).

[270] David Anderson, *A Question of Trust. Report of the Investigatory Powers Review* (June 2015) ('Anderson').

[271] Royal United Services Institute, 'A Democratic Licence to Operate. Report of the Independent Surveillance Review' (Royal United Services Institute for Defence and Security Studies, 2015).

as the 'double lock';[272] and introduces the role of the Investigatory Powers Commissioner to oversee the state agencies' use of investigatory powers.[273] The 'double-lock' authorization requires warrants issued by a Secretary of State to be approved by a Judicial Commissioner before they are signed.[274] Thus, under the IPA regime, a warrant must be issued for bulk powers to intercept,[275] BPDs,[276] equipment interference[277] and communication data acquisition and retention.[278]

In brief, mass cyber surveillance is a preponderant state practice forming part of its national security apparatus aimed at the indiscriminate collection of communications. Based on the type of data collected, it can be sub-divided into two categories: (1) mass interception of communications' content; and (2) bulk communications data collection and retention.[279] The following sections describe each of these methods and outlines the statutory basis for their authorization, with reference to the US and UK legal frameworks.

*3.2.2.1   UK legal regime for mass interception of communications' content*
Bulk or mass interception of communications entails the collection of large volumes of communications in the course of their transition. Describing bulk

---

[272]   IPA (n 201) s 140(2).

[273]   *Ibid* Part 8, Chapter 1.

[274]   *Ibid* ss 140(2) and 176. Bulk interception warrants, bulk personal datasets and bulk equipment interference warrants are subject to the 'double lock' authorization, whereby a warrant issued by the Secretary of State will in addition require the approval of a judge (Judicial Commissioner) who, applying judicial review principles, will review the Secretary of State's decision.

[275]   *Ibid* Part 6 Chapter 1.

[276]   *Ibid* Part 7.

[277]   *Ibid* Chapter 3.

[278]   *Ibid* Chapter 2.

[279]   The IPA legislates for two additional bulk powers: the power to obtain BPDs in s 200 and the power to conduct bulk equipment interference (bulk hacking) in s 176. According to the UK government, the rationale for this is that the use of BPDs is 'an essential way for the security and intelligence agencies to focus their efforts on individuals who threaten our national security, by helping identify or establish links between such individuals and facilitate focusing on the individuals concerned, such as terrorist or spies, removing the need for the use of more intrusive techniques against the innocents' – see BPDs Factsheet (n 261). Bulk equipment interference may be conducted pursuant to a warrant, with the main purpose of obtaining overseas-related communications, equipment data and other information. These types of warrants are foreign focused and aim to identify communications and other information relating to individuals outside of the British Islands. Consequently, the intelligence services must ensure that the main purpose of such a warrant is to obtain communications and other data relating to individuals outside the British Islands – see IPA Equipment Interference Code of Practice (n 245) para 4.2, 22.

interception in practice, the Interception of Communications Code of Practice accompanying the IPA states that this comprises both 'the interception of communications and/or the obtaining of secondary data from such communications in the course of their transmission and the selection for examination of particular intercepted content or secondary data obtained under the [bulk interception] warrant'.[280] The Code also explains that the data obtained on the basis of different processing systems is then filtered; that which is retained is then subject to an additional processes which may 'draw out further communications most likely to be of greatest intelligence value'.[281] These communications, the Code states, 'may then be selected for examination for one or more of the operational purposes specified in the [bulk interception] warrant where the conditions of necessity and proportionality are met'.[282]

Prior to the enactment of the IPA, the interception of foreign (or external) communications was conducted on the basis of a warrant pursuant to Sections 8(4) and 8(5) of the RIPA (known as 'bulk interception warrants'). Unlike a specific warrant pursuant to Section 8(1) of that Act, the authorization granted on the basis of Sections 8(4) and 8(5) by the Secretary of State did not have to specify the intended target of the interception and could be approved if the surveillance was believed to be necessary in the interests of national security, as set out in Section 5(3) of the RIPA. It need not identify a specific person or premises, but only contain a description of the intercepted material.[283] Nevertheless, the Act did provide for a number of safeguards. Among these, Section 16 set out limitations in relation to who could read, look at or listen to the gathered information.[284] These powers were re-enacted in Section 136 of the IPA, which authorizes the use of bulk interception of overseas-related communications on the basis of a warrant. The Interception of Communications Code of Practice explains how bulk warrants may be used, including to establish links between known subjects of interest, improving understanding of their behaviour and their connections, together with 'search[ing] for traces of activity by individuals who may not yet be known but who surface in the course of an investigation, or to identify patterns of activity that may indicate a threat to the United Kingdom'.[285]

---

[280]   UK Home Office, 'Interception of Communications Code of Practice Pursuant to Schedule 7 to the Investigatory Powers Act 2016' (March 2018) para 6.5, 54 ('IPA IC Code of Practice').

[281]   *Ibid* para 6.6, 55.

[282]   *Ibid.*

[283]   RIPA (n 202) s 8(4) and s 8(5)(a).

[284]   *Ibid* s 16.

[285]   IPA IC Code of Practice (n 280) para 6.4, 54.

*3.2.2.2    US legal regime for mass interception of communications' content*
The US surveillance regime, contained in the original 1978 FISA, governed
the electronic surveillance and physical searches of individuals in the US, primarily for the purpose of collecting foreign intelligence. The Act did not apply
to surveillance conducted outside of the US or to foreign telephone communications intercepted within that country.[286] However, technological developments meant that many would-be foreign targets abroad used communication
services based in the US (including US Internet service providers). This
situation required government agencies to obtain traditional FISA surveillance
warrants, which in turn entailed the showing of probable cause for the purposes
of surveillance of foreign suspects located abroad, but using US-based communication providers.[287] As this proved both costly and cumbersome, the US
Congress enacted Section 702 of FISA as part of the 2008 FAA, which permits
the targeting of foreign persons reasonably believed to be located outside the
US for the purpose of acquiring foreign intelligence information.[288] The data is
gathered on the basis of a FISC order approving a certification and accompanying targeting and minimization procedures – which, as mentioned previously,
are aimed at providing protection for US persons' information incidentally
acquired in the course of Section 702 collection. In addition, Executive Order
12333 is the principal US executive branch's authority for all those foreign
operations which are not governed by the FAA. It authorizes the NSA, among
other things, to collect, process and disseminate SIGINT information and data
for foreign intelligence and counterintelligence purposes to support national
and departmental missions, and to provide signals intelligence for the conduct
of military operations.[289] In particular, Section 1.12(b)(13) allows the NSA
to conduct 'such administrative and technical support activities within and
outside the United States as are necessary to perform the functions described in
sections (1) through (12) above, including procurement'[290] – a provision seen
as permitting the NSA's indiscriminate surveillance of both US and foreign
citizens. It is thus the primary governing authority for the US intelligence

---

[286]  FISA AA: Q&A (n 222).

[287]  *Ibid.*

[288]  *Ibid.* The unclassified US government document explains that: 'Title VII of
FISA permits the government to acquire foreign intelligence information about the
plans and identities of terrorists and terrorist organizations, including how they function and receive support. It enables collection of foreign intelligence information about
the intentions and capabilities of spies, weapons proliferators and other foreign adversaries who threaten the United States, and it informs U.S. Intelligence Community (IC)
cybersecurity efforts…'

[289]  Executive Order 12333, 40 Fed Reg 235 (4 December 1981) s 1.12(b)(3)-(7)
('EO 12333').

[290]  *Ibid* s 1.12(b)(13).

agencies' activities outside the US and, similarly to the FAA, provides a different set of standards for the electronic surveillance of non-US persons who are outside the US territory.

To recapitulate, bulk surveillance of foreign communications has been a standard state practice for decades. Usually secretive and often conducted without clear and robust legal bases, it was thrust into the limelight in 2013 as a result of the Snowden disclosures. This method of SIGINT collection involves the indiscriminate and prolific gathering of electronic signals comprising various types of data and is controversial due to its generalized nature. It can therefore be said that such bulk interception of foreign communications is aimed at 'finding a needle in the haystack',[291] as its focus is on patterns of suspicious activities and not on specific individuals or groups.[292]

### 3.2.2.3   Bulk communications data collection

Communications data, also referred to as 'metadata', is described as 'information about the time and location of a phone call or email, as opposed to the actual content of those conversations or messages'.[293] It consists of the 'where', 'when', 'who', 'how' and 'with whom' of communications, and has traditionally been associated with the acquisition of telephone data relating to domestic and international calls (typically call numbers and the time of a call, but not its content).[294] In terms of electronic communications such as emails, it refers to the 'to' and 'from' lines in the email and its technical details. In legal terms, 'communications data' is defined as 'any traffic data comprised in or attached to a communication' and 'any information which includes none of the contents of a communication'.[295] Metadata has a significant value to security and law enforcement agencies, as it can help to build a detailed picture of an individual's contacts, personality and habits. In addition, unlike content data, it is not misleading.

Until the 2013 Snowden revelations, the bulk acquisition and retention of metadata received relatively scant attention. However, this changed when the 2013 leaked documents revealed a secret court order showing that the NSA was collecting telephone records of millions of American customers of US telecommunication giant Verizon, together with metadata collection using

---

[291]   A/HRC/27/37 (n 252) 25.
[292]   William C Banks, 'Programmatic Surveillance and FISA: Of Needles in Haystacks' (2010) 88(7) *Texas Law Review* 1633–67, 1635.
[293]   CoE, Mass Surveillance Memorandum (n 119) 6.
[294]   Patrick F Wash and Seumas Miller, 'Rethinking "Five Eyes" Security Intelligence Collection Policies and Practice Post Snowden' (2015) *Intelligence and National Security* 1–24, 7.
[295]   RIPA (n 202) s 21(4)(a)–(b).

PRISM.[296] It is reported that since 9/11, the NSA has relied extensively on such collection, pursuant to the now defunct Section 215 of the Patriot Act 2001.[297] In 2013 alone, the NSA allegedly gathered up to 97 billion pieces of intelligence or metadata from computer networks worldwide.[298]

The acquisition and retention of metadata also became the subject of some controversy within the EU. Until the seminal judgment of the CJEU in *Digital Rights Ireland Ltd v Minister for Communications, Marine and Natural Resources (Digital Rights Ireland)*,[299] the collection and retention of such data by EU member states was enabled on the basis of the Data Retention Directive.[300] The CJEU Grand Chamber's decision in that case annulled that Directive, which created uncertainty within the EU in relation to the legal validity of such powers. In spite of this judgment, the UK enacted the Data Retention and Investigatory Powers Act 2014 (DRIPA),[301] which allowed the Secretary of State to mandate communications service providers to retain metadata in bulk. The Act was subsequently challenged in the UK High Court in *David Davis v Secretary of State*,[302] where it was found that Sections 1 and 2 of the DRIPA were incompatible with the right of UK citizens to privacy and the protection of personal data. The decision was then appealed to the UK Court of Appeal,[303] which reverted to the CJEU for clarification of its *Digital Rights Ireland* decision. In its ruling of 21 December 2016 in Joined Cases C203/15 and C698/15 (*Tele-2/Watson*),[304] the CJEU confirmed that the general and indiscriminate retention of metadata legislated under the Data Retention and Investigatory Powers Act was unlawful. The Act was repealed in December 2016, when its sunset provision took effect, but much of its data retention functions have been incorporated into Part 4 of the IPA. This

---

[296]   CoE, Mass Surveillance Memorandum (n 119) 6.

[297]   *Ibid.* See also Chapter 3, section 4.3.1.2.

[298]   These include over 14 billion collected from Iran; 13.5 billion from Pakistan; 12.7 billion from Jordan; 70.3 million from France; 471 million from Germany; 45.9 million from Italy; and 60.5 million from Spain – see *ibid* 7.

[299]   C-293/12 and C-594/12 *Digital Rights Ireland Ltd v Minister for Communications, Marine and Natural Resources and Others* (8 April 2014) ('*Digital Rights Ireland*').

[300]   Directive on the Retention of Data Generated or Processed in Connection with the Provision of Publicly Available Electronic Communications Services or of Public Communication Networks 2006/24/EC. Data Retention and Investigatory Powers Act 2014 c 27.

[301]   Data Retention and Investigatory Powers Act 2014 c 27.

[302]   *David Davis and Others v Secretary of State for the Home Departments* [2015] EWHC 2092.

[303]   *Secretary of State for the Home Departments v Watson and Others* [2018] EWCA Civ 70.

[304]   C-203/15 and C-698/15 *Tele2 Sverige AB v Post- och telestyrelsen and Secretary of State for Home Departments v Tom Watson and Others* ('*Tele-2/Watson*').

provides UK government agencies with access to communications data and, among other things, requires communication service providers to retain such data for a maximum period of 12 months for access without a warrant.[305]

The above analysis sought to identify the *sui generis* features of mass cyber surveillance, which can be encapsulated in four key points. First, mass cyber surveillance is a state's indiscriminate monitoring and capture of digital communications, comprising their content and metadata, aimed at identifying future rather than investigating known threats. Second, unlike the targets of cyber espionage, which often comprise selected government organizations, entities and the industrial sector, mass cyber surveillance predominantly focuses on the interception of entire populations or their significant segments. Third, it is sustained and constant, rather than sporadic and selective. Finally, it includes all forms of bulk acquisition methods, such as bulk interception of communications, bulk equipment interference and the compiling of bulk personal datasets.

# 4. CYBER ESPIONAGE AND INTERNATIONAL LAW

## 4.1 Peacetime Espionage and International Law – General

Despite the preponderance of the practice of espionage in international relations, including in times of peace, states have been consistently cautious to subject this activity to direct international law regulation. International law does not regulate espionage *per se*[306] and consequently, the rules relating to peacetime espionage are strikingly unclear. Indeed, it has been observed that 'traditional international law is remarkably oblivious to the peacetime practice of espionage. Leading treaties overlook espionage altogether or contain a perfunctory paragraph that defines a spy and describes his hapless fate upon capture'.[307]

This lack of explicit regulation can be explained on the basis of the realist theory in international relations, which holds states as principal actors in the global arena, concerned with their security and therefore acting in pursuit of their own national interests and struggle for power.[308] It follows that states spy on one another to achieve goals dictated by their own policy agendas, which include the ability to ascertain threats to national security before they

---

[305] IPA (n 201) s 87.
[306] Buchan (n 2) 192.
[307] Richard A Falk, 'Foreword' in Roland J Stanger and Quincy Wright, *Essays on Espionage and International Law* (Creative Media Partners LLC, 2015).
[308] Buchan (n 2) 7.

materialize and to detect, prevent and help to prosecute acts of serious crime and terrorism.[309] Some commentators even venture that peacetime espionage is 'a necessary and desirable feature of international relations', as it 'actually promote[s] the potential for peace and reduce[s] international tension'.[310] In short, most states partake in spying and therefore it is simply not in anyone's interest to permit its regulation.

While international law has long addressed wartime espionage,[311] its peacetime counterpart has traditionally been seen as an issue for domestic law. At an international level, only an oblique acknowledgement of intelligence-gathering activities features in the treaties, including in the context of diplomatic and consular relations,[312] arms control regimes[313] and the law of the sea.[314]

---

[309] Christopher Baker, 'Tolerance of International Espionage: A Functional Approach' (2003) 19 *American University International Law Review* 1091–13, 1094.

[310] Glenn Sulmasy and John Yoo, 'Counterintuitive: Intelligence Operations and International Law' (2007) 28 *Michigan Journal of International Law* 625–38.

[311] Unlike peacetime espionage, wartime espionage is regulated by the rules of international humanitarian law set out in the Hague Regulations 1907, the Geneva Conventions 1949 and the Additional Protocols to the Geneva Conventions 1977, together with customary international law. For a detailed analysis of how international humanitarian law applies to cyber exploitation activities in wartime, see Marco Longobardo, '(New) Cyber Exploitation and (Old) International Humanitarian Law' (2017) 77 *Zeitschrift für ausländisches öffentliches Recht und Völkerrecht* 809–34.

[312] Treaty law on diplomatic relations tacitly acknowledges intelligence gathering in the context of diplomatic activities and seeks to delineate its limits. Thus, Article 3(1)(d) of the Vienna Convention on Diplomatic Relations 1961 states that the functions of a diplomatic mission include the 'ascertaining by all lawful means conditions and developments in the receiving State, and reporting thereon to the Government of the sending State'; Article 11 provides that the receiving state may limit a mission's size and composition; Article 27(1) stipulates that the receiving state's consent is required to install a wireless transmitter and to establish regional officer; while Article 26 provides that the freedom of movement of diplomats may be restricted on national security grounds – see UN Vienna Convention on Diplomatic Relations 1961 (18 April 1961) (entered into force 24 April 1964) UNTS 500, 95.

[313] The basic regulation in the context of the arms control regime was established in the 1970s. Two agreements – the Treaty on the Limitation of Anti-Ballistic Missile Systems (Art 12(1)) and the Interim Agreement on Certain Measures with Respect to the Limitation of Strategic Offensive Arms (Art 5(1)) – refer to 'national technical means of verification' and thus establish the right to gather intelligence in order to assess compliance with arms control obligations.

[314] Article 19 of the United Nations Convention on the Law of the Sea 1982 provides states with the right of innocent passage through the territorial waters of other states. According to Article 19(2)(c), passage of a foreign ship is prejudicial to the peace, good order or security of the coastal state if, in the territorial sea, it engages in 'any act aimed at collecting information to the prejudice of the defence or security of the coastal state' – see UNGA, Convention on the Law of the Sea (10 December 1982) (entered into force 16 November 1994).

However, an explicit prohibition of this practice is made at the sub-regional plain in the African 2006 Protocol on Non-Aggression and Mutual Defence in the Great Lakes Region (Great Lakes Protocol),[315] which forms part of[316] the Pact on Security, Stability and Development in the Great Lakes Region 2006.[317] The Protocol is both a non-aggression and mutual defence treaty, with core aims of resolving and preventing internal and inter-state armed conflicts and renouncing the threat or use of force. To achieve these purposes, the instrument imposes a duty to refrain from 'acts or threats of aggression as defined in Article 1(2) and (3) of this Protocol, as well as any propaganda relating to such acts and threats'.[318] The definition of 'aggression' under Article 1(3) is broad and comprises: (1) the use of armed force (Paragraphs a–f); and (2) other hostile acts (Paragraphs g–k). The protocol makes an explicit reference to espionage as it stipulates that acts of aggression include 'acts of espionage, which could be used contrary to Article 7(4) for military aggression against a Member State'.[319] A number of observations are in order in relation to this provision. First, the treaty does not specifically define 'espionage' and seems to indicate that this relates only to situations of 'military aggression', thus excluding other forms of spying, such as for economic gain in situations not involving military operations. Second, the inclusion of espionage within the ambit of 'aggression' does not sit well with the definition of 'aggression' pursuant to Article 1 of UNGA Resolution 3314, which describes this concept as the use of force.[320] Thus, as noted by Professor Roscini, the hostile activities

---

[315] Second Summit of the International Conference on the Great Lakes Region, Protocol on Non-Aggression and Mutual Defence in the Great Lakes Region (30 November 2006) ('Great Lakes Protocol').

[316] The Pact, apart from the main treaty, also comprises the Dar-es-Salaam Declaration; ten Protocols (including the Great Lakes Protocol); four Programmes of Action; and a set of implementing mechanisms and institutions. For a detailed account of the Pact in the context of *jus ad bellum*, see Marco Roscini, 'Neighbourhood Watch? The African Great Lakes Pact and *Ius ad Bellum*' (2009) 69 *Zeitschrift für Ausländisches öffentliches Recht und Völkerrecht* 931–59 ('Roscini').

[317] International Conference on the Great Lakes Region, The Pact on Security, Stability and Development in the Great Lakes Region (14–15 December 2006). The Great Lakes Region, to which the Pact relates, comprises 11 core countries: Angola, Burundi, Central African Republic, Republic of Congo, Democratic Republic of Congo, Kenya, Rwanda, Sudan, Tanzania, Uganda and Zambia.

[318] Great Lakes Protocol (n 315) Art 5(1).

[319] *Ibid* Art 1(3)(i).

[320] Article 1 of UNGA Resolution 3314 defines 'aggression' as 'the use of armed force by a State against the sovereignty, territorial integrity or political independence of another State, or in any other manner inconsistent with the Charter of the United Nations' – see UNGA Resolution 3314, 'Definition of Aggression' (14 December 1974) UN Doc A/RES/3314.

referred to in Articles 1(3)(g–k) of the Protocol, which include espionage, 'technically amount to preparatory conduct or threats and not acts of aggression'.[321] Finally, the treaty stipulates that such acts 'shall be punishable individually as an international crime against peace as set out in the regional and international legal instruments'[322] and urges states to 'criminalize them when [they] are conducted against other States by individuals or groups operating in their respective States'.[323] The main onus thus seems to be placed on individuals and their criminal responsibility for acts of espionage (by obliging states to criminalize them) and not on states *per se* and their responsibility for spying against other states.

In addition to the aforementioned instruments, general principles of international law apply to the practice of peacetime espionage, including that of territorial sovereignty and non-intervention (both briefly outlined below), forming a 'chequerboard' of international rules that collectively, albeit indirectly, regulate – or at least seek to limit – these practices.

Acts of espionage in the context of the rule of territorial sovereignty have been subject to judicial considerations by, among others, the ICJ in *East Timor v Australia*, and the ECtHR in *Weber v Germany*.[324] The former case related to arbitral proceedings involving East Timor and Australia, administered by the Permanent Court of Arbitration in respect of a dispute over the validity of the 2006 Treaty on Certain Maritime Arrangements in the Timor Sea. The allegation before the ICJ by East Timor was that Australia had not conducted the treaty negotiations in good faith by engaging in espionage. This assertion related to the seizure by agents of the Australian Security Intelligence Organization, acting under a warrant issued by that country's Attorney General, of documents and data in the offices located in Australia of an Australian lawyer acting for East Timor. The seized documents and data contained correspondence relating to the pending arbitration between the government of East Timor and its legal advisers.[325] The ICJ was asked to declare, among other things, that 'the seizure by Australia of the documents and data violated ... the sovereignty of [East Timor]' and to order Australia to immediately return to that country the documents and data in question,

---

[321]   Roscini (n 316) 940.

[322]   Great Lakes Protocol (n 315) Art 5(3).

[323]   *Ibid* Art 3(4).

[324]   *Questions Relating to the Seizure and Detention of Certain Documents and Data (Timor-Leste v Australia)* (Provisional Orders) [2014] ICJ Rep 147 ('*Timor-Leste*'); see also the ECtHR decision in *Weber* (n 258).

[325]   ICJ Press Release, 'Timor-Leste Institutes Proceedings Against Australia and Requests the Court to Indicate Provisional Measures' (18 December 2013) 2013/41.

together with destroying any copies made of them.[326] The ICJ found for East Timor and granted the provisional order, which both governments confirmed had been carried out in 2015, prompting East Timor to observe that it 'has successfully achieved the purpose of its Application to the Court … and therefore implicit recognition by Australia that its actions were in violation of [East Timor's] sovereign rights'.[327] The incident has been widely reported as a case of espionage,[328] but such claims are exaggerated. This is because the ICJ framed the issue in a more nuanced manner, pertaining to the confidentiality of correspondence between a party to legal proceedings (in this case East Timor) and its counsel. To this end, the ICJ considered that country's principal claim – namely, that 'a violation has occurred of East Timor's right to communicate with its counsel and lawyers in confidential manner with regard to issues [relating to] the pending arbitral proceedings'.[329] The ICJ noted that:

> this right might be derived from the principle of sovereign equality of States, which is one of the fundamental principles of the international legal order and is reflected in Article 2, paragraph 1, of the Charter of the United Nations.[330]

The ICJ stressed that when a state is engaged in peaceful settlement of a dispute (through negotiation or arbitration), it is entitled to undertake such proceedings without interference by the other party and therefore has a right to the protection of communications with its counsel.[331] In short, the ICJ recognized the importance of confidentiality between a state and its legal representatives and considered Australia's actions as an interference with this right. The ICJ did not expressly engage with the issue of whether espionage breaches the principle of sovereign territoriality *per se*. As explained by a lawyer acting for East Timor, 'this is not the case about spying or espionage. The Court will not have to pronounce on such activities generally'.[332] Indeed, this was the case, as the ICJ dealt with the issue from a much narrower perspective – namely the duty of one state not to interfere with another state's lawyer/client confidentiality of communications when involved in legal proceedings with that other state.

---

[326]  *Ibid.*
[327]  ICJ Press Release, 'Questions Relating to the Seizure and Detention of Certain Documents and Data (Timor-Leste v Australia)' (12 June 2015) 2015/15.
[328]  See, for example, Kate Lamb, 'Timor-Leste v Australia: What Each Country Stands to Lose', *The Guardian* (23 January 2014).
[329]  *Timor-Leste* (n 324) para II.
[330]  *Ibid.*
[331]  *Ibid.*
[332]  Oral Proceedings, Verbatim Record 2014/1, Case Concerning Questions Relating to the Seizure and Detention of Certain Documents and Data (Timor-Leste v Australia) CR 2014/1 (2014) 15-16, Sir Elihu Lauterpacht.

Although some commentators have reflected on the outcome of this case as constituting 'the first step in limiting the legality of spying under international law [which] would be a pretty big deal',[333] a more cautious approach is preferable. The decision should not be viewed as an unequivocal pronouncement on the part of the ICJ that acts of espionage violate the rule of territorial sovereignty; but rather that 'through the virtue of their sovereignty [S]tates possess a right under international law to maintain a confidential relationship with their advisors'.[334] A similar judicial reticence to hold a state in violation of the rule of territorial sovereignty was expressed by the ECtHR in *Weber v Germany*.[335] Addressing the compatibility of German legislation authorizing strategic surveillance with Article 8 of the ECHR, the ECtHR held that the interception of foreign communications did not violate that obligation.

The precise contours of the practice of espionage and how it implicates the rule against non-intervention[336] in the internal or external affairs of another state, which derives from the principle of sovereignty, are also subject to uncertainty. An essential element of non-intervention, apart from the requirement that the conduct complained of falls within the state's exclusive authority, is that of coercion. While the precise definition of this term has not yet crystallized in international law, it in essence means compelling a state to take a cause of action which it would not voluntarily undertake. Although it is accepted that the use of force will meet the definition of 'coercion',[337] it has been argued that acts of espionage do not fulfill this requirement because they do not compel a state to act or to abstain from acting in a particular way.[338]

The uncertainty of how peacetime espionage engages international law and, consequently, the matter of its legality, has been the subject of much debate in international scholarship.[339] The issue has traditionally been viewed from two

---

[333] Ashely Deeks, 'Can the ICJ Avoid Saying Something on the Merits About Spying in Timor-Leste vs Australia', *Lawfare* (12 March 2014) https://www.lawfareblog.com/can-icj-avoid-saying-something-merits-about-spying-timor-leste-vs-australia.

[334] Buchan (n 2) 60.

[335] *Weber* (n 258) para 81.

[336] For the ICJ's description of the meaning of the principle of non-intervention, see *Nicaragua* (n 58) 205.

[337] See, for example, International Law in Cyberspace –The Netherlands (n 55) 3.

[338] Buchan (n 2) 64.

[339] See, for example, Baker (n 309); A John Radsan, 'The Unresolved Equation of Espionage and International Law' (2007) 28 *Michigan Journal of International Law* 595–23. Radsan concludes that espionage is neither legal nor illegal under international law, and exists 'between the tectonic plates of legal system'. Advocating the tolerance of its ambiguities and paradoxes, and the acceptance that espionage is beyond the law, he proposes to 'move to other projects – with grace'. Demarest (n 9) asserts that peacetime espionage should be narrowly defined to exclude acts of technical intelligence gathering and states that clandestine information gathering constitutes an unfriendly

perspectives: whether collecting secret intelligence is prohibited or whether it is regulated by international law.[340] Thus, two schools of thought can be discerned. The first holds that the collection of secret intelligence remains illegal despite its consistent practice; while according to the other, its 'apparent toleration may have led to a reluctant admission of its lawfulness' under customary international law.[341] This has become known as the permissive customary law exception. The question is far from resolved and an in-depth analysis of whether peacetime espionage can be said to form a rule of customary international law is beyond the scope of this book. However, some legal scholars, including Russell Buchan, doubt that this practice is permissible on the basis of a customary international law exception.[342] This is because although there is ample evidence of states routinely engaging in espionage, the secrecy and the policy of silence that accompany these practices preclude the formation of the requisite *opinio juris* to support the existence of such an exception.[343] That being the case, Buchan argues that political espionage may 'constitute a threat to international peace and security because it violates the principle of the sovereign equality of [S]tates and human dignity';[344] while economic espionage 'threatens the maintenance of national security [thus also] the maintenance of international peace and security'.[345]

**4.2     Cyber Espionage and International Law**

The lack of clarity relating to the applicability of international law to peacetime espionage is even more acute in the context of cyber espionage. As

---

act between nations, but does not violate international law. Chesterman (n 17) observes that as 'intelligence gathering continues to increase, it will demand more effective political and legal mechanisms to avoid abuse and protect valid interests. In the meantime, intelligence will continue to exist in a legal penumbra lying at the margins of diverse legal regimes and at the edge of international legitimacy'.

[340]   Chesterman (n 17).

[341]   *Ibid.* The US government's position in relation to espionage in the context of cyberspace is that 'international law does not prohibit espionage per se even if it involves some degree of physical or virtual intrusion into foreign territory. There is no anti-espionage treaty, and there are many concrete examples of States practicing it, indicating absence of a customary international law norm against it' – see US DoD Views on International and Domestic Law in Cyberspace (n 55).

[342]   See Buchan (2); Iñaki Naverrete and Russell Buchan, 'Out of the Legal Wilderness: Peacetime Espionage, International Law and the Existence of Customary Exceptions' (2019) *Cornell International Law Journal* 897–953.

[343]   For a detailed analysis of cyber espionage as customary international law exception, see Buchan (n 2) chapter 7.

[344]   *Ibid* 191.

[345]   *Ibid.*

previously noted, a broad agreement was reached in 2013 by the UN Group of Government Experts that international law, and in particular the UN Charter, is applicable to states' use of ICTs. It is also essential to maintain peace and stability and to promote an open, secure, peaceful and accessible ICT environment.[346] In addition, 'States' efforts to address the security of ICTs must go hand-in hand with respect for human rights and fundamental freedoms'.[347] However, it remains unsettled exactly how existing international law applies to low-level cyber intrusions. Therefore, it is also acknowledged that the common understanding requires further study.[348] To date, given the failure of the 2017 GGE to arrive at a consensus on how international law applies and the subsequent splintering of the diplomatic efforts, resulting in the UNGA mandating the Open-Ended Working Group on Developments in the Field of ICTs, this remains the subject of ongoing debate. This is exacerbated by states often being ambiguous in invoking the relevant rules, as exemplified by the unwillingness of the UK and the US to engage the vocabulary of international law in response to Russia's cyber electoral interference campaigns, which can be gleaned from both the Muller and Russia Report, referred to *supra*.[349]

That said, some states have begun to voice opinions as to how they consider the principles of international law apply to cyber activities;[350] but the matter

---

[346] GGE 2013 (n 63) para 19. See, for example, US DoD Views on International and Domestic Law in Cyberspace (n 55); Cyber and International Law – UK (n 55); International Law in Cyberspace – The Netherlands (n 55); International Law Applicable to Operations in Cyberspace – France (n 55); Application of International Law to State Conduct in Cyberspace – Australia (n 55); Application of International Law in Cyberspace – New Zealand (n 55); Israel's Perspective on the Application of International Law to Cyber Operations (n 55).

[347] GGE 2013, *ibid* para 21.

[348] *Ibid* para 16. The cyber norms-building approach promulgated by the UN GGE proved to be protracted, with the fifth session in 2017 concluding without the release of a consensus report due to fundamental disagreements among the GGE's 25 members in relation to, *inter alia*, the right to self-defence and the applicability of international humanitarian law. For more details, see Chapter 7.

[349] See Dan Efrony and Yuval Shany, 'A Rule Book on the Shelf? Tallinn Manual 2.0 on Cyber Operations and Subsequent State Practice' (2018) *American Journal of International Law*, 583–657, 588. Efrony and Shany refer to 'a "policy of silence and ambiguity" that is designed to preserve high levels of operational flexibility within the cyber domain'. The UK has, however, acknowledged that cyber electoral interference may breach the principle of non-intervention – see Cyber and International Law – UK (n 55).

[350] See, for example, US DoD Views on International and Domestic Law in Cyberspace (n 55); Cyber and International Law – UK (n 55); International Law in Cyberspace – The Netherlands (n 55); International Law Applicable to Operations in Cyberspace – France (n 55); Application of International Law to State Conduct in Cyberspace – Australia (n 55); Application of International Law in Cyberspace – New

is far from settled. An example of this is states' lack of agreement pertaining to the application of the principle of territorial sovereignty – a postulate set out in the *Island of Palmas* arbitral award,[351] establishing the state's exclusive competence to take legal and factual measures within its territory and prohibiting foreign governments from exercising authority in the same area without consent.[352] Following the two successful GGE processes in 2013 and 2015, there appeared to be a broad consensus reached that 'State sovereignty and international norms and principles that flow from sovereignty apply to State conduct of ICT-related activities, and to their jurisdiction over the ICT infrastructure within their territory'.[353] Since then, however, two opposing views have emerged in relation to whether and how territorial sovereignty applies to cyber operations: one articulated by France in 2019 and the other by the UK in 2018. Issuing an official document titled *International Law Applicable to Operations in Cyberspace,* France confirmed that 'State sovereignty and international norms and principles that flow from sovereignty apply to the conduct by States of ICT-related activities'.[354] Thus, the French position is that it exercises sovereignty over information systems located within its territory. Consequently:

> any cyberattack against French digital systems or any effects produced on French territory by digital means by a State organ, a person or an entity exercising elements of governmental authority or by a person or persons acting on the instructions of or under the direction or control of a State constitutes a breach of sovereignty.[355]

This standpoint suggests that a violation of sovereignty occurs not only when effects are produced on the French territory, but also at the point at which French computer systems are penetrated.[356] By contrast, the UK stance, presented by Attorney-General Jeremy Wright QC, is that the UK does not recog-

---

Zealand (n 55); Israel's Perspective on the Application of International Law to Cyber Operations (n 55).

[351] *Island of Palmas* 2 RIAA (Perm CT Arb 1928) 828.

[352] *Ibid* 839.

[353] GGE 2013 (n 63) para 20; UNGA, 'Group of Governmental Experts on Developments in the Field of Information and Telecommunications in the Context of International Security' (22 July 2015) UN Doc A/70/174 para 28(b).

[354] International Law Applicable to Operations in Cyberspace – France (n 55).

[355] *Ibid,* 7.

[356] Przemyslaw Rogulski, 'France's Declaration on International Law in Cyberspace: The Law of Peacetime Cyber Operations, Part I', *Opinio Juris* (24 September 2019) ('Rogulski').

nize a rule of sovereignty in cyberspace altogether. To this end, the Attorney General stated that:

> some have sought to argue for the existence of a cyber specific rule of a 'violation of territorial sovereignty' in relation to interference in the computer networks of another [S]tate without its consent. Sovereignty is of course fundamental to the international rules-based system. But I am not persuaded that we can currently extrapolate from that general principle a specific rule or additional prohibition for cyber activity beyond that of a prohibited intervention. The UK Government's position is therefore that there is no such rule as a matter of current international law.[357]

Consequently, the UK official standpoint is that the only appropriate rule to apply to state cyber operations below the use of force threshold is that of non-intervention. It follows that a cyber operation will not breach territorial sovereignty unless it constitutes a violation of the principle of non-intervention. By way of comparison, the view expressed in the *Tallinn Manual 2.0* is that 'cyber operations that prevent or disregard another State's exercise of its sovereign prerogatives constitute a violation of … sovereignty and are prohibited by international law'.[358] However, the approach adopted by the experts is that a violation of sovereignty will occur only in a situation where a cyber operation penetrating a foreign system meets a threshold of harm – that is, it results in physical damage or harm. In relation to cyber espionage, Rule 32 states that although it does not *per se* violate international law, the method by which it is carried out might do so.[359] Accordingly, the lawfulness of a cyber operation 'depends on whether the way in which the operation is carried out violates any international law obligations that bind the State'.[360] Thus, the experts agreed that where an individual acting for one state penetrates the physical territory of another state in order to collect confidential data stored on the latter's computers, this amounts to a breach of that state's sovereignty.[361] As stated in the Manual, this is 'not because cyber espionage is involved, but rather by virtue of the fact that the individual is on another State's territory while non-consensually engaging in the operation'.[362] But where a state performs a cyber intrusion remotely, the view is that this constitutes a violation of sovereignty only if the operation results in physical damage or injury,[363] or

---

[357] Cyber and International Law – UK (n 55).
[358] *Tallinn Manual 2.0* (n 1) Rule 4, 17.
[359] *Ibid* 168.
[360] *Ibid* para 6.
[361] *Ibid* Rule 32, 171.
[362] *Ibid.*
[363] *Ibid* Rule 4 para 20.

loss of functionality of cyber infrastructure.[364] The experts could not agree on whether a cyber activity that results in neither physical damage nor the loss of functionality amounts to a violation of sovereignty.[365] The majority view was that remote access without consent of, for example, another state's military cyber systems and exfiltration of classified data would not violate the 'international law prohibition irrespective of the attendant severity'.[366] Yet, this seems exactly the position adopted by France: any cyber operation penetrating a foreign system or producing effects over it constitutes a violation of sovereignty.[367] The argument has its merits – the penetration of a computer system located on the territory of another state could be viewed as the exercise of state power within that territory.[368] Support for this view can be gleaned from some academics. For example, Professor Roscini suggests that:

> cyber exploitation operations … may be a violation of the sovereignty of the targeted State when they entail an unauthorised intrusion into cyber infrastructure located in another State (be it governmental or private), although not intervention (and even less a use of force) as they lack the coercive element.[369]

Similarly, Russell Buchan argues that 'acts of cyber espionage … that penetrate computer networks and systems supported by cyber infrastructure situated within the territory of another State constitute a violation of that State's territorial sovereignty, irrespective of whether that operation causes damage or harm', concluding that 'economic and political cyber espionage transgress the rule of territorial sovereignty [because they are] the unauthorised intrusion into a domain protected by State sovereignty'.[370] Having said that, the official position taken by New Zealand in the 2020 Application of International Law to State Activity in Cyberspace (Application of International Law in Cyberspace),[371] introduces an additional lawyer of uncertainty, since:

> New Zealand considers that territorial sovereignty prohibits states from using cyber means to cause significant harmful effects manifesting on the territory of another state. However, New Zealand does not consider that territorial sovereignty prohibits every unauthorised intrusion into a foreign ICT system or prohibits all cyber activity which has effects on the territory of another state. There is a range of circumstances – in addition to pure espionage activity – in which an unauthorised

---

364   *Ibid.*
365   *Ibid* Rule 4 para 20.
366   *Ibid* Rule 32, 171.
367   Rogulski (n 357).
368   *Ibid.*
369   Roscini (n 44) 66.
370   Buchan (n 2) 54.
371   Application of International Law in Cyberspace – New Zealand (n 55).

cyber intrusion, including one causing effects on the territory of another state, would not be internationally wrongful. For example, New Zealand considers that the rule of territorial sovereignty as applied in the cyber context does not prohibit states from taking necessary measures, with minimally destructive effects, to defend against the harmful activity of malicious cyber actors.[372]

Thus articulated, New Zealand's position indicates that violations of sovereignty occur only when the cyber intrusions have 'significant harmful effects' on another state's territory. 'Unauthorised intrusions' – including espionage – do not seem to amount to internationally wrongful acts. While this view appears to align more closely with that articulated in the *Tallinn Manual 2.0* than the more lenient approach adopted by the French government, what remains unclear is what exactly amounts to 'effects' on the territory of another state and how severe or significant such 'effects' must be to trigger state responsibility. The issue has been tentatively addressed in the Application of International Law in Cyberspace, since the document acknowledges that:

> detailed factual enquiry is required in each case to determine whether state cyber activity that has effects manifesting on the territory of another state, but which does not amount to a use of force or a prohibited intervention, nonetheless involves a violation of the standalone rule of territorial sovereignty. That factual enquiry should take into account the scale and significance of the effects, the objective of the activity, and the nature of the target.[373]

With more states putting forth their official views on these issues in the future, finding common ground in relation to what 'effects' cyber operations must have to qualify as potentially violating state sovereignty will likely be challenging, but necessary not least to articulate the range of response options states may lawfully resort to when faced with hostile cyber operations on their territories.

A matter closely related to the above deliberations is whether other cyber operations, such as mass surveillance and electoral interference may constitute a violation of territorial sovereignty and/or other international law rules. In relation to the former, this state practice was officially condemned by at least one country, Brazil, as such a breach.[374] Furthermore, the *Tallinn Manual 2.0* experts observed that the bulk collection of Internet traffic and cyber sur-

---

[372]   *Ibid* para 14, 2.

[373]   *Ibid* para 15, 3.

[374]   See Dilma Rousseff's Statement (n 2). The former Brazilian President accused the NSA of violating international law by its indiscriminate collection of personal information of that country's citizens and economic espionage, stating that 'in the absence of the respect for sovereignty, there is no basis for the relationship among nations'.

veillance may implicate a whole host of other rules, such as those pertaining to the law of the sea (Rule 54), diplomatic and consular law (Rule 41) and international human rights law (Chapter 6); but that every cyber surveillance operation must be assessed on its individual merits.[375] In addition, 'if cyber operations that are undertaken for espionage purpose violate the international human right to privacy (Rule 35), the cyber espionage operation is unlawful'.[376] Similarly, cyber election meddling may implicate the principles of territorial sovereignty, non-intervention, breach of duty of due diligence and human rights obligations.[377]

The need for greater clarity as to how international law applies to states' cyber intelligence gathering operations is unquestionable – not least because a coherent and explicit legal basis is necessary both to carry out these activities and to respond to them within the legal parameters. It is therefore desirable that states develop bespoke international legal frameworks to specifically and separately regulate the three areas of cyber espionage, cyber electoral interference and mass cyber surveillance. In the context of online disinformation and manipulation, the European Union has recognized that there is a pressing need to protect European democracies and human rights in light of more sophisticated techniques being deployed to maximize influence and manipulate public debate online. To this end, the European Commission in December 2020 put forward the European Democracy Action Plan (EDAP), which complements the proposed Digital Services Act and Digital Markets Act. These efforts represent a welcome step towards addressing disinformation, information influence operations and 'foreign interference', which the EDPA defines as 'coercive and deceptive efforts to disrupt the free formation and expression of individuals' political will by a foreign state actor or its agent'. There is no doubt, however, that until comprehensible rules on a global scale are established, manipulative practices will continue to be utilized with more prevalence and notoriety. Similar reasoning applies to state mass cyber surveillance and its implications for international human rights law – in particular the right to privacy of communications, which is the focus of this book.

In summary, based on the aims, scope and the targets involved, three broad categories of intelligence operations may be distinguished: (1) cyber espionage, which is further subdivided into political and economic – the former also comprising foreign cyber electoral interference through 'doxing' operations;

---

[375] *Tallinn Manual 2.0* (n 1) Rule 32, para 7.
[376] *Ibid* Rule 32, 170.
[377] These include the individual's right to political participation under Article 25 of the ICCPR; the right to freedom of opinion and expression under Article 19 of the ICCPR; the right to privacy under Article 17 of the ICCPR; and the collective right to self-determination.

(2) cyber surveillance, consisting of targeted and mass interception and collection of communications content and metadata, including in bulk; and (3) foreign cyber electoral interference, including cyber tempering with a state's election infrastructure and information operations constituting malinformation and disinformation. This is not to say that all current SIGINT operations will fall neatly within these categories. The boundaries are fluid and certain cyber exploitation operations will always be difficult to compartmentalize with precision. However, what needs to be acknowledged is that the broad classification of peacetime espionage into HUMINT and SIGINT collection no longer accurately reflects states' cyber-enabled intelligence activities in the twenty-first century.

## 5.    CONCLUSION

Cyberspace has become a fertile ground for a whole spectrum of operations collectively referred to as 'cyber espionage', which aim to gather information for political, economic and security purposes. This chapter has identified three categories of these practices: cyber espionage, mass cyber surveillance and foreign cyber electoral interference campaigns. While to date there is no international treaty or customary law that directly regulates cyber espionage, the political uproar that accompanied the 2013 Snowden disclosures brought to the fore the need for the development of a *lex specialis* to set out the legal parameters circumscribing the operational methods of states' intelligence agencies. This chapter has argued that the first step towards achieving such a framework is to develop a more doctrinally nuanced categorization of cyber espionage – in particular to distinguish mass cyber surveillance from other methods of intelligence collection. To this end, it defined 'mass cyber surveillance' as a state's indiscriminate monitoring and capture of digital communications in bulk, aimed at identifying future rather than investigating known threats. Henceforth, this book shall discuss the legality of mass cyber surveillance in relation to individuals' right to privacy of communications as set out under international human rights law.

# 3. The right to online privacy as a customary international law rule

## 1. INTRODUCTION

Privacy is a basic human need, which allows us to live our lives away from unwanted scrutiny and intrusion by others. It affords us a space dedicated solely to ourselves, uninterrupted by anyone else if we so choose – a 'right to be left alone'.[1] It thus gives us a degree of autonomy and makes it possible for us as individuals to lead a dignified existence, free in the knowledge that some of the aspects of what we do and think, and how we interact with the surrounding environment, are guaranteed to be ours and ours alone. At its core is the notion of freedom, which – as observed in *Novak's Commentary to the International Covenant on Civil and Political Rights*[2] – sees 'the human being as autonomous subject, i.e. the individual alone, who is absolutely sovereign over himself or herself and all of his or her actions that do not interfere with others'.[3] Privacy is also vital to society as a whole, as it permits and facilitates the making of democratic choices; protects against the state's arbitrary interference; and enables the exercise of other rights, including those of free expression and assembly. As such, privacy is recognized as a fundamental human right at the international, regional and domestic levels.

It has been argued that advancements in digital technology – in particular, in the first decades of the twenty-first century – have prompted profound social changes on a scale matching or exceeding that of the Industrial Revolution.[4] Unquestionably, this 'digital revolution' has yielded benefits that have enriched and transformed almost every sphere of modern life, from interpersonal interactions to work, mobility, entertainment, banking and finance. However, it has also facilitated hitherto unparalleled intrusions into private life through

---

[1]  Samuel D Warren and Lewis D Brandeis, 'The Right to Privacy' (1890) 4 *Harvard Law Review* 193–220.

[2]  William A Schabas, *U.N. International Covenant on Civil and Political Rights. Novak's CCPR Commentary* (N.P. Engel, 2019) ('Schabas').

[3]  *Ibid* 459.

[4]  Alexandra Rengel, *Privacy in the 21 Century* (Martinus Nijhoff Publishers, 2013) 41.

the collection of information about individuals and its manipulation for commercial and political ends. This has been especially keenly felt in the years that followed the 2013 Snowden revelations, as a result of which it became apparent that once narrowly focused communications intelligence gathering has escalated to the ubiquitous monitoring of entire populations in the name of national security. Partly as a result of these concerns, the UN Human Rights Council and the General Assembly asserted that 'the same rights that people have offline must also be protected online'.[5] This 'normative equivalence paradigm' equates respect and protection of offline rights with their online counterpart.[6] The conceptual online parallel of the right to privacy can thus be understood as 'the level of privacy protection an individual has while connected to the internet'.[7] The question that arises in this context is: what is the source of this right? More specifically, does it derive from international treaty[8] and/or customary law? While privacy of electronic communications is an entrenched principle under the former, its international customary law status is less certain. However, were online privacy established as such a rule, this may potentially have far-reaching consequences, as a legal challenge to states' mass cyber surveillance could be brought on this legal basis – even where a particular country is not a party to the relevant international convention protecting privacy or where such an instrument does not apply.

This chapter engages with this enquiry as follows. Section 2 considers privacy within the broader context of public international law. Section 3 discusses whether the right to online privacy can be said to have crystallized into a customary law rule by applying a two-stage test: uniform and consistent state practice; and a belief that that practice is law (*opinio juris*). To this end, section 4 engages with the first element of this requirement, while section 5

---

[5]     UN Human Rights Committee (UNHRC), 'The Promotion, Protection and Enjoyment of Human Rights on the Internet' (16 July 2012) UN Doc A/HRC/Res/20/8 para 1 ('A/HRC/Res/20/8'); UNHRC, 'The Promotion, Protection and Enjoyment of Human Rights on the Internet' (14 July 2014) A/HRC/Res/26/13 para 1 ('A/HRC/ Res/26/13'); UNGA Resolution, 'The Right to Privacy in the Digital Age' (21 January 2014) UN Doc A/Res/68/167 para 3 ('A/Res/68/167'); and UNGA Resolution, 'The Right to Privacy in the Digital Age' (10 February 2015) A/Res/69/166 para 3 ('A/Res/ 69/166').

[6]     Yuval Shany, 'Contribution to Open Consultation on UN GGE 2015 Norm Proposal' in UN Office for Disarmament Affairs, *Voluntary, Non-binding Norms for Responsible State Behaviour in the Use of Information and Communications Technology. A Commentary* (UN Office for Disarmament Affairs, 2017) 110 ('UNODA Commentary').

[7]     Wilson and Strawn LLP, 'What is the Definition of Online Privacy?', www .winston.com/en/legal-glossary/online-privacy.html.

[8]     As discussed in Chapter 5, the scope of the right to privacy under the main international human rights treaties has been interpreted to include privacy of communications.

enquires into the presence of *opinio juris*. Section 6 then evaluates whether, on the basis of the aforementioned criteria, online privacy has attained customary international law status. Section 7 concludes that, despite the prominence that online privacy has been given at both international and national level, it cannot be said that it has already become a rule of customary law, but is rather an emerging right.

## 2.    PRIVACY AND INTERNATIONAL LAW

### 2.1    Privacy as a Fundamental Human Right

Privacy has been valued and protected in most societies since antiquity, with numerous references found in, *inter alia*, the Bible,[9] the Code of Hammurabi,[10] classical Roman law and ancient Chinese texts.[11] These early citations focused primarily on the right to solitude in certain areas of human activity as not being suitable for general observations and knowledge.[12] Today, privacy is recognized as a much more complex notion, vital both at a personal level and for society *sensu lato*.

As a concept, it encapsulates the individual's right to protect a sphere of his or her life from unwanted intrusion of the state or of others with whom he or she does not wish to share its certain aspects. It includes, among other things, control over personal information; freedom from surveillance; protection from invasion into one's home; personal autonomy; and control over one's body.[13] However, the value of privacy lies not only in the preservation of a person's sense of self, and his or her dignity and individuality. It also plays a vital role for the entire community, as it safeguards liberty and freedom of choice, including in the context of political decision making and freedom of expression.[14] As such, it allows both individuals and societies to develop and

---

[9]    Richard F Hixson, *Privacy in a Public Society: Human Rights in Conflict* (Oxford University Press, 1987) 3.

[10]    Encyclopaedia Britannica, 'Code of Hammurabi. Babylonian Law', www .britannica.com/topic/Code-of-Hammurabi.

[11]    Cao Jingchun, 'Protecting the Right to Privacy in China' (2005) 36(3) *Victoria University of Wellington Law Review* 645–64.

[12]    Alexandra Rengel, 'Privacy as an International Human Right and the Right to Obscurity in Cyberspace' (2014) 2(2) *Groningen Journal of International Law* 33–54, 37.

[13]    For a useful overview of the various aspects of what privacy is and what it protects, see Daniel J Solove, *Understanding Privacy* (Harvard University Press, 2009) 12–13 ('Solove').

[14]    See the Australian Privacy Charter Council, *The Australian Privacy Charter* (December 1994): 'a free and democratic society requires respect for the autonomy of

flourish in the knowledge that some aspects of both the singular and the collective spheres are shielded from unwarranted encroachment and attack. Yet, a definition of what exactly this concept is and what it encompasses has eluded social scientists, jurists, philosophers and legal scholars alike,[15] leading one commentator to observe with exasperation that: 'privacy is a value so complex, so entangled in competing and contradictory dimensions, so engorged with various and distinct meanings, that I sometimes despair whether it can be usefully addressed at all.'[16]

Likewise, there is no universal legal definition of this right, as its abstract and complex nature makes this both difficult and undesirable. Nevertheless, it has been referred to as 'the presumption that individuals should have an area of autonomous development, interaction and liberty free from State intervention and excessive intrusion by other uninvited individuals'.[17] Privacy has been recognized as a fundamental human right in the Universal Declaration of Human Rights[18] and stipulated as a legally binding rule in several international conventions and treaties, including the International Covenant on Civil and Political Rights (ICCPR)[19] and could therefore be said to be an integral part of the International Bill of Rights.[20]

---

individuals and limits on the power of both State and private organisations to intrude on that autonomy.'

[15]    Solove (n 13) 1.

[16]    Robert C Post, 'Three Concepts of Privacy' (2001) 89 *Georgetown Law Journal* 2087–98, 2087.

[17]    UNGA, 'Report of the Special Rapporteur on the Promotion and Protection of Human Rights and Fundamental Freedoms While Countering Terrorism, Ben Emmerson' (23 September 2014) UN Doc A/69/397 para 28, ('A/69/397'). See also David Calcutt, 'Report on Privacy and Related Matters' (1990) London HMSO, defining 'privacy' as 'the right of an individual to be protected against intrusion into his personal life or affairs, or those of his family, by direct physical means or by publication of information'.

[18]    Universal Declaration of Human Rights (adopted 10 December 1948) UNGA Res 217 A(III) Art 12 ('UDHR').

[19]    UNGA, International Covenant on Civil and Political Rights (adopted 16 December 1966, entered into force 23 March 1976) 999 UNTS 999, 171 Art 17 ('ICCPR'); see also Convention on the Right of the Child (adopted 20 November 1980, entered into force 2 September 1990) 1577 UNTS Art 16; and International Convention on the Protection of All Migrant Workers and Members of Their Families (adopted 18 December 1990 UNGA Res 45/158) Art 14.

[20]    The International Bill of Rights comprises: the UDHR (n 18); the ICCPR (n 19); the International Covenant on Economic Social and Cultural Rights (adopted 16 December 1966, entered into force 3 January 1976) 993 UNTS 3 ('ICESCR'); the Optional Protocol to the International Covenant on Civil and Political Rights (adopted 16 December 1966, entered into force 23 March 1976) 999 UNTS 171 ('OP1'); the Optional Protocol to the International Covenant on Economic, Social and Cultural

By becoming parties to international treaties, states are obliged to respect, protect and fulfil the rights set forth therein. Thus, Article 2(1) of the ICCPR provides that each 'State Party [must undertake] to respect and to ensure to all individuals within its territory and subject to its jurisdiction the rights recognized in ... the Covenant'.[21] The extent of this duty is both positive and negative in nature. The obligation to respect is negative and means that states must refrain from interfering with the enjoyment of ICCPR rights where such interference is not expressly permitted by its relevant provision (depending on the formulation of the given right).[22] Where restrictions on any of the ICCPR's entitlements are permissible, states are obliged to demonstrate the necessity of such limitations and take only measures which are proportionate to the pursuit of legitimate aims in order to ensure continuous and effective protection of the ICCPR rights.[23] Conversely, the duty to ensure is positive and requires that states take proactive steps to give effect to and facilitate the enjoyment of those rights.[24] To this end, General Comment 31 explains that states must adopt legislative, judicial, administrative, educative and other measures in order to fulfil their obligations.

The importance of human rights protection and its universal reach are reiterated in Article 55 of the Charter of the United Nations ('UN Charter'), which provides that the 'United Nations shall promote ... universal respect for, and observance of, human rights and fundamental freedoms for all without distinction as to race, sex, language or religion'.[25] This universalist approach is also reflected in the ICCPR, since the nature of the general obligations is to guarantee the Covenant's rights to all. Furthermore, the commitments of state parties to the ICCPR can be summarized as comprising two man aspects. First, it imposes duties on states primarily with regard to individuals. To this end, Article 2(1) expressly provides that states parties to the ICCPR must respect

---

Rights (adopted 5 March 2009, entered into force 5 March 2009); and the Second Optional Protocol to the International Covenant on Civil and Political Rights, Aiming at the Abolition of the Death Penalty (adopted 15 December 1989, entered into force 11 July 1991).

[21]   ICCPR (n 19) Art 2(1).

[22]   Schabas (n 2) 42. Some rights are absolute, which means that states must refrain from engaging in a particular activity, such as the prohibition of torture in Article 7 of the ICCPR. Other rights are qualified and allow states to impose certain limitations on their exercise (eg, ICCPR Arts 17, 18, 19, 21 and 22).

[23]   UNHRC, 'General Comment No. 31. The Nature of the General Obligations Imposed on States Parties to the Covenant' (26 May 2004) UN Doc CCPR/C/21/Rev.1/Add.1326 para 6 ('General Comment 31').

[24]   Schabas (n 2) 42.

[25]   UN, Charter of the United Nations (24 October 1945) 1 UNTS XVI Art 55(c) ('UN Charter').

and ensure the rights of individuals rights holders set out therein.[26] Second, the Human Rights Committee (HRC) in its General Comment 31 further elucidated on this point, stating that:

> while article 2(1) is couched in terms of the obligations of State Parties towards individuals as the right holders under the Covenant, every State Party has a legal interest in the performance of every other State Party of its obligations.[27]

This, the HRC stated:

> follows from the fact that the "rules concerning the basic rights of the human person" are *erga omnes* obligations and that, as indicated in the fourth preambular paragraph of the Covenant, there is a United Nations Charter obligation to promote universal respect for, and observance of, human rights and fundamental freedoms.[28]

This therefore suggests that the ICCPR obligations, including the protection of the right to privacy, may be binding on all states, irrespective of whether a given nation has ratified that treaty.

In view of this, since both the UN General Assembly (UNGA) and the HRC have recognized that individuals enjoy the same rights online as offline, the question is whether online privacy can be said to have the status of a customary law rule in addition to being derived from treaty law. This is of particular importance in the context of mass surveillance, as digital technologies enable states to gather data of entire populations extraterritorially but, as discussed in Chapter 4,[29] without affording them the same legal safeguards as in the case of domestic interception of communications. In addition, states' human rights treaty obligations in cases of extraterritorial mass surveillance have been contested by some governments and, as discussed in Chapter 4 *infra*, the issue of the extent of their jurisdiction remains unsettled. Therefore, determining the source of this right may shed light on whether individuals could legally challenge foreign governments' mass surveillance on the basis of a breach of customary international law rule, where a legally binding treaty protecting this right does not apply and/or the state in question has not ratified it.

---

[26]   Schabas (n 2) 37.
[27]   General Comment 31 (n 23) para 2.
[28]   *Ibid.* See also Schabas (n 2) 37.
[29]   See Chapter 4, section 2.

## 3. THE RIGHT TO ONLINE PRIVACY AS A CUSTOMARY INTERNATIONAL LAW RULE

Customary international law is a body of legal rules that has evolved through both continued state practice and a belief that that practice is law. As a primary source of international law, it is binding on all member states of the international community. Article 38(1)(b) of the Statutes of the International Court of Justice (SICJ) enumerates various sources of international law, among which is 'international custom as evidence of a general practice accepted as law'.[30] Unlike international treaties – which, as provided in Article 38(1)(a) of the SICJ, stipulate rules expressly recognized by the contracting states – customary law is predicated on states' performance and the convergence of practice based on a belief that they are under a legal obligation to act in that manner. Consequently, in order to ascertain whether a particular rule can be said to have such status, two conditions set out in Article 38(1)(b) of the SICJ must be met: (1) the establishment of general state practice (*usus* or *diuturnitas*); and (2) the subjective belief that such practice is law (*opinio juris sive necessitates*, or 'an opinion of law or necessity'). This two-stage test has been recognized as 'the dominant position in the mainstream theory of customary international law'.[31] It follows that the presence of each of these two conditions is regarded as indispensable. To this end, Special Rapporteur Sir Michael Wood, in his 2013 report on the formation and evidence of customary international law, clarified that to establish the existence of customary law rule, 'we must look at what States actually do in their relations with one another, and attempt to understand why they do it, and in particular whether they recognize an obligation to adopt a certain course'.[32] This approach has become known as the inductive method to determining the existence of a new custom, and has been embraced both by the ICJ in a number of celebrated decisions and by the International Law Commission (ILC), a body established by the UNGA in 1947[33] to promote the progressive development and codification of international law. Thus, in *Libya/Malta*, the ICJ held that for a new customary international law rule to be formed, the behaviour in question must amount to a settled practice, which must be followed by the *opinio juris sive necessitatis*.[34] Likewise, in

---

[30] Statute of the International Court of Justice (18 April 1946) Art 38(1)(b) ('SICJ').
[31] International Law Commission, 'First Report on Formation and Evidence of Customary International Law by Sir Michael Wood Special Rapporteur' 65 Session of the ILC (2013) (17 May 2013) UN Doc A/CN.4/663 para 96 ('A/CN.4/663').
[32] *Ibid.*
[33] UNGA Resolution 174(II) (21 November 1947) UN Doc A/Res/147(II).
[34] *Continental Shelf, Libya v Malta* [1985] ICJ Rep 13 at para 27: 'It is of course axiomatic that the material of customary international law is to be looked for primarily

*Nicaragua*, the ICJ reiterated that in order to ascertain whether a particular rule of customary law is applicable, the ICJ 'has to direct its attention to the practice and *opinio juris* of States'.[35] The ILC adopted this approach in its report on the identification of customary law[36] and confirmed that each of these elements must be separately identified. Furthermore, it involves a careful examination of available evidence to ascertain their presence in any given case.[37] Based on this two-pronged formulation, this chapter considers whether the right to privacy online could be said to have crystallized into customary international law rule by examining first state practice and then *opinio juris*.

## 4.    STATE PRACTICE – GENERAL

'State practice' is 'the "objective" (material) element and concerns the consistency and uniformity of practice over time'.[38] In determining whether particular state behaviour can be accepted as customary rule, such factors will be taken into account as duration, consistency uniformity and generality.[39]

There is no exhaustive list of what exactly comprises state practice; but certain manifestations of the judicial, executive and legislative branches are commonly regarded as suitable for furnishing proof of its existence.[40] These include administrative acts; national legislation; decisions of national courts; governmental activities on the international stage, such as treaty making; diplomatic acts and correspondence; together with executive actions, including official manuals and orders.

In order to satisfy these requirements for the purposes of establishing whether online privacy can be said to have crystallized into custom, what must be determined is how its protection offline translates into the safeguarding of this right online. To this end, the following analysis draws, *inter alia*, on domestic legislation and the jurisprudence of selected courts, in addition to a number of reports pertaining to current trends and developments in this field.

---

in the actual practice and *opinio juris* of States …'. See also *Legality of the Threat or Use of Nuclear Weapons*, Advisory Opinion (8 July 1996) ICJ Rep 226, 253 ('*Nuclear Weapons Advisory Opinion*').

[35]   *Military and Paramilitary Activities in and Against Nicaragua* (*Nicaragua v United States of America*) (Merits) [1986] ICJ Rep 14, para 183 ('*Nicaragua*').

[36]   ILC, 'Identification of Customary International Law with Commentaries' (2018) UN Doc A/73/10 (ILC Draft Conclusions) General Commentary para 3 ('ILC Identification of Customary Law').

[37]   *Ibid* Conclusion 2, Commentary para 2.

[38]   A/CN.4/663 (n 31).

[39]   Ian Brownlie, *Principles of Public International Law* (Oxford University Press, 2012) 6–12 ('Brownlie').

[40]   See ILC Identification of Customary Law (n 36) Conclusion 6; *ibid* 6.

## 4.1    Duration

Although the passage of time is a pertinent factor, the duration of relevant conduct over a prolonged period is not paramount. Rather, the essence of customary law rule is that states' practice within the timeframe in question, 'including that of States whose interests are specifically affected, should have been both extensive and virtually uniform in the sense of the provision invoked'.[41] Indeed as noted by Professor Ian Brownlie, a long-immemorial practice is not necessary.[42] For example, rules relating to airspace and the continental shelf have emerged from the fairly quick maturation of practice. What is required, however, is that both its consistency and generality be proven.[43]

The right to the protection of privacy in national legal systems has a long and well-documented pedigree, with examples of some domestic privacy protection laws dating back to as early as the fourteenth century.[44] However, its lengthy development throughout history does not in itself attest to its extension to the online environment as a customary law rule. What is important is the generality, uniformity and consistency of states' protection of this right in the digital context.

## 4.2    Generality

The requirement of generality stipulates that state practice must be 'widespread'[45] within the international society – meaning that 'it must have been applied by the overwhelming majority of States, which hitherto had an opportunity of applying it',[46] so that 'any remaining inconsistent practice will be

---

[41] *North Sea Continental Shelf Cases (Federal Republic of Germany v Denmark, Federal Republic of Germany v Netherlands)* [1969] ICJ Rep 3 para 74 (*'North Sea Continental Shelf Cases'*).

[42] Brownlie (n 39) 7.

[43] *Ibid.*

[44] Early examples of privacy protection include the English Justice of the Peace Act 1361, which provided for the arrest of 'peeping toms' and eavesdroppers; the Swedish Access to Public Records Act 1776, which required that all government-held information be used for legitimate purposes; together with the 1858 prohibition of the publication of private facts in France and the imposition of stringent fines (*The Rachel Affaire*, Judgment 16 June 1885) Trib Pr inst de la Seine, 1858 DP III 62.

[45] *Maritime Delimitation and Territorial Questions between Qatar and Bahrain (Qatar v Bahrain)* [2001] ICJ Pep 40 para 205.

[46] Josef L Kunz, 'The Nature of Customary International Law' (1953) 47 *American Journal of International Law* 662–69, 666 in Russell Buchan, *Cyber Espionage and International Law* (Hart Publishing, 2019) 151 ('Buchan').

marginal and without legal effect'.[47] In addition, even if such conduct is wide-spread, it must be 'representative' of its members – 'namely that States with different political, economic and legal systems [and] States of all continents, [must participate] in the process'.[48]

Currently, out of 193 UN sovereign states, 64 per cent (107 countries) have put in place privacy and/or data protection legislation; whereas only 18 per cent have not.[49] As noted by Lee Bygrave, recent years have witnessed exponential growth in the rate at which governments are enacting data privacy statutes;[50] while the Special Rapporteur on the right to privacy commented that: 'there has been a great increase in the number of countries introducing privacy/data protection laws, with 2018 being a particularly active year around the world.'[51] However, these prolific legislative efforts alone are not sufficient to conclude that the right to privacy online has obtained the status of customary international law, for at least two reasons. First, it is questionable whether its domestic protection meets the requirement of uniformity. Second, states' behaviour testifies to a lack of consistency in relation to the protection of this right in the digital context. This is marked by a legislative pull in the opposite direction, which is evidenced by numerous governments enacting draconian mass surveillance legislation and/or conducting communications intelligence without any specific legal basis. This suggests that – at least for now and prob-ably for the foreseeable future – nations attach greater value to safeguarding security at the expense of online privacy. Both of these points are discussed below.

### 4.3    Uniformity and Consistency

The condition as to uniformity dictates that customary rule must be 'in accord-ance with a constant and uniform usage practiced by States in question'.[52] However, only substantial, as against complete, uniformity is necessary. Thus, in *Nicaragua*, the ICJ observed that there is no need for 'an absolutely rigorous

---

[47]    Mark E Villiger, *Customary International Law and Treaties: Manual on the Theory and Practice of the Interrelation of Sources* (Kluwer International Law, 1997) 30; in Buchan *ibid.*

[48]    *North Sea Continental Shelf Cases* (n 41) para 73, 227.

[49]    UN Conference on Trade and Development, 'Data Protection and Privacy Legislation    Worldwide';    https://unctad.org/en/Pages/DTL/STI_and_ICTs/ICT4D -Legislation/eCom-Data-Protection-Laws.aspx.

[50]    Lee A Bygrave, *Data Privacy Law. An International Perspective* (Oxford University Press, 2014) 99 ('Bygrave').

[51]    Special Rapporteur Joseph A Cannataci, 'Right to Privacy' (17 October 2018), UN Doc A/73/45712 para 43, 7 ('A/73/45712').

[52]    *Asylum* Case *(Colombia v Peru)* [1950] ICJ Rep 284 (*'Asylum Case'*).

conformity'[53] of a particular behaviour of states. Nor is there a requirement that all of them have participated in a certain act. Rather, there must be a general practice; while that of the most influential or powerful countries in a particular field in question will carry the most weight.[54]

### 4.3.1 Domestic legislation as manifestation of state practice

Given space constraints, it is impossible to provide a detailed appraisal of every country's laws pertaining to privacy to ascertain the extent to which its protection represents constant and uniform state practice. Nevertheless, the picture that emerges is one of marked disparity of approaches to the safeguarding of this right from unwarranted intrusions. Broadly speaking, four different trends can be discerned – namely, where this right is (1) explicitly laid down in the constitution; (2) set out in the constitutional order, but not directly referred to in the constitution and also protected by other means, such as tort law and through statutes; (3) protected by data privacy laws; or (4) not expressly recognized by the legal system as an autonomous right.

#### 4.3.1.1 *Constitutions with an express right to privacy*

In a number of countries – such as Israel, Costa Rica,[55] Spain, Poland, Germany, some Scandinavian states,[56] South Africa and Brazil – the right to privacy is explicitly set out in the constitution. Thus, Article 7(a) of the Israeli Basic Law provides that 'all persons have the right to privacy and intimacy';[57] while Section 18.1 of the Spanish Constitution guarantees 'the right to honour, to personal and family privacy'.[58] Likewise, the Polish Constitution refers to this right in Articles 47 and 49. The former provision stipulates that 'everyone has the right to legal protection of his private and family life, of his honour and good reputation and to make decisions about his personal life';[59] the latter postulates that 'the freedom and privacy of communications shall be ensured. Any limitations thereon may be imposed only in cases and in a manner specified by

---

[53]    *Nicaragua* (n 35) para 186.

[54]    Malcolm N Show, *International Law* (Cambridge University Press, 2008) 80 ('Show').

[55]    Costa Rica's Constitution of 1949 (as amended in 2011) Art 24.

[56]    See Instrument of Government (SFS nr 1974:152): 1974 (as amended on 7 December 2010) (Sweden [se]) SFS 1974:152, Main Text, Chapter 8 Acts of Law and Other Provisions, Provisions adopted by means of an act of law Art 2(6); Constitution of the Kingdom of Norway as amended in 2018 (17 May 1814) Art 102; Constitution of Finland (11 June 1999) s 10.

[57]    Basic Law: Human Dignity and Liberty 1992 Art 7(a).

[58]    Constitution of Spain (31 October 1978) s 18(1).

[59]    Constitution of the Republic of Poland (2 April 1997) Art 47.

statute'.[60] An example of a successful constitutional challenge on the basis of these guarantees is Case K23/11[61] heard by the Polish Constitutional Tribunal in 2014, concerning the working methods of the intelligence and security services. The Tribunal concluded that the provisions regulating their operational and investigative activities were contrary to the rights stipulated in Articles 47 and 49, as they did not provide for independent supervision of the process of granting access to telecommunications data. As a result of this judgment, the relevant authorities were requested to take measures to fill in some legal gaps that threatened these rights.

Another example of a successful challenge of state surveillance breaching the right to privacy enshrined in the constitution is the German case of *1 B v R*,[62] heard by the German Federal Constitutional Court in 2020. The case involved the surveillance of non-German individuals outside of Germany by that country's Federal Intelligence Service on the basis of the Federal Intelligence Service Act 2016 (BND Act). This new amendment to the Federal Intelligence Service Act[63] created a statutory basis for the practice of strategic surveillance and established divergent regimes which apply to different categories of individuals depending on their nationality and location. The legal challenge was brought by journalists and civil society groups, who asked the Tribunal to determine whether that statute violated the rights protected under the German Constitution – in particular, the right to privacy (Article 10(1))[64] and the freedom of the press. The Tribunal declared the BND Act 2016 as unconstitutional, thus necessitating its amendment. Significantly, it held that the intelligence services are bound by the constitutional duty to respect the right to privacy not only within their own territory, but also with regard to foreigners in other countries.[65]

Mention must also be made of the Brazilian Constitution, which in Articles 5.X and 5.XII explicitly protects the right to personal intimacy, private life, honour and reputation, together with the secrecy of correspondence, telegraphic, telephone and data communications.[66] Brazil has also pioneered the further development of this area of law by granting access to personal information gathered by government bodies. This constitutional remedy (set out in Article 5.LXIX) – known as the writ of *habeas data* – was established in

---

[60]   *Ibid* Art 49.
[61]   Constitutional Tribunal Case K23/11 (30 July 2014).
[62]   *1 B v R 2835/17* (Judgment 19 May 2020) ('*1 B v R*').
[63]   The Federal Intelligence Service Act dates back to 1968 and was subject to numerous revisions.
[64]   Germany: Basic Law for the Federal Republic of Germany (23 May 1949).
[65]   For a full discussion of this case, see Chapter 4, section 2.3.1.
[66]   Constitution of the Federative Republic of Brazil (2010) Arts 5.X and 5.XII.

response to social demand after the end of the 1964–85 military dictatorship.[67] It primarily facilitates the gaining of permission to review an individual's information stored in governmental or public databases to correct, update, annotate or clarify that data.[68] The writ has attracted some criticism as being costly and slow.[69] Nevertheless, there is no doubt that Brazil has played a vital role in the development of this principle, paving the way for its adoption by other Latin American countries, including Paraguay, Peru and Argentina.

### 4.3.1.2　*Constitutions that indirectly protect the right to privacy*

The second trend – evident in countries such as the US – is to protect privacy through an amalgam of principles embodied in the constitutional law and other means, such as tort law and statute. Two approaches can be discerned, depending on whether the violation of privacy is alleged to have been committed by the state or a private party. Where the infringement is committed by another individual, this gives rise to common law liability in tort. The concept of privacy as a tort was developed in the nineteenth century and provides a right to a private action to recover damages or to obtain an injunction for its unjustifiable invasion.[70] Conversely, where the violation has been perpetrated by the state, an individual is granted constitutional protection and may also base a course of action on statutes such as the Privacy Act 1974,[71] which regulates information-handling practices of federal agencies.

The guarantees against the government's unjustifiable invasion of privacy are set out in the US constitutional order, albeit not explicitly enshrined in the

---

[67]　See Marcos Napolitano, 'The Brazilian Military Regime, 1964–1985' (April 2018), https://oxfordre.com/latinamericanhistory/view/10.1093/acrefore/9780199366439.001.0001/acrefore-9780199366439-e-413.

[68]　Constitution of Brazil (n 66) Arts 5.LXIX and LXXII.

[69]　Privacy International, 'State of Privacy Brazil' (26 January 2019), https://privacyinternational.org/state-privacy/42/state-privacy-brazil.

[70]　At common law, the tort of invasion of privacy covers four interests – namely, protection from: (1) unreasonable intrusion on one's seclusion; (2) the appropriation of one's name or likeness; (3) unreasonable publicity given to one's private life; and (4) publicity which unreasonably places one in a false light before the public – see Restatement (Second) of Torts §§ 652A-6521 (1977).

[71]　Privacy Act 1974 5 USC §5520 (2012). The Act has been described as 'an omnibus code of fair information practices that attempts to regulate the collection of personal information by federal executive branch agencies', and requires that the agencies give the public notice of their system of records by publication in the Federal Register – see US Department of Justice, 'Overview of the Privacy Act' (27 July 2015), www.justice.gov/opcl/overview-privacy-act-1974-2015-edition; and US Department of Justice, 'Privacy Act of 1974' (15 January 2020), www.justice.gov/opcl/privacy-act-1974.

Constitution.[72] Privacy protection is commonly regarded as being created by other provisions, particularly the Fourth Amendment to the Constitution.[73] This safeguards the rights of US citizens to be secure in their 'persons, houses, papers and effects' against unreasonable searches and seizures, preventing government authorities from conducting such searches or seizures without a warrant based on probable cause.[74] Despite being widely acknowledged as the main bulwark against unjustifiable interference with privacy rights, the Fourth Amendment has a number of limitations when applied to Internet-related technologies. First, it does not extend to private action. This is particularly problematic in the context of digital communications, as most data is under the control of private companies, rather than government agencies. Consequently, powerful corporations such as Google, Facebook and Twitter – which have been exposed as having tracked, collected and handed data over to the US government[75] – are generally not bound by the constitutional restrictions. Second, the Fourth Amendment rights are subject to the limitations imposed by the so-called 'third-party' doctrine. This dictates that where an individual voluntarily discloses information to third parties, he or she has no reasonable expectation of privacy.[76] First stipulated by the US courts in the 1970s, this principle creates a tangled set of exceptions to the Fourth Amendment and thus often produces conflicting results. While a detailed analysis of the jurisprudence in this area is beyond the scope of this book, the uncertainty and complexity that result from the application of this rule can nonetheless be illustrated by four high-profile cases: *United States v Jones*,[77] *American Civil Liberties Union v Clapper*,[78] *Klayman v Obama*[79] and *Carpenter v United States*.[80]

The third-party doctrine originates from the US Supreme Court decisions in *United States v Miller*[81] and *Smith v Maryland*.[82] In *Miller*, the Supreme Court

---

[72]    US Constitution (17 April 1787).
[73]    Fourth Amendment, Search and Seizure (passed by Congress 25 September 1789; ratified 15 December 1791) ('Fourth Amendment').
[74]    *Ibid.*
[75]    See Council of Europe, 'Mass Surveillance. Who is Watching the Watchers', Report Doc 13734 (18 March 2015).
[76]    *Katz v United States* 389 US 347 (1967). The Supreme Court held that the Fourth Amendment protects a person's reasonable expectation of privacy. Justice Halan stipulated that in order to fulfil this requirement, an individual must satisfy a two-pronged test: that he or she has 'exhibited an actual (subjective) expectation of privacy and [that] that expectation [is] one that society is prepared to recognize as "reasonable"'.
[77]    *United States v Jones* 132 S Ct 945 (2012).
[78]    *ACLU et al v Clapper* 959 F Supp 2d 724 (SDNY 2013).
[79]    *Klayman v Obama* 957 F Supp 2d 1 (DDC 2013).
[80]    *Carpenter v United States* 585 US (2018).
[81]    *United States v Miller* 425 US 435 (1976).
[82]    *Smith v Maryland* 442 US 735 (1979).

held that the defendant had no right to privacy in his banking records, as they constituted business information belonging to the bank, not his private papers. In *Smith*, the Court decided that the right to privacy was also lost in relation to information pertaining to phone numbers that the defendant had dialled which were held on a pen register,[83] as that data was shared with the phone company, a third party. While the content of communications is protected following the Supreme Court's decision in *Katz v United States*, their metadata has proved a thornier issue, because this can be accessed without a warrant. The 2013 Snowden disclosures revealed that the third-party doctrine has provided the government with a powerful investigatory tool, enabling the National Security Agency (NSA) to bulk collect such data from millions of phone customers, leading to number of lawsuits,[84] including *Clapper* and *Klayman*. The programs were authorized by Foreign Intelligence Surveillance Court orders issued pursuant to the now defunct Section 215 of the Patriot Act 2001 and compelled US telecommunications company Verizon Business Network Services to hand over to the NSA the metadata of all its customers without a warrant on an ongoing basis. This allowed NSA analysts to query the collected metadata using 'selectors' considered applicable to the terrorists abroad. In *Clapper*, the plaintiffs – the American Civil Liberties Union (ACLU) *et al* – alleged that this exceeded the statutory authority granted by Section 215 of the Patriot Act 2001 and violated the First and Fourth Amendments. At first instance, the District Court for the Southern District of New York dismissed the case, finding, *inter alia*, that the program did not breach the Fourth Amendment protection. Relying on *Smith,* Judge Pauley reasoned that a subscriber has no legitimate expectation of privacy in telephony metadata created by third parties and that this has not changed due to the ubiquity of cell phones or the different relationship that now exists between individuals and their phones as opposed to when *Smith* was decided.[85] However, this decision was reversed following ACLU's successful appeal to the Second Circuit Court of Appeals in 2015. The Court held that the telephone metadata program exceeded the scope of what Congress had authorized and therefore violated Section 215 of the Patriot

---

[83]   'A pen register is a device that traces outgoing signals from a specific phone or computer to their destination. [It] produces a list of the phone numbers or Internet addresses, but does not include substantive information transmitted by the signals' – see Cornell University Legal Information Institute, 'Pen Register', www.law.cornell.edu/wex/pen_register.

[84]   The cases followed the 2013 publication by British newspaper *The Guardian* of a series of articles on the NSA's intelligence surveillance and collection programs – see, for example, Glen Greenwald, 'NSA Collecting Phone Records of Millions of Verizon Customers Daily', *The Guardian* (6 June 2013).

[85]   *Clapper* (n 78) 752.

Act,[86] but declined to rule on whether it also constituted a breach of the First and Fourth Amendments.

*Klayman* (a pair of lawsuits combined by joinder) similarly concerned a legal challenge to the NSA's bulk collection of domestic telephone call and Internet records on the basis of, *inter alia*, the Fourth Amendment. The plaintiffs complained of 'a secret and illegal government scheme to intercept and analyse vast quantities of domestic telephone communications and communications from the Internet and electronic service providers',[87] and to store them for up to five years. They brought the case in the District Court for the District of Columbia, seeking an injunction prohibiting future surveillance, declaratory relief and expungement of any metadata already collected. The District Court concluded that the program constituted a search that likely violated the Fourth Amendment and granted the injunction. Importantly, the Court observed that: 'due to our phone centric culture, telephone metadata can potentially reveal an entire mosaic-a vibrant and constantly updating picture of the person's life.'[88] These trends, the Court explained, have led to a 'greater expectation of privacy and a recognition that society views [those] expectation[s] as reasonable'.[89] The Court also distinguished *Smith* on the basis that that case concerned the gathering of call details using a pen register, whereas the present case involved the bulk collection of all telephone records by the NSA. Crucially, the Court held that the bulk collection of call records was unreasonable and likely to violate the Fourth Amendment, specifically pointing out that the government had not shown a single instance in which metadata collection had prevented an imminent terrorist attack and thus doubting whether such tools serve an important government interest. However, the order granting the injunction was subsequently stayed pending appeal to the Circuit Court of Appeals for the District of Columbia. In its 2019 judgment, the Circuit Court upheld the District Court's finding, affirming, *inter alia*, that the challenge to Section 215 surveillance was moot, as the telephony metadata collection program was

---

[86]   On 1 June 2015, Section 215 of the Patriot Act briefly expired and the US Congress passed the Uniting and Strengthening America by Fulfilling Rights and Ensuring Effective Discipline over Monitoring Act of 2015 (2 June 2015) Public Law 114-23 ('Freedom Act'). The Act modified certain provisions of the Patriot Act, including s 215, replacing it with a narrowly circumscribed authority for collecting 'call detail records'. Commenting on the Freedom Act, former US President Obama stated that 'this legislation will strengthen civil liberty safeguards and provide greater public confidence in the [Patriot Act] programs, including by prohibiting bulk collection through the use of s. 215' – see the White House, 'Statement by the President on the US FREEDOM Act' (2 June 2015).

[87]   *Klayman* (n 79) Background, 5.

[88]   *Ibid* para 36, 28.

[89]   *Ibid.*

terminated by the Freedom Act 215, which specifically prohibits the government from conducting this type of bulk collection. The Court also held that the appellants lacked standing to seek the expungement of metadata previously collected under Section 215. The outcome has been declared a victory for the NSA, with the Court apparently legitimizing such intrusions into personal privacy.[90] In legal terms, the two cases (*Clapper* and *Klayman*) – albeit based on similar facts – represent seemingly conflicting outcomes, thus leaving the matter of the impact of digital technologies on Fourth Amendment protection polarized and uncertain.

The difficulties that the third-party doctrine introduces in relation to Fourth Amendment rights is evident not only in the context of the NSA collection, but also in relation to obtaining metadata by the law enforcement agencies pursuant to criminal investigations, where this often occurs without a warrant. As individuals inadvertently share information with Internet service providers (third parties) without much choice in the matter, they risk being deprived of their Fourth Amendment protection. Two cases illustrate this problem: *Jones* and *Carpenter*. In *Jones*, law enforcement officers attached a Global Positioning System device to the suspect's car without a warrant and tracked his movements for 28 days. The Supreme Court held that this was a search within the meaning of the Fourth Amendment, as the use of this method constituted a physical intrusion for the purpose of obtaining information and thus breached a reasonable expectation of privacy. Two further points are notable about this case. First, it did not overrule *Smith,* which means that it remains good authority. Second, Justice Sotomayor (one of the presiding judges) engaged more generally with the right to privacy, showing apparent hostility towards the application of the third-party doctrine in the digital age. Observing that long-term monitoring generates a precise and comprehensive record of an individual's public movement that reflects a wealth of detail about his or her familial, political, professional, religious and sexual associations,[91] she critiqued the doctrine, stating that:

> it may be necessary to reconsider the premise that an individual has no reasonable expectation of privacy in the information voluntarily disclosed to third parties. This approach is ill suited to the digital age, in which people reveal a great deal of information about themselves to third parties in the course of carrying out mundane tasks … I would not assume that all information voluntarily disclosed to some members

---

90  Columbia University Global Freedom of Expression, 'Obama v Klayman', https://globalfreedomofexpression.columbia.edu/cases/klayman-v-obama-the-electronic-frontier-foundation-eff-and-the-american-civil-liberties-union-appellate-amicus-brief-not-the-district-court-opinion/.
91  *Jones* (n 77) 955.

of the public for a limited purpose is, for that reason alone, disentitled to the Fourth Amendment Protection.[92]

A further illustration of the Supreme Court's efforts to grapple with these issues is *Carpenter*, where the Court undertook the challenge of addressing whether the third-party doctrine is still appropriate in a world dominated by digital technologies. In that case, the defendants Timothy Carpenter and Timothy Sander were suspected of several robberies that took place in and around Detroit. To gather the necessary evidence against them, the Federal Bureau of Investigation (FBI) requested Carpenter's call site location information (CSLI) from his telephone company on the basis of an order made under Section 2703(d) of the Stored Communications Act, part of the Electronic Communications Privacy Act 1986. The metadata obtained from the CSLI allowed the FBI to assemble a map of Carpenter's movements, which proved critical to securing his conviction. Carpenter sought to supress the CSLI evidence, relying on the Fourth Amendment, but was denied the motion and consequently prosecuted. The case reached the Supreme Court in 2017, where a year later it was decided that in order to access the data collected from cell towers by wireless carriers, a search warrant is required. Chief Justice Roberts, delivering the majority opinion, found that such information is private and subject necessarily to the Fourth Amendment protection. Of particular note in this regard is his observation that cellphones and the services they provide are such a pervasive and insistent part of daily life that carrying one is indispensable to participation in modern life. To this end, he observed that:

> while a third-party doctrine applies to telephone numbers and bank records, it is not clear whether its logic extends to the qualitatively different category of cell-site records. After all [in 1979] few could have imagined a society in which a phone goes wherever its owner goes, conveying to the wireless carrier not just dialled digits, but a detailed and comprehensive record of the person's movements ... When the government tracks the location of a cellphone, it achieves near perfect surveillance, as if it had attached an ankle monitor to the phone's user.[93]

*Carpenter* undoubtedly strengthens the protection of privacy of the US citizens and represents a further step towards modernizing the rather antiquated third-party rule. Judge Roberts emphasized, however, that the decision is narrow, in that it relates only to the collection of cell phone tower data. Nevertheless, it may have future implications for other information inevitably

---

[92]   *Ibid* 957.
[93]   *Carpenter* (n 80) para III (2).

produced by digital technology users and held by third parties, such as brows-ing histories, text messages and emails.

What the above cases illustrate is a polarized legal landscape – a result of the US courts engaging with the application of the third-party principle to digital communications. Invariably, the need for a clear stance in relation to how this rule impacts on privacy rights in the context of rapidly changing technologies looms large.

### 4.3.1.3    Data protection laws

The third method of privacy protection utilized in a growing number of coun-tries is through data protection legislation. This concept and that of privacy are interlinked, but not identical. Compared to privacy, data protection is a narrow and relatively recent notion, which has developed since the advent of Internet technologies in the 1960s in order to regulate all or most stages of the processing of certain kinds of data. This branch of law is primarily concerned with the management of personal information and addresses the ways in which data is gathered, registered, stored, exploited and disseminated.[94] Its main aim is to safeguard certain interests and rights of individuals in their role as data subjects, including when data about them is processed by others.[95] The primary rules of data protection law embody a set of procedural principles, such as that personal information should be collected by fair and lawful means; that the amount of the gathered data should be limited to what is necessary to achieve the specified purpose, which must be legitimate; and that the data should not be used in ways that are incompatible with the purpose limitation.[96]

A variety of legally binding and non-binding instruments[97] have been put in place at international and regional levels, significantly influencing the development and adoption of domestic data privacy laws worldwide. Thus, at the international level, Article 17 of the ICCPR, despite not specifically referring to data processing, has been interpreted by HRC General Comment 16 to include the collection and storage of personal information on computers,

---

[94]    Bygrave (n 50) 1.

[95]    *Ibid.*

[96]    *Ibid.*

[97]    A number of guidelines, declarations and resolutions of regional and global application, together with sector-specific instruments, apply to both the private and public sphere – see, *inter alia,* Organization for Economic Co-operation and Development, *Guidelines Governing the Protection of Privacy and Transborder Flows of Personal Data, Recommendation of the Council Concerning Guidelines Governing the Protection of Transborder Flows of Personal Data,* C(80)58/FINAL as amended on 11 July 2013 by C(2013)79; Asia-Pacific Economic Cooperation (APEC) Privacy Framework 2005 Publication APCE#205-50-01.2; APEC Cross Border Privacy Rules (2011).

in databanks and on other devices by public authorities, private individuals and bodies.[98] The Comment stipulates that such collection or storage must be regulated by law.[99] In the regional sphere, the three main data protection legally binding regimes that specifically regulate data privacy are: (1) the 1981 Council of Europe (CoE) Convention for the Protection of Individuals with regard to Automatic Processing of Personal Data (as modernized);[100] (2) the EU data protection legal framework; and (3) the African Union Convention of Cyber Security and Personal Data Protection.[101]

The EU legal framework is one of the most ambitious, comprehensive and complex in the field.[102] Data protection is a binding fundamental right under Article 7 of the EU Charter of Fundamental Rights,[103] which lays down the right to respect for private and family life, including communications;[104] and Article 8, which stipulates that everyone has the right to the protection of personal data.[105] The regime's central instrument, the General Data Protection Regulation 2016 (GDPR),[106] sets out data protection rules in relation to the processing of individuals' information within the EU, modernizing the previous standards,[107] in order to harmonize data privacy laws across all EU

---

[98]   UNHRC, 'CCPR General Comment No. 16: Article 17 (Right to Privacy). The Right to Respect of Privacy, Family, Home and Correspondence, and Protection of Honour and Reputation' (8 April 1988) UN Doc HRI/Gen/1/Rev.9 (Vol 1) ('General Comment 16').

[99]   *Ibid* para 10. More recently, the UN Commissioner for Human Rights has also acknowledged that data privacy is subsumed within the broader notion of the right to privacy under the human rights treaties – see Office of the UN High Commissioner for Human Rights (OHCHR), 'The Right to Privacy in the Digital Age. Report of the United Nations High Commissioner for Human Rights' (30 June 2014) UN Doc A/HRC/27/37 47 ('A/HRC/27/37').

[100]   Convention for the Protection of Individuals with Regard to the Automatic Processing of Personal Data (28 January 1981) CETS 108 as modernized by the Protocol amending the Convention for the Protection of Individuals with Regard to Automatic Processing of Personal Data (10 October 2018) CETS No 223.

[101]   African Union Convention of Cyber Security and Personal Data Protection (27 June 2014) EXCL/846 (XXV).

[102]   Bygrave (n 50) 53.

[103]   Charter of Fundamental Rights of the European Union (2012) OJ C 326/391 ('EU Charter').

[104]   *Ibid* Art 7.

[105]   *Ibid* Art 8(1).

[106]   European Parliament and the Council of the European Union, General Data Protection Regulation (4 May 2016) L119 ('GDPR').

[107]   Directive 95/46 on the protection of individuals with regard to the processing of personal data and on the free movement of such data (1995) OJ L281/31.

member states, which must implement it in their legal systems.[108] The GDPR is regarded as the world's strongest set of data protection rules, enhancing how individuals can access information about them and imposing limits on what organizations can do in relation to data handling. To this end, Article 5 of the GDPR requires that this be done in accordance with six main principles: (1) lawfulness, fairness and transparency; (2) purpose limitation; (3) minimization; (4) accuracy; (5) storage limitations; and (6) integrity and confidentiality.[109] Unquestionably, the GDPR is a landmark statute, which has not only affected European countries, but also served as inspiration around the globe, with a number of nations either introducing new or updating existing laws in its wake – examples include Brazil, Benin, Mauritius and the US state of California. Thus, in 2020, California enacted a comprehensive new set of rules on consumer protection. The California Consumer Privacy Act 2020 (CCPA)[110] is said to have been influenced by the GDPR[111] and grants consumers a number of entitlements, including the right: (1) to know what personal information is collected and used; (2) to delete personal information held by businesses; (3) to opt out of the sale of personal information; and (4) to non-discrimination in terms of price or service when a customer exercises his or her right to privacy under the CCPA.[112] Brazil's 2018 General Data Privacy Law is likewise substantially based on the GDPR, setting out requirements for data exports limited by adequacy requirements relating to the destination, data protection impact assessments, data protection officers, data breach notifications, limits on automated processing and administrative fines of up to 2 per cent of a company's revenue in the previous year.[113] Benin's 2017 *Code du numérique* is perhaps the statute outside of the EU that most closely resembles the GDPR, with many similar provisions on matters such as extraterritorial

---

[108]   Between 2017–18, 23 of the then 28 EU member states introduced new domestic data privacy laws, with legislation still in draft in only five countries: Bulgaria, the Czech Republic, Greece, Portugal and Slovenia – see Graham Greenleaf, 'Global Data Privacy Laws 2019: 132 National Laws and Many Bills' (2019) 157 *Privacy Laws and Business International Report* 14–18 ('Greenleaf').

[109]   GDPR (n 106) Art 5.

[110]   California Consumer Privacy Act 2020 AB-375 ('CCPA').

[111]   *Ibid.* The CCPA has different scope, definition and requirements from those set out in the GDPR and imposes additional obligations on businesses that are subject to this statute- see California Department of Justice, 'California Consumer Privacy Act (CCPA), Fact Sheet', www.oag.ca.gov/system/files/attachments/press_releases/CCPA%20Fact%20Sheet%20%2800000002%29.pdf.

[112]   *Ibid.*

[113]   Greenleaf (n 108) 2.

application, privacy by design, direct liability of processors and data breach notifications.[114]

The GDPR significantly strengthen the rights of individuals, charities and businesses in relation to how their information is handled by companies world-wide. However, as national security is outside the scope of EU law, the processing of personal data for national security purposes is not within the ambit of the GDPR. Consequently, the provisions of that Regulation were not designed to be applicable to data processing by intelligence and law enforcement services. A specific data protection regime for these purposes is contained in the modernized Convention 108. The treaty, drafted under the auspices of the CoE, is the only international legally binding instrument on the protection of private life and data privacy open to any country in the world, with a diverse range of countries – including Mexico, Argentina and Tunisia – ratifying it between 2013–19. The Convention aims to protect individuals against abuse when their personal data is collected and processed by both the private and the public sector. To this end, it sets out a number of guarantees (such as data security now contained in Article 7 and transparency of processing set out in Article 8 of the modernized Convention 108). It outlaws the processing of 'sensitive data' on such matters as a person's race, political inclinations, health, religion, or criminal record in the absence of appropriate legal safeguards. It also stipulates for an individual's right to know that information is stored on him or her and, if necessary, to have it corrected. In addition, it also provides rules on transborder data flows, limiting such transfers to states where domestic laws do not ensure its adequate protection. The rights laid down in the Convention may only be restricted when such overriding interests as state security or defence are at stake.

There is no doubt that governments the world over are actively enacting and modernizing their data protection regimes. Indeed, in his 2019 report, Professor Graham Greenleaf pointed to the exponential increase in such domestic measures between 2017–18, with 132 out of 231 countries having enacted them, including 12 additional countries with new laws.[115] This figure was predicted

---

[114]   *Ibid* 5.

[115]   *Ibid* 1–4. These are: the Cayman Islands (Data Protection Law 2017, Law 33/2017); Mauritania (*Loi 2017-020 sur la protection des données à caractère personnel*); Niger (*Loi 2017-28 relative à la protection des données à caractère personnel*); Guinea-Conakry (*Loi L/2016/037/AN relative à la cyber-sécurité et la protection des données à caractère personnel*); Algeria (Law 18-07 10 June 2018); Panama (Law of Protection of Personal Data 24 October 2018); St Kitts & Nevis (Data Protection Act 2018); Lebanon (Electronic Transactions and Personal Data Law October 2018); Bahrain (Law on Protection of Personal Data 19 July 2018); Bhutan (Information, Communications and Media Act of Bhutan 2018); and China (E-commerce Law of the People's Republic of China 2018).

to increase to 137 by 2020.[116] However, he also cautioned that although these laws meet the minimum requirements for data privacy, little is known as to whether they are effectively enforced. Furthermore, the surveillance context within which they exist may largely nullify their potential benefits.[117]

### 4.3.1.4    Legal systems with no general right to privacy

Finally, a brief outline must be made of those countries whose legal systems do not recognize a general right to privacy, such as the UK and China. Thus, there is no explicit constitutional right to privacy in the UK and no specific Privacy Act. There is also no general tort of privacy at common law. Historically, English courts have been reluctant to recognize such a tort and consequently any right of action for invasion of privacy had to be based on other torts, such as defamation, passing off, malicious falsehood or trespass to the person.[118] However, in recent years this area of law has been significantly developed through the introduction of a tort of misuse of private information following the case of *Campbell v Mirror Group Newspapers*[119] and the adoption of the Human Rights Act 1998,[120] which makes it possible for the courts to enforce Article 8 of the ECHR. The developments at common law suggest that although there is no independent tort of privacy, there has been a shift towards judicial recognition of the protection of human autonomy and dignity, thus allowing an aggrieved party to recover damages or seek injunctive relief from another private party.[121] In relation to privacy infringements by the state, the

---

[116]   Greenleaf (n 108) 4.

[117]   *Ibid.*

[118]   *Kaye v Robertson* [1991] FSR 62. In that case Gidwell LJ stated that 'in English law there is no right to privacy and therefore there is no right of action for breach of person's privacy. It is for Parliament to decide whether legislation should be enacted to protect individual's privacy'.

[119]   *Campbell v Mirror Group Newspapers* [2002] All ER (D) 448 (Mar) (QB). Where an individual's complaint is brought against another for wrongfully publishing his or her private information, the courts must apply a two-stage test. First, they must establish whether the information is private, in the sense that it is protected by Article 8 of the ECHR; if so, they must then balance the interests of the owner of that information against the right of freedom of expression conferred on the publisher under Article 10 of the ECHR. See also *Douglas v Hello! Ltd* [2005] EWCA Civ 595 and *Prince of Wales v Associated Newspapers* [2006] EWCA Civ 1776.

[120]   Human Rights Act 1998 c 42.

[121]   Additional means of safeguarding privacy in the UK include the Data Protection Act 2018 c 12, implementing the GDPR into English law, which controls how personal information is used by organizations, businesses and the government; the Prevention from Harassment Act 1997 c 40; and non-legally binding, sector-specific codes of practice, such as the Independent Press Standards Organization's Editor's Code of Practice (2018).

course of action is predominantly based on the Human Rights Act, which gives effect to Article 8 of the ECHR. However, as noted by Anderson QC, there are some striking differences between decisions of the UK judges and those of the European Court of Human Rights (ECtHR) pertaining to the degree of protection to be accorded to privacy, with the former taking an altogether more permissive attitude to the issue of its violations.[122] To this end, in *R (Catt) v CPM*, Lord Sumption observed that in the past, the ECtHR has taken exception to the English courts' characterization of interferences with private life as 'minor', before designating the retention by the police of electronic data in that case as such.[123] This difference in approach is so striking that it caused Anderson QC to observe that:

> it is hard to think of any other area of human rights law that is characterised by such marked and consistent differences of opinion between the European courts and the British judges who in most respects rank among their most loyal and conscientious followers.[124]

Likewise, privacy is not recognized as an autonomous right in China. There is no single legal provision in Chinese national law that defines the right to privacy.[125] Notwithstanding the introduction of a number of laws, regulations, judicial interpretations and administrative rules adopting such concepts as 'personal privacy' and 'personal information',[126] privacy protection is still treated as incidental to other rights.[127] For example, personal privacy has been acknowledged in the context of open court hearings and the right to a fair trial; but there is no indication as to what this amounts to – or indeed that it is a right of any kind.[128]

---

[122]   David Anderson, *A Question of Trust. Report of the Investigatory Powers Review* (June 2015) 31 ('Anderson').

[123]   In *R (Catt) v Commissioner of Police of the Metropolis and Others* [2015] UKSC 9, Lord Sumption stated at para 26: 'I am conscious that the Strasbourg court has in the past taken exception to the characterisation of interferences by English courts with private life as being minor (see, notably, *MM*, at para 170), but the word seems to me to be appropriate to describe what happened in this case' – see Anderson, *ibid* 32.

[124]   Anderson, *ibid.*

[125]   Privacy International, *The Right to Privacy in China. Stakeholder Report. Universal Periodic Review 17th Session –China* (10 March 2013) ('*The Right to Privacy in China*').

[126]   *Ibid.*

[127]   *Ibid.*

[128]   *Ibid.* This can be gleaned from China's numerous attempts at formulating and implementing human rights policies on the instigation of the HRC. These policies are set out in National Human Rights Action Plans for the periods of 2009–10, 2012–15 and 2016–20. The first Action Plan does not mention privacy at all; while the second

The Chinese Constitution[129] does not stipulate for a right to privacy *per se*, but it does recognize a number of related rights, such as human dignity (Article 38)[130] and privacy and freedom of correspondence (Article 40).[131] This latter right is also reflected in Article 4 of China's Postal Law 1984, which provides that 'freedom and privacy of correspondence of citizens are protected by law'. This is nevertheless significantly limited, as if state secrets or criminal investigations are involved, the police and other authorities can intercept communications where necessary almost without restriction. In addition, the concept of 'state secrets' is broad and gives the government extensive powers to review and monitor communications. Similarly, Chinese civil law does not recognize the right to privacy as such, treating it as part of the right to identity and protection of reputation. To this end, Article 101 of the 1986 General Principles of Civil Law provides that: 'The personality of citizens shall be protected by law and the use of insults, defamation and other means to damage the reputation of citizens or legal persons shall be prohibited.'[132] Furthermore, according to the Judicial Interpretation of General Principles of Civil Law 1988, 'an unauthorised revelation of privacy of another constitutes an infringement upon his reputation'.[133] Therefore, under current law, an action for privacy infringement can be brought only if the claimant can show that his or her reputation has also been affected. Generally, this makes the protection of this right both inadequate and sporadic.

That said, some important legislative changes have taken place and are afoot to replace China's patchwork governance of the data sector with a sweeping new legal framework. To this end, four important statutes have been introduced. The first is the 2016 Cybersecurity Law, which requires users to provide real-name information and obliges networks to store Chinese data on mainland servers.[134] The second is the Data Security Law,[135] released for public

---

refers to it, but offers no meaningful definition or protection of this right, stating only that the government will not make public any information that involves individual privacy.

[129]   Constitution of the People's Republic of China (4 December 1982).

[130]   *Ibid* Art 38.

[131]   *Ibid* Art 40.

[132]   The National People's Congress, General Principles of Civil Law of the People's Republic of China (12 April 1986) Order No 37 [1987] Art 101.

[133]   Opinions of the Supreme People's Court on Several Problems Concerning the Application of the General Principles of Civil Law (for Trial Implementation) (adopted and effective on 16 January 1988) Art 140.

[134]   Cybersecurity Law of the People's Republic of China 2016. For more details, see Chapter 7, section 2.3.2.

[135]   Draft Data Security Law (2 July 2020) ('DSL'), www.pkulaw.cn/staticfiles/fagui/20200702/09/19/5/34f52a05583e352871fa38da6c354174.pdf.

consultation in July 2020 by China's National People's Congress, which aims to regulate the access and sharing of data, with a specific focus on the governance of 'important data' – that is, data which, if leaked, would directly affect China's national security, economic security, social stability or public health and security.[136] Although the Data Security Law applies to 'data activities' in China, any outside individual or organization that conducts data activities which may harm national security, the public interest or the rights of Chinese citizens may be subject to the law.[137] 'Data activities' are defined as the collection, storage, processing, use, provision, transmission and disclosure of data;[138] but do not extend to state secrets or personal or military information.[139] Thus, regional and central government departments must first determine what constitutes 'important data' and then implement measures to protect it. The Data Security Law specifically states that law enforcement bodies that collect data for national security purposes should comply with the necessary procedural laws; but individuals and organizations are obliged to comply with a request to access such data. The third important change, which will take effect from 2021, is the Chinese Civil Code, which guarantees individuals the right to privacy of personal information, but purportedly lacks clarification on how that is to be protected or regulated.[140] Finally, the Personal Information Protection Law is still being drafted, but is expected to establish regulation and legal mechanisms for the protection of individuals' personal information. These statutes are important primarily from the perspective of regulating China's data industry – in particular, in the context of data security, its management and cross-border transfers. However, they seem to focus on preventing harm to national security and other state interests, rather than protecting individuals' fundamental rights.

Overall, privacy protection is China is minimal. When placed in the context of China's broader state policy of mass surveillance, including online, both the current constitutional safeguards and the possibility of civil action are wilfully inadequate, for political and legal reasons. The Chinese government is notorious for its widespread use of closed-circuit television and for the mass interception of telephone conversations, fax transmissions, emails and text messages. Perhaps most importantly, the authorities have long sought to exert almost complete control over the Internet *sensu lato* and in respect to

---

[136]   Yan Luo and Zhijing Yu, 'China Issued the Draft Data Security Law', *Hunton* (3 July 2020), www.huntonprivacyblog.com/2020/07/07/china-issues-draft-data-security-law/.

[137]   DSL (n 135) Art 2.

[138]   *Ibid* Art 3.

[139]   *Ibid* Arts 49 and 50.

[140]   Civil Code of the People's Republic of China (to take effect from 1 January 2021).

users' online activities.[141] China is renowned for its stringent controls in the online domain, dictated by a wider state centric command and control ideology, fuelled by the government's policy of establishing a sovereign 'virtual territory', termed 'cyber sovereignty'.[142] To achieve this, the authorities have deployed a variety of tools and methods,[143] building the Great Firewall of China[144] to censor Internet content, block selected foreign websites (eg, Facebook, Twitter and Wikipedia) and restrict online access.[145]

### 4.4     The Protection of Online Privacy as State Practice – an Evaluation

It will be recalled that in order to satisfy the first requirement to establish the existence of customary international law rule under Article 38(1) of the SICJ, state practice must be general, consistent and uniform. While there is undoubtedly evidence of a widespread practice – in that the overwhelming majority of countries across all continents, with divergent political, economic and legal systems, have enacted privacy and/or data privacy laws – this in itself is not conclusive. One of the fundamental aspects of establishing state practice is its uniformity and this requirement cannot be said with all certainty to have been satisfied. Closer examination of the status quo reveals that domestic laws adopt a disparate and often inadequate stance on the issue of privacy protection. This is largely due to the broad spectrum of approaches taken by states, as outlined earlier in this chapter. Thus, at the far end of the scale, some countries have constitutionally guaranteed the right to privacy. The middle ground is occupied by those nations in which the right to privacy is recognized in their constitutional orders, but not explicitly set out in the constitution. It may also be protected by other means, such as tort law and specific privacy/data protection legislation. At the opposite end of the scale are those countries in which privacy is not recognized as a legal right *per se*, but is nonetheless afforded some indirect protection in their legal systems through other means. A case in point is the UK, where legal recourse can be obtained through a limited

---

[141] *The Right to Privacy in China* (n 125). See also Paul Mazur, 'Inside China's Dystopian Dreams: A.I., Shame and Lots of Cameras', *The New York Times* (8 July 2018).

[142] Niels N Schia and Lars Gjesvic, 'China's Cyber Sovereignty', Norwegian Institute of International Affairs (2017).

[143] *The Right to Privacy in China* (n 125).

[144] See Elizabeth C Economy, 'The Great Firewall of China: Xi Jinping's Internet Shutdown', *The Guardian* (29 June 2018).

[145] See Amnesty International, 'Pho Noodles and Pandas: How China's Social Media Users Created a New Language to Beat Government Censorship on COVID-19' (6 March 2020).

tort action, under the Human Rights Act 1998 and the Data Protection Act 2018. In countries with less well-entrenched democratic political traditions, such as China, the right to privacy is not yet explicitly recognized and is ostensibly protected indirectly, but in reality is almost entirely disregarded.[146] Nevertheless, an overwhelming majority of governments have enacted data protection legislation, which aims to capture and respond to the changes in communication introduced by digital technologies.

That said, doubts have been expressed as to the reasons for the adoption of such laws within a relatively short timeframe, with one commentator suggesting this has been dictated by economic needs or coercion, since:

> the assumption that an accelerated adoption of data privacy represents a high acceptance among states (or even *opinio juris* in strict sense) may be undermined if states do adopt such legislation solely due to external pressure, rather than persuasion or acculturation.[147]

This scepticism towards both privacy and data protection is compounded by differences in the implementation of such laws, together with the disparate range of remedies available to aggrieved individuals.[148] In addition, legal recourse depends on whether the alleged privacy violation has been perpetrated by the state or by a private party. In some countries, such as the US, constitutional protection is granted only in relation to government infringements, which excludes Fourth Amendment rights in relation to actions by the powerful corporate sector; whereas in the context of government surveillance, protection is curtailed by the application of the third-party doctrine. The judicial application of this principle to Internet communications has produced a convoluted legal landscape, with some scholars calling for a complete recon-

---

[146] See, for example, Sarah Cook, 'China's Ever-Expanding Surveillance State, *The Diplomat* (25 April 2018). Reportedly, the Chinese authorities' use of surveillance technologies is prevalent and unconstrained by privacy considerations. For example, in Xinjiang, the police in recent years have allegedly collected residents' biometrics without their consent to use these and other data to evaluate the political loyalty of the region's 12 million Turkic Muslim minority residents and determine how much freedom of movement to allow them. See also Maya Wang 'China: Fighting COVID-19 with Automated Tyranny', *The Diplomat* (1 April 2020), the Chinese government's response in the wake of the 2020 Covid-19 pandemic ('Wang').

[147] See Monika Zalnieriute, 'An International Constitutional Moment for Data Privacy in the Times of Mass-Surveillance' (2015) 23 *International Journal of Law and Information Technology* 99–133, 116–17 ('Zalnieriute').

[148] EU Agency for Fundamental Rights, 'Access to Data Protection Remedies in the EU Member States' (European Union Agency for Fundamental Rights, January 2014).

ceptualization of how the Fourth Amendment works in the digital world.[149] In other countries, such as the UK, state measures that violate privacy must be challenged on the basis of Article 8 of the ECHR, incorporated into English law by the Human Rights Act 1998, but its interpretation by the English courts seems not to align with that of the ECtHR. Where the breach of privacy rights has been committed by a private party, the course of action may lie in tort law or in other instruments, such as data protection legislation.

This lack of uniformity and consistency is exacerbated by the context in which the guarantee of privacy exists – which, as observed by Professor Greenleaf, may largely nullify the potential benefits.[150] This is evidenced by, *inter alia*, the proliferation of mass surveillance legislation in response to the increase in terrorist attacks of recent years;[151] the adoption by a large number of states of artificial intelligence (AI) tools to monitor, track and scrutinize their citizens;[152] and a reportedly alarming disregard for privacy obligations, even where this right is guaranteed constitutionally or through other means. Thus, according to a 2017 survey[153] of a representative sample of 14 states from different continents, privacy is guaranteed in principle, but disregarded in practice through loopholes, secret laws and extra-legal proceedings; while governments often interface with network operators and telecommunications service providers to weaken privacy safeguards.[154] Another report pertaining solely to EU member states attests to their unwillingness to comply with recent CJEU judgments in the area of data retention. According to that report, most EU countries (21) have reportedly shown little interest in relinquishing their data retention capabilities, having thus far failed to comply with the CJEU's

---

[149] See, for example, Monu Bedi, 'Facebook and Interpersonal Privacy: Why the Third Party Doctrine Should Not Apply' (2013) 54(1) *Boston College Law Review* 1–71; Monu Bedi, 'Social Networks, Government Surveillance and the Fourth Amendment Mosaic Theory' (2014) 94 *Boston College Law Review* 1809–80.

[150] Greenleaf (n 108).

[151] These include the UK IPA 2016 c 25; the French Intelligence Act 2015 (Law 2015-912) and the German BND Act 2016.

[152] See Steven Feldstein, *The Global Expansion of AI Surveillance* (Carnegie Endowment for International Peace, 2019). According to this report, at least 75 of 176 countries are actively using AI technology for surveillance purposes, including facial recognition (64 countries) and smart policing (52 countries). China and the US are the major driver of AI surveillance worldwide. Chinese companies – including Huawei, Hikvision, Dahua and ZTE – reportedly supply surveillance technologies to 63 countries, 36 of which have signed up to China's 'Belt and Road' Initiative. AI technology supplied by US companies such as IBM and Cisco is present in 32 countries.

[153] Douwe Korff, Ben Wagner, Julia Powles, Renata Avila and Ulf Buermeyer, *Boundaries of Law: Exploring Transparency, Accountability and Oversight of Government Surveillance Regimes* (University of Cambridge Faculty of Law, 2013).

[154] *Ibid* 5.

decisions[155] in *Digital Rights Ireland*[156] and *Tele-2/Watson.*[157] In these rulings, the CJEU prohibited the general and indiscriminate retention of communications data and mandated that all domestic regimes reflect this.[158] While these findings may merely be indicative of a general reticence on the part of states towards renouncing their data acquisition and retention schemes, they nevertheless raise significant privacy, transparency and security concerns and shed light on the current state practice of a large number of EU member states. Perhaps unsurprisingly, the concerns of some EU member states that they have been deprived of an instrument (ie, the powers of indiscriminate retention of traffic and location data) which they consider necessary to safeguard national security and combat crime, were recognized by the CJEU in its 2020 combined judgments in *La Quadrature du Net and Privacy International* (discussed in Chapter 6). The CJEU held that although EU law precludes national legislation from requiring electronic communications service providers to carry out general and indiscriminate transmission or retention of such data, member states may derogate from the obligation to ensure the confidentiality of data by putting in place such legislative measures for a limited time where these are strictly necessary.

As the above discussion indicates, positioning privacy/data privacy protection laws in the wider policy context is vital in order to ascertain the extent to which states' actions exhibit uniformity in terms of the safeguarding of this right. This point can be further illustrated by the global response to the 2020 Covid-19 pandemic. The Covid-19 virus is a new infectious respiratory disease that predominantly affects the lungs and airways, which was first discovered in 2019 in Wuhan, China. Due to a combination of deficient immunity and the lack of a cure and/or vaccine, the disease spread rapidly around the world, with 111,593,583 confirmed cases and 2,475,020 deaths reported on 24 February 2021 by the World Health Organization.[159] Many governments responded to

---

[155] Privacy International, *National Data Retention Laws Since the CJEU's Tele-2/Watson Judgement* (Privacy International, 2017) ('*National Data Retention Laws*').

[156] C-293/12 and C-594/12 *Digital Rights Ireland Ltd v Minister for Communications, Marine and Natural Resources and Others* (8 April 2014) ('*Digital Rights Ireland*').

[157] C-203/15 and C-698/15 *Tele2 Sverige AB v Post- och telestyrelsen and Secretary of State for Home Departments v Tom Watson and Others* ('*Tele-2/Watson*').

[158] *National Data Retention Laws* (n 155). The report revealed that of the following 21 states, none is compliant with current data retention standards: Austria, Belgium, Bulgaria, Croatia, Cyprus, the Czech Republic, France, Germany, Hungary, Ireland, Italy, Luxembourg, the Netherlands, Poland, Portugal, Romania, Slovakia, Slovenia, Spain, Sweden and the United Kingdom.

[159] World Health Organization, *Coronavirus Disease (COVID-19) Dashboard* (24 February 2021), https://covid19.who.int/?gclid=EAIaIQobChMI_PLF4I2b6wIVhu7tCh0 3QwQIEAAYASAAEgKvfvD_BwE.

the pandemic by declaring a state of national emergency and using special powers to attempt to limit transmission of the virus, including through putting in place travel/movement restrictions; the cancellation of public events; the closure of schools, universities and public facilities; and the imposition of social distancing and self-isolation measures (collectively known as 'lockdown'). The legal bases for the adoption of these measures also vary: some countries – such as Canada[160] and New Zealand[161] – have relied on existing emergency legislation; while others have adopted bespoke legal frameworks to fight the pandemic.[162] While the exact emergency response has differed from state to state, some governments – including China and Israel[163] – have also moved towards the deployment of a range of cyber surveillance tools in order to fight the disease, including contact tracing technology through the use of smartphone applications (mobile apps).[164] These methods rely on personal location data and big data analysis to identify patterns in the population's movements, disseminate health alerts to specific locations and inform public health decision making. The reliance on smartphones to trace infections is not new: the UK, the US, Germany and Ireland, among others, have already developed such software.[165] However, it is expected that its use will be expedited around the globe, with Apple and Google joining forces in April 2020 to

---

[160]   See Emergencies Act RSC 1985 c 22 as amended by SC 2001 c 27.

[161]   See Dean Knight, 'Lockdown Bubbles Through Layers of Law, Discretion and Nudges', *Verfassungsblog on Matters Constitutional* (7 April 2020), https://verfassungsblog.de/covid-19-in-new-zealand-lockdown-bubbles-through-layers-of-law-discretion-and-nudges/.

[162]   A case in point is Hungary: on 30 March 2020, in the immediate aftermath of the outbreak of the pandemic, the government introduced the Act on Protecting Against Coronavirus, a statute widely perceived as an attempt by President Orbán at a power grab and the aggrandizement of the executive at the time of crisis – see Kriszta Kovács, 'Hungary's Orbánistan: A Complete Arsenal of Emergency Powers' *Verfassungsblog on Matters Constitutional* (6 April 2020), https://verfassungsblog.de/hungarys-orbanistan-a-complete-arsenal-of-emergency-powers/.

[163]   See Tamar Hostovsky Brandez, 'Israel's Perfect Storm: Fighting Coronavirus in the Midst of a Constitutional Crisis', *Verfassungsblog on Matters Constitutional* (7 April 2020), https://verfassungsblog.de/israels-perfect-storm-fighting-coronavirus-in-the-midst-of-a-constitutional-crisis/. The *Knesset* Service Affairs Committee approved the employment of military cellular tracking technology pursuant to Article 7(B)(6) of the General Security Services Law, 5762-2002.

[164]   Barrie Sander, *COVID-19 Symposium: COVID-19, Cyber Surveillance Normalization and Human Rights Law* (1 April 2020), http://opiniojuris.org/2020/04/01/covid-19-symposium-covid-19-cyber-surveillance-normalisation-and-human-rights-law/ ('Sander').

[165]   *The Economist*, 'Contact Tracing. A Global Microscope, Made of Phones' (18 April 2020).

build contact tracing apps to track transmission of Covid-19[166] in order to help countries to emerge from lockdown. The very use of this technology raises substantial privacy and economic concerns.

Digital contact tracing was pioneered in late March 2020 in Singapore[167] and has since been reportedly deployed in at least 28 other countries around the globe. For example, the Chinese authorities introduced a mobile app called Health Code, which allows technology companies to gather vast quantities of mobile phone and geolocation data to help make decisions in relation to the quarantine of individuals.[168] The UK government also announced the deployment of a contact tracing app as part of its efforts to prevent a second wave of infections once the initial lockdown restrictions were lifted.[169] The government's immediate response was to enact bespoke legislation, the Coronavirus Act 2020,[170] which sets out a diverse range of powers – including enhanced surveillance – in a bid to contain the pandemic. The Act is intended as temporary emergency legislation, with Section 89 limiting the duration of most of its provisions to two years – although this may be extended by a further six months. The powers of interception are set out in Sections 22 and 23, which provide that their statutory basis is the Investigatory Powers Act 2016 (IPA). However, these provisions allow for temporary changes to be made to the IPA in relation to the appointment of Judicial Commissioners (Section 22)[171]

---

[166]  *Ibid.*

[167]  See Alex Hern, 'Data Contact Tracing Will Fail Unless Privacy is Respected, Experts Warn', *The Guardian* (20 April 2020).

[168]  The Health Code system requires that individuals first provide their personal information, including ID number; home address; details of whether they have been in contact with people infected with the virus and their symptoms. The app then assigns users one of three colours: green (movement is unrestricted); yellow (seven-day quarantine); or red (14 days in insolation). Local authorities across China require people to show the app when moving around – for instance, when visiting a supermarket, entering or exiting residential areas, or using the subway – see Wang (n 146). The app allegedly also shares people's location data with the police, which according to the *New York Times* 'set[s] a template for new forms of automated social control that could persist long after the epidemic subsides' – see Sander (n 164).

[169]  The original plan to develop an NHS app was abandoned following trial failures on the Isle of Wight in favour of a new system devised by Apple and Google – see Matt Burgess, 'Everything You Need to Know About the NHS Test, Track and Trace App', *Wired* (11 August 2020), www.wired.co.uk/article/nhs-covid-19-tracking-app-contact-tracing.

[170]  Coronavirus Act 2020 c 7. The Act sets out a diverse range of powers to deal with various challenges stemming from the pandemic and consists of 102 Sections and 29 Schedules. See also Legislation UK, 'Coronavirus Act 2020. Explanatory Notes' (2020) ('CVA Explanatory Notes') 7.

[171]  See CVA Explanatory Notes *ibid*, para 50, 13 and para 52, 13.

and time limits pertaining to urgent warrants under the Act (Section 23).[172] These emergency provisions, alongside other measures, have raised human rights concerns, with leading UK non-governmental organizations (NGOs) condemning them as 'the most draconian powers ever proposed in peace-time Britain';[173] and eminent human right lawyer Kirsty Brimelow QC warning that the Act 'lacks basic human rights safeguards and so is open to abuse in implementation'.[174] The specific problems in the context of state surveillance relate to both the appointment of temporary Judicial Commissioners and the renewed timespan of urgent warrants. The criticisms raised in relation to the latter issue centre on the unilateral nature of such appointments – that is, by the Investigatory Powers Commissioner alone and not by joint appointment, as set out in Section 227 of the IPA. With regard to the relaxation of the rules on the procedures for issuing urgent warrants, it is feared that this may lead to such warrants being used inappropriately; while their time extension to 12 working days is unjustifiable and should therefore be removed.[175]

Governments have a legal obligation to take unprecedented steps to save lives and combat the spread of life-threatening diseases such as Covid-19. Extraordinary times require extraordinary measures. However, certain methods – particularly those which aim to track, collect and share personal data (especially smartphone contact tracing apps) – raise significant ethical and legal questions, specifically in relation to the protection of privacy. While the official assurance is that these measures are only temporary, 'the possibility [of governments using] the COVID-19 crisis as a pretext to expand and normalize these surveillance powers' has nonetheless been recognized.[176] Thus, Barrie Sander aptly observes that:

> whilst government surveillance systems have been established, history suggests that they are seldom relinquished. Surveillance normalisation may result from bureaucratic inertia or mission creep, but it is not unreasonable to suspect that the exploitation of emergency circumstances to enact measures that would otherwise be unthinkable amounts to an explicit choice on the part of many governments. After all, surveillance represents a seemingly 'easier' policy lever in contrast to establishing a robust healthcare system that is adequately equipped to protect the public in the longer term.[177]

---

[172]  *Ibid* para 54, 13.
[173]  *Big Brother Watch*, 'Big Brother Watch Briefing on the Coronavirus Bill' (March 2020), https://bigbrotherwatch.org.uk/wp-content/uploads/2020/03/briefing -coronavirus-bill-final.pdf 2.
[174]  *Ibid.*
[175]  *Ibid* 11.
[176]  Sander (n 164).
[177]  *Ibid.*

Yuval Noah Harari likewise wans that 'many short-term emergency measures will become a fixture of life. That is the nature of emergencies'.[178]

For the reasons outlined above, there appears to be a lack of uniform and consistent state practice relating to the protection of privacy, despite this being guaranteed as a fundamental right in international treaties and given constitutional and/or statutory protection by the vast majority of countries worldwide.[179] This conclusion is based on an overview of the differing approaches to privacy protection in divergent legal traditions[180] and the broader context within which these guarantees currently exist, characterized by the practice of mass surveillance for national security and public health reasons. All this seems to suggest that states' obligation to protect privacy online works better in theory than in practice.

## 5.    OPINIO JURIS

Article 38(1)(b) of the SICJ dictates that the second element that must be satisfied in order to establish the formation of customary international law rule is *opinio juris*, which has been explained by Special Rapporteur Wood as 'the "subjective" (psychological) element [relating] to the motives behind [the] behaviour of States'.[181] Thus, even if a certain widespread, uniform and consistent practice has been established, that in itself will not suffice. There must also be a belief that there exists among states an acceptance as law that this practice is legally binding. This requirement has been confirmed in the judgments of the Permanent Court of International Justice (PCIJ) and the ICJ. Thus, in *Lotus*, the PCIJ held that international law is based on the will of states expressed in conventions or in 'usages generally accepted as expressing

---

[178] Yuval Noah Harari, 'The World After Coronavirus', *Financial Times* (20 March 2020).

[179] See A/73/45712 (n 51) para 43, 7. Professor Cannataci noted a 'great increase in the number of countries introducing privacy/data privacy protection laws with 2018 having been a particularly active year around the world'.

[180] See also Zalnieriute (n 147) 116, suggesting that when state practice in relation to data privacy is assessed through the application of the traditional doctrinal methods, its status under international law is unclear, for three reasons. First, it is not known what proportion of states have comprehensive data privacy regimes (and there are no agreed criteria how to measure the 'comprehensiveness') and whether that proportion is sufficient to imply high acceptance among states. Second, states' exponential adoption of data privacy legislation might still be insufficient per se, as state practice is often understood to require uniform application and enforcement in practice. Third, the scandals of unprecedented levels of governmental surveillance might suggest that governments do not value their official data privacy commitments codified in national laws to an extent necessary to establish *opinio juris*.

[181] A/CN.4/663 (n 31) para 96, 45.

principles of law'.[182] In *Nicaragua*, the ICJ stated that 'for a new customary rule to be formed not only must the acts concerned "amount to a settled practice", but they must be accompanied by the *opinio juris sive necessitates*'.[183] Likewise, in *Gulf of Mine* the ICJ reiterated that the customary international law rule emerges where its 'presence is the *opinio juris* of States [which] can be tested by induction based on the analysis of sufficiently extensive and convincing practice and not by deduction from preconceived ideas'.[184] The ILC, in its Draft Conclusions on Identification of Customary International Law, has further elaborated on the meaning of *opinio juris*, explaining that it consists of two constituent parts: (1) 'the practice in question must be undertaken with a sense of legal rights or obligations';[185] and (2) it 'is to be distinguished from mere usage or habit'.[186] The former makes it crucial to show in each case that states have acted in a certain way because they believed themselves legally compelled or entitled to do so by reason of a rule of customary law. In other words, they must have pursued the practice as a matter of right or submitted to it as a matter of obligation.[187] This point was addressed by the ICJ in the *North Sea Continental Shelf* cases, in which it held that states' actions:

> not only must amount to a settled practice, but must also be such, or be carried out in such a way, as to be evidence of a belief that this practice is rendered obligatory by the existence of the rule requiring it. The need for such a belief, i.e. the existence of a subjective element, is implicit in the very notion of the *opinio juris sive necessitates*. The States concerned must therefore feel that they are conforming to what amounts to legal obligation.[188]

At the same time, the acceptance as law must be distinguished from other extra-legal motives for state action, such as comity, political expediency or convenience.[189] Thus, as illustrated by the *Asylum* case, the practice in question will not be recognized as a rule of customary international law where it is motivated by political expediency.[190]

---

[182]   *S.S. Lotus (France v Turkey)*, Judgment [1927] PCIJ Rep Series A No 10 18.

[183]   *Nicaragua* (n 35) para 207.

[184]   *Delimitation of the Maritime Boundary in the Gulf of Mine Area*, Judgment [1984] ICJ Rep para 111, 299.

[185]   ICL *Identification of Customary Law* (n 36) Conclusion 9(1).

[186]   *Ibid* Conclusion 9(2).

[187]   *Ibid* Commentary para 2, 138.

[188]   *North Sea Continental Shelf Cases* (n 41) para 77.

[189]   ILC *Identification of Customary Law* (n 36) Conclusion 9, Commentary para 3, 139.

[190]   *Asylum Case* (52) 277. The ICJ addressed Colombia's claim of a local custom in the Latin American region which pertained to the granting of asylum. In refusing to recognize the existence of a rule as customary international law, the ICJ stated, *inter*

Needless to say, the establishment in practice of the subjective element that is embodied in *opinio juris* has been notoriously problematic. In this regard, the ILC has clarified the forms of evidence that may be used as acceptance of *opinio juris*. These include 'decisions of nationals courts ... and conduct in connection with resolutions adopted by an international organization or at an intergovernmental conference'.[191] It follows that the resolutions of the UNGA – albeit generally non-legally binding, but nevertheless putting forward states' opinions on various issues – may play a role in establishing the existence of *opinio juris*, especially when adopted by consensus. To this end, in *Nicaragua*, the ICJ stated that '*opinio juris* may, though with all due caution, be deduced from, *inter alia*, the attitude of the parties and the attitude of States towards certain General Assembly resolutions'.[192] However, in its *Nuclear Weapons Advisory Opinion*, the ICJ cautioned that although an UNGA resolution 'can in certain circumstances provide evidence important for establishing the existence of a rule or the emergence of *opinio juris* ... it is necessary to look at its content and the conditions of its adoption'.[193] Furthermore, 'a series of resolutions may show the gradual evolution of the *opinio juris* required for the establishment of a new rule'.[194] The relevance of UNGA resolutions to the establishment of *opinio juris* was also discussed by the Iran-United States Claims Tribunal in *Sedco*, which stated that they:

> are not as such binding upon States and generally are not evidence of customary law. Nevertheless, it is generally accepted that such resolutions in certain specified circumstances may be regarded as evidence of customary international law or can contribute – among other factors – to the creation of such law.[195]

In this sense, two types of resolutions have been distinguished: law declaring and law developing.[196] The former purports 'to state an existing rule of law. In particular, it may be a means for the determination or interpretation of international law, it may constitute evidence of international custom, or it

---

*alia*, that the practices in question were not shown to have been 'exercised by the States granting the asylum as a right appertaining to them and respected by the territorial States as a duty incumbent on them and not merely for reasons of political expediency'.

[191]  ILC *Identification of Customary Law* (n 36) Conclusion 10(2), 140.
[192]  *Nicaragua* (n 35) 433–34.
[193]  *Nuclear Weapons Advisory Opinion* (n 34) 226 para 70.
[194]  *Ibid.*
[195]  *Sedco* (1986) 25 ILM 629 para 33.
[196]  *Institut de Droit International*, 'The Elaboration of General Multilateral Conventions and of Non-contractual Instruments Having a Normative Function of Objective' (17 September 1987).

may set forth general principles of law'.[197] The latter comprises, *inter alia*, resolutions contributing to the creation of international custom; those adding to the emergence of general principles of law; and those laying down policies that determine the substance of future law, whether customary or treaty.[198] The elements that help to determine whether a resolution falls under one of these categories include: (1) the intent and expressions of states; (2) respect for the procedural standards required; (3) the text of the resolution; (4) the extent of its support; and (5) the context in which it was elaborated and adopted, including relevant political factors.[199]

In the aftermath of the 2013 Snowden disclosures, a number of UN instruments emerged which seem to suggest a common approach among the international community towards the issue of online privacy and state surveillance. The most notable of these include the 2013 and 2014 UN Resolutions on the right to privacy in the digital age (Resolutions 68/167 and 69/166), UN Human Rights Council Resolution 28/16;[200] and two reports of the UN Office of the High Commissioner for Human Rights (OHCHR) (A/HRC/27/37 and A/HRC/39/29).[201] Also of importance are earlier studies of UN Special Rapporteurs Martin Scheinin[202] and Frank La Rue,[203] together with the more recent report of Special Rapporteur David Kaye.[204] In addition, two decisions of the UK and US courts – *Liberty v MI5*[205] and *Jewel v NSA*[206] respectively – are indicative of certain attitudes of the judiciary to the problem of privacy

---

[197] *Ibid* Conclusion 4 (Law Declaring Resolutions).

[198] *Ibid* Conclusion 5 (Law Developing Resolutions). Other types of resolutions define the scope of negotiations on multilateral treaties of general interest – in particular, resolutions setting forth rules to be included in a future treaty.

[199] *Ibid* Conclusion 6 (Relevant Elements). The final factor comprises 'any implementing procedures provided by the Resolution'.

[200] UNHRC Resolution, 'The Right to Privacy in the Digital Age' (26 March 2015) UN Doc A/HRC/Res/28/16 ('A/HRC/Res/28/16').

[201] A/HRC/27/37 (n 99); UNHRC, 'The Right to Privacy in the Digital Age. Report of the United Nations High Commissioner for Human Rights' (3 August 2018) UN Doc A/HRC/39/29 ('A/HRC/39/29').

[202] UNHRC, 'Report of the Special Rapporteur on the Promotion and Protection of Human Rights and Fundamental Freedoms while Countering Terrorism, Martin Scheinin' (17 May 2010) UN Doc A/HRC/14/46 ('A/HRC/14/46').

[203] UNHRC, 'Report of the Special Rapporteur on the Promotion and Protection of the Right to Freedom of Opinion and Expression, Frank La Rue' (17 April 2013) UN Doc A/HRC/23/40 ('A/HRC/23/40').

[204] UNHRC, 'Surveillance and Human Rights. Report of the Special Rapporteur on the Promotion and Protection of the Right to Freedom of Opinion and Expression' (28 May 2019) UN Doc A/HRC/41/35 ('A/HRC/41/35').

[205] *Liberty and Privacy International v SSHD and SSFCA* [27 July 2019] EWHC 2057 ('*Liberty v MI5*').

[206] *Jewel v NSA* 673 F 3d 902 (Ct App, 9th Civ 2011).

and government mass surveillance. All the aforementioned developments are considered next, alongside recent judicial pronouncements of the ECtHR and the CJEU.

## 5.1    UNGA Resolutions

UNGA Resolutions 68/167 and 69/166 represent an important political pronouncement of the international community on mass surveillance practices. However, this does not mean that they amount to a binding rule of customary international law. From the perspective of the crystallization of the right to online privacy as such a rule, as observed above, both their content and the manner of their adoption are significant.

With respect to the content, three points are particularly notable. First, the Resolutions reaffirm the right to privacy,[207] stating that no one shall be subjected to its arbitrary and unlawful interference,[208] and emphasize that 'the same rights that people have offline must also be protected online, including the right to privacy'.[209] In so doing, the Resolutions not only reiterate states' human rights obligations, but also make clear that the protection of privacy is owed to everyone – citizens and foreigners alike – explicitly noting the negative impact of all forms of surveillance, including extraterritorial surveillance. Second, the Resolutions call upon all states 'to respect and promote the right to privacy, including in the context of digital communications'; and to take measures to prevent its violation by ensuring that the relevant national legislation complies with their obligations under international human rights law.[210] To this end, they urge states to establish or maintain independent and effective oversight to ensure transparency of, and accountability for, surveillance and/ or interception of communications and collection of personal data.[211] The Resolutions also attach importance to the gathering of metadata, emphasizing that its certain types of metadata 'can reveal personal information and can give an insight into an individual's behaviour, social relationships, private preferences and identity'.[212] Third, the Resolutions concede that the prevention and suppression of terrorism constitutes a public interest of great importance, but stress that states must ensure that any measures taken to combat this threat

---

[207]   A/Res/68/167 (n 5). The Resolutions referred to Article 12 of the UDHR 1947 and Article 17 of the ICCPR 1966.

[208]   *Ibid* recital 5; A/Res/69/166 (n 5) recital 15.

[209]   A/Res/68/167 paras 1 and 3; A/Res/69/166 para 3.

[210]   A/Res/68/167 paras 4(a)–(b); A/Res/69/166 paras 4(a)–(b).

[211]   *Ibid.*

[212]   A/Res/69/166 recital 14.

comply with their obligations under international law, including human rights law.[213]

These instruments are thus an important high-water mark, representing the international community's collective view that mass cyber surveillance poses a particularly grievous threat to online privacy. However, they are couched in general language, with no specifics as to what standards must be adopted or how the stipulations laid out therein are to be achieved. Also worthy of note is what the Resolutions leave out. For example, they provide no explanation of what precisely comprises 'unlawful and arbitrary' surveillance in the context of digital communications. For these reasons, Resolution 69/166 recognizes the need to examine the principles of non-arbitrariness and lawfulness, and acknowledges that General Comment 16 issued by the HRC in 1988 interpreting Article 17 of the ICCPR is now outdated, due to the vast technological leaps that have since taken place.[214] Furthermore, the Resolutions provide no details on the particular measures that states should take to prevent privacy violations; nor do they elaborate on the features that national laws setting out surveillance powers should incorporate in order to ensure that states comply with their human rights obligations to safeguard individuals' rights to online privacy. However, they do reiterate the well-established principles that these legal frameworks must be publicly accessible, clear, precise, comprehensive and non-discriminatory. Finally, although they acknowledge the need for states to use surveillance powers to combat terrorism, they do not set out exactly how such methods should be used to conform with the requirements of necessity and proportionality, or the extent to which law enforcement and security services may share information in different jurisdictions. The Resolutions nonetheless represent the international community's general condemnation of unrestrained surveillance and its growing interest in online privacy, while also constituting an undertaking by the UN institutions to further explore the impact of digital technologies on this right.

Also important in this context is the fact that, in principle, UNGA resolutions are non-legally binding and as a consequence, states often vote in their favour, which arguably represents a 'fake consensus'[215] dictated by a wish 'to maintain their international image without the expectation that the international community will deem their votes as acceptance of a new rule of law'.[216] The overall tenor and manner of adoption of the Resolutions on the right to privacy in the

---

[213]  *Ibid* recital 22.
[214]  A/Res/69/166 recitals 8–9.
[215]  Stephen Schwebel, 'The Effect of Resolutions of the UN General Assembly on Customary International Law' (1979) *American Society of International Law* 301, 308 in Zalnieriute (n 147) 122.
[216]  *Ibid.*

digital age are therefore of significance in this regard. Thus, Resolution 69/167 gained support from an extensive range of countries, but its original language and tone were substantially watered down in the final version.[217] As initially drafted, the Resolution contained a number of radical provisions which proved unacceptable to US diplomats. As a result of lobbying by the US (including its allies), the final version was couched in more conciliatory terms to suit the US administration's political agenda. One of the main points of contention was the assertion that states' foreign espionage activities – including against online communications – are subject to the right to privacy in international law,[218] thus triggering human rights obligations in relation to extraterritorial surveillance. In rejecting this suggestion, the US diplomats insisted that US electronic surveillance was lawful and compliant with international human rights law.[219] According to a leaked document titled *Right to Privacy in the Digital Age – U.S. Redlines*, the US demanded that clarification be made 'that references to privacy rights are referring explicitly to States' obligations under ICCPR and [any] suggestions that such obligations apply extra-territorially [be removed]'.[220] The document explained that the emphasis placed on a reference to Article 17 of the ICCPR was 'essential in order not to suggest that there are two sets of privacy rights, one under the ICCPR and the other from some other source', which suggests US reluctance to recognize the right to online privacy as a customary law rule.[221] Moreover, the administration's stance that the ICCPR does not apply extraterritorially was seen as an attempt to ensure that the US 'preserves the right to spy overseas'.[222] Likewise, the original language of the same Resolution – according to which 'illegal surveillance of communications, their interception and the illegal collection of personal data constitutes a highly intrusive act that violates the right to privacy and freedom of expression' – was softened. Consequently, the final draft merely reflects the community's 'deep concern' at the 'human rights violations and abuses that *may* [emphasis added] result from surveillance and data collection'.[223] The

---

[217] This relates in particular to A/Res/68/167 (n 5).

[218] David P Fidler, 'Cyberspace and Human Rights' in Nicholas Tsagourias and Russell Buchan (eds), *Research Handbook on International Law and Cyberspace* (Edward Elgar Publishing Inc, 2015) 94–117, 113.

[219] *Ibid.*

[220] *Right to Privacy in the Digital Age – U.S. Redlines*, https://columlynch.tumblr .com/post/67588682409/right-to-privacy-in-the-digital-age-us, in Colum Lynch, 'Exclusive: Inside America's Plan to Kill Online Privacy Rights Everywhere', *The Cable* (20 November 2013), https://foreignpolicy.com/2013/11/20/exclusive-inside -americas-plan-to-kill-online-privacy-rights-everywhere/.

[221] *Ibid.*

[222] *Ibid.*

[223] *Ibid.*

Resolution was finally approved in December 2013 by the UNGA without a vote, which is indicative of the aforementioned disagreements and the compromises reached in order to adopt it.

Undoubtedly, Resolutions 68/167 and 69/166 reflect the widespread acceptance among the majority of the international community that human rights must be protected and respected online. However, the final watered-down text, the US political pressure to moderate their tone and impact and the manner of their adoption suggest that these Resolutions are law developing rather than law declaring. Due to the generality of the obligations expressed therein and the political context within which they were adopted, it cannot be said with utter conviction that they constitute a clear and unwavering commitment of states to the protection of online privacy, thus constituting an unequivocal expression of *opinio juris*. Nevertheless, they contribute to the creation of customary law rule and demonstrate that the UN attaches increasing importance to privacy in the digital age.

The pivotal role that privacy plays, including online, has been reiterated in the Human Rights Council Resolutions, such as Resolution 28/16, and in a number of highly influential reports, including that of the OHCHR[224] and of the Special Rapporteurs, as discussed next.

## 5.2     UN Human Rights Bodies

The OHCHR, in the 2014 report 'The Right to Privacy in the Digital Age', expressed deep concerns about the implications of digital surveillance practices across the globe and their damaging impact on the right to privacy.[225] Having analysed the legality of domestic and extraterritorial surveillance, the interception of digital communications and the collection of personal data based on the international law framework, the study concluded that both national legislation and oversight of digital surveillance programs are inadequate, which contributes to a lack of accountability for arbitrary or unlawful interference with privacy.[226] The report identified a pressing need for states to ensure the compliance of any surveillance policy or practice with the right to privacy through the development of effective safeguards against abuse by, among other things, reviewing their own national laws, policies and practices and, in the case of shortcomings, adopting clear, precise and accessible legislative frameworks.[227] A year later, the UN Human Rights Council adopted

---

[224]  A/HRC/27/37 (n 99).
[225]  *Ibid* paras 2–3.
[226]  *Ibid* para 20.
[227]  *Ibid* para 50.

Resolution 28/16,[228] which not only reaffirmed the right to online privacy, but also noted the ability of governments, companies and individuals to undertake surveillance enabled by rapid advancements in technology. The Resolution recognized that terrorism concerns may justify governments' collection of some data, but emphasized this must be done in full compliance with their human rights obligations.[229] Reflecting the fears associated with arbitrary privacy abuses, the Human Rights Council through Resolution 28/16 decided to create the office of a Special Rapporteur on the right to privacy.[230] The Resolution also made explicit reference to two seminal reports (referenced in Chapter 1): that of Special Rapporteur Scheinin on the protection and promotion of human rights while countering terrorism; and that of Special Rapporteur La Rue on the promotion and protection of the right to freedom of opinion and expression. These documents have not only plucked the right to privacy and data protection from relative obscurity and placed it firmly at the top of the UN agenda, but also substantially contributed to highlighting the detrimental effects of mass surveillance.

However, despite these numerous calls and affirmations, states' actions indicate a pronounced move in the opposite direction. Their apparent failure to heed the calls to comply with human rights obligations when conducting mass surveillance was made explicitly clear by the subsequent reports of UN High Commissioner for Human Rights Michelle Bachelet[231] and of Special Rapporteur David Kaye on freedom of opinion and expression,[232] issued respectively in 2018 and 2019. Thus, the High Commissioner, when addressing the issue of mass surveillance, observed that:

> many States continue to engage in secret surveillance and communications interception, collecting, storing and analysing the data of all users relating to a broad range of means of communications (for example email, telephone and video calls, text messages and website visited). While some States claim that such indiscriminate mass surveillance is necessary to protect national security, this practice is not permissible under international human rights law, as an individualized necessity and proportionality analysis would not be possible in the context of such measures.[233]

The scale of the problem was also confirmed by Special Rapporteur Kaye, who, commenting on the problem of targeted surveillance in the context of private surveillance industry, called 'for an immediate moratorium on the

---

[228]  A/HRC/28/16 (n 200).
[229]  *Ibid* recitals 12–13.
[230]  *Ibid* para 4.
[231]  A/HRC/39/29 (n 201).
[232]  A/HRC/41/35 (n 204).
[233]  A/HRC/39/29 (n 201) para 17.

export, sale, transfer, or servicing of privately developed surveillance tools until a human rights-complaints safeguards regime is in place'.[234] The report also found that: 'In environments subject to rampant illicit surveillance, the targeted communities know of or suspect such attempts at surveillance, which in turn shapes and restricts their capacity to exercise the rights to freedom of expression, association, religious belief, [and] culture...'[235]

All of the above examples reflect the unwavering dedication and commitment of the UN human rights machinery to privacy protection. The same cannot be said of states' actions on the domestic level, which appear to disregard their legal obligations to respect and protect privacy, continually engaging in mass surveillance. Indeed, as aptly observed by Christopher Kuner, writing in the context of data privacy, 'there seems to exist a kind of "parallel universe" concerning the collection and sharing of electronic surveillance data for law enforcement purposes and operates independently of the regular legal standards for data protection'.[236]

## 5.3    Court Practice

Finally, mention must be made of the attitudes of the judiciary when confronted with privacy violations by government agencies through the use of mass surveillance technologies. Two recent cases are illustrative of this point: *Liberty v MI5*, decided by the UK High Court in July 2019; and *Jewel v NSA*, appealed to the US Ninth Circuit Court of Appeals from the 2019 decision of the District Court (undecided at the time of writing).

The former was a joint legal challenge by two UK NGOs – Liberty and Privacy International – concerning the use by UK agencies (including MI5) of bulk surveillance powers under the IPA to extract and store information. The NGOs alleged that the data surveillance capabilities allowed under the Act are 'unlawfully wide' – in particular, that the data gathered under warrants granted by a judge or a Home Secretary can comprise: (1) intimate data, including an individual's browsing history; (2) the apps that users have downloaded to their phone; (3) usernames and passwords; and (3) call sites that can pinpoint an individual's location at a given time. The claimants argued that these surveillance methods breach UK citizens' rights under Article 8 and Article 10 (freedom of expression) of the ECHR. In resisting the claim, the UK government asserted that the powers provided by the IPA strike 'a fair

---

[234]  A/HRC/41/35 (n 204) para 66(a).
[235]  *Ibid* para 21.
[236]  Christopher Kuner *et al*, 'Prism and Privacy: Will the Change Anything?' (2013) 3(4) *International Data Privacy Law* 2017–19.

balance between the rights of the individual and the general interest of the community'.[237] Despite revealing some serious lapses in compliance by MI5 in adhering to the necessary protections under the Act, the case was dismissed. The High Court concluded that 'the safeguards in the IPA are sufficient to prevent the risk of abuse of discretionary power and the Act is therefore not incompatible with the [ECHR] on the ground that it does not comply with the concept of law'.[238] In handing down this decision, the High Court was satisfied that the new safeguards introduced by the IPA created a system of supervision, through the Office of the Investigatory Powers Commissioner, which provides sufficiently robust independent oversight of the use of surveillance powers. In the view of the High Court, this was demonstrated by the fact that these safeguards had brought to light MI5's failings.

*Jewel v NSA* is a legal challenge brought in 2008 by US NGO Electronic Frontier Foundation (EFF) on behalf of AT&T customers for alleged violations of the Fourth Amendment and statutory rights by certain NSA surveillance programs – including Upstream – targeting the contents of domestic communications and the collection of metadata, authorized on the basis of the Section 215 of the Patriot Act 2001. The case is more than a decade old and has not yet been decided on the merits, pending resolution of the preliminary issues relating to the claimant's legal standing. The kernel of the argument pertaining to this matter is that a party cannot bring a legal challenge in the US courts unless the court first determines that it was affected in some way by the surveillance in question. This requirement was established by the Supreme Court in *Clapper v Amnesty International*,[239] involving a legal challenge to the PRISM program, in which the Court held that the appellants could not base their alleged injury on bare speculation that their contacts abroad would be targeted merely because they resided 'in geographic areas' that they believed to be 'a special focus' of the US government. Instead, they had to show that the alleged injury was 'certainly impending' or actual, not simply possible. However, it is often impossible to factually establish whether a particular person was a government target, unless the relevant agency admits to this. In *Jewel*, this has been denied on the basis that such information concerns state secrets. In a rare step, a court order was issued to hand over details from the NSA's domestic surveillance program; but subsequently, the organization declared that it had accidently deleted the data relating to the litigation. The issue in relation to standing will be decided only when the court reviews the relevant evidence. The legal battle continues, with the NSA protracting the

---

[237]  *Liberty v MI5* (n 205) para 8,4.
[238]  *Ibid.*
[239]  *Clapper v Amnesty International* 568 US 396 (2013) paras 406 and 410.

process. Of note in this context is the 2019 appeal decision in *Klayman*, where the Court of Appeals for the District of Columbia decided that the appellants lacked standing to challenge the collection under the PRISM program as they were only able to evidence communications with various individuals in countries that they imagined might attract government surveillance. They could provide no specific reason to suspect that their contacts were in fact the targets of the PRISM interception, or indeed that their own communications were collected. While it would be too speculative to assume that similar reasoning will be applied in *Jewel*, it is worth mentioning that thus far, very few of the NSA surveillance programs put in place since the 9/11 attacks have been pronounced illegal or unconstitutional by the US courts.[240]

In considering these cases and their outcomes, there appears to be a certain degree of judicial reluctance to rule on the unlawfulness of mass surveillance *per se*. Although this is by no means necessarily the situation in every jurisdiction, it is nevertheless indicative of certain attitudes in those countries with the most advanced surveillance apparatus. However, this is not an isolated tendency, as the *Liberty* ruling seems to be in line with the recent approach taken by the ECtHR in its 2018 landmark decisions in *Big Brother Watch* and *Centrum För Rättvisa v Sweden*.[241] Both of these cases embraced the policy of mass surveillance. In *Centrum För Rättvisa*, the ECtHR held that: 'the decision to operate a bulk interception regime in order to identify hitherto unknown threats to national security is one which continues to fall within States' margin of appreciation.'[242] The ECtHR went even further than this in *Big Brother Watch*, stating that: 'it is clear that bulk interception is a valuable means to achieve the legitimate aims pursued, particularly given the current threat level from both global terrorism and serious crime.'[243]

This stance can be contrasted with that taken by the CJEU in cases such as *Digital Rights Ireland, Tele-2/Watson, Schrems v Data Protection Commissioner (Schrems I)*[244] and *Schrems v Data Protection Commissioner*

---

[240]　Kieren McCarthy, 'NSA Takes One-Two Punch to the Face', *The Register* (23 May 2017), www.theregister.co.uk/2017/05/23/nsa_takes_onetwo_to_the_face/.

[241]　*Centrum För Rättvisa v Sweden* App no 35252/08 (19 June 2018) ('*Centrum För Rättvisa*').

[242]　*Ibid* para 112.

[243]　*Big Brother Watch and Others v the United Kingdom* App no 58170/13; *Bureau of Investigative Journalism and Alice Ross v the United Kingdom* App no 62322/14; *10 Human Rights Organizations and Others v the United Kingdom* App no 24960/15 (12 October 2018) para 386 ('*Big Brother Watch*').

[244]　C-362/14 *Maximilian Schrems v Data Protection Commissioner* [2015] ECJ ('*Schrems I*').

(*Schrems II*),[245] which taken together represent a higher standard of privacy/ data privacy protection than that adopted by the ECtHR. Thus, in *Digital Rights Ireland*, the CJEU annulled Directive 2006/24/EC,[246] which set out rules on the retention of metadata by private companies for the purposes of its later use by law enforcement agencies. The CJEU explained that the Directive's scope was very wide, as it included all persons, all means of communication and all traffic data, without differentiations or limitations. It also did not impose satisfactory limits in relation to access by the competent national authorities or provide for tailored retention periods *vis-à-vis* the categories of crimes concerned. The CJEU reaffirmed and expanded this dictum in its 2016 *Tele-2/ Watson* decision. According to that judgment, the minimum legal standards of EU law must be prescribed in all national data retention legislation. In particular, the CJEU held that the EU Charter must be read as precluding 'national legislation, which for the purpose of fighting crime, provides for general and indiscriminate retention of all traffic and location data of all subscribers and registered users relating to all means of electronic communication'.[247] Finally in *Schrems I*, the CJEU declared that transfers of the data of EU citizens pursuant to the EU-US Safe Harbour agreement were unsafe, thus invalidating that scheme,[248] as the US does not afford adequate levels of protection to the personal data of EU citizens. In this regard, the CJEU noted that US national security, public interest and law enforcement requirements prevail over the Safe Harbour agreement, so that US companies are bound to disregard, without limitation, the agreement's protective rules where these conflict with US national security requirements. The scheme was subsequently replaced by another non-legally binding data transfer agreement, the Privacy Shield, which was also invalidated following the CJEU's 2020 decision in *Schrems II*.[249] Having said that, as discussed in Chapter 6, the judicial attitudes of the ECtHR and the CJEU may be converging, following the latter's judgment in the four cases of *La Quadrature du Net and Privacy International*.

---

[245]   C-311/18 *Data Protection Commissioner v Facebook Ireland and Maximilian Schrems* [2020] ECJ in which the CJEU invalidated the data transfers on the basis of US-EU Privacy Shield ('*Schrems II*'). For more details, see Chapter 6, section 4.

[246]   Parliament and Council Directive 2006/24, 2006 OJ (L105) 54 (EC).

[247]   *Tele-2/Watson* (n 157) para 134.

[248]   *Schrems I* (n 244). The complaint was brought to the CJEU by Maximilian Schrems, who alleged that, following the Snowden disclosures in relation to the NSA's activities, the transfer of his Facebook data from its Irish subsidiary to the US under the EU-US Safe Harbour Agreement was unsafe, as US law does not afford sufficient protection against surveillance by the public authorities.

[249]   For more details, see Chapter 6, section 4.

## 5.4      Protection of Online Privacy as *Opinio Juris* – an Evaluation

Establishing *opinio juris* is predicated on the subjective belief that a given practice is accepted as law. In the context of online privacy, this means that there must be an overall conviction on the part of states that they have a legal obligation to protect it. This, it is submitted, is lacking, for three reasons. First, states' convergence on the issue of online privacy in the age of surveillance, resulting in UNGA Resolutions 68/167 and 69/166, was a welcome development. However, considering the content, the manner and the political context of the adoption of those instruments, it cannot be said that they have law-declaring value and thus constitute evidence of international custom. Rather, they should be viewed as law-developing mechanisms, indicative of the substance of future law – whether customary or treaty. Second, the activism of UN mandate holders, underpinned by the general condemnation of mass surveillance, is at odds with states' behaviour 'on the ground': mass surveillance has become the preferred method of intelligence collection, routinely undertaken in practice and increasingly legislated for. Finally, the relevant legal standards are diffuse and lack clarity.[250] This is evident from the recent case law of the ECtHR and some national courts (including in the UK and US), whereby mass surveillance appears to have been accepted as a staple of states' security toolbox. By contrast, until its 2020 decision in the *La Quadrature du Net and Privacy International*, the CJEU has repeatedly and unequivocally affirmed online privacy and data privacy, condemning mass data interception and retention, and banning transatlantic data transfers twice, where such data is subject to unrestricted access by the US intelligence and security apparatus.

## 6.      ONLINE PRIVACY AS A CUSTOMARY LAW RULE

It follows that the status of online privacy as a customary international law rule must be considered with caution. Some legal scholars have shown willingness to embrace data privacy as such a rule – probably influenced by the tendency exhibited in the early part of this decade towards greater data privacy protection in international instruments, at the regional level, in the activism of national legislatures and in the jurisprudence of both the ECtHR and the CJEU.[251] However, this optimism requires circumscription in light of incon-

---

[250]   These issues are discussed further in Chapters 4, 5 and 6.

[251]   Zalnieruite (n 147) concluded at 133 that: 'given the constitutionally increasing amount of recognition in international instruments, the prominent place that the topic of data privacy occupies in the writings and commentary, and the treatment as a binding norm that the right to data privacy has received in both national and international legal

sistent state practice and the difficulties of unequivocally establishing *opinio juris*. This uncertainty is underscored by the scepticism of the International Law Association Committee on the Enforcement of Human Rights Law, which had already noted back in 1995, commenting on the right to privacy, that 'the content of [this] right varies considerably among States and the contours of that realm of privacy which is beyond the reach of government is perhaps too vague to be deemed a useful part of customary law'.[252] More recently, the experts who drafted the *Tallinn Manual 2.0* counselled that 'it is unclear as to whether certain human rights reflected in the treaty law have crystallised as rules of customary law'.[253] Some provisions found in, *inter alia*, the ICCPR are regarded as reflective of customary law, but the drafters of the Manual reasoned that 'no definitive catalogue of customary international law exists', and that not all states are parties to the same international human rights law treaties; while the rights accorded to individuals under regional human rights instruments and the scope of those rights vary.[254] Commenting specifically on the right to privacy, the experts observed that:

> The right to be free from arbitrary interference with one's privacy is of central importance in the cyber context. The International Group of Experts concluded that the right is of a customary international law character, but cautioned that its precise scope is unsettled and that a number of States that accept the existence of the right take the position that it does not extend extraterritorially [Rule 34]. The Experts further noted that privacy is not an absolute right and may be subject to limitations … They also acknowledged the existence of a view that the right to privacy has not yet crystallised into a customary norm.[255]

In summary, it has been agreed that human rights, including the right to privacy, apply to both the online and offline environments. However, there is no consensus as to the exact legal contours of this right; while substan-

---

systems, it can be concluded that there is a general fundamental right to data privacy under customary international law.' See also Rengel (n 12) at 42, stating that: 'given the recognition of the right to privacy in the most important international treaties, the legal acknowledgement of the right to privacy in the majority of legal systems, and the generalized belief among jurists and scholars of the importance of privacy, it can be concluded that this right has become part and parcel of customary international law.'

[252] International Law Association Committee on the Enforcement of Human Rights Law, 'Final Report on the Status of the Universal Declaration of Human Rights in National and International Law' (Report of the Sixty-Six Conference) (Buenos Aires 1995) 525, 547.

[253] Michael N Schmitt (ed), *Tallinn Manual 2.0 on the International Law Applicable to Cyber Operations* (Cambridge University Press, 2017) para 1, 179 ('*Tallinn Manual 2.0*').

[254] *Ibid* paras 2–3, 179–80.

[255] *Ibid* Rule 35 para 6, 189.

tial differences exist in national traditions in relation to how it is protected and enforced. For these reasons, the status of the right to online privacy in international law must be considered as an emergent rule, which may in time gain customary law status. Until then, the relevant international human rights treaties are the main source of states' obligations both to protect and to respect privacy online. Consequently, a matter that is of importance in this context is whether and how these treaties apply to cyber surveillance – particularly when conducted outside of state borders. This point is addressed in the following chapter.

## 7. CONCLUSION

This chapter has traced the development of privacy as a social concept and as a fundamental legal right, in order to determine whether online privacy has become a rule of customary international law. The right to privacy is enshrined in international human rights treaties and domestic laws, with most countries now providing for its direct or indirect protection through varied routes, including constitutional, common law, statutory and data protection norms, or a combination thereof. Following the 2013 Snowden revelations, a global dialogue ensued, with online privacy finding a prominent place at the UN and within the broader human rights apparatus, prompting the question as to whether it can be said to constitute a customary law rule. This chapter engaged with this issue by applying a doctrinal approach pertaining to the establishment of such rules. The conclusion reached is that although it has gained in prominence and visibility, the right to online privacy has probably not yet crystallized into customary international law rule, for the following reasons. First, the content of this right is broad, while its scope remains undefined. Second, state practice relating to its protection is inconsistent and lacks uniformity: there is considerable variation in the safeguards offered, whilst numerous states have subjugated this right in favour of indiscriminate surveillance. Third, although privacy is not an absolute right, any restrictions must be necessary and proportionate. However, when pressing needs emerge – such as fighting terrorism or deadly global pandemics – these safeguards are readily disregarded and relaxed, causing concerns that this may in time become normalized. Finally, there is a pronounced lack of cohesion in the courts' attitudes to the issue of privacy/surveillance in the digital context, indicating a certain degree of schism in judicial thinking on the subject. For these reasons, online privacy remains an emerging standard, which may yet become a customary law rule that is legally binding on all states. Consequently, any challenge to the legality of mass surveillance programs must necessarily be based on the international human rights treaties that specifically enshrine the right to privacy of communications.

# 4. The principle of non-discrimination and the extraterritorial application of human rights treaties

## 1. INTRODUCTION

Human rights treaties impose binding obligations on those states which choose to accept them by the process of ratification or accession. In becoming parties to these instruments, nations commit themselves to respect and guarantee the rights and freedoms stipulated therein without discrimination to all individuals within their territory and subject to their jurisdiction. In the context of state surveillance, this means that, in principle, those who are the 'victims' of violations of privacy rights are entitled to bring a legal challenge directly in their national courts and seek redress. In addition, provided that all domestic remedies have been exhausted, such a person, a group or a non-governmental organization may issue proceedings before the relevant human rights treaty body or an international judicial organ alleging a breach of stipulated rights.[1]

---

[1] See, *inter alia*, Optional Protocol to the International Covenant on Civil and Political Rights (adopted 16 December 1966, entered into force 23 March 1976) 999 UNTS 171 ('OP1'). Article 1 of the OP1 allows individual communications alleging a violation of the International Covenant on Civil and Political Rights (ICCPR) to be brought to the attention of the Human Rights Committee (HRC) against states parties to the OP1. Communications may be submitted only by individuals who are subject to the jurisdiction of a state party to the OP1 and who claim to be victims of a violation of an ICCPR right by that state. Articles 2 and 5(2)(b) of the OP1 provide that the HRC may consider an individual's communications only once it has ascertained that 'all available domestic remedies' have been exhausted. Similarly, according to Article 35(1) of the European Convention on Human Rights, prior to a victim of violation bringing a claim against the contracting state before the European Court of Human Rights (ECtHR), he or she must first exhaust all domestic remedies – see Council of Europe (CoE), European Convention for the Protection of Human Rights and Fundamental Freedoms amended by Protocols Nos 11 and 14 (4 November 1950) Art 35(1) ('ECHR'). Article 34 of the ECHR allows for individuals to make an application to the ECtHR claiming to be a victim of a state's violation of the Convention rights. The word 'victim' in the context of Article 34 'denotes the person or persons who are directly or indirectly affected by the alleged violation' – see CoE/ECtHR, 'Practical Guide on Admissibility

States may conduct interception of communications; but to prevent abuse, they can do so only with lawful authority derived from a legislative framework circumscribing where this is allowed, which must be compatible with their human rights obligations. As states' practice attests to continued extraterritorial bulk surveillance of communications, this is likely to have a detrimental effect on individuals' human rights across the globe and thus becomes a concern of international law. However, whether this triggers states' obligations to respect and protect privacy rights of persons outside of their borders is not entirely settled. Related to this is the tendency of domestic legislatures towards the adoption of surveillance laws with a distinct asymmetric approach to privacy protection, based on nationality and/or nature of communications, which seems to have been endorsed by the European Court of Human Rights (ECtHR) in its recent jurisprudence. Consequently, greater procedural safeguards are granted to citizens as against foreigners, resulting in different treatment based on nationality and/or location. These matters give rise to two vexatious and contested questions. The first is whether the differential rules on domestic and foreign cyber surveillance violate the fundamental international human rights law principles of equality of treatment and non-discrimination. The second is whether the duty to protect the right to privacy enshrined in the human rights treaties applies to states' extraterritorial surveillance and, if so, on what legal basis.

To engage with these issues, this chapter is divided into four sections. Section 2 analyses the doctrines of non-discrimination and equality of treatment by first outlining the general principles pertaining to these core values, as set out under the international and European legal frameworks, in particular Articles 2(1) and 26 of the International Covenant on Civil and Political Rights (ICCPR), together with Article 14 of the European Convention on Human Rights (ECHR) and Article 1(2) of Protocol 12 to the ECHR. It then highlights the disparity in treatment under selected domestic surveillance legislation, namely the Foreign Intelligence Surveillance Act 1978 (FISA) (as reauthorized) and the UK Regulation of Investigatory Powers Act 2000 (RIPA)/ Investigatory Powers Act 2016 (IPA). The choice of these regulatory regimes stems from these countries' continued dominant role on the Internet and in the global communications sector. It is also dictated by the extent of their intelligence-gathering capabilities, together with the current UK surveillance regime (the IPA) serving as an example of one of the most draconian surveillance laws in the world. The discussion proceeds to evaluate the lawfulness of these statutes *vis-à-vis* the aforementioned international law standards. Section

---

Criteria' (30 April 2020), para 3(a), https://www.echr.coe.int/documents/admissibility _guide_eng.pdf

3 engages with the issue of the applicability of the ICCPR, the ECHR and the American Convention on Human Rights (ACHR) to states' extraterritorial cyber surveillance. Having outlined the principal criterion devised by the judicial organs pertaining to the establishment of extraterritorial jurisdiction – that is, the 'effective control' test – the chapter queries its suitability in the context of mass cyber surveillance. Consequently, it advocates supplementing this standard with one befitting this domain, based on the state's 'control over rights' doctrine. Section 4 summarizes and concludes the discussion.

## 2.   NON-DISCRIMINATION, EQUALITY OF TREATMENT AND DOMESTIC SURVEILLANCE LEGISLATION

Information technology has significantly challenged the right to privacy, increasingly enabling states to conduct mass surveillance at home and abroad. Although state practice attests to signals intelligence collection being frequently undertaken without any specific legal basis, in recent years a number of countries have specifically legislated for the interception of foreign communications on a mass scale, including the UK,[2] France,[3] Germany[4] and Sweden.[5] Further, in 2018, the US reauthorized its foreign surveillance powers, previously under Section 702 of the FISA and now contained in Section 139 of the FISA Amendments Reauthorization Act (FISA ARA), which allows

---

[2]   Investigatory Powers Act 2016 c 25 sets out bulk powers of (1) interception of communications; (2) retention and examination of bulk personal datasets; (3) equipment interference; and (4) communications data collection and retention – see Chapter 2, section 3.2.2–3.2.2.1 ('IPA').

[3]   French Intelligence Act 2015 (Law 2015-912) introduced a chapter on surveillance of international communications, defined in Article L.854-1 as 'communications emitted from or received abroad'. The legislation, colloquially known as the 'Big Brother Act' and enacted in the wake of the 2015 Paris terrorist attacks (including at satirical newspaper *Charlie Hebdo*), paved the way for very intrusive surveillance powers, state approved eavesdropping and computer hacking.

[4]   German Act on the Federal Intelligence Service 2016 ('BND Act'); *1 B v R 2835/17* (Judgment 19 May 2020) ('*1 B v R*').

[5]   Swedish Signals Intelligence Act 2016 (*Lagen om signalspaningiförsvarsunderrättelseverksamhet* (entered into force in 2009 and subsequently amended in 2009, 2013, 2015 and 2016) is discussed in more detail *infra* ('SIA'). Other countries with such laws include India, Israel, Italy, Japan and South Korea – see Ira Rubinstein *et al, Systemic Government Access to Personal Data: A Comparative Analysis*, Center for Democracy and Technology (13 November 2013) in Asaf Lubin, '"We Only Spy on Foreigners": The Myth of a Universal Right to Privacy and the Practice of Foreign Surveillance' (2018) 18(2) *Chicago Journal of International Law* 502–52, 513–14 ('Lubin').

the intelligence community to conduct surveillance of communications of foreigners located outside of the US territory.[6] These laws' common feature is that they offer greater procedural protection to privacy rights of citizens as opposed to non-citizens, or on the basis of the communications being internal or external/overseas in nature.[7] However, from a technological viewpoint, it is very difficult, or even impossible, to classify digital communications along these lines.[8] Two interrelated issues therefore give cause for concern. The first is the lack of the same privacy safeguards as are applicable to citizens when it comes to foreigners whose data is subject to extraterritorial cyber surveillance. The second is the interception and collection of domestic communications performed on the same legal bases as those pertaining to foreigners – for example, pursuant to Section 702 of the FISA/Section 139 of the FISA ARA – with lower procedural protections. This is often referred to as 'incidental collection' and results in the acquisition, on these legal grounds, of the communications of Americans who may interact with foreign targets. Similarly, in the context of UK collection enabled by Section 8(4) of the RIPA/Section 136 of the IPA pertaining to the acquisition of 'external/overseas communications', by the UK government's own admission, the ambit of this type of information may encompass all activities of UK residents conducted through such platforms as Facebook, Twitter and Google, as their headquarters are located in the US.[9] This most likely enables the UK intelligence agencies to intercept communications in and out of the UK indiscriminately. It also means that UK residents may potentially be deprived of the essential legal safeguards that would otherwise apply to them.

These issues therefore likely engage states' obligations of equality of treatment and non-discrimination, both in relation to the lower protection standards applicable to foreigners and in view of the fact that large volumes of domestic communications seem to be routinely 'caught up' in the process of bulk interception and collection of foreign communications.

---

[6] The White House, 'Statement by the President on FISA Amendments Reauthorization Act of 2017' (19 January 2018) ('Statement by the President on FISA ARA').

[7] The UK and the US are by no means the only countries whose surveillance regimes apply substantially lower protection to the interception directed at foreigners. The other Five Eyes partners also make this differentiation – see New Zealand Government Security Bureau Act 2003 s 15A; Australian Intelligence Services Act 2001 s 9; and Canadian National Defence Act 1985 s 273.64(1).

[8] The UK government has acknowledged this in, *inter alia*, UK Home Office, 'Interception of Communications Code of Practice Pursuant to Schedule 7 to the Investigatory Powers Act 2016' (March 2018) para 6.9 ('IPA IC Code of Practice').

[9] *Privacy International v GCHQ*, Witness Statement of Charles Blandford Farr on Behalf of the Respondent (16 May 2014) IPT/13/92/CH paras 36-37 ('Farr').

## 2.1    The Principles of Equality and Non-Discrimination in International Law

The international human rights law regime is built upon the essential postulates of equality of treatment and non-discrimination first proclaimed in Article 2 of the Universal Declaration of Human Rights 1946, according to which:

> Everyone is entitled to all the rights and freedoms set forth in this Declaration without distinction of any kind, such as race, colour, sex, language, religion, political or other opinion, national or social origin, property, birth or other status. Furthermore, no distinction shall be made on the basis of the political, jurisdictional, or international status of the country or territory to which a person belongs, whether it be independent, trust, non-self-governing or under any other limitations of sovereignty.[10]

The recognition that fundamentally all persons, by virtue of their humanity, are equal and should enjoy all human rights without discrimination[11] was subsequently reiterated in Articles 2(1) and 26 of the ICCPR; Articles 1 and 2 of the International Covenant on Economic Social and Cultural Rights 1976 (ICESCR);[12] and Article 14 of the ECHR.

### 2.1.1    The ICCPR

Article 2(1) of the ICCPR obliges states parties to respect and ensure the protection of the rights stipulated therein to all individuals within their territories and subject to their jurisdiction, prohibiting distinction of any kind on the basis of race, colour, gender, language, religion, political or other opinion, national or social origin, property, birth or other status. This obligation is violated where the discrimination concerns a right recognized elsewhere in

---

[10]    Universal Declaration of Human Rights (adopted 10 December 1948) UNGA Res 217 A(III) Art 2(1) ('UDHR').

[11]    The HRC, in General Comment 18, noted that the ICCPR neither defines the term 'discrimination' nor specifies what it constitutes. However, the Comment points out that Article 1 of the International Convention on the Elimination of All Forms of Racial Discrimination 1969 provides that the term 'racial discrimination' means 'any distinction, exclusion, restriction, or preference based on race, colour, descent, or national or ethnic origin, which has the purpose or effect of nullifying or impairing the recognition, enjoyment or exercise, on an equal footing, of human rights and fundamental freedoms in the political, economic, social, cultural or any other field of public life' – see UNHRC, 'CCPR General Comment No. 18: Non-Discrimination' (10 November 1989) UN Doc HRI/GEN/1/Rev.1, para 6 ('General Comment 18').

[12]    UNGA, International Covenant on Economic Social and Cultural Rights (adopted 16 December 1966, entered into force 3 January 1976) 993 UNTS 3 ('ICESCR').

the ICCPR.[13] Additional safeguards are stipulated in Article 26 of the ICCPR, which enshrines the rule of equality and non-discrimination, thus recognizing the basic philosophical and political tenets underpinning the concept of human rights – namely that liberty exists only 'when it is equal for all'.[14] This is reflected in the text of Article 26, which not only entitles all persons to equality before the law and to its equal protection, but also prohibits any discrimination under the law and guarantees to all persons equal and effective protection against such discrimination on a number of grounds, including nationality.[15] Unlike Article 2(1) (which limits the scope of the rights to be protected against discrimination to those provided for in the ICCPR), Article 26 is an autonomous right in that it provides protection against discrimination on any of the enumerated grounds and forbids such discrimination in law or in fact in any field regulated and protected by public authorities.[16] Article 26 is 'therefore concerned with the obligations imposed on States parties in regard to their legislation and the application thereof'.[17] This means that when a state party adopts legislation, it must comply with the requirement of Article 26 that its content not be discriminatory.[18] Consequently, states are required not to discriminate in their laws, 'regardless of whether this has to do with rights protected by the Covenant, other human rights or other legal rights or duties'.[19] The Article 26 obligation is thus directed at the national legislature, which is bound to protect the right to equality without any discrimination.[20] *Novak's Commentary* explains that this obligation has both negative and positive aspects, in that the legislature must refrain from any discrimination when enacting laws and also prohibit discrimination by enacting special laws and afford effective protection against it.[21]

---

[13]    William A Schabas, *U.N. International Covenant on Civil and Political Rights. Novak's CCPR Commentary* (N.P. Engel, 2019) para 48, 55 ('Schabas').

[14]    Cicero, *De re publica* (51 BC) I 47 in *ibid*, 738.

[15]    UNGA, International Covenant on Civil and Political Rights (adopted 16 December 1966, entered into force 23 March 1976) 999 UNTS 999, 171 ('ICCPR'). Article 26 of the ICCPR provides that: 'All persons are equal before the law and are entitled without any discrimination to the equal protection of the law. In this respect, the law shall prohibit any discrimination and guarantee to all persons equal and effective protection against discrimination on any grounds such as race, colour, sex, language, religion, political or other opinion, national or social origin, property, birth or other status.'

[16]    General Comment 18 (n 11) para 12.

[17]    *Ibid*.

[18]    *Ibid*.

[19]    Schabas (n 13) para 9, 742.

[20]    *Ibid* para 21, 749.

[21]    *Ibid*.

It has been observed that Article 26 'runs like a red thread throughout the International Covenant on Civil and Political Rights'. Although this rule is not deemed a non-derogable provision by Article 4(2)[22] of the ICCPR, abrogations from the principles of equality and non-discrimination are extremely rare, with only two countries (Nicaragua and Turkey) purporting to do so.[23] It could therefore be said that Article 26 is fundamentally of a non-derogable nature,[24] which testifies to the foundational importance of the values enshrined therein to the international community as a whole and to international law.

In connection with the Optional Protocol I procedures, the Human Rights Committee (HRC) has established violations of Article 26 mostly on the grounds of sex, political opinion, religion and citizenship/nationality.[25] In the context of bulk surveillance of foreign communications, the latter basis is the most pertinent to the current analysis.

### 2.1.1.1    Grounds of prohibited discrimination – nationality

Nationality has been expressly recognized by the HRC as grounds for discrimination.[26] In General Comment 15, the HRC explained that the ICCPR's rights apply to everyone, irrespective of their nationality and the general rule is that each one of these rights must be guaranteed without discrimination between citizens and aliens.[27] The HRC also stressed that non-citizens are entitled to equal protection by the law and equality before the law.[28] In addition, the ICESCR established that governments shall take progressive measures to the extent of available resources to protect the rights of everyone, regardless of their citizenship.[29] Thus, as a general rule, human rights are presumptively owed to citizens and non-citizens alike. This is, however, qualified by a stipulation that a particular treaty (or customary rule) may in some circumstances allow for differential treatment. Thus, both the ICCPR and the ICESCR permit

---

[22]    Article 4(1) of the ICCPR permits states to take measures derogating from the obligations under the Covenant in time of public emergency, which threatens the life of the nation. Article 4(2) provides that derogations are not permissible from Articles 6, 7, 8 (paragraphs 1 and 2), 11, 15, 16 and 18 of the ICCPR.

[23]    Schabas (n 13) para 10, 742.

[24]    *Ibid.*

[25]    *Ibid* para 25, 751.

[26]    See, for example, *Ibrahima Gueye et al v France* (13 April 1989) UN Doc CCPR/C/35/D/196/195; *Müntaz Karakurt v Austria* (29 April 2002) UN Doc CCPR/C/74/D/965/2000; *Alina Simunek et al v Czech Republic* (19 July 1995) UN Doc CCPR/C/54/D/516/1992.

[27]    UNHRC, 'General Comment No. 15. The Position of Aliens under the Covenant' (1986) UN Doc HRI/Gen/1/Rev.9/(Vol.1) para 1-2 ('General Comment 15').

[28]    *Ibid* paras 2, 7, 9.

[29]    ICESCR (n 12) Art 2.

states to draw distinctions between citizens and non-citizens, but only with respect to political rights, freedom of movement and economic rights in developing countries. It follows that under Article 25 of the ICCPR, the entitlement to participate in public affairs, to vote, to hold office and to have access to public services is guaranteed to citizens only.[30] Similarly, Article 12(4) of the ICCPR provides that no one shall be arbitrarily deprived of the right to enter his or her own country;[31] while Article 2(3) of the ICESCR allows developing counties to 'determine to what extent they would guarantee the economic rights recognized in the present Covenant to non-nationals'.[32] States therefore may not draw a distinction between citizens and non-citizens as to social and cultural rights, with the exception of the right to public participation and that of freedom of movement. Having said that, international law, as well as state practice, consistently sanctions distinctions on the basis of nationality, which means that some discrimination on these grounds is permissible.[33] The HRC in its General Comment 18 clarified this, stating that 'the enjoyment of rights and freedoms on an equal footing ... does not mean identical treatment in every instance'.[34] Indeed, the HRC confirmed that 'not every differentiation of treatment will constitute discrimination, if the criteria for such a differentiation are reasonable and objective and if the aim is to achieve a purpose, which is legitimate under the Covenant'.[35] In relation to the latter point, *Novak's Commentary* explains that:

> what is considered reasonable... depends on the specific circumstances, the general situation in the country concerned (including its cultural and religious background, specific social traditions and customs), the sometimes rapidly changing social values and moral standards in modern societies ... and personal convictions of those applying the test to the facts in often highly controversial cases.[36]

In short, the prohibition of non-discrimination under Article 2(1) of the ICCPR means that states cannot, as a matter of principle, differentiate in ensuring the rights under the Covenant. In addition, Article 26 of the ICCPR creates an autonomous right to guarantee equality before the law and equal protection of the law, including in relation to legislative provisions with a discriminatory impact on other human rights. However, not all differentiation in treatment will be considered as prohibited discrimination. Different treatment is permis-

---

[30]  ICCPR (n 15) Art 25.
[31]  *Ibid* Art 12(4).
[32]  ICESCR (n 12) Art 2(3).
[33]  General Comment 15 (n 27) paras 23–30.
[34]  General Comment 18 (n 11) para 8.
[35]  *Ibid* para 13.
[36]  Schabas (n 13) para 22, 750.

sible where it is based on reasonable and objective criteria[37] and in pursuit of an aim that is legitimate under the ICCPR.[38]

### 2.1.2   The ECHR

As a general rule, Article 14 of the ECHR guarantees the enjoyment of Convention rights without discrimination on any grounds, such as gender, race, colour, language, religion, political or other opinion, national or social origin, association with a national minority, property, birth or other status. This principle is accompanied by Article 1(2) of Protocol No 12 to the ECHR, which extends its application to public authorities.[39] According to the case law of the European Court of Human Rights, Article 14 merely complements the other substantive provisions of the ECHR,[40] meaning that it does not prohibit discrimination as such, but only discrimination in the enjoyment of the 'rights and freedoms set forth in the Convention'.[41] It follows that the guarantee provided by Article 14 has no independent existence[42] and forms an integral part of each of the Convention articles laying down the rights and freedoms.[43] In practice, the ECtHR always examines Article 14 in conjunction with other substantive Convention rights.[44] However, the applicability of Article 14 is not necessarily dependent on the existence of a violation of the substantive provision guaranteed by the ECHR, and this the ECtHR has recognized even

---

[37]   See, for example, *Broeks v the Netherlands* (1 June 1984) UN Doc CCPR/C/ OP/2, para 13; *Zwaan-de Vries v the Netherlands* (9 April 1987) UN Doc CCPR/ C/29/D/182/1984 para 13; *Vos v the Netherlands* (29 March 1989) UN Doc CCPR/ C/35/D/218/1986 para 11.3; *Dietmar Pauger v Austria* (29 March 1992) UN Doc CCPR/C/44/D/415 para 7.3.

[38]   *G v Australia* (2 December 2011) UN Doc CCPR/C/119/D/2172/2012 para 7.2; *O'Neill et al v Ireland* (24 July 2006) UN Doc CCPR/C/87/D/1314/2004 para 8.3; General Comment 18 (n 11) para 8.

[39]   Protocol No 12 to the Convention for the Protection of Human Rights and Fundamental Freedoms (4 November 2000) ETS 177 (opened for signature on 4 November and entered into force on 1 April 2005).

[40]   See, for example, *Molla Sali v Greece* [GC] App no 20452/14 (2018) para 123; *Carson and Others v the United Kingdom* [GC] App no 42184/05 (2010) para 63; *EB v France* [GC] App no 43546/02 (2008) para 47.

[41]   CoE, *Guide on Article 14 of the European Convention on Human Rights and on Article 1 of the Protocol No. 12 to the Convention. Prohibition of Discrimination* (31 December 2019) 6 ('CoE *Guide on Article 14*').

[42]   *Case 'relating to certain aspects of the laws on the use of languages in education in Belgium' v Belgium* ('*Belgium Linguistic Case*') App no 1474/62 (1968) para 9; *Carson* (n 40) para 63; *EB v France* (n 40) para 47.

[43]   *Belgian Linguistic Case*, *ibid* para 9; *Marckx v Belgium* App no 6833/74 (1979) para 32.

[44]   CoE *Guide on Article 14* (n 41) 50.

in cases where there has been no violation of the substantive right itself.[45] Therefore, for Article 14 to be applicable, it is necessary that the facts of the case fall within the broader ambit of one or more of the ECHR's provisions. As a consequence, a sizeable body of jurisprudence based on the large number of grounds of prohibited discrimination set out in Article 14 of the ECHR and Article 1 of Protocol No 12 has arisen, with the ECtHR applying the former provision to a broad spectrum of divergent areas, ranging from employment[46] and social security[47] to freedom of expression, assembly and association,[48] together with eligibility for tax relief.[49]

In similar vein to the ICCPR, the ECHR regime recognizes that not all differences in treatment are unlawful and therefore that some discrimination is allowed. To that end, a number of exceptions to the non-discrimination provisions set out in Article 14 and Article 1 of Protocol No 12 have been made, including in cases of qualified rights where discrimination may be allowed because the needs of society may be at stake.[50] It follows that since not all differences in treatment constitute discrimination, the ECtHR will have to determine whether the treatment in question amounts to discrimination under Article 14. This the ECtHR does by applying a two-stage test. It first asks whether there has been a difference in treatment of persons in similar situa-

---

[45]   *Sommerfeld v Germany* [GC] App no 31871/96 (2003); *Marckx* (n 43); *Belgium Linguistic Case* (n 42) para 4.

[46]   *Bigaeva v Greece* App no 26713/05 (2009).

[47]   *Andrejeva v Latvia* [GC] App no 55707/00 (2009); *Gaygusuz v Austria* App no 17371/90 (1996); *Koua Poirrez v France* App 40892/98 (2003); *Stummer v Austria* App no 37452/02 (2011).

[48]   *Bączkowski and Others v Poland* App no 1543/06 (2007).

[49]   *Guberina v Croatia* App no 23682/13 (2016).

[50]   Other circumstances which form the basis for the exception to Article 14 include: (1) Article 57 of the ECHR, which allows states to 'make a reservation in respect of any particular provision of the Convention'; and (2) Article 15, which allows states to take measures derogating from their obligations under the ECHR, that may only be taken to the 'extent strictly required by the exigencies of the situation' and may not be taken against Articles 2, 3, 4(1) and 7 of the ECHR, or rights under Protocol No 6 and Protocol No 13 – see Hélène Lambert, 'The Position of Aliens in Relation to the European Convention on Human Rights' (2007) CoE, *Council of Europe Human Rights Files* No 8.

tions,[51] which may occur in the form of direct[52] or indirect discrimination.[53] In relation to this criterion, the ECtHR has acknowledged that the source of the treatment may be based, *inter alia*, on domestic legislation.[54] Second, if a difference is found, the ECtHR will then consider whether it can be objectively and reasonably justified.[55] This part of the assessment requires the state to show that the treatment in question pursues a legitimate aim, and that there is a reasonable relationship of proportionality between the means employed and the aims sought to be realized.[56] In relation to the former requirement, the ECtHR has recognized a number of bases to be considered as constituting a legitimate aim for the state's adoption of a particular measure,[57] including the protection of national security.[58] Having established that a legitimate basis exists, the ECtHR will then examine whether the difference in treatment strikes a fair balance between the protection of the interests of the community and respect for the rights and freedoms of the individual (the proportionality requirement).[59] In considering this latter criterion, the ECtHR has recognized that states have a margin of appreciation in assessing whether and to what

---

[51]   For examples of different treatment, see *Varnas v Lithuania* App no 42616/06 (2013); *Cusan and Fazzo v Italy* App no 77/07 (2014); *Fabris v France* [GC] App no 16574/08 (2011).

[52]   The notion of direct discrimination is not defined in Article 14 of the ECHR. However, in *Biao v Denmark* [GC] App no 38590/10 (2016) at para 80, the ECtHR described it as 'a difference in treatment of persons in analogous, or relatively similar, situations'. See, for example, *Ēcis v Latvia* App no 12879/09 (2019); *Bączkowski* (n 48).

[53]   Indirect discrimination may be a result of a policy or measure which, although couched in neutral terms, has a discriminatory effect on a particular group (*Biao ibid*, para 81; *DH and Others v the Czech Republic* [GC] App no 57325/00 (2007) para 187; *Sampanis and Others v Greece* App no 32526/05 (2008) para 67).

[54]   *Ēcis* (n 52). The source of the difference in treatment was also found to originate from the vocabulary used by a national court to motivate its decision (*Carvalho Pinto de Sousa Morais v Portugal* App no 17484/15 (2017)) and a purely private action (*Identoba and Others v Georgia* App no 73235 (2015)).

[55]   *Molla Sali* (n 40) para 135; *Fabris* (n 51) para 56; *DH v the Czech Republic* (n 53) para 175; *Hoogendijk v the Netherlands* App no 58641/00 (2005).

[56]   *Molla Sali ibid* para 135; *Fábián v Hungary* [GC] App no 78117/13 (2017) para 113; *Abdulaziz Cabalez and Balkanali v the United Kingdom* App nos 9214/80; 9473/81; 9474/81 (1985) para 72; *Belgium Linguistic Case* (n 42) para 10.

[57]   Other aims that the ECtHR has identified include achieving the effective implementation of policy developing linguistic unity (*Belgian Linguistic Case ibid*); legal certainty of completed inheritance arrangements (*Fabris* (n 51)); and restoration of peace ((*Sejdic and Finci v Bosnia and Herzegovina* [GC] App nos 27996/06 and 34836/06 (2009)) – see CoE *Guide on Article 14* (n 41) 17–18.

[58]   *Konstantin Markin v Russia* [GC] App no 30078/06 (2012) para 137.

[59]   *Belgian Linguistic Case* (n 42) para 10.

extent differences in otherwise similar situations justify different treatment.[60] This will depend on the circumstances, the subject matter and the background of the case.[61] The rationale for the ECtHR allowing for such discretion is based on its acceptance that national authorities are better placed than international judges to determine the appropriateness of a particular measure, as they can better ascertain what is in the public interest stemming from the knowledge of their society's needs.

Three key points summarize the above discussion. First, in essence, international human rights treaties are founded on the principles of equality and non-discrimination, which apply to all individuals, nationals and aliens alike. These postulates extend to states' obligations in regard to their legislation and its application. Second, international law does not mandate absolute equality or identical treatment in every situation. In certain circumstances, differential treatment between nationals and aliens is allowed, but it must pursue a legitimate aim (ie, it must have an objective and reasonable justification), and a reasonable relationship of proportionality must exist between the aims sought and the means employed. Third, states do enjoy a margin of appreciation in determining whether and to what extent differences in similar situations justify differential treatment.

## 2.2    Domestic Surveillance Regimes

### 2.2.1    The US

One country which has always held a robust position regarding the issue of the extent of its human rights obligations is the US. According to the well-entrenched view rooted in the social contract theory,[62] US citizens are entitled to constitutional rights, whereas non-citizens/residents simply are not. As noted by Professor Marko Milanovic, this citizenship-orientated approach 'stems from the conception of governments as having legitimacy because of the consent of the governed, which triggers rights and obligations to and from

---

[60]    *Burden v United Kingdom* [GC] App no 13378/05 (2008) para 60.

[61]    *Molla Sali* (n 40) para 136; *Stummer* (n 47) para 88; *Burden ibid*, para 60; *Carson* (n 40) para 61.

[62]    Rooted in seventeenth century political philosophy, the social contract theory underpins the legitimacy of the state over the individual. It 'purports to define the terms on which [the] society is to be governed: the people have made a contract with their ruler which determines their relations with him. They promise him obedience, while he promises his protection and good government. While he keeps his part of the bargain, they must keep theirs, but if he misgoverns the contract is broken and allegiance is at an end' – see JW Gough, *The Social Contract* (Clarendon Press 1936) 2–3; see also Thomas Hobbs, *Leviathan* (Oxford University Press, Reissue edition, 2008).

its citizens and those in its territorial borders'.[63] What underpins this notion is a long-standing tradition in American legal thought, which perceives the US Constitution as such a social contract, binding only between the American people and the state.[64] It is thus the source of both the guarantees of human rights to US citizens and the limitations on the government's powers.[65] As noted in Chapter 3, it is predominantly the Fourth Amendment to the US Constitution that affords protection to US citizens by prohibiting government agencies from conducting warrantless searches and seizures. It was affirmed by the US Supreme Court in *United States v Verdugo-Urquidez*[66] that these guarantees apply only to US citizens. The case concerned a warrantless search by US law enforcement agents of Mexican property owned by a Mexican defendant on trial in the US, who objected to the thus obtained evidence. Having rejected his complaint, the Supreme Court held that the Fourth Amendment was intended to protect only US citizens – that is, those persons 'who are part of the national community or who have otherwise developed sufficient connection with this country to be considered part of that community'.[67]

The US surveillance regime authorizing foreign communications' interception echoes this approach, as it is premised on the principle that those individuals who are protected against untargeted surveillance are only US citizens and non-US citizens located within the US territory. Non-citizens and Americans outside the US borders at the time of the surveillance do not benefit from the Fourth Amendment guarantees. Thus, the basis for making the so-called PRISM and Upstream collection orders is Section 702 of the FISA,[68] as reauthorized. In a nutshell, Section 702 approves the domestic interception of foreigners' communications when the subjects of the interception are believed to be outside of the US[69] and permits their targeting without the need to obtain a detailed court order specifying the person or place to be intercepted.[70] Section

---

[63]   Marko Milanovic, 'Human Rights Treaties and Foreign Surveillance: Privacy in the Digital Age' (2015) 56(1) *Harvard International Law Journal* 81, 89 ('Milanovic').

[64]   *Ibid.*

[65]   US Constitution (17 April 1787).

[66]   *United States v Verdugo-Urquidez* 494, US 259 (1990).

[67]   *Ibid*, Chief Justice William Rehnquist.

[68]   US Office of the Director of National Intelligence, 'The FISA Amendment Act: Q&A' (17 April 2017) 9 www.dni.gov/files/icotr/FISA%20Amendments%20Act%20QA%20for%20Publication.pdf ('FISA AA: Q&A'). The document states that: 'For most Section 702 collection, the government acquires data from the company providing the electronic communication service to the user. Some of NSA's Section 702 collection, however, has been obtained via "upstream" collection, in which the NSA obtains communications directly from the Internet backbone ...'

[69]   50 US Code §1881a(a).

[70]   50 US Code §1881a(h).

702 allows for joint authorization to target foreign persons to be made by the Attorney General (AG) and the Director of National Intelligence (DNI). Thus authorized, the surveillance may last for a period of up to one year.[71] The acquisition is conducted pursuant to a Foreign Intelligence Surveillance Court (FISC) order approving the certification and accompanying targeting and minimization procedures. However, unlike in the case of 'traditional FISA' authorization (outlined below), instead of issuing individual court orders, the FISC approves annual certifications submitted by the AG and the DNI that set out categories of foreign intelligence information that the government is authorized to acquire on the basis of Section 702.[72] Once the FISC has approved the certification, the AG and DNI can compel electronic communications service providers to assist the intelligence community's collection in relation to the authorized Section 702 targets.[73] The statute does stipulate a number of limitations pertaining to the interception. However, these are mainly aimed at the protection of the constitutional rights of US citizens, including the prohibition from intentionally targeting any person known at the time of the acquisition to be located in the US[74] and any US person reasonably believed to be located outside the US.[75] The targeting and minimization procedures impose additional limitations aimed at protecting US citizens.[76] Thus, the former require the AG and the DNI to ensure that any authorized acquisition is limited to targeting persons reasonably believed to be located outside the US[77] and to 'prevent the intentional acquisition of any communication as to which the sender and all intended recipients are known at the time of the acquisition to be located in the United States'.[78] The latter aim to protect US persons' communications from 'incidental' acquisition of the information when the target of the interception communicates with a US person.[79] The purpose of targeting persons located outside the US set out in Section 702 is to 'acquire foreign intelligence information'.[80] However, this concept, as noted by the Council of Europe's (CoE) Commissioner for Human Rights, is sweepingly defined, as it includes any 'information with respect to a foreign power ... that relates to ... the

---

[71]　50 US Code §1881a(a).
[72]　FISA AA: Q&A (n 68).
[73]　*Ibid.*
[74]　50 US Code §1881a(b)(1).
[75]　*Ibid* §1881a(b)(3).
[76]　*Ibid* §1881a(c)(1)(A)-(B).
[77]　*Ibid* §1881a(d)(1)(A).
[78]　*Ibid* §1881a(d)(1)(B).
[79]　*Ibid* §1881a(e); FISA AA: Q&A (n 68).
[80]　*Ibid* §1801(e).

conduct of the foreign affairs of the United States'.[81] The term 'foreign power', according to the same paragraph, comprises, *inter alia*, a foreign government, a foreign entity or political organization, or a group engaged in terrorism.[82] Thus formulated, the concept subsumes within its ambit any 'foreign-based political organization', including political entities associated with the state (eg, political parties) and any politically active non-governmental organizations.[83] Arguably, therefore, the statute provides the legal basis in the US to conduct purely political surveillance on foreigners' data accessible in US clouds, together with economic espionage, as these authorizations are subject to very limited review by the FISC.[84] In any case, the FISC operates in secret and the review of Section 702 orders is primarily focused on a verification that not too much information on 'US persons' is incidentally obtained thereunder.[85]

The procedures for targeting individuals outside the US and non-US persons can be contrasted with so-called 'traditional FISA' orders under Title I, which require the filing of a detailed application asking the FSIC to authorize the electronic surveillance of domestic communications.[86] According to these standards, electronic surveillance will be approved only if the application is made in writing upon oath or affirmation to a judge and approved by the AG as meeting the stated requirements.[87] These include the identification (if known) or description of the specific target of the electronic surveillance.[88] In addition, the application must demonstrate probable cause that the target of surveillance is 'a foreign power or an agent of a foreign power',[89] and that a significant purpose of the surveillance is to obtain 'foreign intelligence information'.[90] Furthermore, it must contain 'a description of the nature of the information sought and the type of communications, or activities to be subjected to the surveillance'.[91] It must also confirm that appropriate 'minimization procedures are in place'.[92] If the FISC is satisfied that there is a probable cause and that the government's proposed collection methods and minimization procedures adequately protect US persons' information acquired during the collection,

---

[81]   CoE Commissioner for Human Rights, 'The Rule of Law on The Internet and in the Wider Digital World' (December 2014) 49 ('CoE *The Rule of Law*').
[82]   50 US Code § 1801(a).
[83]   *Ibid.*
[84]   *Ibid.*
[85]   *Ibid.*
[86]   50 US Code § 1804.
[87]   *Ibid* § 1804(a).
[88]   *Ibid* § 1804(a)(2).
[89]   *Ibid* § 1804(a)(3)(A).
[90]   *Ibid* § 1804(a)(6)(B).
[91]   *Ibid* § 1804(a)(5).
[92]   *Ibid* § 1804(a)(4).

then it may grant the authorization to conduct the electronic surveillance. Thus, unlike Section 702 authorization, one of the critical aspects of this type of surveillance is the government's satisfying the requirement that there be some level of probable involvement in a criminal activity if a US person is suspected to be an agent of a foreign power.

Although intended for the domestic interception of foreign communications, Section 702 has purportedly been used to monitor, collect and search US citizens' communications for terrorist or other criminal activities. According to civil liberties groups, legal analysts, members of Congress and media accounts, the National Security Agency (NSA) is notorious for the collection of domestic communications on the basis of Section 702 unrelated to foreign intelligence.[93] Reportedly, in 2014 'the NSA was collecting far more data on ordinary Internet users than on legally targeting foreigners'.[94] Acting on these legal grounds, the US government is allegedly able to amass, without showing probable cause, great volumes of information pertaining to US citizens[95] and aliens alike. Section 702 was due to expire on 31 December 2017 unless the US Congress passed legislation extending its sunset provisions. The provision was reauthorized in 2018, despite the controversy associated with incidental collection and criticisms voiced by members of the judiciary, technology companies and numerous privacy and civil liberties groups.[96] The new Section 139

---

[93]  See, for example, Thorsten Wetzling and Kilian Vieth, *Upping the Ante on Bulk Surveillance. An International Compendium of Good Legal Safeguards and Oversight Innovations* (Heirich Böll Stiflung Publication Series on Democracy, 2018), reporting at p 20 that in 2018, Section 702 had more than 100 000 designated targets, which were not just limited to terrorists, but also foreigners whose communications might relate to the conduct of US foreign affairs, including diplomats and officials from friendly nations. The document notes that 'the implications of this are profound as section 702 can monitor innocent foreigners and in the process, may sweep up communications of the average Americans they are talking to' ('*Upping the Ante*'); see also Laura K Donohue, 'The Case for Reforming Section 702 of U.S. Foreign Intelligence Surveillance Law' (26 June 2017) *Council on Foreign Relations*; Electronic Frontier Foundation, 'Decoding 702: What is Section 702?', www.eff.org/ 702-spying ('Donohue').

[94]  Donohue, *ibid.*

[95]  *Ibid.* This has raised concerns in relation to, *inter alia*, the violation of Fourth and Fifth Amendment rights, together with posing a risk of the executive branch using Section 702 to monitor political opposition.

[96]  See US House Committee on the Judiciary, Chairman Jerrold Nadler, 'Fact Sheet: s. 139, FISA Amendments Reauthorization Act' (10 January 2018), https:// judiciary.house.gov/news/documentsingle.aspx?DocumentID=221.

of the 2017 FISA ARA, due to lapse in 2023, was endorsed by the former US President Donald Trump, who commented that:

> in order to detect and prevent attacks before they happen, we must be able to intercept communications of foreign targets who are reasonably believed to possess foreign intelligence information. Section 702 provides the necessary authority, and it has proven to be among the Nation's most effective foreign intelligence tools. It has enabled our Intelligence Community to disrupt numerous plots against our citizens at home and our war fighters abroad, and it has unquestionably saved American lives. The act ... preserves and extends this critically important national security tool.[97]

In summary, there are a number of important differences between the 'traditional FISA' authorized collection of communications and that pursuant to Section 702. The latter permits state agencies to target foreigners located outside of the US borders for the purposes of acquiring foreign intelligence information on the basis of generalized orders. In contrast to 'traditional FISA' surveillance, Section 702 does not require the government to obtain an order which specifies the person or place that it intends to place under surveillance. Instead, the statute allows the US AG and DNI to jointly authorize the targeting of foreigners abroad on the basis of FISC-approved annual certifications. The oversight regime pertaining to this type of targeting aims to protect the constitutional rights and privacy of US persons whose communications may be incidentally acquired during the process. Thus, it can be said that the US surveillance regime is based on a legislative asymmetry. Commenting on this disparity, Professor Milanovic observed that:

> for FISA's drafters ... the physical presence of an individual on U.S. territory, and his or her citizenship or residence status were criteria of categorical normative relevance with regard to enjoyment of the right to privacy. For the Supreme Court in *Verdugo-Urquidez*, a citizen is entitled to privacy no matter where he is located, but the same does not apply for an alien.[98]

Put succinctly, US persons benefit from the protection of the Fourth Amendment to the US Constitution, while foreigners are treated as 'fair game'.[99] This status quo not only constitutes different treatment on the basis of nationality, but also seems to provide the government with a tool to acquire large volumes of US citizens' communications on the basis of much-reduced procedural safeguards, through the process of so-called 'incidental collection'.

---

[97] Statement by the President on FISA ARA (n 6).
[98] Milanovic (n 63) 89.
[99] CoE, 'Mass Surveillance. Who is Watching the Watchers', Report Doc 13734 (18 March 2015) 45 ('CoE Mass Surveillance Report').

## 2.2.2 The UK

The IPA likewise distinguishes between different categories of interception based on the nature of communications. An example of such a variance is the regime pertaining to the interception of communications issued under Part 2 (targeted interception warrants) and Chapter 1 of Part 6 (bulk interception warrants) of that statute. The IPA Interception of Communications Code of Practice explains the distinction between targeted and bulk interception. It states that 'bulk interception is a strategic intelligence gathering capability, whereas targeted interception is primarily an investigative tool that is used once a particular subject for surveillance has been identified'.[100] Thus, the latter form of surveillance, operated within the UK, may be conducted only on the basis of targeted warrants, which are authorized if a detailed description in relation to whom or what is the subject of the interception is provided in order to aid the proper assessment of the necessity, proportionality and level of intrusion with privacy involved in the intelligence gathering.[101] In contrast, overseas communications[102] may be intercepted on the basis of bulk interception warrants,[103] with no obligation to name or describe the person, organization or set of premises in relation to which the interception is to take place.[104]

---

[100] IPA IC Code of Practice (n 8) para 6.8, 22.

[101] IPA (n 2) Part 2 Chapter 1; IPA IC Code of Practice (n 8) paras 4.1–4.17, 17–21.

[102] The distinction between internal and external communications under the RIPA 2000 was reiterated in the IPA s 136(3), which defines 'overseas communications' as (1) communications sent by individuals who are outside of the British Islands, or (2) communications received by individuals who are outside of the British Islands.

[103] The IPA IC Code of Practice (n 8) explains at para 2.21 that the purpose of defining 'overseas communications' is to 'ensure that bulk interception warrants are foreign focused and cannot have as their main purpose the interception of communications sent between individuals in the British Islands'.

[104] IPA (n 2) Part 6 Chapter 1; IPA IC Code of Practice para 6.8. The Code specifies that such warrants must provide the following general information: (1) the background to the application for a bulk warrant; (2) a description of the communications to be intercepted, including details of any telecommunications operator that may be required to assist in the operation; (3) a description of the conduct to be authorized, which must be restricted to the interception of overseas-related communications; (4) the operational purposes for which the content may be selected for examination; (5) a consideration of whether the intercepted content may be made available to any other security/intelligence agency; (6) an explanation as to why the conduct is considered necessary and proportionate for one or more of the statutory purposes; (7) an assurance that material obtained under the warrant will be selected for examination only so far as it is necessary for the specified operational purposes; and (8) an assurance that all content and intercepted data will be retained for no longer than necessary – see IPA IC Code of Practice (n 8) para 6.20, 67–58.

The Interception of Communications Code of Practice to the IPA clarifies the circumstances for the lawful issuance of such a warrant, stating that:

> A bulk interception warrant may only be issued to the intelligence services and must meet two conditions. The first is that its main purpose must be limited to the interception of overseas-related communications and/or the obtaining of secondary data from such communications. Overseas related communications are defined at section 136(3) of the Act as those that are sent or received by individuals outside the British Islands. This condition prevents the issue of a bulk interception warrant with the primary purpose of intercepting communications between people in the British Islands. The second condition is that the warrant authorises ... the person to whom it is addressed [to] intercept communications described in the warrant, to obtain secondary data from such communications, to select for examination the intercepted content or secondary data, or the disclosure of anything obtained under the warrant.[105]

The bulk warrant must specify the operational purposes[106] for which any intercepted conduct or secondary data obtained under it may be selected for examination.[107] However, the Act does not impose a limit on the number of communications which may be intercepted. Furthermore, according to the Code, if the requirements for issuing such a warrant are met, then 'the interception of all communications transmitted on a particular route or cable, or carried by a particular telecommunications operator, could, in principle be lawfully authorized'.[108] As a consequence, the communications of UK nationals may also be intercepted on this legal basis. This has been recognised by the UK government, as the Code concedes that:

> Due to the global nature of the internet, the route a particular communication will take is hugely unpredictable. This means that a bulk interception warrant may intercept communications between individuals in the British Islands. Section 136(5) of the Act makes clear that a bulk interception warrant authorises the interception of communications that are not overseas-related to the extent this is necessary in order to intercept the overseas-related communications to which the warrant relates.[109]

The document thus acknowledges that interception on the basis of a bulk warrant could result in the collection of large volumes of communications and/or data, because such intelligence gathering may encompass all communica-

---

[105]   IPA IC Code of Practice *ibid* paras 6.1 and 6.2, 54.
[106]   IPA (n 2) s 142(4).
[107]   *Ibid* s 143(3); IPA IC Code of Practice (n 8) para 6.14.
[108]   IPA IC Code of Practice *ibid* para 6.8, 22.
[109]   *Ibid* para 6.9, 55.

tions transmitted on a particular route or cable, or carried out by a particular operator.[110]

What transpires from the above discussion can be encapsulated in three main points. First, varied levels of privacy protection are applied, depending on nationality/nature of communications, resulting in different treatment of citizens and aliens. This is exemplified by the UK and the US surveillance regimes, although these are not isolated instances of such differentiation. Second, digital communications of foreigners and citizens are often collected on the legal basis designed for foreigners'/overseas communications. Third, as a consequence of this, both citizens and aliens are likely to be deprived of more stringent procedural guarantees against arbitrary interference with the right to privacy.

## 2.3    Domestic Surveillance Laws and the Principles of Equality and Non-discrimination – an Evaluation

States are obliged to ensure that measures taken in the struggle against terrorism do not discriminate in purpose or effect on grounds of nationality. Furthermore, the principle of non-discrimination must be observed in all matters – in particular, those concerning liberty, security and dignity of the person, equality before the courts and due process of law, as well as international cooperation in judicial and police matters.[111]

The surveillance legislation outlined above facilitates the continued efforts to combat terrorism and serious crime that most communities now face. However, these frameworks are *prima facie* discriminatory, as they provide for different treatment on the grounds of nationality or location. Whether this difference in treatment constitutes a violation of the principles of non-discrimination and equality of treatment depends on it being justified on the grounds of legitimate aim and proportionality, as discussed next.

### 2.3.1    Legitimate aim
The relevant UK and US surveillance laws appear to satisfy the requirement of legitimate aim, as they seek to protect national security. That national authorities may in principle conduct extraterritorial (or strategic) surveillance to further such objectives has been recognized by the ECtHR in, *inter alia*, *Weber v Germany*, and more recently in the *Big Brother Watch v UK* and

---

[110]    *Ibid* para 6.7, 55.

[111]    UNCHR (Sub-Commission), 'Report by Special Rapporteur David Weissbrodt' (2003) UN Doc E/CN.4/Sub.2/2003/23 para 28.

*Centrum För Rättvisa v Sweden* cases (as discussed in more detail below and in Chapters 5 and 6).

Some domestic courts have also engaged with the issue of extraterritorial surveillance as a means of furthering national security goals and its impact on foreigners' right to privacy. A case in point is the 2020 decision of the German Federal Constitutional Court in the *1 B v R*[112] case. It will be recalled[113] that the legal challenge to the Federal Intelligence Service's (BND) surveillance pursuant to the BND Act 2016 was based on, *inter alia*, the breach of the right to privacy set out in the German Constitution. The case focused on three issues: (1) the BND's collection, storage and analysis of data in the context of foreign communications surveillance; (2) the transfer of data thus obtained to other entities; and (3) cooperation with foreign intelligence services.[114] A significant point for the purposes of the present discussion is that the Constitutional Court has in principle approved strategic communications surveillance conducted by Germany in other countries, stating that this form of interception as a 'a special tool for gathering foreign intelligence is in principle compatible with article 10(1)' of the Basic Law (GG).[115] The powers to do so, the Court stated, derive from Germany's legislative competence for 'foreign affairs' pursuant to Article 73(1) no 1 of the GG.[116] This competence confers on the BND the task of providing the government with intelligence not only to prepare for genuine political decision making, but also to detect any dangerous developments originating from abroad.[117] Importantly, however, the Court held for the first time that the constitutional safeguards against the German state's surveillance are not restricted to that country's territory, but that the right to privacy stipulated in the GG also extends beyond its borders to foreigners subject to its interception. To that end, the Court held that:

> under Article 1(3) GG German State authority is bound by the fundamental rights of the Basic Law not only within the German territory. At least Art. 10(1) and Art. 5(1)

---

[112] *1 B v R* (n 4). See also *amaBhungane Centre for Investigative Journalism v Minister of Justice and Correctional Services* [2019] ZAGPPHC 384. In this landmark decision, the High Court of South Africa held that secret, unregulated mass surveillance was unlawful, as it lacked a legal basis and therefore was unconstitutional.

[113] See Chapter 3 *supra*, section 4.3.1.1.

[114] Press Release No 37/2020, 'In Their Current Form, Surveillance Powers of the Federal Intelligence Service Regarding Foreign Telecommunications Violate Fundamental Rights of the Basic Law' (19 May 2020) ('*1 B v R* Press Release'), www .bundesverfassungsgericht.de/SharedDocs/Pressemitteilungen/EN/2020/bvg20-037 .html.

[115] *Ibid* para III(1).

[116] *Ibid* para II(1).

[117] *Ibid*.

second sentence GG, which afford protection against telecommunications surveillance as rights against State interference, also protect foreigners in other countries. This applies irrespective of whether surveillance is conducted from within Germany or from abroad ...[118]

Having outlined the aims of the Basic Law – namely comprehensive protection of human rights and placing the individual at the centre of such protection – the Court found that: 'fundamental rights as rights of an individual ought to provide protection whenever the German State acts and thus [the Basic Law] potentially creates a need for protection-irrespective of where, towards whom and in what manner it does so.'[119] In the Court's view, such applicability of fundamental rights even in relation to foreigners in other countries reflects Germany's participation in the international community.[120] As a consequence, the fact that the legislature, in drafting the BND Act 2016, assumed that German state authorities are not bound by the Basic Law in relation to the protection of rights against interference with the privacy of foreigners abroad renders the statute unconstitutional, necessitating its amendment in particular to reflect the requirements of the principle of proportionality. The Court thus concluded that the BND Act 2016 applies provisionally and only until 31 December 2021.[121]

This is an important development, as it clearly upholds the principle of non-discrimination and equality. It also represents rare judicial discontent with the legislature's failure to recognize that foreigners abroad deserve protection when a state engages in activities that may affect their human rights, even where they pursue a legitimate aim. Furthermore, the case supports the view that in the context of bulk interception of foreign communications, states' obligations are not restricted purely to their territories. As such, it calls into question the validity of other countries' legislation based on different treatment – the UK IPA being a case in point. Serious doubts pertaining to the lawfulness of the UK and US regimes in the context of discrimination and equality before the law had been expressed in international human rights forums on a number of occasions prior to this landmark ruling. Thus, the CoE Commissioner for Human Rights in its 2014 report emphasized that the universal application of human rights guarantees in the ECHR and the ICCPR has been consistently affirmed by the ECtHR and the HRC,[122] but that the US has failed to ensure that its FISA Section 702 surveillance regime complies with its ICCPR obli-

---

[118] *Ibid* para 2.
[119] *Ibid* para I(1).
[120] *Ibid*.
[121] *Ibid* para VII.
[122] CoE *The Rule of Law* (n 81) 48.

gations or international human rights law generally.[123] Furthermore, the HRC, in its 2015 Periodic Report on the UK, commenting on that country's surveillance powers under the then RIPA, stated that: 'there shall be no discrimination between aliens and citizens in the application of these rights.'[124] The HRC was quite critical of the discriminatory nature of that law, reminding the UK of its obligations under Article 17 of the ICCPR and stating that:

> The Regulation of Investigatory Powers Act 2000, which makes a distinction between "internal" and "external" communications, provides for untargeted warrants for the interception of external private communications and communications data that are sent or received outside the United Kingdom without affording the same safeguards as apply to the interception of internal communications.[125]

Consequently, the HRC urged the UK to:

> review the regime regulating the interception of personal communications and retention of communications data ... with the view to ensuring that such activities both within and outside the State party, conform to its obligations under the [ICCPR], including Article 17.[126]

Regrettably, this call has not been heeded, since the IPA reiterates the RIPA's bipolarity based on the nature of communications. Subsequently, the CoE, in its 2015 report, commenting on the US and UK mass surveillance powers, recognized that the varied level of protection based on nationality constitutes a violation of the principle of equal treatment, noting that:

> the unique position of the United States (and the United Kingdom) with regard to the physical infrastructure of the Internet and the fact that private companies based in the United States collect and store huge amounts of data of persons residing anywhere in the world makes the exclusion of 'non-US [and UK] persons' from any legal protection against mass surveillance simply intolerable ... it may lead to the destruction of the Internet as we know it...[127]

Thus, in a nutshell, the conducting of extraterritorial surveillance of communications is accepted in international jurisprudence as a means of states' pursuing their national security goals and thus meets the requirement of legitimate aim.

---

[123]  *Ibid* 50.
[124]  General Comment 15 (n 27) para 7.
[125]  UNHRC, 'Concluding Observations on the Seventh Periodic Report of the United Kingdom of Great Britain and Northern Ireland' (17 August 2015) UN Doc CCPR/C/GBR/CO/7 para 24.
[126]  *Ibid* para 24(a).
[127]  CoE Mass Surveillance Report (n 99) para 103, 29.

However, such surveillance must be undertaken in such a way, as to respect the fundamental rights of all individuals, regardless of where they are located.

### 2.3.2 Proportionality

Turning to the second limb of the non-discrimination test, this requires the establishment of a reasonable relationship of proportionality between the means employed and the aims sought to be realized. In relation to this assessment, the *1 B v R* decision also provides a number of insightful guidelines. In that case, the German Constitutional Court criticized the disproportionality of the BND's strategic surveillance of foreigners' communications, noting its exceptionally broad scope and indiscriminate effect as being particularly aggravating.[128] Moreover, the Court commented that such an unrestricted practice can be used against anyone, 'without specific grounds; [as] objective thresholds for the use of these powers are not required, neither with regard to the situations that can give rise to surveillance measures nor to the individuals that may be affected by them'.[129] Furthermore, the Court noted their exceptional breadth, which allows for the analysis and collection of 'highly private and spontaneous communication processes reaching far into everyday life', together with the possibility to identify interests, desires and preferences as reflected in Internet usage.[130] Based on these concerns, the Court held that the powers of strategic surveillance must be designed in line with the task of gathering foreign intelligence – that is, early detection of dangers originating from abroad. For these reasons, strategic surveillance must be restricted in accordance with the principle of proportionality, which in the Court's view the BND Act 2016 does not satisfy.[131]

Were this line of reasoning to be applied to the bulk powers under the UK IPA and Section 702 of the US FISA (as reauthorized), the inevitable conclusion would be that these statutes and the manner in which the powers they confer are exercised do not satisfy the proportionality requirement – not least because of the large volumes of routinely collected data and the authorization of surveillance not restricted to sufficiently specific purposes or linked to particular grounds for suspicion. Such an acquisition of general intelligence from abroad is to a certain extent facilitated by the stance taken by previous statutes (eg, the RIPA) and reiterated in the subsequent surveillance laws (particularly the IPA) pertaining to the technological nature of the means of communication. Thus, the IPA places reliance on separating domestic from foreign

---

[128] *Ibid* para III(1)(a).
[129] *Ibid.*
[130] *Ibid.*
[131] *Ibid* para III(2).

communications – a condition that was suitable for modes of communications based on telephone switching systems which pre-date the Internet era. By the UK government's own admission, such differentiation in the digital context is difficult, if not impossible, in practice. This is because digital technology dictates that electronic communications travel in packets though fibre-optic cables. These packets are broken into smaller suitably sized blocks for their fast and efficient transmission.[132] These smaller packets are sent across the network and may travel by different routes before reaching their ultimate destination, where they are reassembled in order. As a result of this technique, known as 'packet switching', the data does not necessarily take the most direct path, but rather the fastest one, consequently making it almost impossible to confidently distinguish between purely domestic and international traffic. This phenomenon is exploited by state organs, as acknowledged by the UN High Commissioner for Human Rights, who noted that:

> if there is uncertainty around whether data are foreign or domestic, intelligence agencies will often treat data as foreign (since digital communications regularly pass 'off-shore' at some point) and thus allow them to be collected and retained. The result is significantly weaker – or even non-existent – privacy protection for foreigners and non-citizens, as compared with those of citizens.[133]

Arguably, therefore, from the perspective of the second limb of the non-discrimination test, legislation which does not take account of the highly complex technological nature of the Internet, dictated by different routing patterns, makes the measures (allowing for the collection of all data in bulk) disproportionate to the aims sought to be realized, even if the stipulation as to legitimate aims pursued by the legislation is satisfied.

Additional difficulties pertaining to the satisfaction of the proportionality criterion stem from the frequently made assertions that foreigners axiomatically pose a greater threat to national security than a state's own citizens,[134] and therefore that the collection of communications *en masse* facilitates

---

[132] Techopeida, 'Packet Switching' (2 February 2017), www.techopedia.com/definition/5603/packet-switching.

[133] Office of the UN High Commissioner for Human Rights, 'The Right to Privacy in the Digital Age. Report of the United Nations High Commissioner for Human Rights' (30 June 2014) UN Doc A/HRC/27/37 47 para 35 ('A/HRC/27/37').

[134] See Neil MacFarquhar, 'As Domestic Terrorists Outpace Jihadists, New U.S. Law is Debated', *The New York Times* (25 February 2020), discussing the high-level threat in the US posed by home-grown extremists compared with that originating from international terrorism; see also Uri Friedman, 'Where America's Terrorists Actually Come From' *The Atlantic* (30 January 2017), www.theatlantic.com/international/archive/2017/01/trump-immigration-ban-terrorism/514361/.

early detection and often pre-empts serious crimes from being committed. This assumption has, however, been challenged by, *inter alia*, the Special Rapporteur on the right to privacy, who – commenting in the context of the 2016 BND Act prior to the German Constitutional Court proclaiming it as unconstitutional – observed that:

> The way this reflects reality is not clear at all. Most of the terrorist attacks carried out in Europe during the past two years and more were carried out by European Union citizens, most often by citizens of the State where the attack was carried out. If the major risk lies there, (i.e. with the citizens of one's own State) what is the true value of laws that discriminate between nationals and non-nationals? Especially since, in terms of Article 17 of the International Covenant on Civil and Political Rights, everybody enjoys a right to privacy irrespective of nationality or citizenship, so one must ask how useful or appropriate, never mind legal such types of provisions may be.[135]

That said, the scepticism regarding the unequal treatment of individuals' communications in the digital context does not seem to be reflected in the recent ECtHR jurisprudence pertaining to mass surveillance of foreign communications. A case in point is the *Big Brother Watch* decision, where the ECtHR was presented with an opportunity to determine that the UK interception regime under Section 8(4) of the RIPA breached Article 14 of the ECHR (read in conjunction with Articles 8 and 10), but declined to do so. In this context, the applicants alleged that Section 8(4) of the RIPA was indirectly discriminatory on grounds of nationality because persons outside the UK were disproportionately likely to have their private communications intercepted. Further, Section 16 of that Act (outlined in Chapter 2, section 3.2.2.1) provided safeguards only to persons known to be in the British Islands, in that it prevented the intercepted material from being selected for examination without a warrant.[136] The ECtHR found that the complainants had not substantiated their claim pertaining to foreigners outside of the UK being likely to be disproportionately intercepted under Section 8(4).[137] This is because, first, the definition of 'external communications' includes 'a communication sent or received outside of the British Islands'.[138] The ECtHR reasoned that this therefore does not exclude the interception of communications where one of the parties is in the British

---

[135] UNGA, 'Report of the Special Rapporteur on the Right to Privacy' (30 August 2016) UN Doc A/71/368, para 36 ('A/71/368').

[136] *Big Brother Watch and Others v the United Kingdom* App no 58170/13; *Bureau of Investigative Journalism and Alice Ross v the United Kingdom* App no 62322/14; *10 Human Rights Organizations and Others v the United Kingdom* App no 24960/15 (12 October 2018) para 514, 182 ('*Big Brother Watch*').

[137] *Ibid* para 516.

[138] *Ibid.*

Islands.[139] Second, '"internal communications" (where both the sender and the receiver are in the British Islands) are frequently – and lawfully – intercepted by a by-catch of a section 8(4) warrant'.[140] In relation to Section 16 of the RIPA, the ECtHR observed that this prevented the intercepted material from being selected for examination based on the individual being in the British Islands. Therefore, any resulting difference in treatment would be founded on geographical location, not directly on nationality or national origin.[141] Relying on its dictum in *Magee v the United Kingdom*,[142] the ECtHR held that as such a difference in treatment could not be explained in terms of personal characteristics, it was not a relevant difference in treatment for the purposes of Article 14 of the ECHR and therefore did not amount to discriminatory treatment within the meaning of that provision.[143] Accordingly, the ECtHR held that the complaint under Article 14 in conjunction with Articles 8 and 10 was 'manifestly ill-founded' pursuant to Article 35(3)(a) of the ECHR (the latter provision setting out the admissibility criteria).

This outcome could perhaps be best rationalized when read in the light of the ECtHR's previous decision in *Centrum För Rättvisa*, which shortly preceded the *Big Brother Watch* judgment. Although the ECtHR in *Centrum För Rättvisa* did not directly address the issue of discrimination, the judgment is significant for a number of reasons. First, it is one of the few cases in which the ECtHR was directly confronted with legislation aimed at mass surveillance of foreign communications. Second, it signalled the ECtHR's departure from its previous robust stance regarding the legality of mass surveillance represented by a consistent line of case law since the 1970s (discussed in more detail in Chapter 5).

In *Centrum För Rättvisa*, rather than condemning bulk surveillance of foreign communications, the ECtHR seems to have legitimized this practice. Significantly, this apparent embracing of mass interception measures the ECtHR explained on the basis of 'the present-day threats being posed by global terrorism and serious cross border crime as well as the increased sophistication of communications technology'.[144] In view of this, the ECtHR held that 'the decision to set up a bulk interception regime in order to identify such threats was one which fell within the respondent State's margin of

---

[139]  *Ibid.*

[140]  *Ibid.*

[141]  *Ibid* para 517, 182.

[142]  *Magee v the United Kingdom* App no 18135/95 (2000) para 50.

[143]  *Big Brother Watch* (n 136) para 517, 182.

[144]  *Centrum För Rättvisa v Sweden* App no 35252/08 (19 June 2018) para 179 (*'Centrum För Rättvisa'*).

appreciation'.[145] When considered from the perspective of the principle of non-discrimination, what is remarkable about this outcome is that the ECtHR seems to have endorsed different treatment upon which the Swedish law in question (the Signals Intelligence Act (SIA)) is founded.[146] Having reviewed the SIA and the related scheme, the ECtHR concluded that the Swedish regime provides adequate and sufficient guarantees against arbitrariness and the risk of abuse. The Court held that the relevant legislation meets the 'quality of law' requirement, while 'interference' with the right to privacy is necessary in a democratic society.[147] It also ruled that both the structure and the operation of the system are proportionate to the aims sought to be achieved.[148] On this basis, the ECtHR concluded that the surveillance regime falls within Sweden's discretion, noting that there were sufficient minimum safeguards in place to protect the public from abuse, while identifying nevertheless some areas where there is scope for improvement.[149]

In consequence, by holding that, in principle, bulk interception schemes of foreign communications fall inside a state's margin of appreciation (*Weber, Centrum För Rättvisa, Big Brother Watch*), and that surveillance laws which differentiate on the basis of geographical location fall outside the scope of Article 14 of the ECHR (*Big Brother Watch*), the ECtHR seems to have endorsed legislation setting out different standards of protection for domestic and foreign surveillance. As this could be the ECtHR's new line of approach, and in view of current state practice clearly evidencing that a double standard has emerged in this area, some academics argue that any attempt at applying the same criteria to domestic and foreign surveillance in the name of universalism is doomed to fail.[150] Indeed, it has been proposed that certain legal differences in treatment between domestic and foreign surveillance should be recognized and allowed, justified, *inter alia*, by practical limitations in the way foreign surveillance is conducted, particularly in the digital age.[151] Furthermore, this type of interception, being a 'unique creature', requires specific tailoring and therefore the thinking based on 'one-size-fits-all' human

---

[145] *Ibid.*

[146] SIA (n 5) s 1(2).

[147] *Centrum För Rättvisa* (n 144) para 181.

[148] *Ibid.*

[149] *Ibid* paras 150 and 173–77. These include (1) the regulation of the communication of personal data to other states and international organizations; and (2) the practice of not giving public reasons following a review of individual complaints.

[150] Asaf Lubin, 'Legitimising Foreign Mass Surveillance in the European Court of Human Rights', *Just Security* (2 August 2018), www.justsecurity.org/59923/legitimizing-foreign-mass-surveillance-european-court-human-rights/.

[151] See Lubin (n 5) 502–52.

rights standards for all surveillance practices must be abandoned.[152] These arguments are unconvincing, being at variance with international law's mantle of equality and non-discrimination. They seem also to gloss over the problem of how to reconcile ubiquitous surveillance with the aims that surveillance powers seek to realize – that is, to facilitate the early detection and prevention of serious crime and cross-border terrorism. For example, in the US, bulk telephone data collection pursuant to the repealed Section 215 of the Patriot Act 2001 has been criticized for not being a useful counterterrorism tool. An independent executive body, the Privacy and Civil Liberties Oversight Board, found that such collection not only raises constitutional and legal concerns, but also has no material counterterrorism value, concluding that:

> based on the information provided to the Board, including classified briefings and documentation, we have not identified a single instance involving a threat to the United States in which the program made a concrete difference in the outcome of a counterterrorism investigation. Moreover we are aware of no instance in which the program directly contributed to the discovery of a previously unknown terrorist plot or the disruption of a terrorist attack.[153]

In *Centrum För Rättvisa* and *Big Brother Watch*, the ECtHR explicitly recognized that the combination of global terrorist threats, the trans-border nature of criminal activities and the ease of communication enabled by digital technologies justify granting to states wide discretion in respect of the measures they adopt when it comes to safeguarding national security. In so doing, the ECtHR seems to have dangerously enlarged the scope of this margin, which is of particular concern bearing in mind the ongoing debate pertaining to the factual utility of the foreign communications surveillance apparatus. It is submitted, therefore, that as a result of the broadening of this margin of appreciation in national security matters, the pendulum has swung too far towards achieving greater security, thus shifting the balance at the expense of safeguarding individuals' privacy. Rather than rejecting the universalist approach to human rights protection, what seems necessary is the careful recalibration of this balance to reflect the principles of equal treatment and non-discrimination. One way to achieve this is for domestic legislatures to adjust their existing laws (or enact new ones where none are in place) to recognize that foreigners' privacy rights must be safeguarded on a par with those of the intercepting state's nationals. Perhaps a cue can be taken from the German Constitutional

---

[152]  Lubin (n 150).

[153]  See, for example, Privacy and Civil Liberties Oversight Board, 'Report on the Telephone Records Program Conducted under Section 215 of the USA PATRIOT Act and on the Operations of the Foreign Intelligence Surveillance Court' (Privacy and Civil Liberties Oversight Board, 23 January 2014) 11.

Court, which in *1 B v R* set out six criteria that the legislature must meet to satisfy the proportionality requirement. These include the surveillance statute placing restrictions on the volume of data to be acquired from the transmission channels and on the geographical area covered by the surveillance; the duty to determine the purpose of surveillance with sufficient precision and legal clarity; and the obligation to take account of the 'core' of private life.[154]

In summary, one of the distinct characterises of domestic statutes allowing for extraterritorial surveillance of communications is their discriminatory nature, which is difficult to justify on objective and reasonable grounds, particularly in relation to the proportionality requirement. Looking to the future, the conclusion drawn from this must be that:

> given the unresolved technical challenges to accurately distinguish between national and non-national communications data, let alone the constitutional and human rights challenges to such an approach, [granting the same privacy protection to domestic and foreign communications] appears to be the most consistent and right solution to the problem.[155]

After all, we are all foreigners to someone.

This reinforces the need to clarify the legal basis in relation to the extent of states' obligations under human rights treaties when they engage in extraterritorial surveillance practices. The next section of this chapter turns to an analysis of this issue.

## 3. THE EXTRATERRITORIAL APPLICATION OF HUMAN RIGHTS TREATIES

### 3.1 The Scope of Application of Human Rights Treaties

As already observed, the system of protection created by human rights treaties enables an individual or a group to directly enforce its rights in national courts. States are required to adopt all legislative and other measures necessary to give effect to these instruments and persons whose rights have been violated are to be ensured an effective remedy directly before domestic and other judi-

---

[154] See *1 B v R* Press Release (n 114) para 2(a)–(i). In the context of the legislature taking account of the 'core of privacy' to discharge the obligation of proportionality, the German Constitutional Court explained that the 'analysis must cease as soon as it becomes apparent that surveillance is encroaching on the core of private life; even where mere doubts arise, the measure may only be continued in the form of recordings that are examined by an independent body prior to analysis. Intelligence relating to the highly personal domain may not be used and must be deleted immediately'.

[155] *Upping the Ante* (n 93) 23.

cial organs.[156] The question as to whether a particular complaint falls within the ambit of a treaty and therefore triggers states' human rights obligations is determined on the basis of a jurisdictional clause stipulated therein. In the human rights context, jurisdiction can be understood as a responsibility giving rise to specific legal obligations,[157] which functions as a threshold criterion.[158] Consequently, establishing the jurisdiction of a contracting state is a necessary condition for determining responsibility for acts or omissions imputable to it.[159] The ICCPR, the ECHR and the ACHR circumscribe their jurisdictional ambit in Article 2(1), Article 1 and Article 1(1) respectively. Thus, Article 2(1) of the ICCPR provides that: 'each State Party to the present Covenant undertakes to respect and to ensure to all individuals within its territory and subject to its jurisdiction the rights recognized in the present Covenant, without distinction of any kind ...'[160] In comparison, Article 1 of the ECHR provides that: 'the High Contracting Parties shall secure to everyone within their jurisdiction the rights and freedoms defined in Section 1 of this Convention.'[161] Similarly, Article 1(1) of the ACHR stipulates that states parties 'undertake to respect the rights and freedoms recognized herein and to ensure to all persons subject to their jurisdiction the free and full exercise of those rights and freedoms ...'[162]

As a general rule, the jurisdictional clauses set out in the human rights conventions oblige states to secure the listed rights to persons within their own jurisdiction, which means that if the infringement is committed within their territory, the relevant treaty will apply. In the context of states' cyber operations implicating individuals' human rights, the view expressed by the experts drafting the *Tallinn Manual 2.0* is that 'such law applies to all persons on a State's territory irrespective of where the State's cyber activities that implicate the human right in question occur'.[163] An example of how such obligations would apply is where the communications of an individual who is located within a state's territory are intercepted abroad by that state, or 'when the State acquires access to the individual's data that is stored electronically

---

[156] Schabas (n 13) para 13, LXV.

[157] Cedric Ryngaert, *Jurisdiction in International Law* (Oxford University Press 2015) 22–26.

[158] *Catan and Others v Republic of Moldova and Russia* App nos 43370/04; 8252/05; 18454/06 (19 October 2012) para 103.

[159] *Ibid.*

[160] ICCPR (n 15) Art 2(1).

[161] ECHR (n 1) Art 1.

[162] Organization of American States, The American Convention on Human Rights (The Pact of San José, Costa Rica) (entered into force 18 July 1978) Art 1(1) ('ACHR').

[163] Michael N Schmitt (ed), *Tallinn Manual 2.0 on the International Law Applicable to Cyber Operations* (Cambridge University Press, 2017) 183–84 ('*Tallinn Manual 2.0*').

beyond its borders'.[164] Thus, the obligations under the treaties will be triggered because the rights bearer is both within the state's territory and subject to its jurisdiction, allowing him or her to seek domestic redress. However, as mass cyber surveillance predominantly involves the interception of often entire populations outside the intercepting states' territories, the question that arises is whether and, if so, how human rights treaties apply in such situations.

The problem remains unresolved and is particularly troubling because of the a-territorial nature of the Internet and the consequences this has for the global rule of law in the digital environment. Some countries[165] have long asserted and continue to insist that their human rights obligations are *sensu stricto* territorially constrained. The US in particular has held a long-entrenched view that it is not bound by its ICCPR obligations in relation to non-US resident foreigners and with respect to acts done outside of its territory. Whether this view can be justified on the basis of the pertinent rules of treaty interpretation is explored next.

## 3.2     Extraterritorial Application of Human Rights Obligations

The territorial scope of treaties is set out in Article 29 of the Vienna Convention on the Law of Treaties 1968 (VCLT),[166] which provides the principal rule that a treaty is binding upon each state party in respect of its entire territory.[167] As this provision applies to human rights treaties, a state will be legally responsible for infringements that occur within its borders. However, with the rise of nations' involvement in the international arena through a plethora of activities – from military operations and economic globalization to transnational terrorism (to name but a few) – it has been acknowledged that their conduct may affect the rights of individuals who are located outside of their physical frontiers and thereby trigger their human rights obligations extraterritorially. The issue of the scope of such obligations has gained in prominence, with the leading judicial institutions recognizing that in certain circumstances, states may be liable for acts or omissions that occur outside their territories. However, the exact extent to which they will be accountable has not yet been fully settled. This is for a number of reasons – not least because no two jurisdictional clauses contain the same wording, as exemplified by Article 2(1) of

---

[164]  *Ibid.*

[165]  These countries include the US, Israel and Turkey – see footnote 174 *infra*.

[166]  UN, Vienna Convention on the Law of Treaties 1969 (23 May 1969) UN TS Vol 1155 ('VCLT').

[167]  *Ibid.* Article 29 states that: 'Unless a different interpretation appears for the treaty or is otherwise established, a treaty is binding upon each part in respect of its entire territory'.

the ICCPR, Article 1 of the ECHR and Article 1(1) of the ACHR, which results in their variable interpretation by the relevant human rights organs. In addition, states do not maintain a uniform approach to the issue of the extraterritorial scope of their human rights commitments, with some countries actively opposing such an approach. Both of these issues are discussed next.

### 3.2.1 The interpretation of jurisdictional clauses
Human rights treaties are subject to the general rules of interpretation set out in Articles 31 to 33 of the VCLT. In the *Alberta Union* case,[168] the HRC confirmed that the ICCPR must be interpreted in the light of these rules. Likewise, the ECtHR in *Loizidou v Turkey*[169] affirmed that the ECHR is subject to the principles of treaty construction set out in the VCLT, with account taken of any relevant principles of international law.

As a fundamental rule of interpretation, Article 31(1) of the VCLT stipulates that an international treaty 'shall be interpreted in good faith in accordance with the ordinary meaning to be given to the terms of the treaty in their context and in the light of its object and purpose'.[170] Based on this stipulation, two main interpretative methods can be distinguished: (1) the textual approach, which centres on the actual text of the agreement and calls for the natural and ordinary meaning be given to its words; and (2) the teleological method, which adopts a wider perspective, 'emphasiz[ing] the object and purpose of the treaty as the most important backcloth against which the meaning of any particular treaty provision should be measured'.[171] If the interpretation in accordance with Article 31 leads to an ambiguous, manifestly absurd or unreasonable result, Article 32 of the VCLT provides that recourse may be had to supplementary means of interpretation, including the *travaux préparatoires* of the treaty and the circumstances of its conclusion. The International Court of Justice (ICJ), in the *Competence of the General Assembly for the Admission of a State to the United Nations* case, observed that 'the first duty of a tribunal, which is called upon to interpret and apply the provisions of a treaty is to endeavour to give effect to them in their natural and ordinary meaning in the context in which they occur'.[172]

When it comes to the interpretation of the ICCPR, the ECHR and the ACHR jurisdictional clauses, two trends can be discerned: (1) the narrow premise

---

[168] *JB et al v Canada* (18 July 1996) UN Doc CCPR/C/28/D/18/1982 para 6.3.
[169] *Loizidou v Turkey* App no 15318/89 (18 December 1996) 2231.
[170] VCLT (n 166) Art 31(1).
[171] Malcolm N Show, *International Law* (Cambridge University Press, 2008) 933 ('Show').
[172] *Competence of the General Assembly for the Admission of a State to the United Nations* (1950) ICJ Reports, 4-8.

based on the textual approach held by some countries, including the US, consistently rejecting the view that the ICCPR places human rights obligations outside its territory – this approach has also recently been adopted by the UK Investigatory Powers Tribunal (ITP) in relation to GCHQ foreign surveillance; and (2) the expansive stance, rooted in the teleological school and postulated by the major international courts and human rights bodies,[173] firmly holding that in certain circumstances states do have human rights obligations outside their borders. Each view is discussed below.

### 3.2.2   The narrow interpretation

This standpoint is reflected in the policy of a small number of countries, including the US[174] and has recently been adopted by the UK IPT. According to this view, Article 2(1) of the ICCPR should be read to reflect the textual approach taken to treaty interpretation as set out in Article 31(1) of the VCLT, namely in accordance with the ordinary meaning given to its text. Consequently, the US stance is that Article 2(1) must be construed to mean that that country's human rights obligations are triggered only if an individual is both within its territory *and* subject to its jurisdiction, thus proffering the conjunctive reading of this provision. Based on this interpretation, the US rules out the extraterritorial application of the ICCPR altogether. This position the US government first made known to the HRC in its 1995 statement.[175] There, it argued that the wording of Article 2(1) restricted the ICCPR's scope of application to persons who are simultaneously under the jurisdiction and within the territory of the US. Subsequent administrations reiterated this stance in the Consolidated Second and Third Periodic Reports to the HRC.[176] By this reasoning, the US

---

[173] That is, the ICJ, the HRC and the ECtHR, and the Inter-American Court of Human Rights.

[174] The US ratified the ICCPR in 1992. Israel also holds the view that the ICCPR does not apply outside of its sovereign territory. In the *Wall Advisory Opinion*, the ICJ, when considering the extraterritorial application of the ICCPR, took note of Israel's position in relation to the applicability of the Covenant, which that country expressed in 1998 in its communications to the HRC. Israel stated then that the 'Covenant and similar instruments did not apply directly to … the situation in the occupied territories' – see *Legal Consequences of the Construction of a Wall in the Occupied Palestinian Territory,* Advisory Opinion ('*Wall Advisory Opinion*') [2004] ICJ Rep para 110. Likewise, Turkey, upon ratification of the ICCPR, declared that 'this Convention is ratified exclusively with regard to the national territory where the Constitution and the legal and administrative order of the Republic of Turkey are applied' – see Schabas (n 13) para 36, 49.

[175] UNHRC, Fifty-Third Session, 'Summary Record of the 1405th Meeting' (24 April 1995) UN Doc CCPR/C/SR.1405, para 20.

[176] UNHRC, 'Consolidation of Reports Submitted by States Parties Under Article 40 of the Covenant' (28 November 2005) UN Doc CCPR/C/USA/3.

maintains that it is not legally bound to comply with the ICCPR for its surveillance activities in relation to non-US communications. As a result, anyone who is not simultaneously within that country's territory and subject to its jurisdiction does not benefit from the ICCPR protection.[177]

To date, the ECtHR has not directly commented on states' extraterritorial obligations under the ECHR in the context of mass cyber surveillance. However, the matter was given attention by the UK IPT in *Human Rights Watch and Others v The Secretary of State for the Foreign and Commonwealth Office and Others*.[178] In that case, the IPT rejected the extraterritorial application of the right to privacy under Article 8 of the ECHR to claimants abroad who had alleged that they were subject to secret surveillance by the UK government. The case concerned the interception, storage and use of information and communications by Government Communications Headquarters (GCHQ) of two groups of applicants – those who at the time were resident in the UK and those who were not. With regard to the latter category, the IPT ruled that the UK 'owes no obligation under article 8 ECHR to persons [who] are situated outside its territory in respect of electronic communications between them, which pass through that State'.[179] The IPT reasoned that foreigners not physically present in the UK, but subject to GCHQ's interception under Section 8(4) of the RIPA, do not have a right to privacy under Article 8 of the ECHR, as they have not enjoyed private life in that country. Therefore, the UK is under no obligation to respect it.[180] In rejecting the extraterritorial application of the ECHR, the IPT adopted the textual approach to treaty interpretation, thus construing it narrowly, and relied on the ECtHR's decision in *Banković v Belgium*.[181] The case is discussed in more detail below, but of note at this juncture is that the ECtHR held that human rights can apply extraterritorially only where the state exercises effective control over the territory in which the individual is located. This interpretation can be contrasted with the more progressive approach discussed next.

### 3.2.3    The expansive interpretation

As already noted, the jurisdictional competence of a state is primarily territorial.[182] However, based on the case law of the ICJ and that of the international

---

[177]  *Ibid* para 20.

[178]  *Human Rights Watch Inc and Others v The Secretary of State for the Foreign and Commonwealth Office and Others* [2016] ALL ER (D) 105.

[179]  *Ibid* para 60.

[180]  *Ibid* para 58.

[181]  *Banković and Others v Belgium* App No 52207/99 (19 December 2001) 57 ('*Banković*').

[182]  VCLT (n 166) Art 29.

human rights adjudicating bodies – namely the HRC, the Inter-American Court of Human Rights (IACtHR) and the ECtHR – a shift towards a more functional approach to jurisdiction is unquestionable. Thus, the ICJ, in the *Wall Advisory Opinion*, addressed the meaning of the phrase 'within its territory and subject to its jurisdiction' stipulated in Article 2(1) of the ICCPR. The ICJ observed that while states' jurisdiction is primarily territorial, it may sometimes be exercised outside their national territories.[183] Having taken into account the ICCPR's object and purpose, the ICJ held that it 'would seem natural' that even when such is the case, state parties should be bound to comply with the ICCPR when they exercise jurisdiction outside their territory.[184] The ICJ reasoned not only that the HRC's practice is consistent with this approach, but also that the *travaux préparatoires* to the ICCPR confirm that the Covenant's drafters did not intend to allow states to escape from their obligations when they exercise jurisdiction outside of their national borders.[185] This interpretation therefore favours the disjunctive reading of Article 2(1) and holds that a state is bound by human rights obligations in relation to individuals who are either within its borders or subject to its jurisdiction.

A similar view has been adopted by the ECtHR, with the Court affirming that although states' jurisdictional competence under Article 1 of the ECHR is primarily territorial,[186] acts of contracting states performed or producing effects outside their territories can, in exceptional circumstances, constitute an exercise of jurisdiction within the meaning of Article 1.[187]

Finally, the IACtHR has held that the use of the word 'jurisdiction' in Article 1(1) of the ACHR signifies that a state's obligations to respect and ensure human rights apply to every person who is within that state's territory or who is in any way subject to its authority, responsibility or control.[188] Further, it held that the term 'jurisdiction' is not limited to the notion of national territory, but covers a broader concept that includes certain ways of exercising jurisdiction beyond the territory of the state in question.[189] Thus, in line with Article 31

---

[183]  *Wall Advisory Opinion* (n 174) para 109.
[184]  *Ibid.*
[185]  *Ibid.*
[186]  See, for example, *Soering v the United Kingdom* App no 14038/88 (7 July 1989) para 86; *Banković* (n 181) para 61; *Ilaşcu and Others v Moldova and Russia* [GC] App no 48787/99 (8 July 2004) para 312; *Al-Skeini and Others v the United Kingdom* [GC] App no 55721/07 (7 July 2011) para 131; *Catan* (n 158) para 104.
[187]  See *Banković ibid* para 67; *Al-Skeini ibid* para 131; *Catan ibid.*
[188]  *Rights and Guarantees of Children in the Context of Migration and/or in Need of International Protection*, Advisory Opinion OC-21/14 Inter-American Court of Human Rights (19 August 2014) para 61.
[189]  *State Obligations in Relation to the Environment in the Context of the Protection and Guarantee of the Rights to Life and to Personal Integrity: Interpretation and*

of the VCLT, 'jurisdiction' should be given its ordinary meaning, interpreted in good faith and taking into account the context, object and purpose of the ACHR. This, the Court held, is obvious from the ACHR's *travaux prépara-toires*, which reveal that the original text of Article 1(1), containing a reference to both states' territory and their jurisdiction, was rejected at the stage of the ACHR's adoption (ie, during the Inter-American Specialized Conference on Human Rights) in favour of states being obliged to respect and ensure the ACHR rights 'to all persons subject to their jurisdiction'.[190] Consequently, the margin of the ACHR's rights protection was extended, meaning that states' obligations are not restricted to the geographical space corresponding to their territory, but encompass those situations where – even outside of a state's borders – a person is subject to its jurisdiction.[191] In other words, states may be found internationally responsible not only for acts or omissions attributed to them within their geographical confines, but also for acts or omissions committed outside of their borders which fall within their jurisdiction.[192] For these reasons, a state's obligations under the ACHR extend to circumstances in which its extraterritorial conduct constitutes an exercise of its jurisdiction.[193]

To determine the scope of extraterritorial jurisdiction, a broadly similar approach based on 'effective control' has been devised. Thus, in General Comment 31, the HRC stated that:

> a State Party must respect and ensure the rights laid down in the [International] Covenant [of Civil and Political Rights] to anyone within the power, or effective control of that State Party, even if not situated within the territory of the State Party.[194]

This standard has also been adopted by both the ECtHR and the IACtHR as the appropriate criterion to establish an exception to the general rule dictating that jurisdiction is territorially limited.[195] Furthermore, in conceptualizing when and how the international human rights obligations may arise outside a state's

---

*Scope of Articles 1(1) and 2 of the American Convention on Human Rights,* Advisory Opinion OC-23/17 Inter-American Court of Human Rights (15 November 2017) para 74 (*'Advisory Opinion on the Environment and Human Rights'*).

[190] *Ibid* para 77.
[191] *Ibid.*
[192] *Ibid.*
[193] *Ibid* para 78.
[194] UNHRC, 'General Comment No 31. The Nature of the General Obligations Imposed on States Parties to the Covenant' (26 May 2004) UN Doc CCPR/C/21/Rev.1/Add.1326 para 10 ('General Comment 31').
[195] *Catan* (n 158) para 104; *Banković* (n 181) para 67; *Al-Skeini* (n 186) para 131; *Advisory Opinion on the Environment and Human Rights* (n 189).

borders, two types of extraterritorial jurisdiction have been distinguished, that is, the spatial model and the personal model.

### 3.2.3.1   The spatial model

According to this doctrine, a state will be held accountable for its human rights violations in relation to those individuals who are located within a geographical locality outside of that state's territory, but over which it has effective overall control – for instance, as a result of a military occupation.[196] This approach has been adopted by, and is now well established in, the jurisprudence of the ICJ, the HRC and the ECtHR. Thus, in the *Wall Advisory Opinion*[197] and in *DRC v Uganda*,[198] the ICJ concluded that the international human rights instruments are applicable 'in respect of acts done by a State in the exercise of its jurisdiction outside its own territory', particularly in occupied territories. The ECtHR in *Loizidou v Turkey*[199] held that a state's responsibility was engaged when, as a consequence of lawful or unlawful military action, it exercised effective control of an area outside its national borders. This approach the ECtHR subsequently applied in *Banković v Belgium*, holding that as the states concerned did not exercise effective control over the territory within which the human rights violations took place, the extraterritorial application of the ECHR could not be established. The case concerned a complaint brought by six individuals living in Belgrade (Serbia) against NATO for its bombing campaign during the Kosovo conflict, resulting in damage to numerous buildings and several deaths. The ECtHR held that as a general rule, jurisdiction was defined and limited by the sovereign territorial rights of the other relevant states, and that the other bases for jurisdiction were exceptional. It found that since the respondent states did not have 'effective' control over the area in question, Article 1 of the ECHR did not apply. Moreover, it introduced the concept of legal space (*espace juridique*), whereby the ECHR, being a regional treaty, applied only inside the territorial borders of its contracting states.[200] Based on this reasoning, the ECtHR held that as the former Federal Republic of Yugoslavia did not fall within this legal space, the ECHR did not apply.[201] The *Banković* decision

---

[196]   *Wall Advisory Opinion* (n 174) paras 107–13.

[197]   *Ibid*, paras 107–13.

[198]   *Armed Activities on the Territory of the Congo (Democratic Republic of Congo v Uganda)* [2005] ICJ Rep, paras 178–80 (*'DRC v Uganda'*). The ICJ noted that: 'Uganda at all times [had] responsibility for all actions and omissions of its own military forces in the territory of the DRC in breach of its obligations under the rules of international human rights law and international humanitarian law which are relevant and applicable in the specific situation.'

[199]   *Loizidou* (n 169).

[200]   *Banković* (n 181) para 80.

[201]   *Ibid*.

sparked controversy and criticism, with leading commentators concluding that it was built on erroneous legal foundations and ran contrary to both the previous case law and core human rights values.[202] Unsurprisingly, the ECtHR in a number of subsequent decisions declined to follow the approach stipulated therein. Thus, it did not apply the rule that Article 1 jurisdiction is limited to the European 'legal space', finding instead that the ECHR applies in a broad range of circumstances, including the alleged acts of Turkish agents in Iraq in *Issa v Turkey*;[203] the killings at the Turkish-Iranian border in *Pad v Turkey*[204] and the actions of Armenia denying Azerbaijani refugees the right of return to their homes following the Armenia-Azerbaijan 1992 conflict over the Nagorno-Karabakh province in *Chiragov v Armenia*,[205] to name but a few examples. Furthermore, in *Issa*, the ECtHR disregarded the principle that jurisdiction under Article 1 does not apply to states' acts outside their territorial borders, unless the state exercises 'effective control' over the region or an area in question. Rather, the Court followed the line of case law[206] based on the personal model advanced by, *inter alia*, the HRC to find that:

> a State may also be held accountable for violations of the Convention rights and freedoms of persons who are in the territory of another State, but who are found to be under the former State's authority and control through its agents operating – whether lawfully or unlawfully – in the latter State.[207]

It is this model of jurisdiction, that seems to have gained traction in the subsequent ECtHR jurisprudence in particular.

### 3.2.3.2   The personal model

This concept dictates that a state may be held accountable for its human rights infringements when it exercises authority and control over an individual – for example, while such a person is held in its physical custody. The HRC in General Comment 31 explained this principle, stating that 'a State Party must respect and ensure the rights laid down in the Covenant to anyone within [its] power or effective control ..., even if not situated within [its] territory'; and that this 'applies also to those within the power or effective control of the forces of a State Party acting outside its territory, regardless of the circum-

---

[202] See Marko Milanovic, *Extraterritorial Application of Human Rights* (Oxford University Press 2011).

[203] *Issa and Others v Turkey* App no 31821/96 (16 November 2004).

[204] *Pad and Others v Turkey* App no 60167/00 (28 June 2007).

[205] *Chiragov and Others v Armenia* App no 13216/05 (16 June 2015).

[206] *Lopez Burgos v Uruguay* (1 January 1979) UN Doc CCPRC/13/D/52/1979; *Lilian Celiberti de Casariegeo v Uruguay* (29 July 1981) UN Doc CCPR/C/13/D/56/1979.

[207] *Issa* (n 203) para 71.

stances in which such power or effective control was obtained'.[208] The HRC applied this model of jurisdiction in, *inter alia*, *Lopez Burgos v Uruguay*,[209] a case concerning the kidnapping and torture by Uruguayan security forces of a Uruguayan citizen living in Argentina. The HRC held that Uruguay had violated its duties under the ICCPR, stating that the obligation placed on states by Article 2(1) to ensure an individual's rights within their territory and subject to their jurisdiction does not mean that a state cannot be held accountable for violations of its agents in the territory of another state. The HRC concluded that it would be:

> unconscionable to so interpret the responsibility under Article 2 of the [ICCPR] as to permit a State Party to perpetrate violations of the Covenant on the territory of another State, which violations it could not perpetrate on its own territory.[210]

On the European level, the divergent approaches adopted by the ECtHR to establishing jurisdiction in the *Banković* and *Issa* cases resulted in an inconsistent and confusing state of law on extraterritorial jurisdiction. An opportunity to address the issue arose in *Al-Skeini v UK* (*Al-Skeini*).[211] In that case, the Grand Chamber (GC) of the ECtHR clarified and arguably expanded the scope of the ECHR's application. The GC confirmed the primarily territorial nature of jurisdiction under the ECHR, but recognized two exceptions to this principle: (1) where state agents exercise authority and control extraterritorially; and (2) where a state exercises effective control of an area outside its national territory. State agent authority is particularly pertinent to military operations, where physical authority and control are very often exercised in prisons or in formal detention centres. However, the ECtHR emphasized that it is not the control over the place of detention, but rather in relation to an individual that establishes jurisdiction. To this end, the GC asserted that it would be erroneous to assume that jurisdiction arises 'solely from the control exercised by the State over the buildings, aircraft, or ship in which the individuals were held. What is decisive in such cases is the exercise of physical power and control over the person in question'.[212] The application of this approach can be seen in *Öcalan v Turkey*,[213] a case which concerned the handover in Kenya to Turkish officials of an individual suspected in Turkey of terrorist-related crimes. The ECtHR held that as soon as the transfer took place, the suspect was effectively

---

[208]   General Comment 31 (n 194) para 10.
[209]   *Lopez* (n 206).
[210]   *Ibid* paras 12.2–12.3.
[211]   *Al-Skeini* (n 186).
[212]   *Ibid*, para 136.
[213]   *Öcalan v Turkey* App no 46221/99 (12 March 2003).

under Turkish authority and therefore within its jurisdiction. Most notably, however, in the subsequent cases of *Hassan v UK* (*Hassan*)[214] and *Jaloud v the Netherlands* (*Jaloud*),[215] the ECtHR seems to have moved further away from the first limb articulated in *Al-Skeini,* based on effective control of an area, towards state agent authority. Thus, *Hassan* concerned the capture of an Iraqi national, Tarek Hassan, by the British armed forces, his detention and subsequent death at Camp Bucca in Iraq in 2003. The application alleged that at that time, Mr Hassan was under the control of the British military, and that his dead body was found bearing marks of torture and execution. The UK government argued that Mr Hassan was not within its jurisdiction, in particular because the UK did not have exclusive or primary control over him. The ECtHR disagreed with this contention. The point of departure for the Court was the dictum in *Al-Skeini.* Thus, the ECtHR noted that in that case, jurisdiction was established on the basis of state agent authority, not effective control over an area,[216] and held that this jurisdictional doctrine also applied to Mr Hassan because 'he was within the physical power and control of the [UK] soldiers'.[217] This preference for state agent authority over the spatial model was subsequently affirmed in *Jaloud.* That case centred on the fatal shooting of Azhar Sabah Jaloud, who was killed when the car in which he was travelling was fired upon by a Dutch soldier while being driven through a military checkpoint established pursuant to Security Council Resolution 1483. That Resolution mandated a military mission, termed 'Stabilization Force in Iraq' (SFIR), between July 2003 and March 2005. The victim's father claimed that the Netherlands had failed to properly investigate the circumstances of his son's death and therefore was in breach of its procedural obligations under Article 2 of the ECHR (right to life). The Netherlands resisted the allegations, asserting, *inter alia,* that the case did not fall within that country's jurisdiction within the meaning of Article 1 of the ECHR. The ECtHR dismissed these objections, finding that the case did fall within the ambit of the ECHR and holding the Netherlands in breach of Article 2 of the ECHR. Two of the grounds upon which the Dutch government based its jurisdictional challenge are particularly pertinent to the present context. The first is that at the time of the shooting, the vehicle checkpoint was under the authority of Iraq's security forces; while the second is that the Dutch troops had at no time exercised physical control over Mr Jaloud and the firing of the

---

[214]   *Hassan v the United Kingdom* App no 29750/09 (16 September 2014).
[215]   *Jaloud v the Netherlands* App no 47708/08 (26 November 2014).
[216]   *Hassan* (n 214) para 75.
[217]   *Ibid* para 76.

shots was not in itself sufficient to establish jurisdiction. In rejecting both of these arguments, the ECtHR held that:

> The checkpoint had been set up in the execution of SFIR's mission … to restore the conditions of stability and security conducive to the creation of an effective administration in the country. The Court is satisfied that [the Netherlands] exercised its 'jurisdiction' within the limits of its SFIR mission and for the purpose of asserting authority and control over persons passing through the checkpoint. That being the case, the Court finds that the death of Mr Azhar Sabah Jaloud occurred within the 'jurisdiction' of the Netherlands, as that expression is to be construed within the meaning of Article 1 of the Convention.[218]

Thus, the ECtHR appears to have accepted that the Netherlands' exercise of its jurisdiction was based on the Dutch military personnel asserting authority and control over the individual, even absent physical control in relation to him. That being the case, the decision not only falls within the state agent authority exception (limb (a) of the *Al-Skeini* test), but also expands it. This is because the ECtHR seems to have endorsed the idea that a state may be held accountable for its human rights violations where it exercises effective control over the enjoyment of an individual's rights. Termed 'effective control over persons' rights', this doctrine has found support in recent years from both the HRC and the IACtHR.

Thus, the HRC, in its General Comment 36 pertaining to the right to life set out in Article 6 of the ICCPR, endorsed this approach, stating that:

> In light of article 2 paragraph 1 of the Covenant, a State party has an obligation to respect and to ensure the rights under article 6 of all persons who are within its territory and all persons subject to its jurisdiction, that is, all persons over whose enjoyment of the right to life it exercises power or effective control. This includes

---

[218] *Jaloud* (n 215) para 152. However, see *Georgia v Russia (II)* GC App no 38263/08 (21 January 2021). The judgment concerned interstate proceedings during the international armed conflict between the two states in August 2008. The ECtHR decided *inter alia* that 'military operations' during 'the active phase of hostilities' during international armed conflict are beyond the jurisdiction of the state and therefore the purview of the Court (para 138). In such situations, neither the spatial nor the personal model applies (para 137). However, jurisdiction may be established following the ceasing of the active phase of hostilities on the basis of the spatial model. The judgment has been criticized for representing a regressive step from *Al-Skeini* to *Bankovic* and for going 'against the expansive general trend in international human rights law regarding both extraterritoriality and the application of human rights to armed conflicts', but its impact remains uncertain at the time of writing – see Marko Milanovic, 'Georgia v Russia No. 2: The European Court's Resurrection of Bankovic in the Context of Chaos' (25 January 2012) EJIL:Talk!, https://www.ejiltalk.org/georgia-v-russia-no-2-the-european-courts-resurrection-of-bankovic-in-the-contexts-of-chaos/.

persons located outside any territory effectively controlled by the State, whose right to life is nonetheless impacted by its military or other activities in a direct and reasonably foreseeable manner.[219]

Within the inter-American human rights system, the interpretation of the term 'jurisdiction' in Article 1(1) of the ACHR aligns with that adopted by the HRC pertaining to actions of state agents abroad.[220] To this end, the Inter-American Commission on Human Rights has indicated that the exercise of jurisdiction may include instances where 'the person [is] present in the territory of a State but is subject to the control of another State generally through the actions of that State's agents abroad'.[221] The IACtHR, in, *inter alia*, *Alejandre v Cuba*, established that to determine whether a person is within a state's jurisdiction, 'the inquiry turns not on the presumed victim's nationality, or presence within a particular geographical area, but on whether under specific circumstances, the State observed the rights of a person subject to its authority and control'.[222] Consequently, extraterritorial jurisdiction has been recognized in cases relating to military interventions,[223] military operations in international air space[224] and in the territory of another state,[225] and military facilities outside of a state's territory.[226]

Following the IACtHR's landmark 2017 *Advisory Opinion on the Environment and Human Rights*, the scope of the word 'jurisdiction' in Article 1(1) was further expanded to encompass acts outside of a state's territory where that state exercises authority over the person or has effective control over activities that cause human rights violations.[227] The Opinion concerned the interplay of environmental protection and human rights law in the context of an application made by the Republic of Colombia to clarify the scope of state responsibility for environmental harm under the ACHR, in particular in light of the Convention for the Protection and Development of the Marine

---

[219] UNHRC, 'General Comment No 36, Article 6 (Right to Life)' (30 September 2019) UN Doc CCPR/C/GC/36 para 66 ('General Comment 36').

[220] *Franklin Guillermo Aisalla Molina (Ecuador v Colombia)* (21 October 2011) UN Doc CCPR/C/28/D/118/192 para 91 ('*Ecuador v Columbia*').

[221] *Case of Armando Alejandre Jr et at v Cuba* Merits Report no 86/99 (29 September 1999) para 23 ('*Alejandre v Cuba*').

[222] *Ibid*, para 37.

[223] *Case of Salas et al v United Sates* Admissibility Report no 31/93 (14 October 1993) paras 14, 15 and 17.

[224] *Alejandre v Cuba* (n 221).

[225] *Ecuador v Colombia* (n 220).

[226] *Djamel Ameziane v United States* Admissibility Report no 17/12 (20 March 2012) para 35.

[227] *Advisory Opinion on the Environment and Human Rights* (n 189) para 81.

Environment of the Wide Caribbean Region (Cartagena Convention) and customary international law.[228] The IACtHR held that since human rights depend on the existence of a healthy environment, states must take measures to prevent environmental damage both inside and outside of their territories. The IACtHR provided detailed guidance on the interaction between international human rights law and international environmental law. One of its key findings[229] was the articulation of a pioneering test to determine the ACHR's extraterritorial application in cases involving trans-border environmental harm. The IACtHR's starting point was to note that the scope of application of human rights treaties has been interpreted to involve either: (1) a state's exercise of effective control over a foreign territory (spatial model); or (2) control over a particular person by state agents acting abroad (personal model).[230] The IACtHR then observed that since no human rights tribunal had previously considered the issue of transboundary environmental harm, no test existed to establish states' responsibility in that context; while the application of the well-established model based on effective control was not suitable, as if applied to the present context, it would preclude claims of transboundary environmental damage altogether.[231] With this in mind, the IACtHR devised a new test, holding that the term 'jurisdiction' encompasses any situation in which a state exercises 'authority' over a person or subjects him or her to its 'effective control', whether within or outside its territory.[232] On this basis, a state may be held responsible for its actions or omissions where the activities of that state have a cross-border effect. This then raises states' obligations to take all necessary measures to avoid activities in their territory or under their control which

---

[228] *Ibid* para 1. Specifically, the IACtHR was asked: 'how the Pact of San José should be interpreted when there is a danger that the construction and operation of major new infrastructure projects may have severe effects on the marine environment in the Wider Caribbean Region and, consequently, on the human habitat that is essential for the full enjoyment and exercise of the rights of the inhabitants of the coasts and/ or islands of a State Party to the Pact, in light of the environmental standards recognized in international customary law and the treaties applicable among the respective States.'

[229] *Ibid*. The IACtHR has recognized for the first time the right to the healthy environment under the ACHR as an independent right and clarified the content of a duty to prevent transboundary harm.

[230] *Ibid* para 79.

[231] *Ibid* para 80. The IACtHR considered that most of the instances establishing extraterritorial jurisdiction of the ECHR and the ICCPR 'involve military actions or actions by State security forces that indicate "control" or "power" or "authority" in the execution of the extraterritorial conduct. However, these are not to situations described by the requesting State and do not correspond to the specific context of environmental obligations referred to in this request for advisory opinion'.

[232] *Ibid* para 81.

may affect the rights of persons within or outside their borders.[233] The IACtHR explained the application of this approach, stating that:

> when transboundary harm or damage occurs, a person is under the jurisdiction of the State of origin *if there is a causal link between the action that occurred within its territory and the negative impact on the human rights of persons outside its territory The exercise of jurisdiction arises when the State of origin exercises effective control over the activities that caused the damage and the consequent human rights violation* [emphasis added].[234]

Thus, based on this premise, jurisdiction may arise where: (1) a state has effective control over the activities that have caused the damage; (2) it is in a position to prevent harm from occurring, but has not done so; and (3) this, as a consequence, has a negative impact on foreigners' rights. What is noteworthy is the change of focus when it comes to the interpretation of the jurisdictional clause, as proposed by the IACtHR. Instead of analysing a state's control over foreign areas or persons outside its borders, the enquiry turns on a state's control over activities within its own domain, asking whether its territory was used in such a way as to cause significant external damage,[235] affecting others' fundamental rights. This is an innovative reconceptualization of the test, with potentially far-reaching consequences. First, on this basis states may be found responsible for the failure to prevent transboundary environmental harm emanating from their geographical areas, which they are duty bound to prevent. Second, the subsequent IACtHR practice shaping the contours of this new approach may also influence how extraterritorial obligations are determined by other courts and bodies in divergent contexts.

In summary, as a general rule, states will be held liable for human rights violations occurring within their territories. The exercise of jurisdiction outside their physical borders remains an exception. However, progressively, it has been accepted that states will be held accountable for their human rights violations where they exercise 'effective control' over an area (spatial model) or a person (personal model). This latter approach seems to have been further redefined, and recent developments at the HRC, the ECtHR and the IACtHR attest to a closer alignment of the extraterritorial jurisdiction test based on the 'control over rights' doctrine. In addition, the IACtHR has held that jurisdiction will be established where there is a causal nexus between the action that has occurred within the state's territory and its detrimental impact on the human rights of persons outside its borders.

---

[233]  *Ibid* para 104(g).
[234]  *Ibid* para 104(h).
[235]  *Ibid* para 104(f).

### 3.3 Applicability of Human Rights Treaties to Extraterritorial Cyber Surveillance

Numerous UN human rights bodies and mandate holders have favoured the expansive interpretation of jurisdictional clauses when it comes to states' human rights obligations in relation to their extraterritorial cyber surveillance activities. To this end, the HRC, when addressing NSA surveillance pursuant to Section 702 of the FISA conducted through, *inter alia*, the PRISM and Upstream programs, stated that the US does hold a duty under the ICCPR to 'take all necessary measures to ensure that its surveillance activities, both within and outside the United States, conform to its obligations under the Covenant, including article 17'.[236] The HRC urged the US to take measures 'to ensure that any interference with the right to privacy complies with the principles of legality, proportionality and necessity regardless of the nationality or location of the individuals whose communications are under direct surveillance'.[237] Furthermore, in its report on the right to privacy, guided by the principle that states may not avoid their international human rights obligations by taking action outside their territory that they would be prohibited from taking at home, the UN Office of the High Commissioner for Human Rights (OHCHR) confirmed that states' human rights obligations are triggered where they conduct extraterritorial surveillance.[238] Similarly, the CoE Commissioner for Human Rights observed that:

> A State that uses its legislative and enforcement powers to capture, or otherwise exercise control over personal data that are not held on its physical territory but on the territory of another State, for example by using the physical infrastructure of the Internet and global e-communications systems to extract those data from servers, personal computers or mobile devices in the other State, or by requiring private entities that have access to such data abroad to extract those data from the servers or devices in another country and hand them over to the State, is bringing those data – and in respect of those data, the data subjects – within its 'jurisdiction' in the sense in which that term is used in the ECHR and the ICCPR. Such a State must, in this extraterritorial activity, comply with its obligations under those treaties.[239]

In addition, according to the *Tallinn Manual 2.0*, 'as a general principle, customary international human rights law applies in the cyber context beyond

---

[236] UNHRC, 'Concluding Observations on the Fourth Periodic Report of the United States of America' (23 April 2014) UN Doc CCPR/C/USA/CO/4 para 22, 10.

[237] *Ibid.*

[238] A/HRC/27/37 (n 133) para 33.

[239] CoE *The Rule of Law* (n 81) 54.

a State's territory in situations in which that State exercises "power or effective control", as it does offline'.[240]

Thus, there seems to be a consensus that, in principle, states' treaty obligations extend to their extraterritorial cyber surveillance operations on the basis of the 'effective control' test (the spatial and personal model).[241] However, the utility of the thus conceived jurisdictional doctrine is problematic for a number of reasons. First, cyber surveillance operations do not depend on the state being actually physically present on the territory where the monitored individuals reside.[242] Second, a foreign state cannot be said to exercise 'effective control' over a person abroad when intercepting, storing and sharing that individual's data. Nor can it be argued that such a state has control over the area where the interception is taking place. As noted by some commentators,[243] the shortcomings of the 'traditional' effective control approach centre on the fact that some intelligence services – particularly the NSA – exert effective remote, rather than physical, control over much of the communications of foreign nationals abroad.[244] This occurs through eavesdropping on their communications, filtering or altering their content, and breaking many forms of encryption by installing 'back doors' engineered in many software systems.[245] The NSA also has the capacity to gain control of computers not directly connected to the Internet, due to the implantation of transmitting devices in hardware manufactured in the US and elsewhere;[246] and has relationships with Internet and telecommunication companies that facilitate data access.[247] The US does not recognize the extraterritorial application of human rights, but its virtual power is reputed to be unprecedented.[248] Consequently, the dual model requiring physical control over an area or a person to establish jurisdiction creates a lacuna, allowing some states to continue to exploit it. For these reasons, the traditional 'effective control' test seems unsuitable in the context of extraterritorial cyber surveillance, as it does not take account of the fact that in the digital age, a person can also be subject to the exercise of a foreign state's authority through the control over his or her communications and, by extension, over his or her right to privacy.

---

[240]    *Tallinn Manual 2.0* (n 163) Rule 34, para 5, 183.

[241]    *Ibid.*

[242]    See Ashley Deeks, 'An International Legal Framework for Surveillance' (2015) 55 *Virginia Journal of International Law* 291, 298–300.

[243]    See Peter Margulies, 'The NSA in the Global Perspective: Surveillance, Human Rights and International Counterterrorism' (2014) 82 *Fordham Law Review* 2137.

[244]    *Ibid* 2151.

[245]    *Ibid.*

[246]    *Ibid.*

[247]    *Ibid.*

[248]    *Ibid.*

That said, to date, the international human rights courts and bodies have not devised a suitable model for establishing jurisdiction, although the OHCHR did consider how states' obligations might be triggered, stating that:

> digital surveillance ... may engage a State's human rights obligations if that surveillance involves the State's exercise of power or effective control in relation to digital communications infrastructure, wherever found, for example, through direct tapping or penetration of that infrastructure. Equally, where the State exercises regulatory jurisdiction over a third party that physically controls the data, that State also would have obligations under the Covenant. If a country seeks to assert jurisdiction over the data of private companies as a result of the incorporation of those companies in that country, then human rights protections must be extended to those whose privacy is being interfered with, whether in the country of incorporation or beyond. This holds whether or not such an exercise of jurisdiction is lawful in the first place, or in fact violates another State's sovereignty.[249]

Thus, according to this reasoning, a state may be held legally responsible for its human rights violations where it exercises control over the digital communications infrastructure or regulatory control over Internet service providers in relation to any person, irrespective of his or her nationality or location. A similar view has been expressed by Special Rapporteur Emmerson, who observed that:

> Certain States have the technical capacity to conduct mass surveillance of communications between individuals not resident within their jurisdiction, and have thus implemented surveillance arrangements that have extraterritorial effect. Some of these activities are physically conducted on the territory of the State concerned and therefore engage the principles of territorial jurisdiction under the Covenant. This is the case not only where State agents place data interceptors on fibre-optic cables travelling through their jurisdictions, but also where a State exercises regulatory authority over the telecommunications or internet service providers that physically control the data.[250]

An opportunity to engage with the extraterritorial application of the ECHR in the context of GCHQ and NSA surveillance arose in 2018 in the *Big Brother Watch* case. However, since the respondents did not raise the issue, the ECtHR did not address this problem and simply applied the relevant ECHR law. Nevertheless, noteworthy is a Written Submission in the context of that litigation, made by the International Commission of Jurists with suggestions con-

---

[249] A/HRC/27/37 (n 133) para 34.
[250] UNGA, 'Report of the Special Rapporteur on the Promotion and Protection of Human Rights and Fundamental Freedoms While Countering Terrorism, Ben Emmerson' (23 September 2014) UN Doc A/69/397 para 41 ('A/69/397').

cerning this matter.[251] Addressing the extraterritorial dimensions of the right to privacy applied to surveillance activities, the Commission argued that, due to the transborder nature of the Internet, the obligations of states (both positive and negative) with regard to the mass interception of Internet data necessarily apply extraterritorially in certain situations.[252] In particular, the Commission was of the view that:

> in cases of mass surveillance, the State's authority, or control over the information and therefore of an important element of the private sphere of the persons concerned, is sufficient to establish jurisdiction irrespective of the location of the individual concerned.[253]

This view of the Commission was based on the general principles of jurisdiction established by the ECtHR in, *inter alia*, the *Al-Skeini* case, according to which a state's jurisdiction under Article 1 of the ECHR may extend to the acts of its authorities producing effects outside its own territory. The Commission noted that the ECtHR has held that such jurisdiction may arise either 'when, through consent, invitation or acquiescence of the Government of that territory, it exercises all or some of the public powers normally to be exercised by that Government' on the territory; or in situations where a contracting party, in the absence of territorial control, nevertheless 'exercises control and authority over an individual'.[254] Importantly, the document concluded that the ECtHR jurisprudence on Article 8 of the ECHR recognizes that privacy rights extend to aspects of the personal sphere of an individual beyond his or her physical integrity, and consequently submitted that:

> jurisdiction as regards mass surveillance should be interpreted such that, even where a State exercises authority and/or control over personal information of an individual physically outside the territory of the Contracting Party, the person should be recognized as coming within the authority and/or control of the State, for the purposes of rights that relate to such information, in particular under article 8 ECHR.[255]

The thorny issue of the circumstances in which states' human rights obligations are triggered in the context of extraterritorial cyber surveillance remains unsettled. However, there seems to be a convergence of the human rights courts and bodies all moving away from the traditional effective control model towards

---

[251] *Big Brother Watch and Others v the United Kingdom*, Written Submission on Behalf of the International Commission of Jurists (9 February 2016).
[252] *Ibid* 8.
[253] *Ibid*.
[254] *Ibid*.
[255] *Ibid* 9.

a more expansive conception of jurisdiction focusing on states' control over the rights of individuals. An important development is the IACtHR's reconceptualization of jurisdiction, which boils down to the principle that where environmental pollution travels across borders, legal responsibility must follow. From the perspective of transboundary pollution, the planet's physical environment can be considered a-territorial. Cyberspace likewise is characterized by its borderless nature. If the IACtHR's test is applied by analogy to that domain, then a state's responsibility for extraterritorial mass surveillance will be triggered when (1) it has control over domestic activities that have a detrimental effect on individuals' rights abroad; and (2) it fails to prevent violations of human rights (including the right to privacy of communications) emanating from its territory.

Devising a suitable mechanism is bound to be replete with difficulties and will have far-reaching consequences – especially bearing in mind the 'inevitable ripple effects on other scenarios such as extraterritorial use of lethal force through, for example drone strikes'[256] were a more permissive approach to this issue to be adopted. Nevertheless, states' theatre of operations will increasingly involve actions in the cyber domain, impacting on an array of human rights and fundamental freedoms. Articulating how governments' responsibility is triggered in such circumstances is an onerous, but a necessary task.

## 4.    CONCLUSION

This chapter engaged with two pivotal aspects of the treaty-based privacy protection regime. First, it addressed the overriding obligations on all states of non-discrimination and equal treatment. Having noted that these principles are a fundamental premise upon which the international human rights apparatus is predicated, the chapter observed that not all forms of different treatment will automatically be considered as amounting to discrimination. Having applied the two-limb test dictating that for a given measure not to be discriminatory, it must both pursue a legitimate aim and be proportionate, it concluded that satisfying the latter criterion in relation to the asymmetric treatment of foreigners who are subject to extraterritorial surveillance is particularly problematic. Furthermore, given the foundational importance attached to the principle of equality under Article 26 of the ICCPR, it is difficult to justify why nations should be permitted to legislate for lower standards of privacy protection in

---

[256] Marko Milanovic 'UK Investigatory Powers Tribunal Rules that Non-UK Residents Have No Right to Privacy under the ECHR' *EJIL: Talk!* (2016), www .ejiltalk.org/uk-investigatory-powers-tribunal-rules-that-non-uk-residents-have-no -right-to-privacy-under-the-echr/.

relation to foreigners, which they would not be allowed to do in relation to their own nationals. Consequently, the chapter embraced a proposition that a higher standard of protection – that is, one pertaining to the targeted interception of communications – should equally apply to bulk surveillance of foreign communications. Such an approach may also address the problem of incidental collection of domestic communications.

Further, it was observed that the varied privacy safeguards adopted by some states when conducting surveillance outside their borders necessitate the establishment of clear standards in relation to the extraterritorial applicability of human rights treaties. These issues were discussed in the second part of the chapter and centred on the extent of such obligations, focusing on the ICCPR, the ECHR and the ACHR. Noting that a broad consensus has been reached that human rights treaties apply to cyber surveillance conducted outside of states' borders, the chapter queried the utility of the traditional 'effective control' test and supported the calls for a criterion that befits the digital environment. Although the issue has not yet been fully settled, the recent interpretations of jurisdictional clauses by the major human rights courts and bodies seem to lean towards a test based on 'control over individuals' rights'. This approach, coupled with a standard that states' obligations may be triggered when they fail to prevent harm originating from their territories which has a detrimental effect on foreigners' human rights, could serve as a guiding principle when devising a suitable test for states' extraterritorial cyber surveillance activities.

# 5.    Treaty-based privacy protection
    – interference

## 1.    INTRODUCTION

The right to privacy is said to be 'amongst the essential ingredients of modern human rights law'.[1] The crucial role that this principle plays is recognized in Article 12 of the Universal Declaration of Human Rights 1946.[2] Subsequently restated in similar terms in numerous legally binding international and regional treaties – including in Article 17 of the International Covenant on Civil and Political Rights (ICCPR), Article 8 of the European Convention on Human Rights (ECHR) and Article 11 of the American Convention on Human Rights (ACHR) – its primary purpose is to guarantee the respect for the individual existence of the human being.[3] This includes safeguarding against arbitrary interference by public authorities, requiring in essence that the state refrain from such intrusions unless they are justified on one of the permitted grounds. Online surveillance remains controversial and raises a number of fundamental legal challenges – not least of which are whether it is consistent with international legal standards and what measures are needed to protect individuals against violations of privacy, so that governments do not arbitrarily interfere with this interest.

The formulations of privacy under Article 17 of the ICCPR, Article 8 of the ECHR and Article 11 of the ACHR differ slightly. Nevertheless, all these provisions have been interpreted to protect the confidentiality of communications, free from unwanted intrusion. Furthermore, their structure follows the same pattern. The first part of each article sets out the core right, which has

---

[1]    Javaid Rehman, *International Human Rights Law* (Pearson Education Limited, 2010) 106.

[2]    Universal Declaration of Human Rights (adopted 10 December 1948) UNGA Res 217 A(III) ('UDHR'). Article 12 states that: 'no one shall be subjected to arbitrary interference with his privacy, family, home or correspondence, nor to attacks upon his honour and reputation. Everyone has the right to the protection of the law against such interference or attack'.

[3]    William A Schabas, *U.N. International Covenant on Civil and Political Rights. Novak's CCPR Commentary* (N.P. Engel, 2019) 460 ('Schabas').

been held by the relevant judicial organs to include electronic surveillance and interception of communications by state agencies. This is then followed by a second paragraph which articulates the circumstances in which the right to privacy may be lawfully limited. Typically, therefore, the legality of the state's encroachment is determined on the basis of first establishing whether there has been an interference. If that is the case, the inquiry then turns to ascertaining whether such an interference can be justified.

The aim of this chapter is to engage with the first aspect of this test and delineate what types of cyber surveillance activities amount to an interference with the right to privacy of communications. The chapter is divided into five sections. Section 2 maps out the scope of the right to privacy by focusing on Article 17 of the ICCPR, Article 8 of the ECHR and Article 11 of the ACHR. It first outlines its divergent facets as circumscribed in the case law of the international judicial organs and positions this right within the context of state surveillance activities. Attention is then turned to what constitutes an interference with digital communications, with reference made to the issue of legal standing.[4] Section 3 engages with some contentious matters pertaining to the notion of interference – that is: (1) the operation of mass surveillance programs; (2) the stage at which the interference with privacy takes place; and (3) the collection and retention of metadata. Section 4 circumscribes the contours of the concept of interference with the right to privacy of communications in the digital environment; while section 5 offers some conclusions.

## 2.    TREATY-BASED PRIVACY PROTECTION

### 2.1    The Scope of the Right to Privacy

Privacy has been unequivocally proclaimed as a fundamental human right in international and regional legal frameworks. At the international level, it is enshrined in, among others,[5] Article 17 of the ICCPR. Regionally, it is stipulated in, *inter alia*, Article 8 of the ECHR and Article 11 of the ACHR.[6]

---

[4]    'Standing', or *locus standi*, is defined as 'a party's right to make a legal claim or seek judicial enforcement of a duty or right' – see Bryan A Garner, *Black's Law Dictionary* (West Group, 1999) 1413.

[5]    See also Article 16 of the Convention on the Right of the Child (adopted 20 November 1980, entered into force 2 September 1990) 1577 UNTS; and Article 14 of the International Convention on the Protection of All Migrant Workers and Members of Their Families (adopted 18 December 1990 UNGA Res 45/158).

[6]    Council of Europe (CoE), European Convention for the Protection of Human Rights and Fundamental Freedoms amended by Protocols Nos 11 and 14 (4 November 1950) (European Convention on Human Rights) Art 8 ('ECHR'); Organization of American States, The American Convention on Human Rights (The Pact of San José,

Human rights courts and bodies have not provided a singular definition of 'privacy', primarily in recognition of the complex character of what this concept embodies. For example, the European Court of Human Rights (ECtHR) emphasized that the broad nature of 'private life' does not lend itself to exhaustive definition[7] and that therefore it 'may embrace multiple aspects of the person's physical and social identity'.[8] However, a certain established scope can be discerned and continues to evolve in line with new developments in such areas as data protection, medicine and surveillance.

## 2.2    Article 17(1) of the ICCPR

On the international level, the obligation to protect and respect the right to privacy is set out in Article 17 of the ICCPR, which provides that:

1.  No one shall be subjected to arbitrary and unlawful interference with his privacy, family, home or correspondence, nor to unlawful attacks on his honour or reputation.

---

Costa Rica) (entered into force 18 July 1978), Art 11 ('ACHR'). The right to privacy is also set out in the following documents: (1) the Cairo Declaration on Human Rights in Islam, Art 18 (adopted at the Islamic Conference of Foreign Ministers, Cairo, 5 August 1990); (2) the Arab Charter on Human Rights, Arts 16 and 21 (adopted 16 September 1994); (3) the African Commission on Human and People's Rights Resolution on the Declaration of Principles on Freedom of Expression in Africa (23 October 2002) ACHPR/Res.62 (XXXII)02; (4) the African Charter on the Rights of Welfare of the Child, Art 19 (11 July 1990) CAB/LEG 124.9/49; (5) the Human Rights Declaration of the Association of Southeast Asian Nations, Art 21 (18 November 2012); (6) the Asia-Pacific Economic Cooperation Privacy Framework (2015); (7) Convention for the Protection of Individuals with Regard to the Automatic Processing of Personal Data (28 January 1981) CETS 108 Art 1, as modernized by Protocol amending Convention for the Protection of Individuals with Regard to Automatic Processing of Personal Data (10 October 2018) CETS No. 223 ('Convention 108'); (8) the Additional Protocol to the Convention for the Protection of Individuals with regard to Automatic Processing of Personal Data regarding supervisory authorities and transborder data flows (opened for signature 8 November 2001, entered into force 1 July 2004) ETS No 181; (9) the Council of Europe Recommendation No R(99) 5 for the protection of privacy on the Internet (adopted by the Committee of Ministers on 23 February at the 660th Meeting of Ministers' Deputies); and (10) European Parliament and the Council of the European Union, General Data Protection Regulation (4 May 2016) L119 ('GDPR').

[7]    *Paradiso and Campanelli v Italy* [GC] App no 25358/12 (29 January 2017) 159.

[8]    *S and Marper v the United Kingdom* [GC] App no 30562/04 (4 December 2008) 66.

2.   Everyone has the right to the protection of the law against such interfer-
     ence or attacks.[9]

The extent of the right protected by Article 17 has been circumscribed by the
UN Human Rights Committee (HRC) in its case law to comprise six broad
categories:[10] (1) the safeguarding of one's own identity;[11] (2) a person's physical and psychological integrity;[12] (3) intimacy, including the protection of
personal data;[13] (4) individual autonomy; (5) communications;[14] and (6) sexu-
ality.[15] In addition, the HRC, in its General Comment 16, confirmed that other
areas covered by the right to privacy include: (1) surveillance, whether electronic or otherwise; interceptions of telephonic, telegraphic and other forms of
communications; wiretapping and recording of conversations;[16] (2) searches of
people's homes;[17] (3) personal and body searches;[18] and (4) the gathering and
holding of personal information on computers, data banks and other devices.[19]

### 2.2.1   Article 17(1) of the ICCPR – the right to privacy of communications

Privacy of communications is primarily underpinned by the notion of an individual's autonomy. It defends the right to establish and develop relationships
with other human beings and the outside world.[20] This includes the protection
of the secrecy of correspondence. To this end, according to the HRC's General
Comment 16:

> Compliance with article 17 requires that the integrity and confidentiality of corre-
> spondence should be guaranteed de jure and de facto. Correspondence should be
> delivered to the addressee without interception and without being opened or other-

---

[9]   UNGA, International Covenant on Civil and Political Rights (adopted 16
December 1966, entered into force 23 March 1976) 999 UNTS 999, 171 Art 17
('ICCPR').

[10]   Schabas (n 3) 466–75.

[11]   *Coeriel et al v the Netherlands* App no 435/1991 (9 December 1994).

[12]   *Costello-Roberts v the United Kingdom* App no 13134/87 (25 March 1993).

[13]   UNHRC, 'Concluding Observations on the Sixth Periodic Report of Spain' (5
January 2009) UN Doc CCPR/C/ESP/CO/5 ('Concluding Observations, Spain').

[14]   *Mółka v Poland* App no 56550/00 (11 April 2006).

[15]   *Toonen v Australia* (4 April 1994) UN Doc CCPR/C/50/D/488/1992.

[16]   UNHRC, 'CCPR General Comment No. 16: Article 17 (Right to Privacy),
The Right to Respect of Privacy, Family, Home and Correspondence and Protection
of Honour and Reputation' (8 April 1988) UN Doc HRI/Gen/1/Rev.9 (Vol 1) para 8
('General Comment 16').

[17]   *Ibid.*

[18]   *Ibid.*

[19]   *Ibid.*

[20]   *Shimovolos v Russia* App no 30194/09 (21 June 2011) 64.

wise read. Surveillance, whether electronic or otherwise, interception of telephonic, telegraphic and other forms of communications, wire-tapping and recording of conversations should be prohibited.[21]

At the time of drafting of both Article 17 and General Comment 16 (the latter in the 1980s), methods of correspondence generally comprised written letters transmitted by post. Few could have then anticipated the impact of digital technologies on such means of communication.[22] Nevertheless, although now somewhat outdated, these standards and principles continue to play a vital role in delineating the legal ambit of this right; while the changing means and methods of communication have been reflected in the HRC's case law. To this end, the HRC has interpreted the term 'correspondence' as comprising not only written letters, but also other forms of interchange, such as telephonic, facsimile and electronic messages (emails).[23]

### 2.2.1.1   Interference with privacy of communications – state surveillance activities

Generally, 'every withholding, censorship, inspection of (or listening to) or publication of private correspondence represents an interference within the meaning of Art. 17'.[24] Traditionally, states have enjoyed a monopoly on communications – as was the case, for example, in the UK where the General Post Office established in 1660 was the state's sole postal and telecommunications carrier until 1969. For this reason, secret government surveillance measures such as opening letters,[25] tapping telephones[26] and intercepting post or telegrams[27] for the purposes of preventing crime or combating terrorism have been classed among the most common forms of interference. To this end, the HRC emphasized that: 'all types of surveillance activities and interference with privacy, including online surveillance for the purposes of State security [must be] governed by appropriate legislation that is in full conformity with the Covenant.'[28] In addition, such surveillance must be subject to judicial author-

---

21   General Comment 16 (n 16) para 8.
22   Schabas (n 3) 489.
23   *Angel Estrella v Uruguay* (29 March 1983) UN Doc CCPR/C/18/D/74/1980.
24   Schabas (n 3) 490.
25   UNHRC, Concluding Observations: Zimbabwe' (3 April 1998) UN Doc CCPR/C/79/Add.89 ('Concluding Observations, Zimbabwe').
26   UNHRC, 'Concluding Observations on the Seventh Periodic Report, Poland' (31 October 2016) UN Doc CCPR/C/POL/CO/7 ('Concluding Observations, Poland').
27   *Pinkney v Canada* (2 April 1980) UN Doc CCPR/C/OP/1.
28   UNHRC, 'Concluding Observations on the Second Periodic Report on Turkmenistan' (20 April 2017) UN Doc CCPR/C/TKM/CO/2, 36-37 ('Concluding Observations, Turkmenistan').

ization and an effective and independent oversight mechanism;[29] while those whose rights have been violated must have meaningful access to appropriate remedies in case of abuse.[30] As a consequence, because electronic surveillance by government authorities falls within the meaning of the term 'correspondence' under Article 17, states are obliged to ensure that the gathering, storage and use of personal data is not subject to abuse and that it is not used for purposes contrary to the ICCPR.[31] This means that states should ensure that the processing and gathering of information are subject to review and supervision by an independent (preferably judicial) body, with necessary guarantees of impartiality and independence.[32]

---

[29]    *Ibid*; UNHRC, 'Concluding Observations on the Second Report of Namibia' (23 August 2016) UN Doc CCPR/C/NAM/CO/2 ('Concluding Observations, Namibia'); UNHRC, 'Concluding Observations of the Human Rights Committee, Sweden' (7 May 2009) UN Doc CCPR/C/SWE/CO/6 para 6, 18 ('Concluding Observations, Sweden 2009'); UNHRC, 'Concluding Observations on the Seventh Periodic Report of Sweden' (28 April 2016) UN Doc CCPR/C/SWE/CO/7 paras 36–37 ('Concluding Observations, Sweden 2016'); UNHRC, 'Concluding Observations, Switzerland' (27 July 2017) UN Doc CCPR/C/CHE/CO/4, 47 ('Concluding Observations, Switzerland'); Concluding Observations, Poland (n 26), 39–40; UNHRC, 'Concluding Observations on the Sixth Periodic Report of Morocco' (1 December 2016) UN Doc CCPR/C/MAR/CO/6, 37–38 ('Concluding Observations, Morocco'); UNHRC, 'Concluding Observations on the Fourth Periodic Report of Rwanda' (2 May 2016) UN Doc CCPR/C/RWA/CO/4, 35-36 ('Concluding Observations, Rwanda'); UNHRC, 'Concluding Observations on the Second Periodic Report of Honduras' (22 August 2017) UN Doc CCPR/C/HND/CO/2, 39 ('Concluding Observations, Honduras').
[30]    Concluding Observations, Turkmenistan (n 28) 36–37; Concluding Observations, Honduras *ibid* 39; UNHRC, 'Concluding Observations, Hong Kong Special Administrative Region (China) (21 April 2006) UN Doc CCPR/C/HKG/CO/2 12 ('Concluding Observations, Hong Kong'); Concluding Observations, Sweden 2009 and Concluding Observations, Sweden 2016 *ibid*; UNHRC, 'Concluding Observations on the Fourth Periodic Report of the United States of America' (23 April 2014) UN Doc CCPR/C/USA/CO/4. ('Concluding Observations, US'); UNHRC, 'Concluding Observations on the Third Periodic Report of the Former Yugoslav Republic of Macedonia' (23 July 2015) UN Doc CCPR/C/MKD/CO/3 23; UNHRC, 'Concluding Observations on the Initial Report of South Africa' (27 April 2016) UN Doc CCPR/C/ZAF/CO/1, 42-43 ('Concluding Observations, South Africa').
[31]    Concluding Observations, Sweden 2016 (n 29) 18.
[32]    *Ibid*.

## 2.3    Article 8(1) of the ECHR

At the European level, the main instrument that safeguards civil and political rights is the ECHR and its Additional Protocols.[33] The ECHR sets out the right to privacy in Article 8, which states that:

1. Everyone has the right to respect for his private and family life, his home and his correspondence.
2. There shall be no interference by a public authority with the exercise of this right except such as is in accordance with the law and is necessary in a democratic society in the interests of national security, public safety or the economic well-being of the country, for the prevention of disorder or crime, for the protection of health or morals, or for the protection of the rights and freedoms of others.[34]

In contrast to Article 17(1) of the ICCPR, which refers to 'privacy', Article 8(1) of the ECHR pertains to 'private life', but both of these formulations in essence convey the same meaning.[35] As in the case of Article 17(1), the notion of private life under Article 8(1) lacks an all-embracing definition on account of its multifaceted nature. Indeed, the ECtHR, in clarifying the scope of this provision, observed that 'it does not consider it possible to attempt an exhaustive definition of the notion of private life'.[36] Nevertheless, its meaning extends beyond the protection of the sense of self, as in accordance with the ECtHR:

It would be too restrictive to limit [this] notion to an 'inner circle', in which the individual may live his own personal life as he chooses and to exclude therefrom entirely the outside world not encompassed within that circle. Respect for private life must also comprise to a certain degree the right to establish and develop relationships with other human beings.[37]

Reflecting this observation, the scope of 'private life' as developed in the ECtHR's jurisprudence is broad, as it encompasses a plethora of categories, including: (1) the physical and psychological integrity of a person;[38] (2) the right to establish and develop relationships with other human beings;[39] (3)

---

[33] The ECHR is complemented by 16 additional protocols. See CoE, 'European Convention on Human Rights and Its Protocols', www.coe.int/en/web/compass/the-european-convention-on-human-rights-and-its-protocols.

[34] ECHR (n 6) Art 8.

[35] Schabas (n 3) 466.

[36] *Niemietz v Germany* App no 13710/88 (16 December 1992).

[37] *Ibid* 29.

[38] *X and Y v the Netherlands* App no 8978/80 (26 March 1985).

[39] *Niemietz* (n 36) 29.

State sponsored cyber surveillance

the entitlement to personal development or self-determination;[40] (4) gender identification;[41] (5) the right to protect one's reputation;[42] (6) the right not to be subject to unwarranted searches and seizures;[43] (7) the unwarranted gathering of data by security or other organs of the state;[44] and (8) surveillance of communications and telephone conversations.[45]

### 2.3.1 Article 8(1) of the ECHR – the right to privacy of communications

Similarly to Article 17 of the ICCPR, Article 8(1) of the ECHR explicitly sets out the right to respect for correspondence as an autonomous interest and aims to protect the confidentiality of communications. The term 'correspondence' within the meaning of that provision has been widely construed and includes: (1) letters of a private or professional nature;[46] (2) packages seized by customs officers;[47] (3) telephone conversations between family members[48] or with others;[49] (4) telephone calls from private or business premises;[50] and (5) information relating to such conversations (date, duration, number dialled).[51] Digital methods of communication have also been held by the ECtHR to fall within the scope of 'correspondence' – in particular, in relation to emails,[52] Internet use[53] and data stored on computer servers[54] (including hard drives[55]

---

[40] *Pretty v the United Kingdom* App no 2346/02 (29 April 2002) 61.
[41] *B v France* App no 13343/87 (25 March 1992) 40.
[42] *Chauvy and Others v France* App no 64915/01 (29 June 2004) 175.
[43] *Funke v France* App no 10828/84 (25 February 1993) para 48.
[44] *Rotaru v Romania* App no 28341/95 (4 May 2000) 43–4.
[45] *Halford v the United Kingdom* App no 20605/92 (25 June 1997) 44.
[46] *Niemietz* (n 36) 32.
[47] *X v the United Kingdom* App no 7308/75 (12 December 1978).
[48] *Margareta and Roger Andersson v Sweden* App no 12963/87 (3 October 1990) 72.
[49] *Malone v the United Kingdom* App no 8691/79 (2 August 1984) 38–39; *Klass and Others v Germany* App no 5029/71 (6 September 1978) 21 and 41.
[50] *Amann v Switzerland* [GC] App no 27798/95 (16 February 2000) 44; *Halford* (n 45) 44–46; *Copland v the United Kingdom* App no 62617/00 (3 April 2007) 41; *Kopp v Switzerland* App no 23224/94 (25 March 1998) 50.
[51] *PG and JH v the United Kingdom* App no 44787/98 (25 September 2001) 46.
[52] *Copland* (n 50) 41; *Bărbulescu v Romania* [GC] App no 61496/08 (26 September 2017) 72.
[53] *Copland ibid* 41–42.
[54] *Wieser and Bicos Beteiligungen GmbH v Austria* App no 74336/01 (16 October 2007) 45.
[55] *Petri Sallinen and Others v Finland* App no 50882/99 (27 September 2005) 71.

and floppy disks),[56] together with other forms of electronic communications, such as telexes[57] and pager messages.[58]

### 2.3.1.1    *Interference with privacy of communications – state surveillance*

In accordance with the ECtHR's case law, all forms of censorship, interception, monitoring, seizure and other hindrance with privacy of communications fall within the scope of Article 8 of the ECHR.[59] The scale of the interference with the right to privacy in the context of states' secret surveillance operations has been the subject of extensive analysis by the ECtHR on numerous occasions in the past. A series of early cases dealing with the interception of telephone conversations though the application of various surveillance techniques by law enforcement agencies helped to develop a consistent set of principles in relation to interference with Article 8 rights. The cases of *Klass v Germany,*[60] *Malone v UK,*[61] *Halford v UK*[62] and *Liberty v UK*[63] established, *inter alia,* that wiretapping of telephone conversations constitutes an interference with the right to privacy and the use of covert surveillance technologies invariably engages Article 8, as the notions of 'private life' and 'correspondence' extend not only to the interception of telephone communications, but also to so-called 'metering' practices.[64] The finding that the concept of 'correspondence' covers telephone conversations was extended in *Halford v UK*[65] to include the interception of office telephone calls. The ECtHR's subsequent jurisprudence established that not only such direct methods of surveillance, but also the collection and storage of personal information in relation to an individual's use of the telephone, email and Internet amount to interference with private life and correspondence. Thus, in *Copland v UK*[66] the ECtHR concluded that the collection and storage of personal information relating to the applicant's

---

[56]    *Iliya Stefanov v Bulgaria* App no 65755/01 (22 May 2008) 42.

[57]    *Christie v the United Kingdom* App no 28957/95 (11 July 2002).

[58]    *Taylor-Sabori v the United Kingdom* App no 47114/99 (22 October 2002).

[59]    CoE, 'Guide on Article 8 of the European Convention on Human Rights. Right to Respect for Private and Family Life, Home and Correspondence' (31 August 2019).

[60]    *Klass* (n 49).

[61]    *Malone* (n 49).

[62]    *Halford* (n 45).

[63]    *Liberty & Others v United Kingdom* App no 58243/00 (1 July 2008).

[64]    *Malone* (n 49). 'Metering' involved the use of a meter to register the number dialled on a particular telephone, together with the time and duration of each call. The ECtHR held that there had been an interference with Article 8, as the notion of 'private life' and 'correspondence' extended to the interception of telephone communications and metering practices.

[65]    *Halford* (n 45).

[66]    *Copland* (n 50).

use of the telephone, email and Internet without her knowledge amounted to an interference with her right to respect for private life and correspondence.[67] Likewise, Article 8 was breached when the ECtHR found that the storage of communications amounted to an interference in the cases of *Leander v Sweden*[68] and *Amann v Switzerland*.[69] In *Leander*, the ECtHR held that: 'both the storing and the release of [secret police-register information], coupled with a refusal to allow [the applicant] an opportunity to refute it, amounted to an interference with his right to respect for private life.'[70] In *Amann*, the ECtHR ruled that the interception and/or storage of communications constituted a violation, and that the 'subsequent use of the stored information has no bearing on that finding';[71] nor did it matter 'whether the information gathered on the applicant was sensitive or not or as to whether the applicant had been inconvenienced in any way'.[72]

The ECtHR has also found interference with the right to privacy in a number of cases relating to the storage of electronic data on government databases. In *S and Marper v UK*[73] the applicants' fingerprints and DNA samples were to be held indefinitely in a database, following criminal proceedings against them. The ECtHR held that Article 8 had been violated, as the blanket and indiscriminate nature of the powers of retention of the fingerprints, cell samples and DNA profiles of persons suspected but not convicted of offences failed to strike a fair balance between the competing private and public interests, as they were disproportionate to the aims achieved.[74] A violation of private life was also established in *Shimovolos v Russia*,[75] concerning the collection of information in the so-called 'surveillance database' of a human rights activist's movements by train and air within Russia. In that case, the ECtHR observed that the creation and maintenance of the database and the procedure for its operation were governed by a ministerial order which had never been published or otherwise made accessible to the public. Consequently, the applicable domestic law did not indicate with sufficient clarity the scope and manner of the exercise of the discretion conferred on the domestic authorities to collect and store information on individuals' private lives in the database. Nor did

---

67  ECtHR, 'Factsheet-New Technologies' (June 2015) ('ECtHR Factsheet').
68  *Leander v Sweden* App no 9248/81 (26 March 1987).
69  *Amann* (n 50).
70  *Leander* (n 68) para 22.
71  *Amann* (n 50) para 69.
72  *Ibid* para 70.
73  *S and Marper* (n 8).
74  ECtHR Factsheet (n 67) 1.
75  *Shimovolos* (n 20).

it set out, in a form accessible to the public, any indication of the minimum safeguards against abuse.[76]

The ECtHR continued to find violations of Article 8 in similar fashion in such cases as *MK v France*[77] and *Brunet v France*.[78] In the former decision, the ECtHR held that the retention of the data in question had amounted to disproportionate interference with the applicant's right to privacy. In the latter judgment, the ECtHR considered that the French state had overstepped its discretion, as such withholding of data could be regarded as a disproportionate breach of the applicant's right to privacy and was not necessary in a democratic society. Likewise, an infringement of Article 8 was determined in *Robathin v Austria*,[79] where the applicant's documents and electronic data were searched by the police following a criminal investigation. The ECtHR found interference because the investigation concerned all of his electronic data, rather than that relating solely to the case under investigation. As there were no substantiating reasons given for such an all-encompassing search, the Court held that the seizure and examination of all the data had gone beyond that which was necessary to achieve the legitimate aim, and thus found a violation of Article 8. Most notably, however, in the *Weber v Germany*[80] and *Kennedy v UK*[81] cases, the ECtHR held that legislation which, by its mere existence, entails a threat of surveillance for all those to whom it might apply impacts on the freedom of communications between users of telecommunication services and thereby amounts in itself to an interference with the rights under Article 8.

## 2.4    The Right to Privacy in the Inter-American Human Rights System

### 2.4.1    General

The Inter-American human rights system is based on two disparate, but inter-related mechanisms. The first is the Organization of American States (OAS) Charter system, which relies on the OAS Charter[82] and the American Declaration of the Rights and Duties of Man (ADHR).[83] The second is based

---

[76]   ECtHR Factsheet (n 67) 2.

[77]   *MK v France* App no 76100/13 (24 September 2015).

[78]   *Brunet v France* App no 21010/10 (18 September 2014).

[79]   *Robathin v Austria* App no 30457/06 (3 October 2012).

[80]   *Weber and Saravia v Germany* App no 54934/00 (29 June 2006).

[81]   *Kennedy v the United Kingdom* App no 26839/05 (18 May 2010).

[82]   Charter of the Organization of American States (signed 1948, entered into force 13 December 1951) 119 UNTS 3 ('OAS Charter').

[83]   American Declaration of the Rights and Duties of Man (Bogotá Declaration) (adopted 2 May 1948) ('ADHR').

on the ACHR[84] and is binding on those OAS member states which have become parties to that Convention.

The functioning of both regimes is supported by an inter-related organ, the Inter-American Commission on Human Rights (IACHR), with jurisdiction extending to all OAS member states, since Article 1(2) of the Statutes of the Inter-American Commission on Human Rights 1997 provides that: 'human rights are understood to be … the rights set forth in the American Convention on Human Rights and … in the American Declaration of the Rights and Duties of Man.'[85] The IACHR was created by the OAS and, following the amendment of the OAS Charter by the 1967 Buenos Aires Protocol, has been recognized as one of the OAS's 'principal organs'.[86] As an institutional body of the OAS, the IACHR's main functions are set out in Article 106 of the OAS Charter, namely to promote the observance and protection of human rights and to serve as a consultative organ of the OAS in these matters.[87] Its role and powers are set out in Article 41 of the ACHR and include making recommendations to the governments of member states on measures in favour of human rights;[88] preparing studies and reports;[89] and requesting information on human rights issues.[90] The IACHR is also vested with the authority to receive individual communications alleging violations of human rights contained in both the ADRH and the ACHR.[91] Accordingly, the IACHR can analyse and investigate individual petitions that allege human rights violations with respect to both the

---

[84] ACHR (n 6). The other human rights instruments are: (1) the Inter-American Convention to Prevent and Punish Torture (adopted 9 December 1985) OAS TS No 67; (2) the Additional Protocol to the American Convention on Human Rights in the Area of Economic, Social and Cultural Rights (Protocol of San Salvador) (16 November 1999) A-52; (3) the Protocol to the American Convention on Human Rights to Abolish the Death Penalty (8 June 1990) OAS TS No 73; (4) the Inter-American Convention on the Prevention, Punishment and Eradication of Violence against Women (Convention of Belem do Para) (adopted 9 June 1994, entered into force 5 March 1995); and (5) the Inter-American Convention on the Elimination of All Forms of Discrimination Against Persons with Disabilities (adopted 7 June 1999, entered into force 14 September 2001) AG/RES 1608 (XXIX-0/99).

[85] OAS, Statute of the Inter-American Commission on Human Rights (1 October 1997) OAS Off Rec OEA/SerP/IX.0.2/80, Vol 1 at 88 Art 1(2).

[86] OAS Charter (n 82) Arts 53 and 106.

[87] *Ibid* Art 106.

[88] ACHR (n 6) Art 41(b).

[89] *Ibid* Art 41(c).

[90] *Ibid* Art 41(d).

[91] The individual complaint procedures derive from two different sources. Those under the OAS Charter system are set out in Articles 26–48 of the Rules of Procedure of the Inter-American Commission on Human Rights, whereas those under the ACHR stem from Articles 44–55 of the ACHR.

member states of the OAS that ratified the ACHR and those that have not done so. Although it cannot provide legally binding judgments, it may, in case of the alleged violation of ACHR rights, refer the case to the Inter-American Court of Human Rights (IACtHR), provided that the relevant state has accepted that Court's jurisdiction.[92]

### 2.4.2 The OAS Charter system

The OAS is a regional agency[93] established in 1948 with the signing in the same year of the OAS Charter in Bogotá, Colombia, bringing together 35 states of the Americas. The primary objectives of the OAS include the protection of human rights, together with the promotion of solidarity and the defence of the sovereignty, territorial integrity and independence of these states.[94] The OAS has been compared to the Council of Europe, being a body responsible for the promotion and protection of human rights in the Americas.[95]

The OAS Charter (as amended)[96] reflects the OAS' goals of safeguarding peace and justice, promoting solidarity and defending the sovereignty, territorial integrity and independence of the American states.[97] It makes a number of references to fundamental rights, declaring in Article 3(l) that: 'the American States proclaim the fundamental rights of the individual without distinction as to race, nationality, creed, or sex.'[98] Article 17 of the OAS Charter further provides that: 'each State has the right to develop its cultural, political, and economic life freely and naturally. In this free development, the State shall respect the rights of the individual and the principles of universal morality.'[99]

While the OAS Charter sets out the objectives of the American states in broad terms, the document that is focused on providing the normative basis for the development, protection and promotion of human rights is the ADHR.[100] Although adopted as a declaration rather than a legally binding treaty, it nev-

---

[92]  Rehman (n 1) 278.
[93]  OAS Charter (n 82) Art 1.
[94]  *Ibid.*
[95]  Rehman (n 1) 271.
[96]  The OAS Charter has been amended by four protocols: (1) Buenos Aires (entered into force 27 February 1970) 721 UNTS 324, OAS TS 1-A; (2) Cartagena de Indias (entered into force 16 November 1988) OAS TS No 66, 25 ILM 527; (3) Washington (entered into force 25 September 1997) 1_E Rev OEA *Documentos Oficiales* OEA/SerA/2 Add 3 (SEPF), 33 ILM 1005; (4) Managua (entered into force 29 January 1996) 1-F Rev OEA *Documentos Oficiales* OEA/SerA/2 Add4 (SEPF), 33 ILM 1009.
[97]  OAS Charter (n 82) Art 1.
[98]  *Ibid* Art 3(l).
[99]  *Ibid* Art 17.
[100]  The ADHR was adopted in 1948 at the same time as the adoption of the OAS Charter.

ertheless constitutes a source of international obligations for the member states of the OAS.[101] The ADHR proclaims the fundamental principle of equality and universality of human rights, asserting that 'all men are born free and equal in dignity and in rights';[102] and that 'the essential rights of man are not derived from the fact that he is a national of a certain State, but are based upon attributes of his human personality'.[103] The right to privacy is set out in Article 5, according to which 'every person has the right to the protection of the law against abusive attacks upon his honor, his reputation and his private and family life'.[104] Furthermore, Article 10 specifically asserts every individual's right to the inviolability and transmission of his or her correspondence.[105]

### 2.4.3    The ACHR system

The second strand of the Inter-American human rights system of protection is rooted in the ACHR. Adopted in 1969, it is a legally binding international convention, which defines the human rights that the ratifying states have agreed to respect and ensure.[106] It also specifies the means of their protection by declaring that the two principal organs, the IACtHR and the IACHR, are competent 'with respect to matters relating to the fulfilment of the commitments made by the State Parties to this Convention'.[107]

The IACtHR is an autonomous judicial institution whose main function is to apply and interpret the ACHR;[108] while its jurisdiction is both adjudicatory and advisory,[109] in that it may issue judgments and consultative opinions. Only those state parties to the ACHR which have accepted the IACtHR's continuous jurisdiction and the IACHR may submit a case to that Court.[110] Individuals lack direct recourse to the IACtHR and in order to institute proceedings must first present their petition to the IACHR and go through the relevant procedures.[111]

---

[101]    IACHR, 'Basic Documents in the Inter-American System', www.oas.org/en/iachr/mandate/basic_documents.asp.

[102]    ADHR (n 83) Preamble.

[103]    *Ibid* para 2.

[104]    *Ibid* Art V.

[105]    *Ibid* Art X.

[106]    ACHR (n 6) Art 1. At the time of writing, 25 states have ratified/acceded to the ACHR – see OAS, 'American Convention on Human Rights. Pact of San José, Costa Rica (B-32) Signatories and Ratification', www.oas.org/dil/treaties_B-32_American _Convention_on_Human_Rights_sign.htm.

[107]    *Ibid* Art 33.

[108]    OAS, Statute of the Inter-American Court of Human Rights, La Paz Bolivia (October 1979) Art 1.

[109]    *Ibid* Art 2.

[110]    OAS, 'Petition and Case System' (2010), www.oas.org/en/iachr/docs/pdf/HowTo.pdf.

[111]    *Ibid.*

## 2.4.3.1     *Article 11(1) of the ACHR – the right to privacy*
The right to privacy is stipulated in Article 11, which provides that:

1. Everyone has the right to have his honor respected and his dignity recognized.
2. No one may be the object of arbitrary or abusive interference with his private life, his family, his home, or his correspondence, or of unlawful attacks on his honor or reputation.
3. Everyone has the right to the protection of the law against such interference or attacks.[112]

The protection of privacy in Article 11 of the ACHR applies to most Latin American states. The provision prohibits all arbitrary or abusive interference, specifically enumerating a number of categories of privacy protection, including that of correspondence. In a similar vein to the HRC and the ECtHR, the IACtHR has recognized that privacy is a broad concept that should not be subject to exhaustive definition and explained that: 'the sphere of privacy is characterized by being exempt and immune from abusive and arbitrary invasion by third parties, or public authorities.'[113] To this end, the IACtHR has interpreted the right to privacy as:

a series of factors associated with the dignity of the individual, including for example, the ability to develop his or her own personality and aspirations, to determine his or her own identity and to define his or her own personal relationships.[114]

The Court has also acknowledged that privacy is inextricably linked to identity, which it has defined as 'the collection of attributes and characteristics that allow for the individualization of the person in a society'.[115]

The concept of private life has been considered in the IACtHR's jurisprudence in the context of, *inter alia*, journalistic disclosures of personal infor-

---

[112]     ACHR (n 6) Art 11.

[113]     *Escher et al v Brazil* Inter-American Court of Human Rights Series C No 67 (6 July 2009) para 113.

[114]     *Artavia Murillo et al v Costa Rica* Inter-American Court of Human Rights Series C No 257 (28 November 2012) para 43.

[115]     *Gelman v Uruguay* Inter-American Court of Human Rights Series C No 221 (24 February 2011) para 22.

mation of public officials;[116] physical, social[117] and gender identity (including sexual orientation);[118] and the integrity of the home.[119]

*2.4.3.2    Article 11(1) of the ACHR – the right to privacy of communications*
The importance of the protection of the right to privacy of communications as set out in Article 11 of the ACHR has been upheld by both the IACHR and the IACtHR. The former dealt with issues pertaining to privacy in relation to, *inter alia*, an individual's reputation;[120] searches of the home and seizure of documents;[121] together with human rights defenders in the Americas.[122] In this latter context, the IACHR noted that if such individuals or groups are to do their work freely, 'they must enjoy adequate protection from state authorities to guarantee that they will not be victims of arbitrary meddling in their private lives, or of attacks on their honor or reputation'.[123] It further asserted that this right includes 'State protection from harassment and intimidation, assaults, surveillance, interference with correspondence … telephone and electronic communications and illegal intelligence activities'.[124] The IACHR conceded that the law enforcement agencies may necessarily conduct intelligence operations, but this must occur in accordance with the law to combat crime, to protect constitutional order or to facilitate criminal prosecutions.[125] Further, the IACHR emphasized that 'the State cannot maintain intelligence files as means of control over general information related to the citizenry'.[126]

One of the most extensive analyses of the IACtHR pertaining to the right to privacy under Article 11 of the ACHR is that in the cases of *Escher et al*

---

[116]   See *Fontevecchia v Argentina* Inter-American Court of Human Rights Case No 12.524 (29 November 2011).

[117]   *Massacres of El Mozote and Nearby Places v El Salvador* Inter-American Court of Human Rights (25 October 2012) 1544. The IACtHR held that the concept of private life includes the right to privacy of one's sexual life.

[118]   *Atala Riffo and Daughters v Chile* Inter-American Court of Human Rights (24 February 2012).

[119]   *Case of Ituango Massacres v Colombia* Inter-American Court of Human Rights Series C No 148 (1 July 2006) para 194.

[120]   *Francisco Martorell v Chile* Inter-American Commission of Human Rights Rep 11/96 (3 May 1996).

[121]   *Garica v Peru* Inter-American Commission of Human Rights Report No 1/95 OEA/Ser L/V/II.88.rev.1 doc. 9 (1995).

[122]   Inter-American Commission on Human Rights, 'Report on the Situation of Human Rights Defenders in the Americas', www.cidh.org/countryrep/Defenders/defenderschap1-4.htm.

[123]   *Ibid* para 94.

[124]   *Ibid.*

[125]   *Ibid* para 100.

[126]   *Ibid.*

*v Brazil*[127] and *Donoso v Panama*,[128] both relating to the interception of telephone communications conducted by law enforcement agencies. In *Escher v Brazil* the application concerned the illegal wiretapping by the military police of organizations, farmers and land reform activists in the Brazilian state of Paraná. The IACtHR discussed in detail the nature of the obligation set out in Article 11 of the ACHR and spelled out the limits within which the police may intercept private communications. It first noted that although telephone conversations are not expressly mentioned in Article 11, they are nevertheless a form of communications falling within the sphere of the protection of privacy.[129] It therefore ruled that: 'article 11 protects conversations using telephone lines installed in private homes or in offices, whether their content is related to private affairs of the speakers, or to their business or professional activity.'[130] Furthermore, the Court found that Article 11 'applies to telephone conversations irrespective of their content and can even include both the technical operations designed to record this content by tapping it and listening to it, or any other element of the communication process'.[131] An example of the latter method is the recording of the destination or origin of the calls that are made, the identity of the speakers, the frequency, the time and the duration – all of which, the IACtHR noted, are aspects that can be verified without the need to record the content of the call by tapping the conversation.[132] For these reasons, the Court held that: 'the protection of privacy is manifested in the right that individuals other than those conversing may not illegally obtain information on the content of the telephone conversations or other aspects inherent in the communication process.'[133] The case of *Donoso v Panama* was based on similar facts to those of *Escher*, in that it concerned the interception of telephone conversations. In that case, an order was made by the Attorney General for the recording of phone calls between Panamanian lawyer Mr Donoso and his client. The IACtHR held that telephone conversations – whether private or business related – fall within the ambit of Article 11. In this case, as the conversations were between a lawyer and his client, they were subject to professional confidentiality and recording them constituted an interference with the right to privacy set out in Article 11.

---

[127] *Escher* (n 113).
[128] *Donoso v Panama* Inter-American Court of Human Rights Series C No 193 (27 January 2009) para 193.
[129] *Escher* (n 113) para 114.
[130] *Ibid.*
[131] *Ibid.*
[132] *Ibid.*
[133] *Ibid.*

The exceptional capabilities that many states now have at their disposal for conducting surveillance mean that the inter-American human rights system must adjust and adapt to the increased challenges regarding the protection of the right to privacy. The difficulties in facing up to this task are manifold and complex. First, the promotion and protection of individual human rights in the Americas has traditionally focused on the need to safeguard individuals and groups against torture, disappearances and mass killings, as historically the region has been plagued with repressive and violent military regimes and dictatorships, such as those in Chile, Argentina and Nicaragua.[134] As a consequence, the right to privacy of communications has only relatively recently begun to feature prominently within the legal structures of that region. Indeed, as noted by one commentator:

> when it comes to the right to privacy, the OAS treaty sets forth a right which is dear to the hearts of all Latin Americans, but which can best be called an ethical aspiration whose importance is less of an achievement than intent.[135]

Second, as outlined above, human rights protection is rooted in two distinct systems: one based on the OAS Charter and the other on the ACHR. Consequently, those OAS states which have not ratified the ACHR may refuse to accept the obligations stemming from the Convention. In such cases, those individuals whose rights have been violated will lack recourse to the IACtHR. This is particularly problematic in the context of cyber surveillance, as a number of OAS countries – including powerful and technologically advanced nations such as the US and Canada – have not ratified or acceded to the ACHR. This means that any allegations against these states made to the IACHR will be considered only on the basis of the ADHR, and not the ACHR.[136] Third, the system lacks an effective mechanism to ensure compliance with the IACtHR's judgments. This is because although the Court is required to submit to the General Assembly of the OAS an annual report which, *inter alia*, evidences those cases where its decisions have not been complied with, its role is confined to making 'pertinent recommendations'[137] to the states concerned to encourage adherence with its judgments. This limits the enforcement of the ACHR obligations to mainly political sanctions.

---

[134] See Mark Becker, 'Dictatorships in Latin America', https://science.jrank.org/pages/7630/Dictatorship-in-Latin-America.html.

[135] Ann Van Wynen Thomas and AJ Thomas Jr, 'Human Rights and the Organization of American States' (1972) 12(2) *Santa Clara Law Review* 319–76, 357.

[136] ACHR (n 6) Art 61.

[137] *Ibid.*

In summary, all three treaties – the ICCPR, the ECHR and the ACHR – recognize the privacy of communications as an autonomous right. Furthermore, in accordance with the interpretations of their judicial organs, the term 'correspondence' includes all forms of digital communications. A considerable array of activities have been identified as constituting interference with privacy, including: (1) online surveillance for state security purposes; (2) the existence of legislation that allows for secret surveillance; (3) the collection and storage of personal information, including in government databases; (4) the monitoring of Internet use, including emails; and (5) the interception of telephone calls.

## 3.   MASS CYBER SURVEILLANCE AS INTERFERENCE WITH THE RIGHT TO PRIVACY OF COMMUNICATIONS

Mass surveillance poses a unique challenge to the right to privacy of communications, and the first step in assessing whether it amounts to a violation is to ascertain what exactly constitutes an interference with this right. To this end, the views advanced by the HRC, the Office of the UN High Commissioner for Human Rights (OHCHR) and other human rights mandate holders, together with decisions from the European Courts (the ECtHR and the CJEU), the IACHR and the IACtHR, are of particular importance. On assessment of these pronouncements, a number of converging international law principles on privacy in the digital age can be discerned, which circumscribe the contours of the protected interests (outlined in section 4 *infra*). However, there are numerous points of divergence that have contributed to uncertainty in relation to what exactly amounts to an intrusion with privacy, including the following: (1) At what stage does the interference actually occur – at the point of data collection or when the gathered data is then analysed? (2) Does the collection of metadata amount to interference? (3) Does the operation of bulk interception programs constitute interference? All these aspects are explored below within the context of the interpretations of the notion of interference by the UN, European and Inter-American organs.

### 3.1   The Meaning of 'Interference' with the Right to Privacy in the Digital Age – the UN

#### 3.1.1   The UN HRC
It will be recalled that when interpreting the right to privacy of correspondence under Article 17 of the ICCPR, the HRC, in its General Comment 16, explained that 'the integrity and confidentiality of correspondence should be

guaranteed de jure and de facto'.[138] In the digital context, this means that states must 'ensure that e-mails and other forms of online communications are actually delivered to the desired recipient without the interference, or inspection by State organs, or by third parties'.[139]

In recent years, the HRC has reviewed numerous countries' existing surveillance legislation in light of their Article 17 obligations. The common thread in this process is the HRC's concern pertaining to infringements of the right to privacy enabled by these laws, facilitating the excessive use of surveillance methods, since many stipulate sweeping communications and metadata retention powers. Thus, when assessing US compliance with its Article 17 obligations, the HRC raised serious reservations:

> about the surveillance of communications in the interest of protecting national security, conducted by the National Security Agency (NSA) both within and outside the United States, through the bulk phone metadata surveillance programme (section 215 of the USA PATRIOT Act) and, in particular, surveillance under Section 702 of the Foreign Intelligence Surveillance Act (FISA) Amendment Act, conducted through PRISM (collection of communications content from United States-based Internet companies) and UPSTREAM (collection of communications metadata and content by tapping fibre optic cables carrying Internet traffic) and the adverse impact on individuals' right to privacy.[140]

In relation to the UK surveillance legislation, the HRC similarly observed that the now largely defunct Regulation of Investigatory Powers Act 2000 (RIPA), governing the interception of communications and communications data, 'allow[ed] for mass interception of communications and lack[ed] sufficient safeguards against arbitrary interference with the right to privacy'.[141] The HRC made similar observations on a number of subsequent occasions, each time referring to highly intrusive powers resulting in unlimited and indiscriminate surveillance of communications and the collection of metadata, which it clearly regards as an interference with Article 17 rights.[142] For example, when commenting on the French Intelligence Act 2015, the HRC raised concerns

---

[138]   General Comment 16 (n 16).

[139]   *Ibid* para 24.

[140]   Concluding Observations, US (n 30) para 22.

[141]   'Concluding Observations on the Seventh Periodic Report of the United Kingdom of Great Britain and Northern Ireland' (17 August 2015) UN Doc CCPR/C/GBR/CO/7 para 24 ('Concluding Observations, UK').

[142]   See, for example, Concluding Observations, Sweden 2016 (n 29) para 18; UNHRC, 'Concluding Observations on the Sixth Periodic Report of Canada' (20 July 2015) UN Doc CCPR/C/CAN/CO/6 para 10 ('Concluding Observations, Canada'); UNHRC, 'Concluding Observations on the Sixth Periodic Report Denmark' (15 August 2016) UN Doc CCPR/C/DNK/CO/6 para 27; UNHRC, 'Concluding Observations on

about the powers granted to the intelligence services for digital surveillance both within and outside France. In particular, the HRC observed that the Act 'gives the intelligence agencies excessively broad, highly intrusive surveillance powers on the basis of broad and insufficiently defined objectives, without the prior authorisation of a judge and without an adequate and independent oversight mechanism'.[143] The HRC has also commented extensively on other domestic legal regimes which allow for mass interception of communications,[144] by granting the intelligence agencies the authority to, *inter alia*, collect raw or bulk data from intercepted communications and share it with other state agencies.[145] Furthermore, the HRC has reflected on the insufficient transparency with regard to the scope of such laws and the safeguards on their application.[146] For example, in its Concluding Observations on Switzerland,[147] the HRC noted that that country's statutes accord very intrusive surveillance powers to its intelligence services, which operate on the basis of insufficiently defined objectives, such as the 'national interest'; while the period of the retention of data is often not specified.[148] Similarly, commenting on reports about the intrusive use of satellite communications and proposals for a system of bulk data retention in its Concluding Observations on Norway,[149] the HRC urged that all necessary steps be taken to guarantee that surveillance activities within and outside that state's territory are in conformity with the obligations under the ICCPR – in particular, Article 17.[150] To that end, the HRC specifically emphasized that states 'should take measures to guarantee that any interference in a person's private life should be in conformity with the principles of legality, proportionality and necessity'.[151] This means that the collection and use of data on communications must take place on the basis of a 'specific and legitimate objective'; while the 'exact circumstances in which

---

the Seventh Periodic Report on Colombia' (17 November 2016) UN Doc CCPR/C/COL/CO/7 para 32; Concluding Observations, Poland (n 26) para 39.

[143] UNHRC, 'Concluding Observations on the Fifth Periodic Report of France' (17 August 2015) UN Doc CCPR/C/FRA/CO/5.para 12 ('Concluding Observations, France').

[144] See, for example, Concluding Observations, UK (n 141) para 24; UNHRC, 'Concluding Observations on the Fourth Periodic Report of the Republic of Korea' (3 December 2015) UN Doc CCPR/C/KOR/CO/4 para 42; Concluding Observations, Honduras (n 29) para 38.

[145] Concluding Observations, Sweden 2016 (n 29) para 36.

[146] *Ibid.*

[147] Concluding Observations, Switzerland (n 29).

[148] *Ibid* 46.

[149] UNHRC, 'Concluding Observations on the Seventh Periodic Report of Norway' (28 April 2018) UN Doc CCPR/C/NOR/CO/7 ('Concluding Observations, Norway').

[150] *Ibid* 21.

[151] *Ibid.*

such interference may be authorised and the categories of persons likely to be placed under surveillance must be set in detail in law'.[152] States should also 'ensure the effectiveness and independence of a monitoring system for surveillance activities'.[153]

### 3.1.2    The Office of the High Commissioner for Human Rights

In her 2014 report,[154] UN High Commissioner for Human Rights Dr Navi Pillay warned that globally, 'mass surveillance [is] emerging as a dangerous habit rather than an exceptional measure'.[155] The document called for government surveillance to respect the right to privacy. It described the interference with this right as both the interception of communications content and the collection of metadata, thus rejecting a claim made by some countries – including the US[156] – that, unlike the former, the collection of communications data does not amount to an interference with Article 17 rights.[157] The report made it clear that:

> any capture of communications data is potentially an interference with privacy and… the collection and retention of communications data amounts to an interference with privacy whether or not those data are subsequently consulted or used. Even the mere possibility of communications information being captured creates an interference with privacy,[158] with a potential chilling effect on other rights, including those to free expression and association. The very existence of mass surveillance programs thus creates an interference with privacy. The onus would be on the State to demonstrate that such interference is neither arbitrary nor unlawful.[159]

Referencing the Court of Justice of the European Union's (CJEU) landmark decision in *Digital Rights Ireland*, the report explained that: 'the aggregation of information [of communications data] may give an insight into an individual's behaviour, social relationships, private preferences and identity that go beyond

---

[152]    *Ibid*; Schabas (n 3) 492.

[153]    *Ibid*.

[154]    Office of the UN High Commissioner for Human Rights (OHCHR), 'The Right to Privacy in the Digital Age. Report of the United Nations High Commissioner for Human Rights' (30 June 2014) UN Doc A/HRC/27/37 47 ('A/HRC/27/37').

[155]    *Ibid* para 3.

[156]    The position advanced by the US is that the collection of communications data (as against its content) does not amount to an interference with the right to privacy – see 'Transcript: Dianne Feinstein Saxby Chambliss Explain, Defend NSA Phone Records Program' *The Washington Post* (6 June 2013).

[157]    A/HRC/27/37 (n 154) para 19.

[158]    *Weber* (n 80) para 78; *Malone* (n 49) para 64.

[159]    A/HRC/27/37 (n 154) para 20, 7.

even that conveyed by accessing the content of a private communication.'[160] The *Digital Rights Ireland* case has provided a number of insights in relation to what is considered an interference with privacy rights and consequently has become an important benchmark and a reference point outside of the EU legal regime. It is therefore useful to recall at this juncture that the CJEU invalidated the Data Retention Directive (2006/24/EC), which required that providers of electronic communications services and networks retain all traffic and location data for a period of between six months and two years. This was to ensure that the data was available for the purpose of the investigation, detection and prosecution of serious crime. The CJEU held that even though the Directive did not provide for the retention of the content of communications, the traffic and location data covered by it, taken as a whole, may facilitate the drawing of very precise conclusions in relation to the private lives of the persons whose data has been retained.[161] Therefore, the obligation to hold the data constituted in itself an interference with the right to respect for private life and communications guaranteed by Article 7 of the EU Charter and the right to the protection of personal data under its Article 8. Moreover, the access by the competent authorities to the data constituted a further interference with these fundamental rights. The judgment has also made it clear that because the information was retained and subsequently used without the subscriber being informed, this was likely to generate in the minds of the persons concerned the feeling that their private lives were the subject of constant surveillance. Therefore, although the interference satisfied the public security objective, it failed to fulfil the requirement of proportionality.[162]

Both of these conclusions were reiterated in the subsequent OHCHR report issued in 2018. Thus, the mere existence of secret surveillance amounts to an interference with the right to privacy,[163] both at the point of the interception of communications (content and metadata) and when they are subsequently retained.

---

[160]  *Ibid.*

[161]  C-293/12 and C-594/12 *Digital Rights Ireland Ltd v Minister for Communications, Marine and Natural Resources and Others* (8 April 2014) paras 26–27 and 37 ('*Digital Rights Ireland*').

[162]  See, however, the CJEU's decision in four joint cases: C-623-17 *Privacy International*, C-511/18 *La Quadrature du Net and Others*, C-512/18 *French Data Network and Others* and C-520/18 *Ordre des Barreaux Francophones et Germanophone and Others* (6 October 2020) ('*La Quadrature du Net and Privacy International*'), according to which states may enact legislative measures for general and indiscriminate retention of data in exceptional circumstances, discussed further in Chapter 6.

[163]  UNHRC, 'The Right to Privacy in the Digital Age. Report of the United Nations High Commissioner for Human Rights' (3 August 2018) UN Doc A/HRC/39/29 para 7, 3 ('A/HRC/39/29').

### 3.1.3    UN Special Rapporteurs

The report of the UN Special Rapporteur on the promotion and protection of human rights and fundamental freedoms, Ben Emmerson, presented to the UN General Assembly (UNGA) in 2014,[164] built on the work of his predecessors, Martin Scheinin[165] and Frank La Rue.[166] The document asserted that bulk access to communications, mass surveillance of content and metadata, data retention and the use of automated mining algorithms with no prior suspicion or legal/executive authorization amount to 'systematic interference with the right to respect of the privacy of communications and [require] a correspondingly compelling justification'.[167] Furthermore, the report emphasized that: 'the use of mass surveillance technology effectively does away with the right to privacy of communications on the internet altogether.'[168] It also recalled that UNGA Resolution 69/167 confirmed the legal right to respect for the privacy of digital communications and therefore 'the adoption of mass surveillance technology undoubtedly impinges on the very essence of that right'.[169] Noting that the 'very existence of mass surveillance programs constitutes a potentially disproportionate interference with the right to privacy', the report concluded that:

> it is incompatible with the existing concepts of privacy for States to collect all communications, or metadata all the time indiscriminately. The very essence of the right to privacy of communications is that infringements must be exceptional and justified on a case-by-case basis.[170]

Consequently, the document put an onus 'on those States deploying bulk access surveillance technologies to explain promptly, precisely and publicly, why this wholesale intrusion into collective privacy is justified for the prevention of terrorism or other serious crime'.[171]

---

[164] UNGA, 'Report of the Special Rapporteur on the Promotion and Protection of Human Rights and Fundamental Freedoms While Countering Terrorism, Ben Emmerson' (23 September 2014) UN Doc A/69/397 ('A/HRC/69/397').

[165] UNHRC, 'Report of the Special Rapporteur on the Promotion and Protection of Human Rights while Countering Terrorism, Martin Scheinin (28 December 2009) UN Doc A/HRC/13/37 ('A/HRC/13/37').

[166] UNHRC, 'Report of the Special Rapporteur on the Promotion and Protection of the Right to Freedom of Opinion and Expression, Frank La Rue' (17 April 2013) UN Doc A/HRC/23/40 ('A/HRC/23/40').

[167] A/HRC/69/397 (n 164) para 9.

[168] *Ibid* para 12.

[169] *Ibid* para 18.

[170] *Ibid.*

[171] *Ibid* para 19.

In addition to 'interference' being thus circumscribed, the restriction of anonymity of digital communications is also regarded as an interference with the right to privacy, as its comprising impedes free exchange of communications and ideas. This point has been iterated by Special Rapporteur David Kaye, who observed that: 'Encryption and anonymity provide individuals and groups with a zone of privacy online to hold opinions and exercise freedom of expression without arbitrary and unlawful interference or attacks.'[172]

Finally, in addition to recognizing that the interception of communications and the collection of metadata constitute an interference with privacy, the Special Rapporteur on the right to privacy, Professor Joseph Cannataci, referring to the CJEU's decision in *Schrems I*, reiterated the Court's view that: 'legislation permitting the public authorities to have access on a generalized basis to the content of electronic communications must be regarded as compromising the essence of the fundamental right to respect for private life.'[173] The CJEU in that case explained that:

> to establish the existence of an interference with fundamental rights to respect of private life, it does not matter whether the information in question relating to private life is sensitive or whether the persons concerned have suffered any adverse consequences on account of that interference.[174]

In summary, several key points define what amounts to an 'interference' with the right to privacy of digital communications under Article 17 of the ICCPR, including: (1) the existence and operation of surveillance programs; (2) the unlimited and indiscriminate interception of communications contents and metadata at home and abroad; (3) the mere collection of data, even if it is not examined or used by a human or an algorithm; (4) the use of automated mining algorithms; (5) bulk retention of communications data; (6) the collection of raw data and its sharing among government agencies on broadly defined or undefined bases; and (7) the restriction of the anonymity of digital communications. Fundamentally, therefore, within the UN human rights regime, the existence of mass surveillance programs constitutes a disproportionate interference with the right to privacy of communications.

---

[172] UNHRC, 'Report of the Special Rapporteur for the Promotion and Protection of the Right to Freedom of Opinion and Expression, David Kaye' (22 May 2015) UN Doc A/HRC/29/32, para 12 ('A/HRC/29/32').

[173] UNHRC, 'Report of the Special Rapporteur on the Right to Privacy, Professor Joseph Cannataci' (24 November 2016) UN Doc A/HRC/31/64, para 31 ('A/HRC/31/64').

[174] C-362/14 *Maximilian Schrems v Data Protection Commissioner* [2015] ECJ para 87 ('*Schrems I*'); C-311/18 *Data Protection Commissioner v Facebook Ireland and Maximilian Schrems* [2020] ECJ ('*Schrems II*').

**3.2    The Meaning of 'Interference' with the Right to Privacy in the Digital Age – the ECtHR**

National surveillance legislation and measures may be subject to the ECtHR's review once domestic remedies have been exhausted.[175] An individual who alleges that interception interferes with his or her human rights must first satisfy the ECtHR that he or she can be considered to be a 'victim' of such interference (also referred to as 'standing' or '*locus standi*'),[176] so that the ECtHR can determine whether the case is admissible. This creates a problem as, due to the secretive nature of surveillance activities, applicants often struggle to demonstrate that they were indeed in fact their target. The ECtHR thus often jointly considers the question of the applicant's 'victim' status and that of the existence of an interference at the first stage of its review. In recent years, the Court addressed the issue of standing in *Zakharov v Russia*,[177] a decision widely regarded as one updating its previous jurisprudence in relation not only to *locus standi*, but also generally to domestic surveillance. Thus, the ECtHR consolidated a long line of previous case law and clarified the position with respect to who is permitted to bring a claim. The Court's Grand Chamber (GC) held that an applicant can assert to be the victim of an Article 8 violation on the basis of the mere existence of legislation which allows for a system of secret interception of communications, without having to demonstrate that these measures were applied to him or her.[178] In doing so, the GC confirmed that it will consider such applications *in abstracto*, and that the mere existence of a law permitting surveillance may in itself constitute interference. Whether that is the case is decided on the basis of a two-stage test. First, the ECtHR will determine whether the scope of the legislation is such that the applicant is likely to be affected by it – either because he or she belongs to a group of persons targeted by the contested legislation or on the grounds that it directly affects all users of communication.[179] Second, the Court will scrutinize the availability of the effective remedies at the domestic level and adjust the degree of its enquiry depending on the effectiveness of such remedies.[180] Thus,

---

[175]   ECHR (n 6) Art 35(1).

[176]   *Ibid* Art 34.

[177]   *Roman Zakharov v Russia* [GC] App no 47143/06 (4 December 2015).

[178]   *Ibid* para 171, 41.

[179]   *Ibid* para 171. The GC recalled *Kennedy v UK* (n 81) and stated that: 'where the domestic system does not afford an effective remedy to the person that he or she was subjected to secret surveillance, widespread suspicion and concern among the general public that secret surveillance powers are being abused cannot be said to be unjustified.'

[180]   *Ibid.*

where the mere threat of surveillance may in itself restrict communications, this will constitute a direct interference with the right to privacy for all users, thereby justifying the right to challenge the law in the abstract.[181] In such cases, the claimant need not demonstrate that the secret surveillance measures were in fact applied to him or her.

Good illustrations of this two-pronged approach are the cases of *Weber v Germany* and *Liberty v UK*, decided a decade ago; while a more recent application of this method can be seen in *Zakharov v Russia*, *Szabó v Hungary*,[182] *Centrum För Rättvisa v Sweden*[183] and *Big Brother Watch v UK*.[184] Thus, *Zakhorov* concerned Russian legislation granting sweeping surveillance powers to the intelligence and law enforcement agencies to intercept all domestic communications, whereby mobile network operators were required by law[185] to install equipment enabling operational search activities to be carried out, thus permitting the blanket interception of all mobile telephone communications.[186] The applicant claimed that this constituted an interference with his Article 8(1) rights because of the mere existence of legislation permitting secret surveillance measures and the risk of being subjected to them, rather than as a result of any specific surveillance methods applied to him.[187] The GC held that the legislation in question instituted such a secret system, as due to its operation, any person using Russian mobile telephone services could have his or her mobile communications intercepted, without ever being notified of this taking place.[188] To that end, the GC found that the legislation in question directly affected all users of these mobile telephone services; while Russian law did not provide for effective remedies to those who suspected they were subject to surveillance.[189] Having considered the secret nature of the surveillance measures under the statute in question, the broad scope of their applica-

---

[181] *Ibid.*

[182] *Máté Szabó and Beatrix Vissy v Hungary* App no 48725/17 (11 October 2017).

[183] *Centrum För Rättvisa v Sweden* App no 35252/08 (19 June 2018) ('*Centrum För Rättvisa*').

[184] *Big Brother Watch and Others v the United Kingdom* App no 58170/13; *Bureau of Investigative Journalism and Alice Ross v the United Kingdom* App no 62322/14; *10 Human Rights Organizations and Others v the United Kingdom* App no 24960/15 (12 October 2018) ('*Big Brother Watch*').

[185] The relevant national laws in question were the Operational-Search Activities Act of 1995, the Code of Criminal Procedure of 2001 and Order 70 issued by the Ministry of Communications, which required telecommunications networks to install equipment enabling law enforcement agencies to carry out operational search activities.

[186] ECtHR Press Release, 'Arbitrary and Abusive Secret Surveillance of Mobile Telephone Communications in Russia' (4 December 2015).

[187] *Zakharov* (n 177) para 177.

[188] *Ibid* para 175.

[189] *Ibid.*

tion (affecting all users of mobile telephone services) and the lack of effective means to challenge this secret system at the domestic level, the ECtHR held that: 'the mere existence of the contested legislation amounts in itself to an interference with the exercise of [the applicant's] rights under Article 8.'[190] The ECtHR adopted a similar stance on state secret surveillance affecting domestic communications in its subsequent *Szabó v Hungary* decision. That case related to the establishment in 2011 by the Hungarian authorities of a specific Anti-Terrorism Task Force (TEK) within the police force, with powers derived from the Police Act (Section 7E), as amended in 2011, and the National Security Act.[191] Under this framework, the TEK could conduct secret surveillance for two purposes: (1) the prevention, tracking and repelling of terrorist acts in Hungary; and (2) the gathering of intelligence necessary for rescuing Hungarian citizens in distress abroad.[192] The applicants – members of a non-governmental watchdog organization critical of the government – complained that the legislation (in particular, Section 7/E(3) of the Police Act) violated Article 8. This was based on the allegation that the provision in question was not sufficiently detailed and precise, and lacked adequate guarantees against arbitrariness and abuse.[193] The ECtHR found an infringement of Article 8, because a number of measures set out under the Hungarian regime amounted to interference by a public authority with the exercise of the applicants' rights, including conducting secret searches of homes and keeping them under surveillance; recording and opening letters; checking and recording the contents of electronic or computerized communications; and additionally making recordings of any data thus acquired.[194] Particularly noteworthy is the ECtHR's statement pertaining to the dangers of unrestricted surveillance. Recalling *Klass*, the Court observed that:

> in the mere existence of the legislation itself there is involved, for all those to whom the legislation could be applied, a menace of surveillance; this menace necessarily strikes at freedom of communication between users of the postal and telecommunication services and thereby constitutes an "interference by a public authority" with the exercise of the applicants' right to respect for private and family life and for correspondence.[195]

---

[190]  *Ibid* paras 178–79.
[191]  This competence was defined in Act XXXIV of 1994 on the Police, Section 7/e (as amended by Act CCVII of 2011).
[192]  *Szabó* (n 182) para 11.
[193]  *Ibid* paras 26–27.
[194]  ECtHR, Press Release, 'Hungarian Legislation on Secret Anti-Terrorist Surveillance Does Not Have Sufficient Safeguards Against Abuse' (12 January 2016).
[195]  *Szabó* (n 182) para 53.

The ECtHR further noted that: 'given the technological advances since the *Klass and Others* case, the potential interference with email, mobile phone and Internet services as well as those of mass surveillance attract the Convention protection of private life even more acutely.'[196] Following the clarification of the admissibility criterion in *Zakharov* and its application in *Szabó*, the subsequent litigation of *Big Brother Watch* found that the applicants (human rights groups and individual journalists) had standing to bring a claim, as they were sufficiently likely to have been the targets of surveillance in light of the wide scope of the interception program under the RIPA. Likewise, in *Centrum För Rättvisa v Sweden*, the ECtHR found that the mere existence of the Swedish signals intelligence regime amounted in itself to an interference with the applicant's rights under Article 8(1).

The above cases confirm that the ECtHR has taken a pragmatic stance on the issue of admissibility and show that the Court is prepared to hear cases *in abstracto*, provided that the applicant can demonstrate that he or she was sufficiently likely to have been the subject of the interception. This requirement can be satisfied by evidencing the existence of secret surveillance legislation, as this in itself constitutes an interference with the protected right.

### 3.2.1 The stage of interference

This jurisprudence also attests to the fact that for the ECtHR, interference with the right to privacy occurs once the intelligence services intercept the signals and begin collecting the data.[197] This interpretation has not been universally accepted, however. The practice of the intelligence agencies can be described in broad terms as consisting of the collection, filtering and storage of data, which is then accessed when needed for analysis. Consequently, a different interpretation has been advanced, according to which an interference with privacy rights occurs only at the point of the intelligence services actually accessing and analysing the previously gathered information, and not at the stage of amassing it.[198] This approach has been adopted, for example, in the

---

[196]  *Ibid.*

[197]  The same approach to interference transpires from the case law of the CJEU – see C-203/15 and C-698/15 *Tele2 Sverige AB v Post- och telestyrelsen and Secretary of State for Home Departments v Tom Watson and Others* (*'Tele-2/Watson'*) at para 100: 'The interference entailed by such legislation in the fundamental rights enshrined in Articles 7 and 8 of the Charter is very-far reaching and must be considered to be particularly serious. The fact that the data is retained without the subscriber or registered user being informed is likely to cause the persons concerned to feel that their private lives are subject to constant surveillance'; see also *Digital Rights Ireland* (n 161) para 37.

[198]  See, for example, CJEU *Opinion 1/15 on the Draft Agreement between Canada and the European Union on the transfer and processing of Passenger Name Record*

US and advanced by the UK government,[199] whereby the interference is considered to have taken place when the intelligence services use the data, rather than when they acquire it. This is not the case, however, for the ECtHR, the CJEU and the OHCHR, as according to their line of thinking the interference occurs at the point of data collection. To this end, the OHCHR report has confirmed that:

> The right to privacy is not only impacted by the examination or use of information about a person by a human or an algorithm. Even the mere generation and collection of data relating to a person's identity, family, or life already affects the right to privacy, as through those steps an individual loses some control over information that could put his or her privacy at risk.[200]

This divergence in understanding of the meaning of 'interference' is potentially far reaching. For the human rights courts and bodies, it denotes that it is established through the existence of legislation allowing for secret surveillance measures, which then opens up the means for the courts to proceed to analyse the merits of the case. Consequently, under the ECHR law, the mere collection of content and metadata by intelligence services constitutes an interference, regardless of whether the information is then analysed.

---

*data*, Opinion of the Advocate General (8 September 2016), where, in a case concerning the EU-Canada Passenger Name Record Agreement, the UK argued that there is no interference until the intelligence services begin to use the intercepted data. The CJEU held, however, that communication of personal data to a third party, such as a public authority, constitutes an interference with the right to respect for private life, regardless of the subsequent use of the communicated information – CJEU, *Opinion 1/15 on the Draft Agreement between Canada and the European Union on the transfer and processing of Passenger Name Records data*, Opinion of the Court (Grand Chamber) (26 July 2017) paras 124–25 ('CJEU *Opinion 1/15*').

[199] EU Agency for Fundamental Rights, 'Surveillance by Intelligence Services. Fundamental Rights Safeguards and Remedies in the EU. Volume II: Field Perspectives and Legal Update' (Luxembourg Publications Office of the EU, 2017) 35. See also *Liberty v MI5*, where, in the context of Liberty's challenge of MI5's surveillance, the Hight Court observed that: 'There is a fundamental difference of approach as between the Claimant and the Defendants in relation to the obtaining and retention of bulk data, as distinct from its later selection for examination. It is common ground between the parties that there is an interference with the right to respect for private life at all material stages, including at the stage when data is obtained and retained. However, the Defendants submit that there is no "meaningful" intrusion into privacy rights until the stage when the data is selected for examination. The Claimant submits that that is wrong and inconsistent with "decades" of authority from the European Court of Human Rights. It also submits that this is a proposition which is not only "startling" but "dangerous and artificial"' – *Liberty and Privacy International v SSHD and SSFCA* [27 July 2019] EWHC 2057 para 6, 4 ('*Liberty v MI5*').

[200] A/HRC/39/29 (n 163) para 7, 3.

This view can be contrasted with that taken in *Tallinn Manual 2.0*. In considering this issue, the Manual's experts failed to take a unified stance. Having agreed that, in principle, the right to privacy encompasses the confidentiality of communications, including emails, the consensus reached is that this right is implicated when a state accesses the communication's content and when it is subject to human inspection.[201] Opinion was divided on the applicability of the right to machine inspection by algorithmic analysis.[202] In particular, no consensus was achieved on whether an interference occurs where a machine engages in the inspection of content to filter for terms that will result in subsequent inspection.[203] The prevailing view was that the right to privacy is implicated only when the state accesses the content of communications or processes personal data found in them.[204] Only a small number of experts concurred with the belief that the mere collection of communications, even without accessing them, constitutes an interference.[205] The uncertainty relating to the stage in the intelligence cycle at which the interference occurs can have potentially far-reaching consequences. This is because the standpoint that it takes place only when the already collected data is analysed legitimizes the collection and retention of vast troves of data with practically no legal constraints. This thus creates an atmosphere of constant state surveillance, which the ECtHR in particular has long been mindful of in its interpretation of this term.

A related matter concerns the use of bulk interception programs, which also evidences a certain bi-polarity of approaches.

### 3.2.2 Bulk interception of communications

Prior to the decisions in *Centrum För Rättvisa v Sweden* and *Big Brother Watch v UK*, the ECtHR had considered on only two other occasions the compatibility of regimes which expressly permit the bulk interception of foreign communications, namely in *Weber v Germany* and then in *Liberty v UK*. The *Weber* case concerned a complaint regarding the process of strategic surveillance under the amended German G10 Act, which authorized the monitoring of international wireless telecommunications. Interception sites, situated on German territory, collected signals emitted from foreign countries with the aid of certain catchwords listed in the monitoring order. Only communications containing these phrases were recorded and used. The Court considered and

---

[201] Michael N Schmitt (ed), *Tallinn Manual 2.0 on the International Law Applicable to Cyber Operations* (Cambridge University Press, 2017) Rule 35 para 7, 189 ('*Tallinn Manual 2.0*').

[202] *Ibid* para 8, 190.

[203] *Ibid*.

[204] *Ibid* para 9.

[205] *Ibid*.

applied six minimum procedural safeguards for lawful interception (discussed in more detail in Chapter 6). Having established that there existed adequate and effective guarantees against abuses of Germany's strategic monitoring powers, the ECtHR considered the complaint of a violation of Article 8 as ill founded. By contrast, an infringement of this right was found in *Liberty v UK*. The ECtHR reviewed the UK interception regime of external communications under the then Interception of Communications Act 1985, which allowed the British government, through an interception facility also located within its territory, to monitor simultaneous conversations between Ireland and Europe. The legal challenge was brought by two Irish non-governmental organizations, which complained that this violated their Article 8 rights, and the ECtHR GC pronounced in their favour. This is because, unlike in *Weber*, the law in question did not indicate, with sufficient clarity so as to provide adequate protection against abuse of power, the scope or manner of the exercise of the very wide discretion conferred on the state to intercept and examine external communications. Specifically, the GC held that the UK regime did not set out, in a form accessible to the public, any indication of the procedures to be followed for selecting for examination, sharing, storing and destroying the intercepted material. Although these two decisions represent different outcomes, an important aspect that they have in common is that the ECtHR underscored that national authorities enjoy a wide margin of appreciation in choosing how best to achieve the legitimate aim of protecting national security.[206] For this reason, it accepted in both *Weber* and in *Liberty* that bulk interception regimes do not *per se* fall outside states' margin of discretion, meaning that in principle they may conduct strategic surveillance of foreign communications, provided that the methods of doing so adhere to the procedural standards set out by the ECtHR in, *inter alia*, the *Weber* case. This stance the ECtHR subsequently followed in both *Centrum För Rättvisa* and *Big Brother Watch*.

In the much-anticipated *Big Brother Watch* decision, the First Section of the ECtHR was asked to consider three joined applications arising out of the disclosures of classified information made by Edward Snowden in 2013 relating to the GCHQ-run bulk communications interception program Tempora and two NSA surveillance programs – PRISM and Upstream. The applicants argued that the then UK legal framework, the RIPA, regulating the acquisition, use, sharing and destruction of intercepted communications, violated, *inter alia*,[207] Article 8 of the ECHR. The complaint focused on three different surveillance regimes under that legislation, namely: (1) the bulk interception of

---

[206] *Weber* (n 80) para 106.
[207] The applicants also brought complaints in relation to the violation of Article 6, Article 10, Article 14 and Article 41 of the ECHR.

communications pursuant to Section 8(4) of the RIPA, which was alleged to be so complex as to be inaccessible and therefore lacking the necessary quality of law;[208] (2) the obtaining of communications data from communications service providers (CSPs) under Chapter II of the RIPA, which was said to allow for the obtaining of such data in unclear circumstances and without proper safeguards;[209] and (3) intelligence sharing with foreign governments – specifically, information intercepted by the NSA under the PRISM and Upstream programs, for which, the applicants argued, there was no basis in law.[210] Each of these grounds is outlined below.

### 3.2.2.1    The Section 8(4) regime

Having referred to *Weber*, the ECtHR reiterated that it was accepted that bulk interception schemes did not *per se* fall outside national authorities' broad margin of discretion in choosing how best to achieve legitimate aims.[211] The Court then concluded that 'the decision to operate a bulk interception regime in order to identify hitherto unknown threats to national security is one which continues to fall within States' margin of appreciation'.[212] This the ECtHR justified on the basis of:

> current threats facing many Contracting States (including the scourge of global terrorism and other serious crime, such as drug trafficking, human trafficking, the sexual exploitation of children and cybercrime), advancements in technology, which have made it easier for terrorists and criminals to evade detection on the Internet, and the unpredictability of the routes, via which electronic communications are transmitted.[213]

The ECtHR found that there was a clear interference with the applicants' Article 8 rights and proceeded to consider whether this was justified on the basis of the three criteria of 'in accordance with the law', legitimate aim and necessity set out in Article 8(2).[214] By a majority, the First Section held that there was a violation of Article 8 because the regime pursuant to Section 8(4) of the RIPA did not meet the 'quality of law' requirement, and as such was 'incapable of keeping the "interference" to what is "necessary in a democratic society"'.[215]

---

[208]    *Big Brother Watch* (n 184) para 273.
[209]    *Ibid* para 457.
[210]    *Ibid* para 398.
[211]    *Ibid* para 314.
[212]    *Ibid.*
[213]    *Ibid* para 314.
[214]    This is discussed in more detail in Chapter 6.
[215]    *Big Brother Watch* (n 184) para 388.

### 3.2.2.2    The Chapter II regime

The core of the applicants' argument in this context was that Chapter II of the RIPA regime on the acquisition of communications data retained by CSPs permitted such data to be obtained in a wide range of ill-defined circumstances, without proper safeguards. The ECtHR found that that part of the Act and the accompanying Acquisition and Disclosure of Communications Data Code of Practice provided a clear legal basis, but ultimately held that there was a violation of Article 8, as the Chapter II regime was not in accordance with the law within the meaning of Article 8. In reaching this decision, the ECtHR relied on the CJEU's rulings in *Digital Rights Ireland* and *Tele-2/Watson*[216] concerning the retention of data by CSPs, holding that their access must be limited to that which is strictly necessary – namely, fighting serious crime[217] – and be subject to prior review by a court or an independent administrative body. The ECtHR stressed that since at that time the UK was a member of the EU, in case of a conflict between domestic and EU law, the latter should prevail. As the Chapter II regime permitted access for the purpose of combating 'crime', as against 'serious crime' as set out under EU law, and with little *ex ante* scrutiny by a court or an independent administrative body, Article 8 rights were implicated.[218]

### 3.2.2.3    Intelligence-sharing regime

The applicants argued that the UK government's receipt of material intercepted by the NSA under PRISM and Upstream programs was in breach of their rights pursuant to Article 8, as there was no basis in law for the intelligence sharing carried out by the government agencies and no regime which satisfied the 'quality of law' requirement.[219] Having observed that this was the first time that it had been asked to assess the compliance of such a scheme with the ECHR, the First Section found no violation of Article 8.[220] The ECtHR's approach was first to clarify that the alleged interference consisted of the receipt, storage, examination and use of the intercepted material by the UK authorities (rather than the UK agencies being responsible for the interception itself).[221] The ECtHR then assessed the intelligence sharing arrangements in the light of the applicable test under Article 8(2) and decided that the domestic law was sufficiently clear, as it indicated the procedures to be used by the UK

---

[216]   *Tele-2/Watson* (n 197).
[217]   *Big Brother Watch* (n 184) para 463.
[218]   *Ibid* para 467.
[219]   *Ibid* para 398.
[220]   *Ibid* para 416.
[221]   *Ibid* para 420.

services when requesting foreign intelligence agencies to intercept or convey the intercepted material.[222]

Both decisions in the *Big Brother Watch* and *Centrum För Rättvisa* cases were delivered by the First Division and have been appealed to the ECtHR Grant Chamber, with final judgments pending at the time of writing. Nevertheless, based on these and the previous ECtHR case law, the following observations are in order in relation to the meaning of the term 'interference' in the context of digital surveillance: (1) the operation of bulk surveillance programs is an interference, but does not *per se* amount to a violation of Article 8 of the ECHR, as this falls within the state's broad discretion. However, a breach of this provision may be found on the basis of the manner of their operation – that is, if this does not follow the prescribed procedural safeguards; (2) an interference with the protected right occurs not only when the data is accessed for analysis, but also at the point of its interception and collection; and (3) intelligence-sharing arrangements may amount to interference, but will not necessarily violate Article 8 rights if they meet the set criteria under Article 8(2) of the ECHR.

### 3.3 The Meaning of 'Interference' with the Right to Privacy in the Digital Age – the IACtHR

In June 2013, in response to the revelations made by Edward Snowden regarding the NSA's secret surveillance, the UN Special Rapporteur on the protection and promotion of the right to freedom of opinion and expression and the Special Rapporteur for freedom of expression of the Inter-American Commission on Human Rights[223] issued a *Joint Declaration on Surveillance Programs and Their Impact on Freedom of Expression* (Joint Declaration).[224] The document highlighted a series of international legal principles pertaining to the right to privacy and freedom of expression in the context of the programs used by the NSA to collect digital content and metadata and those of a number of other states in the Americas that routinely intercept communications from private parties. The Joint Declaration emphasized the concerns of the Special Rapporteurs regarding the existence of these and other security

---

[222] *Ibid* para 447.

[223] See OAS, 'Office of Special Rapporteur for Freedom of Expression. History' (2011), www.oas.org/en/iachr/expression/showarticle.asp?artID=52&lID=2.

[224] OAS, UN Special Rapporteur on the protection and promotion of the right to freedom of opinion and expression and Special Rapporteur for freedom of expression of the Inter-American Commission on Human Rights, 'Joint Declaration on Surveillance Programs and Their Impact on Freedom of Expression' (2013) ('OAS Joint Declaration').

measures stressing the serious harm that they pose to these fundamental rights. Furthermore, it underlined the need to amend states' surveillance legislation and 'establish improved mechanisms for transparency and public debate on theses practices'.[225] The Declaration recognized that communications surveillance constitutes an interference with the right to privacy, being 'a particularly invasive act that seriously affects [this] right and freedom of expression'.[226] To this end, the document echoed the UN approach – namely that the protection of national security may justify in exceptional cases the surveillance of private communications, but that ensuring human rights protection must be a fundamental part of any counter-terrorism strategy.[227] The rapid technological progress of recent years, the report observed, coupled with the fact that the Internet has facilitated the amassing of large amounts of data on persons – including their locations, online activities and with whom they communicate – means that such information is not only highly revealing, but also easily accessible. Consequently, the use of such data 'by police and security forces running surveillance programs intended to combat terrorism and defend national security has increased without adequate regulation in the majority of the States in [the Latin American] region';[228] while the legislation on intelligence and security 'has remained inadequate as new technologies have been developed in the digital era'. For these reasons, 'the indiscriminate access to information on communications between persons can have a chilling effect on the freedom of expression of thought and the search for and distribution of information in the region'.[229] In view of these concerns, the Joint Declaration called on states to guarantee that their surveillance activities be clearly authorized by law to protect against arbitrary and abusive interference with private interests.[230] It also underscored states' duties of public transparency and accountability in relation to the regulatory framework of surveillance programs, which 'must establish limits with regard to the nature, scope and duration of these type of measures [and] the reasons for ordering them'; while 'any surveillance of communications and interference with privacy that exceeds what is stipulated by law... or is carried out clandestinely, must be harshly punished.'[231]

To summarize, under the inter-American system, interference with the right to privacy occurs when a state intercepts, monitors, collects and discloses communications. The use of surveillance programs to combat terrorism and

---

[225]   *Ibid* Opening Statement para 2.
[226]   *Ibid* para 3.
[227]   *Ibid* para 3.
[228]   *Ibid* para 4.
[229]   *Ibid* para 5.
[230]   *Ibid* para 7.
[231]   *Ibid,* paras 8–12.

in pursuit of other national security goals also amounts to an interference either where it is undertaken on an inadequate or non-existent legal basis, or where there is indiscriminate access to information. Surveillance legislation must therefore clearly specify the criteria to be used to determine when such surveillance may be lawfully undertaken.

## 4. THE CONTOURS OF INTERFERENCE WITH THE RIGHT TO PRIVACY OF COMMUNICATIONS IN THE DIGITAL AGE

Based on the interpretation of the notion of 'interference' with the right to privacy in the context of digital surveillance from the human rights courts, bodies and the various mandate holders on the international and regional levels, interference with the right to privacy of communications is established in the following circumstances: (1) where there is legislation allowing for secret surveillance measures;[232] (2) where both the content of communications[233] and communications data[234] are collected, irrespective of whether that data is examined;[235] (3) where the data, once collected, is analysed; (4) where personal data is collected without the knowledge or permission of the individuals subject to the interception; (5) where the data is retained over time;[236] (6) where raw or processed data is made available pursuant to intelligence-sharing arrangements;[237] and (7) where the anonymity of digital communications is restricted through compromising the methods of their encryption.[238]

However, based on the legal developments at the time of writing, there appears to have emerged an important jurisprudential difference regarding the existence and the use of mass cyber surveillance programs. Thus, for the ECtHR, the operation of bulk interception schemes does not *per se* constitute a violation, as this falls within the state's margin of discretion. It will constitute an infringement with Article 8 rights if it fails to fulfil the minimum procedural requirements – the so-called *Weber* criteria.[239] However, for the UN

---

[232]  *Weber* (n 80); *Liberty* (n 63); *Zakharov* (n 177); *Szabó* (n 182); *Centrum För Rättvisa* (n 183).

[233]  General Comment 16 (n 16); A/HRC/27/37 (n 154); *Malone* (n 49); *Liberty ibid*; *Zakharov ibid*; *Szabó ibid*.

[234]  *Malone ibid*; A/HRC/27/37 *ibid*; *Digital Rights Ireland* (n 161); *Escher* (n 113).

[235]  CJEU *Opinion 1/15* (n 198); *Digital Rights Ireland ibid*; *Tele-2/Watson* (n 197).

[236]  *Amann* (n 50); *Rotaru* (n 44); *S and Marper* (n 8); *Digital Rights Ireland ibid*; *Tele-2/Watson ibid*.

[237]  Concluding Observations, Sweden 2016 (n 29) para 36; *Big Brother Watch* (n 184).

[238]  A/HRC/29/32 (n 172); A/HRC/23/40 (n 166).

[239]  *Centrum För Rättvisa* (n 183); *Big Brother Watch* (n 184).

human rights bodies and mandate holders and the inter-American organs, mass surveillance compromises the very essence of the right to respect for private life,[240] as it is inherently disproportionate and therefore cannot be justified. This apparent legal gap may become less pronounced when the ECtHR GC delivers its final decision in *Big Brother Watch* and *Centrum För Rattvisa* cases. However, predicting the outcome at this stage may be too speculative. It is nevertheless tentatively submitted that, bearing in mind the Court's general acquiescence pertaining to strategic surveillance dating back to the 2006 *Weber* judgment, this seems unlikely.

## 5.    CONCLUSION

The ubiquitous and pervasive nature of mass surveillance has challenged the right to privacy, and the initial response from the UN human rights bodies and the regional courts in the aftermath of the Snowden revelations was to recognize and condemn it as a violation of treaty obligations. Since then, however, many governments have been increasing their powers of surveillance at home and abroad; while the ECtHR has upheld a number of domestic bulk interception regimes, referring to this practice as a 'valuable means' to counter terrorism. In light of these developments, it is likely that these activities are becoming a permanent feature of most states' security tool-box.

The aim of this chapter was to identify the types of cyber surveillance activities that amount to an interference with privacy. Having analysed the approaches taken at the UN, European and inter-American levels, what emerges is a fragmented legal landscape, with the jurisprudence of the ECtHR appearing to be more permissive when it comes to the operation of mass surveillance programs and intelligence-sharing arrangements compared with the position taken by the other courts and bodies. The chapter highlighted a number of key aspects in the debate relating to the meaning of 'interference' in the digital age, most notably the stance adopted – at least for the time being – by the ECtHR, according to which mass surveillance of foreign communications is an indispensable instrument used by states to safeguard national security, when it is undertaken in accordance with the relevant procedural safeguards. It also outlined the approach taken on the issue of *locus standi*. Thus, in order to bring a claim before the international or regional judicial organs, an individual must first exhaust domestic remedies. Under the ICCPR, he or she may bring a complaint against the state before the HRC alleging a violation of

---

[240]  Concluding Observations, US (n 30); Concluding Observations, UK (n 141); Concluding Observations, Sweden 2016 (n 29); Concluding Observations, France (n 143).

Article 17 rights if that state is a party to the Optional Protocol 1. Within the inter-American system, only those individuals whose countries have ratified the ACHR may have access to the IACtHR, but this recourse is indirect, as it necessitates a petition to the IACHR. Finally, on the European level, the ECtHR will hear a complaint pertaining to secret surveillance *in abstracto*, thus affording the applicant 'victim status' where there is a sufficient likelihood that he or she was the target of the interception.

# 6. Treaty-based privacy protection – justifications

## 1. INTRODUCTION

Once it has been established that an interference with the right to privacy has taken place, it must then be determined whether that interference can be justified. This is because, in contrast to a number of absolute rights,[1] such as the right to life or the right not to be subject to torture, the right to privacy is qualified. This means that in some circumstances, states may lawfully restrict its enjoyment in order to protect others or the wider public interest. This is expressly recognized in Article 17(1) of the International Covenant on Civil and Political Rights (ICCPR), Article 11(2) of the American Convention on Human Rights (ACHR) and Article 8(2) of the European Convention on Human Rights (ECHR). Thus, while Article 17(2) prohibits interference that is 'arbitrary and unlawful', Article 11(2) stipulates that it must not be 'arbitrary and abusive'. Unlike these rather general formulations, however, the text of Article 8(2) is more specific, as it articulates that privacy may be limited if it is 'in accordance with the law' and 'necessary in a democratic society'. In addition, the provision enumerates specific instances in which such interference may lawfully take place – that is, where it is necessary (1) in the interest of national security, public safety or the economic wellbeing of the country; (2) for the prevention of disorder or crime; (3) for the protection of health and morals; or (4) for the protection of the rights and freedoms of others.[2] Despite these textual differences, the jurisprudence interpreting all three provisions shares a common approach to determining the issue of justification, based on a three-part test: namely, that the measure in question (1) be in accordance with

---

[1]  The Council of Europe (CoE) explains that 'absolute or unqualified rights are rights, which cannot be balanced against the needs of other individuals or against any general public interest' – see CoE, 'Some Definitions', www.coe.int/en/web/echr -toolkit/definitions.

[2]  CoE, European Convention for the Protection of Human Rights and Fundamental Freedoms amended by Protocols Nos 11 and 14 (4 November 1950) (European Convention on Human Rights) Art 8(2) ('ECHR').

the law; (2) pursue a legitimate aim; and (3) be necessary and proportionate to the achievement of that aim.

This chapter addresses the question of whether mass cyber surveillance of foreign communications is lawful by applying these three criteria. The discussion commences with an evaluation of whether interference with an individual's right to privacy through the deployment of bulk interception and collection surveillance programs is in accordance with the law. Section 3 considers whether these methods can be said to pursue a legitimate aim; while Section 4 assesses bulk intelligence gathering in the light of the requirements of necessity and proportionality. Conclusions on the findings are set out in Section 5.

## 2.    'IN ACCORDANCE WITH THE LAW'

The term 'in accordance with the law' means that the interference with privacy rights must be based in law. In the context of surveillance, this requires not only that domestic legislation authorizing the use of the interception exists (ie, it must have a legal basis), but also that such legislation has certain characteristics – namely, it must be (1) accessible to the public; (2) clear and precise; and (3) foreseeable.

### 2.1    Legal Basis

The requirement that interference with privacy can occur only if conducted pursuant to the state's domestic law is a fundamental condition of international human rights law and broadly of the rule of law.

Under Article 17 of the ICCPR, the principle of legality is closely linked to the notion of 'arbitrary interference'. The Human Rights Committee (HRC) elaborated on the meaning of the terms 'unlawful' and 'arbitrary' in its General Comment 16. Thus, the HRC stated that 'unlawful':

> means that no interference can take place except in cases envisaged by the law. Interference authorised by States can only take place on the basis of the law, which itself must comply with the provisions, aims and objectives of the Covenant.[3]

Moreover, the conjunctive nature of Article 17(1) requires that in addition to not being unlawful, interference must not be arbitrary. This stipulation mirrors that set out in Article 12(1) of the Universal Declaration of Human Rights

---

[3]    UNHRC, 'CCPR General Comment No. 16: Article 17 (Right to Privacy). The Right to Respect of Privacy, Family, Home and Correspondence and Protection of Honour and Reputation' (8 April 1988) UN Doc HRI/Gen/1/Rev.9 (Vol 1) para 3 ('General Comment 16').

and subsumes within its meaning the notions of injustice, unpredictability and unreasonableness.[4] The significance attached to 'arbitrariness' was further elaborated on in the context of Article 9 of the ICCPR (liberty and security of person), where the HRC stated that:

> the notion of 'arbitrariness' is not to be equated with 'against the law', but must be interpreted more broadly to include elements of inappropriateness, injustice, lack of predictability and due process of law, as well as elements of reasonableness, necessity and proportionality.[5]

In addition, 'arbitrariness' suggests an interference with privacy by state organs.[6] Explaining this concept in the context of interference with that right, the HRC commented in General Comment 16 that:

> the expression 'arbitrary interference' is also relevant to the protection of the right provided for in article 17 [and] can also extend to interference provided for under the law. The introduction of the concept of arbitrariness is intended to guarantee that even interference provided for by law should be in accordance with the provisions, aims and objectives of the Covenant and should be, in any event, reasonable in the particular circumstances.[7]

The HRC also specified the characteristics and the meaning of the term 'law', when addressing the right to freedom of expression under Article 19 of the ICCPR, declaring that:

> a norm to be characterised as 'law' must be formulated with sufficient precision to enable an individual to regulate his or her conduct accordingly and it must be made accessible to the public. A law may not confer unfettered discretion for the restriction of expression on those charged with its execution. Laws must provide sufficient guidance to those charged with their execution to enable them to ascertain what sorts of expression are properly restricted and what sorts are not.[8]

In the context of mass surveillance, the HRC found numerous instances involving state agencies falling foul of the aforementioned standards due to the interception of personal communications without explicit statutory authorization or defined safeguards, which as a consequence provide insufficient

---

[4]    William A Schabas, *U.N. International Covenant on Civil and Political Rights. Novak's CCPR Commentary* (N.P. Engel, 2019) 465 ('Schabas').

[5]    UNHRC, 'General Comment No. 35, Article 9 (Liberty and Security of Person)' (16 December 2014) UN Doc CCPR/C/GC/35, 12 ('General Comment 35').

[6]    Schabas (n 4) 465.

[7]    General Comment 16 (n 3) para 4.

[8]    UNHRC, 'General Comment No. 34, Article 19: Freedoms of Opinion and Expression' (21 July 2011) UN Doc CCPR/C/GC/34, 25 ('General Comment 34').

guarantees against abuse.[9] Responding to these shortcomings, the HRC has made a number of recommendations pertaining to the requirement of legality. For example, in its Concluding Observations on South Africa, the HRC urged that country to 'ensure the interception of communications by law enforcement and security services is carried out only according to the law and under judicial supervision'.[10] In a similar vein, Turkmenistan was asked to:

> ensure that ... all types of surveillance activities and interference with privacy, including online surveillance for the purposes of State security, are governed by appropriate legislation that is in full conformity with the Covenant, in particular article 17, including with the principles of legality, proportionality and necessity, and that State practice conforms thereto.[11]

In its comments in relation to Belarus,[12] the HRC was also critical of the legislation in question, which set out broad powers of surveillance of communications, allowing remote access to all users' communications without notifying providers.[13] As the legislation did not afford sufficient safeguards against arbitrary interference with privacy, Belarus was urged to ensure that all types of surveillance activities, including online surveillance, are 'governed by appropriate legislation that is in full conformity with the Covenant, in particular article 17, including with principles of legality, proportionality and necessity'.[14]

The European Court of Human Rights (ECtHR) has adopted a similar approach to the interpretation of the phrase 'in accordance with the law' under Article 8(2) of the ECHR. In *Sunday Times v UK*, the ECtHR held that this involves two preconditions. The first is that the law be accessible; while the second is that a norm cannot be regarded as 'law' unless it is formulated with sufficient precision to enable a citizen to regulate his or her conduct.[15] In a number of early surveillance cases, the ECtHR consistently maintained

---

[9]   See, for example, UNHRC, 'Concluding Observations on the Sixth Periodic Report of Italy' (1 May 2017) UN Doc CCPR/C/IT/CO/6 para 36 ('Concluding Observations, Italy').

[10]   UNHRC, 'Concluding Observations on the Initial Report of South Africa' (27 April 2016) UN Doc CCPR/C/ZAF/CO/1 ('Concluding Observations, South Africa').

[11]   UNHRC, 'Concluding Observations on the Second Periodic Report on Turkmenistan' (20 April 2017) UN Doc CCPR/C/TKM/CO/2, 36-37 ('Concluding Observations, Turkmenistan').

[12]   UNHRC, 'Concluding Observations on the Fifth Periodic Report of Belarus' (22 November 2018) UN Doc CCPR/C/BLR/CO/5 ('Concluding Observations, Belarus').

[13]   *Ibid* para 43.

[14]   *Ibid* para 44.

[15]   *Sunday Times v the United Kingdom* App no 6538/74 (26 April 1979) para 49.

that any interference with privacy must be based on national legislation.[16] Commenting in the context of domestic state surveillance in *Zakharov v Russia*, the ECtHR reiterated this basic requirement, stating that:

> 'in accordance with the law' requires the impugned measure both to have some basis in domestic law and to be compatible with the rule of law, which is expressly mentioned in the Preamble to the Convention and inherent in the object and purpose of Article 8. The law must thus meet quality requirements: it must be accessible to the person concerned and foreseeable as to its effects.[17]

This fundamental condition also features strongly in the inter-American legal tradition. Thus, in *Donoso v Panama*, the Inter-American Court of Human Rights (IACtHR) held that any restriction on privacy must have a legal basis. Having first noted that privacy is not an absolute right, the IACtHR then observed that it may be restricted by the state only if the interference is not abusive or arbitrary. Thus, any restrictions must be statutorily enacted.[18] This condition was reiterated in the Organization of American States' (OAS) Joint Declaration on Surveillance Programs, which demands that states guarantee that:

> the interception, collection and use of personal information, including all limitations on the right of the affected person to access this information, be clearly authorised by law in order to protect them from arbitrary or abusive interference with their private interests.[19]

Signals intelligence (SIGINT) collection of foreign communications was practised by states long before the Snowden disclosures. These operations were likely to have been conducted either without any legal grounds or without a robust legal framework – and in many instances, continue to be so. A case is point is the National Security Agency's (NSA) collection of foreign communications pursuant to Section 702 of the Foreign Intelligence Surveillance

---

[16] See, for example, *Malone v the United Kingdom* App no 8691/79 (2 August 1984) para 67; *Huvig v France* App no 11105/84 (24 April 1990) para 28; *Kruslin v France* App no 11801/85 (24 April 1990) para 27; *Khan v the United Kingdom* App no 35394/94 (12 May 2000) para 26.

[17] *Roman Zakharov v Russia* [GC] App no 47143/06 (4 December 2015) para 228.

[18] *Donoso v Panama* Inter-American Court of Human Rights Series C No 193 (27 January 2009) para 56.

[19] Organization of American States (OAS), UN Special Rapporteur on the protection and promotion of the right to freedom of opinion and expression and Special Rapporteur for freedom of expression of the Inter-American Commission on Human Rights, 'Joint Declaration on Surveillance Programs and Their Impact on Freedom of Expression' (2013) para 8 ('OAS Joint Declaration').

Act (FISA), where this occurs on the basis of annual certifications, also acknowledged to be used to collect Americans' communications without a warrant,[20] and Executive Order 12333. The latter mechanism has been used in an even more opaque manner than Section 702. It is said to serve often as an alternative basis of authority for US surveillance activities above and beyond Section 702.[21] Indeed, little is known even to US government officials about how the NSA uses the Order to conduct its surveillance operations abroad. For example, Senator Dianne Feinstein, the former Chair of the US Senate State Intelligence Committee, commented in 2013 that the Committee 'does not receive the same number of official reports on the NSA surveillance activities directed abroad pursuant to legal authorities outside of FISA (specifically Executive Order 12333)'.[22]

Greater public interest in cyber surveillance practices led many parliaments either to adopt new laws or to reform their existing surveillance legislation in the years that followed the Snowden disclosures. One notable aspect of this process is that while states' targeted surveillance is usually regulated, the bulk interception of foreign communications is seldom put on a statutory footing, in spite of the fact that this is now routinely undertaken in practice. For example, according to the 2017 European Union Agency for Fundamental Rights report, 27 out of the then 28 EU member states have in place specific laws for targeted interception, but only five (ie, France, Germany, the United Kingdom, the Netherlands and Sweden) have adopted detailed legislation governing the use of measures aimed at bulk surveillance of foreign communications.[23] Other European countries may follow this trend; but at present, they do not regulate strategic surveillance in detail.[24]

These developments undoubtedly go a long way towards increasing the transparency of the intelligence services' powers and therefore contribute to

---

[20]   Ron Wyden, Senator for Oregon, 'Wyden, Udall on Revelations that Intelligence Agencies Have Exploited Foreign Intelligence Surveillance Act Loophole', Press Release (1 April 2014), www.wyden.senate.gov/news/press-releases/wyden-udall -on-revelations-that-intelligence-agencies-have-exploited-foreign-intelligence -surveillance-act-loophole.

[21]   Electronic Privacy Information Centre, 'Executive Order 12333', https://epic .org/privacy/surveillance/12333/.

[22]   Diane Feinstein, Senator for California, 'Feinstein on NSA Compliance', Press Release (16 August 2013), www.feinstein.senate.gov/public/index.cfm/2013/8/ feinstein-statement-on-nsa-compliance.

[23]   EU Agency for Fundamental Rights, 'Surveillance by Intelligence Agencies: Fundamental Rights Safeguards and Remedies in the EU-Mapping Member States' Legal Frameworks' (European Union Agency for Fundamental Rights, 2015), 40 ('FRA').

[24]   *Ibid.*

the efforts to regain public trust in their purpose and their operational methods. Since an increasing number of countries routinely conduct mass surveillance, most likely without any specific legal basis, and only a handful do so pursuant to published laws, the activities of the former inevitably fall foul of their international human rights law obligations. For those states that intercept foreign communications pursuant to domestic laws, the criterion of 'legal basis' is not limited to a requirement that the legislation be published on a national level. It must also meet the standards of clarity and precision to a sufficient degree to enable those affected to regulate their conduct with foresight of the circumstances in which intrusive surveillance may occur.[25] In other words, the law in question must be accessible.

## 2.2    Accessibility

The requirement of 'in accordance with the law' does not only dictate the existence of national surveillance legislation, but also relates to its quality. It follows that secret rules and guidelines and their secret (including judicial) interpretation, do not have the requisite quality of law.[26] Simply put, a law that is not public cannot be said to be so, because the rule of law necessitates that it be known and accessible to all. Furthermore, rules that are expressed in general terms, giving unfettered discretion to the executive, likewise do not meet this requirement. Consequently, the scope of the exercise of discretion must be indicated within the statute or the published guidelines with reasonable clarity, so that members of the public can ascertain how it can be applied in practice. This set of basic principles is shared by all three international judicial organs (the HRC, the ECtHR and the IACtHR), and has been reiterated by the various mandate holders.

Thus, the HRC, in General Comment 16, stated that the legislation authorizing interference with private communications 'must specify in detail the precise circumstances in which such interference may be permitted'.[27] The HRC commented on this requirement in, *inter alia*, its Concluding Observations on the US in relation to PRISM and Upstream collection warrants pursuant to Section 702 of the FISA, expressing concerns at the opaque nature of the Foreign Intelligence Surveillance Court's (FISC) authorization process. To this end, the HRC observed that: 'until recently the judicial interpretations of

---

[25]   UNGA, 'Report of the Special Rapporteur on the Promotion and Protection of Human Rights and Fundamental Freedoms While Countering Terrorism, Ben Emmerson' (23 September 2014) UN Doc A/69/397 para 28 ('A/69/397') para 36 ('A/ HRC/69/397').

[26]   *Malone* (n 16) para 67.

[27]   General Comment 16 (n 3) para 8.

FISA and rulings of the Foreign Intelligence Surveillance Court (FISC) had largely been kept secret, thus not allowing affected persons to know the law with sufficient precision.'[28] Similarly, in its observations on Switzerland, the HRC commented that the law in question:

> grants very intrusive surveillance powers to the Confederation's intelligence services on the basis of insufficiently defined objectives such as the national interest, referred to in article 3 [while] the time period for which data may be retained is not specified.[29]

The UN Office of the High Commissioner for Human Rights (OHCHR) emphasized this fundamental requirement too, stating that the protection of the law offered under Article 17(1) of the ICCPR against unlawful or arbitrary interference with privacy necessitates that any communications surveillance program be conducted on the basis of a publicly accessible law. This in turn must comply with the state's own constitutional regime and international human rights law.[30] Accessibility, the High Commissioner explained, 'requires not only that the law is published, but that it is sufficiently precise to enable the affected person to regulate his or her conduct, with foresight of the consequences that a given action may entail'.[31]

The ECtHR interprets the requirement of accessibility along similar lines. In *Malone v UK*, for example, the ECtHR commented on the obscurity and uncertainty of the law in question, stating that it did not indicate with reasonable clarity the scope and manner of the discretion conferred on the public authority. Consequently, the minimum degree of legal protection to which citizens are entitled under the rule of law in a democratic society was lacking. Similar observations have been made on a number of other occasions,[32] including quite recently in *Zakharov v Russia*,[33] in which the ECtHR confirmed that the law

---

[28] UNHRC, 'Concluding Observations on the Fourth Periodic Report of the United States of America' (23 April 2014) UN Doc CCPR/C/USA/CO/4 para 22 ('Concluding Observations, US').

[29] UNHRC, 'Concluding Observations, Switzerland' (27 July 2017) UN Doc CCPR/C/CHE/CO/4, para 46 ('Concluding Observations, Switzerland').

[30] Office of the UN High Commissioner for Human Rights (OHCHR), 'The Right to Privacy in the Digital Age. Report of the United Nations High Commissioner for Human Rights' (30 June 2014) UN Doc A/HRC/27/37 para 28 ('A/HRC/27/37').

[31] *Ibid.*

[32] See, for example, *Rotaru v Romania* App no 28341/95 (4 May 2000) para 52; *S and Marper v the United Kingdom* [GC] App no 30562/04 (4 December 2008) para 95; *Kennedy v the United Kingdom* App no 26839/05 (18 May 2010) para 151.

[33] *Zakharov* (n 17) para 225.

must be accessible to the person concerned and foreseeable as to its effects.[34] Applying these principles in *Szabó v Hungary*, the ECtHR found, *inter alia*, that the Hungarian legislation (specifically Section 7/E(3) of the Police Act) was not sufficiently precise or comprehensive on surveillance and that the government had not proved the practical effectiveness of any supervision arrangements.[35] As a result, the power granted by that provision to Hungary's anti-terrorist organ was unlimited in cases in which intelligence gathering may be used, and thus the ECtHR found a violation of Article 8.[36]

An example of a domestic court's interpretation and application of the 'in accordance with the law' criterion, as stipulated in Article 8(2) of the ECHR, is the UK case of *Privacy International v Secretary of State for Foreign and Commonwealth Affairs*,[37] heard by the Investigatory Powers Tribunal (IPT). The case was brought in 2016 by Privacy International and concerned a challenge to the bulk investigatory powers to obtain communications and communications data ('bulk communications datasets' (BCDs)) from telecommunications operators, together with the retention and examination of bulk personal datasets (BPDs) by MI5, MI6 and Government Communications Headquarters (GCHQ). The IPT found that the obtaining of BCDs was lawful under domestic law (at that time governed by Section 94 of the Telecommunications Act 1984); but that until 2015 (when stricter safeguards were introduced), both the BCD and the BPD regimes violated Article 8, as the rules and arrangements for obtaining the data were not publicly accessible, foreseeable and subject to adequate oversight. The IPT summarized that the proper approach under the ECtHR jurisprudence pertaining to compliance with the 'in accordance with the law' requirement is, first, that there must not be an unfettered discretion of the executive action and therefore there must be effective guarantees against abuse.[38] Second:

> the nature of the rules fettering such discretion and laying down safeguards must be clear and the ambit of them must be in the public domain so far as possible; there

---

[34] *Ibid* para 228; see also *Big Brother Watch and Others v the United Kingdom* App no 58170/13; *Bureau of Investigative Journalism and Alice Ross v the United Kingdom* App no 62322/14; *10 Human Rights Organizations and Others v the United Kingdom* App no 24960/15 (12 October 2018) para 305 ('*Big Brother Watch*').

[35] *Máté Szabó and Beatrix Vissy v Hungary* App no 48725/17 (11 October 2017) para 89 ('*Szabó*').

[36] *Ibid.*

[37] *Privacy International v Secretary of State for Commonwealth Affairs* [27 October 2016] UKIPTrib 15_110-CH.

[38] *Ibid* para 62(i).

must be an adequate indication or signposting, so that the existence of interference with privacy may in general terms be foreseeable.[39]

The approach taken at the inter-American level closely aligns with the afore-mentioned criteria laid down by the HRC and the ECtHR. The legality require-ment is set out in Article 30 of the ACHR, which provides that any restriction on Convention rights must be specifically authorized by law.[40] The IACtHR, in interpreting this provision, defined the term 'law' to mean 'a general legal norm tied to the general welfare, passed by democratically elected legislative bodies established by the Constitution and formulated according to the pro-cedures set forth by the constitutions of the State Parties for that purpose'.[41] Thus, any restriction on human rights must be on the basis of domestic laws and applied in compliance with them.[42] This is reflected in the OAS's Joint Declaration on Surveillance Programs, according to which national law must authorize access to communications and personal information only under the most exceptional circumstances defined by legislation. When national security is invoked as a reason for surveillance, the law must 'clearly specify the criteria to be used for determining the case in which such surveillance is legitimate'.[43] In addition, the document declares that: 'any surveillance of communications and interference with privacy that exceeds what is stipulated by law, has ends that differ from those which the law permits, or is carried out clandestinely must be harshly punished.'[44]

In short, in the context of state surveillance, the mere enactment of a legal framework authorizing surveillance does not make the interception of com-munications lawful. The law in question must be accessible to the public (ie, not secretive) and be clear; while the ambit of the powers it confers on the executive must be sufficiently circumscribed, so that the discretion it grants is not unfettered.

---

[39] *Ibid* para 62(ii).

[40] Organization of American States, The American Convention on Human Rights (The Pact of San José, Costa Rica) (entered into force 18 July 1978), Art 30 ('ACHR').

[41] *The Word 'Law' in Article 30 of the American Convention on Human Rights*, Advisory Opinion OC-6/86 Inter-American Court of Human Rights (9 May 1986) para 38 ('OC-6/86').

[42] See *Escher et al v Brazil* Inter-American Court of Human Rights Series C No 67 (6 July 2009), where the IACtHR set out specific terms in relation to the restrictions imposed on fundamental rights that must be followed.

[43] OAS Joint Declaration (n 19) para 9.

[44] *Ibid* para 10.

## 2.3      Foreseeability

Foreseeability requires that national law be sufficiently clear to give citizens an adequate indication of the circumstances and conditions empowering the public authorities to resort to surveillance. However, this does not mean that an individual should be able to anticipate exactly when interception powers are likely to be exercised, as this would lead to the altering of his or her conduct and thus defeat the purpose of those steps being undertaken. Until recently, all three judicial organs (the HRC, the ECtHR and the IACtHR) shared a similar approach in relation to the qualities that national legislation must display in order to satisfy this criterion. However, following the *Big Brother Watch v UK* judgment, there appears to be a divergence of legal standards in the jurisprudence of the ECtHR, as the Court seems to have taken an altogether more security-friendly outlook to the issue of the use of mass surveillance programs to bulk intercept and collect foreign communications, compared to the more hostile treatment of this issue by the other two judicial organs. This is explored next, starting with the general outline of the interpretation of the foreseeability criterion in the context of state surveillance expressed at the UN level, followed by that taken by the inter-American human rights institutions and the ECtHR.

The HRC, in General Comment 16, explained the extent of the foreseeability requirement, stating that the surveillance legislation must specify in detail the precise circumstances in which the interference may be permitted, while the decision to make use of such authorized interference must be made by a state organ designated under the law and on a case-by-case basis.[45] The HRC has adopted an uncompromising stance in this regard, requesting on numerous occasions that states take the necessary steps to improve the specificity and transparency of their surveillance laws. This can be illustrated by its observations in relation to US surveillance powers, prompting the HRC to urge that country to ensure that any interference with the right to privacy, family, home or correspondence be authorized by laws that are publicly accessible and sufficiently precise.[46] In addition, the laws must specify in detail the precise circumstances in which any such interference may be permitted; the procedures for authorization; the categories of persons who may be placed under surveillance; the limit on the duration of the surveillance; and the procedures for the use and storage of the collected data.[47]

---

[45]   General Comment 16 (n 3) para 8.
[46]   See Concluding Observations, US (n 28).
[47]   See UNHRC, 'Concluding Observations on the Seventh Periodic Report of the United Kingdom of Great Britain and Northern Ireland' (17 August 2015) UN Doc CCPR/C/GBR/CO/7 para 24 ('Concluding Observations, UK'); UNHRC,

The UN High Commissioner of Human Rights confirmed this stance, emphasizing that states must ensure that any interference with privacy is authorized by laws that:

> are sufficiently precise, specifying in detail the precise circumstances in which any such interference may be permitted, the procedure for authorising, the categories of persons who may be placed under surveillance, the limits on the duration of surveillance, and procedures for the use and storage of the data collected.[48]

A similar approach is taken in the inter-American system. In the OAS's Joint Declaration on Surveillance Programs, the UN Special Rapporteur on the protection and promotion of the right to freedom of opinion and expression and the Special Rapporteur for freedom of expression set out some basic parameters in this regard, stating that:

> The law must establish limits with regard to the nature, scope and duration of these types of measures; the reasons for ordering them; the authorities with power to authorise, execute and monitor them; and the legal mechanisms by which they may be challenged. Given the importance of the exercise of these rights for a democratic system, the law must authorize access to communications and personal information only under the most exceptional circumstances defined by legislation.[49]

This therefore not only echoes the well-entrenched international law standards pertaining to the manner in which states may conduct surveillance lawfully, but also reiterates the need to place limits on these practices to avoid arbitrary and abusive interference with private life.

Since the early 1970s, the ECtHR has recognized and reflected in its jurisprudence the threat to democracy posed by states' unbridled secret surveillance. In its early case law, the ECtHR acknowledged that the mere existence of legislation that allows a system to clandestinely monitor communications may give rise to a 'menace of surveillance' that amounts to an interference with privacy.[50] That being the case, the ECtHR reasoned that any discretion granted to the executive must not be expressed in terms of an unfettered power.

---

'Concluding Observations on the Fifth Periodic Report of France' (17 August 2015) UN Doc CCPR/C/FRA/CO/5 ('Concluding Observations, France'); UNHRC, 'Concluding Observations on the Seventh Periodic Report of Sweden' (28 April 2016) UN Doc CCPR/C/SWE/CO/7 ('Concluding Observations, Sweden 2016'); Concluding Observations, Turkmenistan (n 11).

[48] A/HRC/27/37 (n 30) para 28.
[49] OAS Joint Declaration (n 19) paras 8–9.
[50] *Klass and Others v Germany* App no 5029/71 (6 September 1978) para 37.

For these reasons, the Court has developed minimum standards,[51] subsequently reiterated in *Weber v Germany*, which lay down six basic conditions that a surveillance law must meet in order to be compatible with Article 8 of the ECHR to guard against abuse of power (the '*Weber* criteria'). According to this dictum, the domestic law authorizing surveillance must specify: (1) the nature of the offences which may give rise to an interception order; (2) a definition of the categories of people liable to have their telephones tapped; (3) a limit on the duration of telephone tapping; (4) the procedures to be followed for examining, using and storing the data obtained; (5) the precautions to be taken when communicating the data to other parties; and (6) the circumstances in which recordings may or must be erased, or the tapes destroyed.[52] In its *Zakharov* decision, the Grand Chamber of the ECtHR not only updated and consolidated its previous jurisprudence pertaining to these safeguards, but also substantially undermined the conducting of bulk surveillance of domestic communications by introducing the requirement of 'reasonable suspicion'.[53] Thus, in assessing whether authorization procedures are robust enough to ensure that secret surveillance is not ordered haphazardly, irregularly or without due and proper consideration, the ECtHR will take into account a number of factors, including the authority competent to approve the surveillance and its scope of review.[54] This new high threshold dictates that the authorizing body must verify:

> the existence of a reasonable suspicion against [the] person concerned, in particular whether there are factual indications for suspecting that person of planning, committing, or having committed criminal acts, or other acts that may give rise to secret surveillance measures, such as for example, acts endangering national security.[55]

The Grand Chamber further reinforced this standard with an additional requirement that the interception authorization (eg, a court order or warrant) detail (1) a specific person or group to be placed under surveillance; or (2) a single set of premises as the premises in respect to which the authorization is ordered.[56] Such identification, the ECtHR held, may be made by names, addresses, telephone numbers or other relevant information.[57] In this sense alone, the *Zakharov* decision seems to have substantially undermined the

---

[51]  See, for example, *Huvig* (n 16) para 34; *Amann v Switzerland* [GC] App no 27798/95 (16 February 2000) 76; *Prado Bugallo v Spain* App no 58496/00 (18 February 2003) para 30.
[52]  *Weber and Saravia v Germany* App no 54934/00 (29 June 2006) para 95.
[53]  *Zakharov* (n 17) para 260.
[54]  *Ibid* para 257.
[55]  *Ibid* para 260.
[56]  *Ibid* para 264.
[57]  *Ibid.*

practice of unrestricted domestic surveillance, as it attached great importance to the indication of actual involvement in criminal conduct before secret surveillance is authorized and acted upon. However, any hope that states' legislation authorizing foreign interception would also have to meet these high standards was soon quashed by the *Big Brother Watch* decision. In that case, the First Section of the ECtHR not only confirmed the previous stance taken in *Centrum För Rättvisa v Sweden*, whereby bulk interception regimes fall within states' wide margin of appreciation,[58] but also explicitly acknowledged that these constitute 'a valuable means to achieve the legitimate aims pursued, particularly given the current threat level from both global terrorism and serious crime'.[59] That being the ECtHR's default position, the Court rejected the need for 'reasonable suspicion' to be also applicable in cases of bulk surveillance of foreign communications. This criterion, together with two others of prior independent judicial authorization and subsequent notification of surveillance subjects,[60] were advanced by the applicants to update the existing legal standards. In holding that 'reasonable suspicion' is not a necessary requirement, the ECtHR reiterated nevertheless that, as in the case of targeted surveillance, bulk interception regimes must also satisfy the *Weber* test to be sufficiently foreseeable to minimize the risk of abuse of power.[61] However, the similarity of the legal standards pertaining to the foreseeability safeguards between targeted and bulk surveillance ends there. Although the ECtHR acknowledged the impact of modern technology, which has made interception even more invasive, it reasoned that to automatically assume that bulk interception constitutes a greater intrusion into the private life of an individual than targeted interception would be wrong.[62] The Court did concede that some additional safeguards may be beneficial; but ultimately held that in the context of bulk surveillance of foreign communications, reasonable suspicion and subsequent notification are not appropriate, for two reasons. First, this would contravene the ECtHR's previous acknowledgement that the operation of a bulk interception regime in principle falls within states' margin of discretion.[63] Second, and perhaps most interestingly, the First Section observed that:

> bulk interception is by definition untargeted and to require 'reasonable suspicion' would render the operation of such a scheme impossible. Similarly, the requirement

---

[58]   *Big Brother Watch* (n 34) para 112.
[59]   *Ibid* para 386.
[60]   *Ibid* para 316. These two conditions are discussed below.
[61]   *Ibid* para 315.
[62]   *Ibid.*
[63]   *Ibid* para 317.

of 'subsequent notification' assumes the existence of clearly defined surveillance targets, which is simply not the case in a bulk interception regime.[64]

As a result of this judgment, the ECtHR's jurisprudence seems to have bifurcated into separate branches, with one set of rules tailored to targeted (domestic) surveillance and the second applicable to bulk interception of foreign communications. In the first instance, surveillance may be conducted where the *Weber* criteria and the requirement of reasonable suspicion are met. In the context of bulk interception of foreign communications, the onus on an authorizing body is to satisfy the *Weber* criteria alone. Not only does this outcome seem to signal the ECtHR's resolute confidence in the probity of mass surveillance *per se*,[65] which is at odds with its previous stance on the issue in the *Zakharov* and *Szabó* cases; the Court also appears to condone states' legislative trends embracing different treatment of foreign and domestic surveillance by legitimizing this stance. This obfuscation of standards can be contrasted with the observations made by the UN Special Rapporteur on counter terrorism only five years prior to the *Big Brother Watch* judgment, which are worth quoting in full:

> Extraterritorial surveillance operations pose unique challenges for the application of the "quality of law" requirements in article 17 of the Covenant. Domestic legislation governing the interception of external (international) communications often affords less protection than comparable provisions protecting purely domestic communications. Of even greater concern, some States (including the United States) continue to permit asymmetrical protection regimes for nationals and non-nationals. This difference of treatment affects all digital communications since messages are often routed through servers located in other jurisdictions ... Either form of differential treatment is incompatible with the principle of non-discrimination in article 26 of the Covenant, a principle that is also inherent in the very notion of proportionality. Moreover, the use of mass surveillance programmes to intercept communications of those located in other jurisdictions raises serious questions about the accessibility and foreseeability of the law governing the interference with privacy rights, and the inability of individuals to know that they might be subject to foreign surveillance or to interception of communications in foreign jurisdictions. The Special Rapporteur considers that States are legally bound to afford the same protection to nationals and non-nationals, and to those within and outside their jurisdiction.[66]

To summarize, the foreseeability benchmark necessitates that domestic statutes confer a degree of precision and predictability, so that individuals can ascertain the circumstances in which their government may use powers of

---

[64]  *Ibid.*
[65]  *Ibid* para 176.
[66]  A/HRC/69/397 (n 25) paras 42–43.

secret surveillance. However, due to the volatile nature of threats to national security, states are allowed a degree of discretion, whereby the surveillance legislation need not spell out specific instances that may give rise to interception, but nevertheless it must be sufficiently clear to give an indication as to the circumstances and conditions empowering the executive to resort to surveillance. The ECtHR's jurisprudence interpreting how surveillance may be used confirms that national laws must meet six basic standards (the *Weber* criteria). In the context of domestic surveillance, these have been further enhanced in the ECtHR case law by the requirement of reasonable suspicion. When it comes to the bulk interception of foreign communications, however, a more permissive approach to surveillance seems to have emerged, with the ECtHR rejecting the applicability of this criterion to bulk interception regimes. This is at variance with the standards laid out by the UN and inter-American judicial organs and mandate holders, which require that the law be sufficiently detailed and set out the precise circumstances in which surveillance may be permitted, irrespective of whether it is domestic or foreign. Consequently, according to this benchmark, laws allowing for the interception of foreign communications which do not provide this degree of detail are likely not only to fail the test of foreseeability, but also to breach the principle of equality before the law set out in Article 26 of the ICCPR (discussed in Chapter 4 *supra*). It remains to be seen how the ECtHR will craft its future jurisprudence in view of this disparity, in particular following the appeals of the decisions in the *Big Brother Watch* and *Centrum För Rättvisa* cases to the Grand Chamber, together with a number of pending surveillance litigation cases.[67] This, in time, should shed more light on the ECtHR's approach to the issue of states' mass surveillance of foreign communications through cyber means.

### 2.3.1 Effective oversight

A matter closely related to foreseeability is that of effective oversight. As a general rule, domestic laws authorizing surveillance must not only be compatible with the rule of law, but also be able to provide effective means of redress against arbitrary interference with the right to privacy by public authorities. This requires that all surveillance measures be subject to independent supervision and approval to protect against abuse, which in practice

---

[67] There are also a number of pending cases before the ECtHR on the issue of extraterritorial surveillance and Article 8, including *Association confraternelle de la presse judiciaire and 11 Other Applications v France* App nos 49526/15, 49615/15, 49616/15, 49617/15, 49618/15, 49619/15, 49620/15, 49621/15, 55058/15, 55061/15, 59602/15 and 59621/15 – applications communicated to the French government on 26 April 2017; and *Privacy International and Others v the United Kingdom* App no 46259/16 – application communicated to the UK government on 19 November 2018.

comprises independent authorization and oversight mechanisms. To this end, the UN Resolutions on the Right to Privacy in the Digital Age (Resolutions 68/167 and 69/166) repeatedly called on states to 'establish, or maintain existing independent, effective domestic oversight mechanisms capable of ensuring transparency, as appropriate, and accountability for State surveillance of communications, their interception and collection of personal data'.[68]

The scope of privacy protection under Article 17 of the ICCPR, as explained by the HRC in General Comment 16, extends to requiring that contracting states provide the HRC with information pertaining to the authorities entitled to exercise control over the interference with privacy rights with strict regard for the law.[69] The UN Special Rapporteur on counter terrorism, commenting on covert surveillance systems, stated that adequate procedural safeguards protecting against abuse of power may take a variety of forms, but will generally include independent prior authorization and/or subsequent prior review.[70] In addition, the UN Office of the High Commissioner for Human Rights asserted that best practice necessitates the involvement in the process of all three branches of government – the executive, the legislature and the judiciary – together with independent civilian oversight.[71] The OHCHR has reiterated the need for the authorization, review and supervision of surveillance measures by independent bodies at all stages, including when they are first ordered, expressing a preference for the judicial authority carrying out these functions.[72] Such a judicial body must ensure the existence of 'clear evidence of a sufficient threat and that the surveillance proposed is targeted, strictly necessary and proportionate to authorise (or reject) ex ante the surveillance measures'.[73] Thus, while authorization should be entrusted to a judge, an oversight framework may comprise a combination of judicial, administrative and/or parliamentary mechanisms.[74] In any case, oversight bodies must be independent of the authorities carrying out the surveillance and equipped with appropriate and adequate expertise, competencies and resources. Furthermore, authorization and oversight should

---

[68]   UNGA Resolution, 'The Right to Privacy in the Digital Age' (21 January 2014) UN Doc A/Res/68/167, para 4(d) ('A/Res/68/167'); UNGA Resolution, 'The Right to Privacy in the Digital Age' (19 December 2016) UN Doc A/Res/71/199 ('A/Res/71/199').

[69]   General Comment 16 (n 3) para 6.

[70]   A/69/397 (n 25) para 45.

[71]   A/HRC/27/37 (n 30) para 37.

[72]   UNHRC, 'The Right to Privacy in the Digital Age. Report of the United Nations High Commissioner for Human Rights' (3 August 2018) UN Doc A/HRC/39/29 para 39 ('A/HRC/39/29').

[73]   *Ibid.*

[74]   *Ibid* para 40.

be institutionally separated;[75] while the role of the oversight bodies includes proactively investigating and monitoring the surveillance agencies, having access to intercepted communications and carrying out periodic reviews of the agencies' capabilities.[76]

That being the case, on the UN and inter-American levels, the tendency is towards judicial authorization. Thus, the HRC has placed importance on the requirement for the independent monitoring of surveillance powers and has repeatedly insisted that states should guarantee that the processing and gathering of information be subject to review and supervision by an independent body, with a strong preference for judicial authorization of such measures.[77] Support for the judicial authority as the appropriate entity to adjudicate the necessity of surveillance can also be found in the inter-American system. Article 8(1) of the ACHR establishes the right of every person to a hearing by a competent, independent and impartial tribunal, both in the criminal context and in matters relating to the determination of his or her rights and obligations of a civil, labour, fiscal or other nature.[78] The IACtHR interpreted this stipulation as giving individuals the right to access to justice, which is manifested, *inter alia*, by impartial and independent judicial authorities approving all surveillance requests, including search warrants.[79] The OAS's Joint Declaration on Surveillance Programs also emphasizes that surveillance activities 'must be monitored by an independent oversight body and governed by sufficient due process guarantees and judicial oversight, within the limitations permissible in a democratic society'.[80]

---

[75]  *Ibid.*

[76]  *Ibid.*

[77]  See, for example, Concluding Observations, US (n 28); Concluding Observations, UK (n 47); Concluding Observations, France (n 47); Concluding Observations, Italy (n 9); UNHRC, 'Concluding Observations on the Fourth Periodic Report of the Republic of Korea' (3 December 2015) UN Doc CCPR/C/KOR/CO/4 para 42 ('Concluding Observations, Republic of Korea'); 'Concluding Observations, Sweden 2016' (n 47) paras 36–37; UNHRC, 'Concluding Observations on the Sixth Periodic Report of Canada' (20 July 2015) UN Doc CCPR/C/CAN/CO/6 ('Concluding Observations, Canada'); UNHRC, 'Concluding Observations on the Fourth Periodic Report of Rwanda' (2 May 2016) UN Doc CCPR/C/RWA/CO/4 ('Concluding Observations, Rwanda'); Concluding Observations, South Africa (n 10); Concluding Observations: Turkmenistan (n 11); UNHRC, 'Concluding Observations on the Second Periodic Report of Honduras' (22 August 2017) UN Doc CCPR/C/HND/CO/2, 39 ('Concluding Observations, Honduras').

[78]  ACHR (n 40) Art 8.

[79]  See *Escher* (n 42). Commenting on judicial authorization at para 139, the IACtHR stated that: 'decisions adopted by domestic bodies that can affect human rights must be duly founded and justified, otherwise such decisions would be arbitrary.'

[80]  OAS Joint Declaration (n 19) para 9.

The requirement for effective oversight and authorization is of great importance in the European legal system too, but the recent ECtHR case law on bulk surveillance seems to attach more weight to the overall effectiveness of the oversight process rather than it being conducted by a judge. The ECtHR's early approach articulated in the 1970s reflected the principle that the decisions regarding surveillance must be made by a competent judicial authority acting independently of the executive. Thus, in *Klass v Germany*, the Court held that:

> the rule of law implies, *inter alia*, that an interference by the executive authorities with an individual's rights should be subject to an effective control which should normally be assured by the judiciary, at least in the last resort, judicial control offering the best guarantee of independence, impartiality and proper procedures.[81]

Over the course of the following years, the ECtHR confirmed this approach, expressing a preference for prior judicial authorization, but ultimately stopped short of requiring this in every case.[82] In *Klass*, it found that oversight by a non-judicial body is allowed where that body is sufficiently 'independent of the authorities carrying out the surveillance'.[83] In the *Zakharov* and *Szabó* cases, the Court reiterated that the 'requirement of prior judicial authorisation constitutes an important safeguards against arbitrariness',[84] but to date it has not considered this to be a 'necessary requirement'[85] in the context of either targeted or mass surveillance. To this end, responding to the argument put forward in *Big Brother Watch* for updating the surveillance requirements by including an additional safeguard of prior independent judicial authorization, the ECtHR held that (unlike the requirements of reasonable suspicion and the subsequent notification of surveillance subjects), judicial authorization, 'by contrast, is not inherently incompatible with the effective functioning of bulk interception'.[86] Nevertheless, the Court declined making this a mandatory criterion. The ECtHR reasoned that although prior judicial authorization is desirable in principle, and perhaps even 'best practice, by itself it can neither be necessary nor sufficient to ensure compliance with Article 8 of the Convention'.[87] The Court did, however, consider it as an important safeguard

---

[81]   *Klass* (n 50) para 56.

[82]   See, for example, *Weber* (n 52) para 94; *Klass* (n 50) para 56; *Kopp v Switzerland* App no 23224/94 (25 March 1998) para 74; *Association for European Integration and Human Rights and Ekimdzhiev v Bulgaria* App no 62540/000 (2007) para 87.

[83]   *Klass* (n 50) para 56.

[84]   *Zakharov* (n 17) para 248; *Szabó* (n 35) para 75.

[85]   *Zakharov ibid* para 258; *Klass* (n 50) para 51; *Weber* (n 52) para 115; *Kennedy* (n 32) para 31; *Szabó ibid* para 77.

[86]   *Big Brother Watch* (n 34) para 318.

[87]   *Ibid* paras 319–20.

and viewed it as 'perhaps even "best practice"', but nevertheless emphasized that what is crucial is the examination of the actual operation of the system of interception, including the checks and balances on the exercise of the power and the lack of evidence of any abuse.[88] Applying this reasoning to the facts of the case, the ECtHR held that despite the lack of judicial authorization, the British system of supervision and authorization pursuant to Section 8(4) of the Regulation of Investigatory Powers Act 2000 (RIPA) allowing for bulk interception of external communications was capable of providing adequate and effective guarantees against abuse.[89] However, the ECtHR found a violation of Article 8, as the regime under Section 8(4) did not meet the 'quality of law' requirement. This was not due to the lack of authorization to carry out mass surveillance by a judge, but was rather based on the techniques practised by GCHQ.[90] The decision thus leaves the matter of *ex ante* judicial authorization somewhat unclear, in particular when assessed in light of the outcome in relation to this issue in *Zakharov*. Similarly, in that case, the ECtHR did not explicitly mandate prior judicial authorization. It closely scrutinized the manner in which the authorization was conducted by the Russian court and considered it to be an inadequate 'rubber stamping'. The ECtHR held that in practice, the process often disregarded the verification of the reasonable suspicion criterion and the application of the proportionality and necessity tests.[91] By contrast, in *Big Brother Watch*, the ECtHR seems to have been more lenient by not attaching much importance to the fact that there was no judicial authorization in the first place. Quite the contrary, the Court was satisfied that in principle, the independent oversight provided by the Interception of Communications Commissioner (replaced by the Investigatory Powers Commissioner's Office working for the Home Office and staffed by, *inter alia*, inspectors, lawyers and communications experts), together with the IPT, meant that the UK intelligence agencies took their Convention obligations seriously and were not abusing their powers under Section 8(4) of the RIPA.[92] One reason for this outcome is perhaps the ECtHR's recognition that these powers would soon be defunct, replaced by the modernized Investigatory

---

[88]   *Ibid* para 320.
[89]   *Ibid* para 381.
[90]   *Ibid* para 387. The ECtHR held that the two areas of concern in relation to powers under Section 8(4) of RIPA were 'first, the lack of oversight of the entire selection process, including the selection of bearers for interception, the selectors and search criteria for filtering intercepted communications, and the selection of material for examination by an analyst; and secondly, the absence of any real safeguards applicable to the selection of related communications data for examination'.
[91]   *Zakharov* (n 17) paras 262–63
[92]   *Big Brother Watch* (n 34) 387.

Powers Act 2016 (IPA), whose 'double lock' system was expressly referred to by the Court in that case[93] and was announced by the UK government as being the most significant change to the regime. Perhaps unsurprisingly, these new safeguards withstood a subsequent challenge by UK non-governmental organizations and the scrutiny of the IPT, which considered them as compatible with Article 8 of the ECHR in *Liberty v Secretary of State for Home Departments*.[94] Noteworthy is the IPT's finding that the regime created under the IPA is lawful to a large extent because of the rigorous oversight and safeguards put in place by that legislation. To this end, Lord Justice Singh and Mr Justice Holgate concluded that the IPA includes 'several safeguards against the possible abuse of power'.[95]

To date, the UK safeguards pertaining to bulk interception warrants seem to have been accepted by the courts[96] as meeting the necessary threshold. Perhaps these constitute a blueprint of good practice when it comes to the desirable procedures for authorization that other national legislatures ought to follow. What nevertheless remains problematic is not just that, as already noted, only a small number of countries have expressly legislated in detail on bulk surveillance, thus setting out a system of oversight of surveillance powers; but also that, even where such legislation is in place, this is organized in extremely diverse ways.[97] For example, in contrast to the UK 'double lock' system, mandating an amalgam of ministerial and judicial approval for bulk warrants, the 2015 French Surveillance Act allows for the authorization of surveillance of international communications networks and the exploitation of untargeted content and metadata collected from them to be made by the Prime Minister's Office based on a request from, *inter alia*, the Minister of Defence, Interior or Finance.[98] The Prime Minister's Office may issue authorizations without seeking the prior opinion of the National Commission for the Control of Security Interceptions (CNCIS), the main body responsible for the oversight of interception surveillance. When the Prime Minister (or his or her delegate)

---

[93]   *Ibid* para 380.
[94]   *Liberty v Secretary of State for Home Departments* [2019] EWHC 2057 (29 July 2019).
[95]   *Ibid.* At para 397 the High Court observed that: 'the primary focus of the arguments before this Court has been on the ground that the 2016 Act does not contain sufficient safeguards against the risk of abuse of power and that, accordingly it is inconsistent with the requirement that interference with human rights must be "in accordance with the law" … we do not accept these arguments.'
[96]   Liberty announced that it will seek to appeal the High Court decision reached in 2019.
[97]   FRA (n 23) 63.
[98]   *Ibid* 47. See Law No 2015-1556 Art L 854-2.

authorizes the interception, the CNCIS is to review this approval.[99] If it deems that the approval is not justified under the law, it can send a recommendation to the Prime Minister calling for the interruption of the interception, but such recommendations are rare and appear not to be legally binding.[100] Thus, there is no legal requirement that any independent authority be consulted before a bulk collection decision; while the CNCIS can launch investigations only following the formal complaint of an individual or organization.[101]

In her 2014 report, the UN High Commissioner for Human Rights noted that the practice of many states revealed, among other shortcomings, weak procedural safeguards and ineffective oversight, which contributed to the lack of accountability for arbitrary and unlawful interference with privacy.[102] In the following years, intelligence reforms in Europe added a degree of transparency; but the divergent nature of the methods of oversight and authorization through, *inter alia*, the judiciary, expert bodies and parliamentary committees contributes to the complexity and disparity of the system, with additional questions being asked as to their independence and effectiveness.[103] While it is impossible to arrive at a single model of effective oversight and authorization due to nations' disparate political, administrative and judicial structures, there is an obvious need for a common minimum benchmark that oversight and authorization must meet in the context of the bulk interception and collection of foreign communications.

In conclusion, the ECtHR has in principle endorsed judicial authorization of bulk surveillance of foreign communications, but has imposed no explicit requirement that only *ex ante* judicial authorization is an acceptable option to prevent the risk of abuse of power by state agencies. By contrast, both the HRC and the IACtHR seem to lean towards not only independent *ex ante* authorization, but also mandatory judicial involvement in this process.

---

[99] *Ibid* Art L 243-8.

[100] Reportedly, out of 6396 interception authorizations granted in 2011, only 55 received negative recommendations from the CNCIS – see *Commission des lois constitutionnelles, de la législation et de l'administration générale de la République* (Commission on Constitutional Laws, Legislation, and General Administration of the Republic), *Assemblée nationale (*National Assembly) *Rapport d'Information* (Information Report) No 1022 (14 May 2013) 21.

[101] Akin Üner, 'Politics of Digital Surveillance, National Security and Privacy', Centre for Economics and Foreign Policy Studies (2018) 11.

[102] A/HRC/27/37 (n 30) para 37.

[103] *Ibid* 9.

## 3.    LEGITIMATE AIM

In addition to meeting the requirement of 'in accordance with the law', any restriction on the right to privacy must satisfy the condition of pursuing a legitimate aim. Unlike Article 8(2) of the ECHR, which stipulates specific circumstances in which interference with privacy may be compatible with the Convention,[104] neither Article 17(2) of the ICCPR nor Article 11(2) of the ACHR contains such a detailed clause. Nevertheless, a certain commonality of approach can be discerned among the three judicial organs in interpreting this requirement, which have recognized the protection of national security and the prevention of terrorism and other serious crime as legitimate aims.

Elaborating on the requirement of 'legitimate aim' in relation to Article 17 of the ICCPR, the UN Special Rapporteur on counter terrorism and the UN Special Rapporteur on freedom of expression have taken the position that the 'permissible limitations' test stipulated in Article 12(3) of the Covenant (freedom of movement)[105] is equally applicable to Article 17.[106] Thus, the test stipulated in Article 12(3) of the ICCPR sets out four criteria according to which a state may be justified in restricting freedom of movement – namely, where that is necessary to protect national security; public order; health and morals; or the rights and freedoms of others. Of these, national security has been accepted as a legitimate aim for the purposes of Article 17. To this end, numerous reports from various UN mandate holders attest to the fact that the prevention, suppression and investigation of crime and acts of terrorism amount to legitimate aims for the purposes of Article 17.[107] Specifically, the UN High Commissioner for Human Rights has explicitly recognized that digital communications surveillance on the grounds of national security for the prevention of terrorism or other crime constitutes a 'legitimate aim' under Article 17.[108]

---

[104]    ECHR (n 2) Art 8(2)

[105]    This is not the only article in the ICCPR that contains a specific limitation clause. Other provisions setting out such a stipulation are Article 12(3) on the right to liberty of movement and freedom to choose residence; Article 18(3) on the right to freedom of thought, conscience and religion; Article 21 on the right to peaceful assembly; and Article 22(1) on the right to freedom of association.

[106]    See UNHRC, 'Report of the Special Rapporteur on the Promotion and Protection of Human Rights while Countering Terrorism, Martin Scheinin (28 December 2009) UN Doc A/HRC/13/37 paras 17-18 ('A/HRC/13/37'); UNHRC, 'Report of the Special Rapporteur on the Promotion and Protection of the Right to Freedom of Opinion and Expression, Frank La Rue' (17 April 2013) UN Doc A/HRC/23/40 paras 28-29 ('A/HRC/23/40').

[107]    See, for example, A/69/397 (n 25) para 33.

[108]    A/HRC/27/37 (n 30) para 24.

Typically, domestic surveillance laws provide for the restriction of privacy on a broad basis linked to these aims. However, such formulations have been of concern to the HRC for being open-ended, as they provide the potential for abuse of power. Thus, when reviewing a number of statutes, the HRC recommended that states ensure closer alignment between the use of surveillance powers and the needs that these are meant to protect. For example, in the Concluding Observations on the US, the HRC urged that country to ensure that 'the collection of, access to and use of communications data are tailored to specific legitimate aim'.[109] Similarly, in the Concluding Observations on France and Rwanda, the HRC asked that it be guaranteed:

> that the collection and use of data on communications take place on the basis of specific and legitimate objectives and that the exact circumstances in which such interference may be authorised and the categories of persons likely to be placed under surveillance are set out in detail.[110]

In its Concluding Observations on Namibia, the HRC stated that 'the interception of communications may only be justified under limited circumstances'.[111] This suggests that the HRC is not in favour of imprecise categories such as 'national security', which it has repeatedly found to be overtly opaque and far too broad. Likewise, the UN Special Rapporteur on freedom of expression has observed that 'vague and unspecified notions of "national security" have become an acceptable justification for the interception of and access to communications in many countries'.[112] The Special Rapporteur was quite critical of the manner in which communications surveillance is being deployed on this basis, stating that:

> The use of an amorphous concept of national security to justify invasive limitations on the enjoyment of human rights is of serious concern. The concept is broadly defined and is thus vulnerable to manipulation by the State as a means of justifying actions that target vulnerable groups such as human rights defenders, journalists, or activists. It also acts to warrant often-unnecessary secrecy around investigations or law enforcement activities, undermining the principles of transparency and accountability.[113]

---

[109]   Concluding Observations, USA (n 28) para 22(b).
[110]   See Concluding Observations, France (n 47) para 12; Concluding Observations, Rwanda (n 77) para 36.
[111]   UNHRC, 'Concluding Observations on the Second Report of Namibia' (23 August 2016) UN Doc CCPR/C/NAM/CO/2 para 38 ('Concluding Observations, Namibia').
[112]   A/HRC/23/40 (n 106) para 58.
[113]   *Ibid* para 60.

A similar approach in relation to the requirement of 'legitimate aim' can be discerned at the inter-American level. Article 30 of the ACHR stipulates that any restrictions on the rights set out in the Convention 'may not be applied except when that is in accordance with laws enacted for reasons of general interest and in accordance with the purpose for which such restrictions have been established'.[114] In addition, Article 32(2) of the ACHR states that: 'The rights of each person are limited by the rights of others, by the security of all, and by the just demands of the general welfare, in a democratic society.'[115] The IACtHR has interpreted these provisions by holding that:

> the requirement that the laws be enacted for reasons of general interest means they must have been adopted for the 'general welfare' ... a concept that must be interpreted as an integral element of public order in democratic states, the main purpose of which is 'the protection of the essential rights of man and the creation of circumstances that will permit him to achieve spiritual and material progress and attain happiness'.[116]

However, it has also held that a generalized postulation of the 'public good' alone does not suffice to fulfil the requirement of legitimate aim. In its *Compulsory Membership in an Association Prescribed by Law for the Practice of Journalists* Advisory Opinion, the IACtHR held that:

> 'Public order' or 'general welfare' may under no circumstances be invoked as a means of denying a right guaranteed by the Convention or to impair or deprive it of its true content ... Those concepts, when they are invoked as a ground for limiting human rights, must be subjected to an interpretation that is strictly limited to the 'just demands' of 'a democratic society', which takes account of the need to balance the competing interests involved and the need to preserve the object and purpose of the Convention.[117]

As already noted, Article 11 of the ACHR does not provide a list of legitimate aims. This can be contrasted with a number of other Convention provisions,[118] which contain a limitation clause setting out such grounds as public safety, public order, public health, public morals or the rights and freedoms of others.

---

[114]  ACHR (n 40) Art 30.

[115]  *Ibid* Art 32(2).

[116]  OC-6/86 (n 41) para 29.

[117]  *Compulsory Membership in an Association Prescribed by Law for the Practice of Journalists,* Advisory Opinion OC-5/85, IACtHR (13 November 1985) para 67 ('OC-5/85').

[118]  See, for example, ACHR (n 40) – Article 12(3) on freedom to manifest religion or beliefs; Article 13(2) on freedom of thought and expression; Article 16(2) on freedom of association; and Article 22(3) on the exercise of freedom of movement.

However, Articles 30 and 32 of the ACHR clearly apply to the right to privacy. Consequently, the restrictions placed on this right, in light of the aforementioned case law, mean that they must be specific and neither vague nor open ended. In the context of state surveillance, for these reasons, the concept of 'national security' seems insufficiently precise as a legitimate aim to justify the violation of Article 11 rights.

While at the UN and for the inter-American human rights organs, the tendency is for stricter standards pertaining to states' legitimization of surveillance on national security grounds, the approach taken by the ECtHR in its recent jurisprudence seems to be more permissive. The ECtHR has long recognized that governments may restrict the right to privacy under Article 8 in the interest of national security. In its case law, the Court has confirmed that threats to national security include, *inter alia*, espionage,[119] terrorism,[120] incitement to/approval of terrorism,[121] subversion of parliamentary democracy,[122] separatist extremist organizations that threaten the unity or security of a state by violent or undemocratic means[123] and incitement of disaffection of military personnel.[124] It has also established that states have a certain margin of appreciation in choosing the means for achieving the legitimate aim of protecting national security.[125] On examining the ECtHR's case law, what transpires is that the 'legitimate aim' requirement does not *per se* pose a major issue for the Court. This can be illustrated by a reference to the *Zakharov, Centrum För Rättvisa* and *Big Brother Watch* decisions. Thus, in *Zakharov*, the ECtHR accepted that 'the surveillance measures permitted by the Russian law pursue the legitimate aims of the protection of national security and public safety, the prevention of crime and the protection of the economic well-being of the country'.[126] In *Centrum För Rättvisa*, the Court accepted that bulk interception regimes that aim to identify unknown threats to national security continue to fall within states' margin of appreciation.[127] In *Big Brother Watch*, having noted the conclusions of the UK Independent Reviewer of Terrorism

---

[119] *Zakharov* (n 17); *Klass* (n 50).

[120] *Klass ibid*; *Weber* (n 52).

[121] *Zana v Turkey* App no 18954/91 (30 September 1991).

[122] *Leander v Sweden* App no 9248/81 (26 March 1967).

[123] *United Communist Party of Turkey v Turkey* App no 19392/92 (30 January 1998).

[124] *Arrowsmith v the United Kingdom* App no 7050/75 (12 October 1978).

[125] See, for example, *Leander* (n 122) para 59; *S and Marper* (n 32) para 102; *Weber* (n 52) para 106; *Zakharov* (n 17) para 232.

[126] *Zakharov ibid* para 237.

[127] *Centrum För Rättvisa v Sweden* App no 35252/08 (19 June 2018) para 112 ('*Centrum För Rättvisa*').

Legislation[128] and those of the Venice Commission[129] (both of which recognized the value of bulk interception for security operations through allowing the intelligence services to adopt a proactive approach in relation to unknown threats), the ECtHR concluded that: 'bulk interception is a valuable means to achieve the legitimate aims pursued, particularly given the current threat level from both terrorism and serious crime.'[130]

A similar trend can be discerned in the jurisprudence of some domestic courts when specifically dealing with mass surveillance of foreign communications. For example, the German Constitutional Tribunal's 2020 decision in *1 B v R* is broadly in line with the ECtHR's approach in *Big Brother Watch*. In the former case, one of the allegations pertained to the claim that the powers of the German security agencies set out in the Federal Intelligence Service Act 2016 ('BND Act') to access telecommunications transmission routes and networks to collect the data of foreigners in other countries were not aligned to specific grounds or suspicions, but could rather be used broadly to obtain information indicating situations of danger or general intelligence that was of interest to Germany in foreign and security policy matters. Embracing this type of surveillance, the Constitutional Court not only saw the value that it offers in relation to public security, but also stressed that it is in the public interest that the security services supply the federal government with such information, as this 'helps it to assert itself in the power political sphere of international relations and can prevent mistakes that could have serious consequences'.[131] As for public security, in the Court's words:

> the expansion and internationalization of communication possibilities and the resulting accompanying increased politicisation and ability to organise of international criminal gangs mean that domestic situations of danger frequently originate in networks of actors cooperating internationally and that they can easily have foreign and security policy dimensions.[132]

---

[128]  David Anderson, *A Question of Trust. Report of the Investigatory Powers Review* (June 2015) ('Anderson').

[129]  CoE, European Commission for Democracy Through Law, 'Report on the Democratic Oversight of Signals Intelligence Agencies' Study no 719/2013 (Venice Commission, 2015).

[130]  *Big Brother Watch* (n 34) para 386.

[131]  Press Release No 37/2020, 'In Their Current Form, Surveillance Powers of the Federal Intelligence Service Regarding Foreign Telecommunications Violate Fundamental Rights of the Basic Law' (19 May 2020) para III(1)(b) ('*1 B v R* Press Release'), www.bundesverfassungsgericht.de/SharedDocs/Pressemitteilungen/EN/2020/bvg20-037.html.

[132]  *Ibid.*

Although the Court recognized that strategic surveillance has been and continues to be undertaken without specific grounds, it concluded that this is to some extent mitigated by the fact that is it conducted by an agency which in principle is not vested with operational powers.[133] Worthy of note too is that both the language and the approach adopted by the German Constitutional Court in relation to 'legitimate aim' pertaining to strategic surveillance are strikingly similar to those of the ECtHR in both *Big Brother Watch* and *Centrum För Rättvisa*, indicating a degree of symmetry in the broader judicial outlook on these matters.

It appears, therefore, that – at least for now, and in contrast with the more restrictive standards of the UN and inter-American human rights bodies – mass surveillance conducted by Council of Europe states can be justified on the broad basis of identifying dangers to national security emanating from abroad, as this falls within states' margin of appreciation. In other words, a state can in principle seek to find a 'needle in a haystack', since bulk interception appears to have been accepted by the ECtHR as a valuable means to achieve legitimate aims, including that on a broadly defined basis of national security.

## 4.     NECESSITY AND PROPORTIONALITY

The final criterion for determining the legality of a state measure that interferes with the right to privacy is that of necessity and proportionality. This means that any limitation on this right must be necessary to achieve a legitimate aim, and be both proportionate to that aim and the least intrusive option available to achieve it.[134] In addition, authorities seeking to limit privacy rights, including for the purpose of protecting national security, must be able to demonstrate that they have some chance of attaining that goal.[135] This means that in practice, in implementing surveillance measures, states must strike a balance between protecting citizens against terrorist attacks and other serious crimes and safeguarding their fundamental rights. It follows that a measure which is unable to achieve the stated objective or which is ineffective cannot be said to be necessary or proportionate.

The HRC adheres to this approach, despite not specifically addressing the concept of proportionality in the context of Article 17 of the ICCPR. Nevertheless, it has commented on this requirement in relation to Article 12 (freedom of movement), stating that the restrictions must not only serve the

---

[133]  *Ibid.*
[134]  A/HRC/27/37 (n 30) para 23.
[135]  *Ibid.*

permissible purposes, but also be necessary to protect them.[136] In its General Comment 27 on Article 12, the HRC explained what proportionality entails in the following terms:

> Article 12, paragraph 3, clearly indicates that it is not sufficient that the restrictions serve the permissible purposes; they must also be necessary to protect them. Restrictive measures must conform to the principle of proportionality; they must be appropriate to achieve their protective function; they must be the least intrusive instrument amongst those which might achieve the desired result; and they must be proportionate to the interest to be protected ... The principle of proportionality has to be respected not only in the law that frames the restrictions, but also by the administrative and judicial authorities in applying the law. States should ensure that any proceedings relating to the exercise or restriction of these rights are expeditious and that reasons for the application of restrictive measures are provided.[137]

In relation to surveillance, in addition to the above stated criteria, states must show that: (1) there is a 'rational connection between the means employed and the aim sought to be achieved';[138] (2) there is a balance between 'the extent of the intrusion into Internet privacy rights against the specific benefit accruing to investigations undertaken by a public authority in the public interest';[139] (3) 'any limitation to the right to privacy [does] not render the essence of the right meaningless [and is] ... consistent with other human rights, including the prohibition of discrimination';[140] and (4) 'any decision to allow interference with communications [is] taken by the authority designated by law "on a case-by-case basis". The proportionality of any interference with the right to privacy should therefore be judged on the particular circumstances of the individual case'.[141]

When viewing bulk surveillance programs through the prism of the necessity and proportionality criterion circumscribed in this way, the general attitude of the UN human rights bodies is that of antagonism, as this is considered inherently incompatible with Article 17 of the ICCPR. Accordingly, the UN High Commissioner for Human Rights conceded that where there is a legitimate aim and appropriate safeguards are in place, states may be allowed to engage in quite intrusive surveillance.[142] However, the Commissioner stressed that governments must demonstrate that the interference is both necessary and

---

[136] UNHRC General Comment No 27: Article 27 (Freedom of Movement) (2 November 1999) UN Doc CCPR/2/21/Rev1/Add9 ('General Comment 27').

[137] *Ibid* paras 14–15.

[138] A/69/397 (n 25) para 51.

[139] *Ibid* para 51.

[140] A/HRC/27/37 (n 30) para 23.

[141] A/69/397 (n 25) para 51.

[142] A/HRC/27/37 (n 30) para 25.

proportionate to the specific risk being addressed. It follows that mass or bulk surveillance programs may be deemed arbitrary as it is not enough that the measures are targeted to 'find certain needles in a haystack',[143] even if they serve a legitimate aim and are deployed on the basis of an accessible legal regime. The proper assessment is 'the impact of the measure on the haystack, relative to the harm threatened, namely whether the measure is necessary and proportionate'.[144] For these reasons, the Commissioner concluded that at least one feature of bulk surveillance – that is, governments' requirements that telecommunications companies and Internet service providers store communications and location metadata for subsequent access by government agencies – appears neither necessary nor proportionate.[145] The UN Special Rapporteur on counter terrorism has also called into question the use of surveillance programs on a proportionality basis, stating that the technology that enables states to run vast data collection and analysis schemes undoubtedly offers them an additional means to pursue their anti-terrorism and other security goals.[146] However, the assessment of these methods must also take account of the 'collateral damage to collective privacy rights'.[147] For these reasons, 'mass data collection programmes appear to offend against the requirement that intelligence agencies must select the measure that is least intrusive on human rights'.[148] In addition, the lack of opportunity for an individualized proportionality assessment prior to deployment of the measures also means that the vital criterion of case-by-case analysis is not met, which in effect renders the programs arbitrary.[149] Consequently, the Special Rapporteur concluded that such methods can be compatible with Article 17 of the ICCPR only if the relevant states 'are in a position to justify as proportionate the systematic interference with the Internet privacy rights of a potentially unlimited number of innocent people in any part of the world'.[150] Similarly, the Special Rapporteur on the promotion and protection of the right to freedom of opinion and expression reiterated the need for states to ensure that their domestic legal frameworks meet the standards required by international law.[151] Surveillance must not only be authorized in law for the most serious criminal offences, but also be con-

---

[143] *Ibid.*

[144] *Ibid.*

[145] *Ibid* para 26.

[146] A/69/397 (n 25) para 52.

[147] *Ibid.*

[148] *Ibid.*

[149] *Ibid.*

[150] *Ibid.*

[151] UNHRC, 'Surveillance and Human Rights. Report of the Special Rapporteur on the Promotion and Protection of the Right to Freedom of Opinion and Expression' (28 May 2019) UN Doc A/HRC/41/35, para 50 ('A/HRC/41/35').

tained in precise, publicly accessible laws and applied solely when necessary and proportionate.[152]

The above stated principles circumscribing the necessity and proportionality benchmark are also closely followed in the inter-American legal system. Thus, Article 11(2) of the ACHR stipulates that the right to privacy, being qualified, may be restricted by a state where, among other applicable criteria, the interference meets the requirements of suitability, necessity and proportionality. The IACtHR, interpreting these principles in the context of the right to liberty in *Chaparro Álverez and Lap Íñiguez v Ecuador*, explained that:

> it is not sufficient that every reason for deprivation or restriction of the right to liberty is established by law; this law and its application must respect the requirements listed below, to ensure that this measure is not arbitrary: (i) that the purpose of the measures that deprive or restrict liberty is compatible with the Convention ...; (ii) that the measures adopted are appropriate to achieve the purpose sought; (iii) that they are necessary, in the sense that they are absolutely essential to achieve the purpose sought and that, among all possible measures, there is no less burdensome one in relation to the right involved, that would be as suitable to achieve the proposed objective ... and (iv) that the measures are strictly proportionate, so that the sacrifice inherent in the restriction of the right to liberty is not exaggerated or excessive compared to the advantages obtained from this restriction and the achievement of the purpose sought.[153]

In other words, according to the IACtHR, a measure is necessary where there are no other means of achieving the set goal and no other methods exist that would have a lesser impact on an individual's rights. Apart from being necessary, the measure must also be proportionate. In *Kimel v Argentina*, the IACtHR stated that satisfying the proportionality test entails that: 'it is discussed whether the restriction is strictly proportionate, in a manner such that the sacrifice inherent therein is not exaggerated or disproportionate in relation to the advantages obtained from the adoption of such limitation.'[154] Thus, the IACtHR treats the notions of necessity and proportionality as closely connected, observing that:

> if there are various options to achieve [the legitimate] objective, that which least restricts the right protected must be selected. Given this standard, it is not enough to demonstrate, for example, that a law performs a useful or desirable purpose; to be compatible with the Convention, the restrictions must be justified by reference to governmental objectives which, because of the importance, clearly outweigh the

---

[152] *Ibid* para 50(b).

[153] *Chaparro Álverez and Lap Íñiguez v Ecuador* IACtHR (21 November 2007) para 93.

[154] *Kimel v Argentina Inter-American Court of Human Rights* (2 May 2008) para 83.

social need for the full enjoyment of the right ... That is, the restriction must be proportionate and closely tailored to the accomplishment of the legitimate governmental objective necessitating it.[155]

These principles were echoed in the OAS's Joint Declaration on Surveillance Programs, which emphasized that states must adhere to the proportionality requirement when conducting surveillance operations, while the application of the surveillance:

shall be authorised only in the event of a clear risk to protected interests and when the damage that may result would be greater than society's general interest in maintaining the right to privacy and the free circulation of ideas and information[156]

For the ECtHR, the requirement of proportionality has always played a vital role in the assessment of the legality of state surveillance. For example, in *S and Marper*, the ECtHR's Grand Chamber held that the 'blanket and indiscriminate' retention of DNA data amounted to a disproportionate interference with the private lives of the individuals from whom the data had been obtained – mainly because the genetic material was 'retained indefinitely whatever the nature or seriousness of the offence of which the person was suspected'.[157] However, the ECtHR has recognized that governments face a difficult task in seeking to balance national security and human rights interests. To this end, the ECtHR has granted states a wide margin of appreciation with regard to the actual implementation of security measures. In its early case law, the ECtHR recognized that the technical advances that have enabled the conduct of espionage and surveillance, together with the increase in terrorism in Europe, mean that states must be able to effectively counter such threats by undertaking secret surveillance of communications, which in exceptional circumstances is necessary in a democratic society in the interest of national security.[158] Holding that domestic legislatures enjoy some leeway pertaining to the establishment of the conditions under which surveillance systems may operate, the ECtHR stressed nonetheless that states do not have an unlimited discretion to subject persons in their jurisdiction to secret surveillance.[159] Whether a government's actions fall within this band is very much context dependent and the Court will assess this on a case-by-case basis.[160] Specifically addressing strategic

---

[155] OC-5/85 (n 117) para 46.
[156] OAS Joint Declaration (n 19) para 9.
[157] *S and Marper* (n 32) para 118.
[158] See *Klass* (n 50) para 48; *Leander* (n 122) para 59.
[159] *Klass ibid* para 49.
[160] For example, in *Peck v the United Kingdom* App no 44647/98 (28 January 2003), para 77, the ECtHR held that in cases concerning the disclosure of personal data, the

surveillance, the ECtHR in the *Weber* case confirmed that national authorities enjoy a fairly broad discretion in choosing the means to achieve the legitimate aim of protecting national security.[161] However, the Court must be satisfied that there exist adequate and effective guarantees against abuse. In making this assessment, it will take into account such factors as the nature, scope and duration of the possible measures; the grounds on which they can be ordered; the authorities competent to authorize, carry out and supervise them; and the types of remedies provided by national law.[162]

As previously observed, the ECtHR's reasoning in the *Centrum För Rättvisa* and *Big Brother Watch* cases is predicated on the fundamental premise that states' operation of bulk surveillance of foreign communications falls within their margin of discretion. This is because the ECtHR seems to be satisfied that these methods assist governments in identifying unknown threats emanating from abroad. In its *Big Brother Watch* decision, the ECtHR readily accepted that the alternatives to bulk interception – such as targeted surveillance, the use of human sources and commercial cyber-defence products, or a combination thereof – would be insufficient substitutes for bulk interception powers as a method of obtaining the necessary intelligence.[163] This reasoning represents a paradigm shift – not only because it seemingly contradicts the ECtHR's own stance on this issue in earlier cases, particularly in *Zakharov* and *Szabó*, but also due to the disconnect this has created with the jurisprudence of the IACtHR and of the UN human rights bodies. This also appeared to be the case in relation to the stance of the Court of Justice of the European Union (CJEU), as reflected in its jurisprudence pre-dating its decision in the four joint cases of *La Quadrature du Net and Privacy International*,[164] handed down in October 2020.

Perhaps the most startling difference in this regard are the *Digital Rights Ireland* and *Schrems I* decisions, in which the CJEU unequivocally condemned the bulk collection and processing of personal data precisely because their indiscriminate and generalized nature cannot, in the Court's view, be considered as proportionate and strictly necessary in a democratic society.

---

margin of appreciation should be left to the competent national authorities in striking a fair balance between the relevant conflicting public and private interests; and that the scope of the margin depends on such factors as the nature and the seriousness of the interests at stake and the gravity of the interference.

[161] *Weber* (n 52) para 106; see also *Klass* (n 50) para 49; *Leander* (n 122) para 59; *Malone* (n 16) para 81.

[162] *Weber ibid* para 106; *Kennedy* (n 32) para 50.

[163] *Big Brother Watch* (n 34) para 176.

[164] C-623-17 *Privacy International*, C-511/18 *La Quadrature du Net and Others*, C-512/18 *French Data Network and Others* and C-520/18 *Ordre des Barreaux Francophones et Germanophone and Others* (6 October 2020).

The CJEU confirmed this approach in its much-anticipated decision handed down on 16 July 2020 in *Schrems II*. Following the challenge to personal data transfers in the 2015 *Schrems I* judgment, the CJEU invalidated the US-EU Safe Harbour framework, which was subsequently replaced with the US-EU Privacy Shield to comply with the EU data protection requirements. On 12 July 2016 the European Commission deemed the Privacy Shield agreement adequate under EU law to enable data transfers to the US ('Commission's Adequacy Decision').[165] Apart from that framework, organizations transferring personal data to third countries outside of the EU may also rely on data transfer agreements which adopt Standard Contractual Clauses, whose use was affirmed as valid under European Commission Decision 2010/87 (subsequently amended by EU Decision 2016/2297). In a legal challenge in *Schrems II*, the CJEU was asked[166] to review the validity of both these methods – that is, Standard Contractual Clauses[167] and the Privacy Shield – as approved mechanisms to protect the transfers of EU citizens' personal data from the EU to third countries in light of the requirements set out in the EU Charter and the General Data Protection Regulation (GDPR). One of the key aspects that the CJEU was requested to pronounce on was whether the GDPR applies to data transfers between economic operators in situations where that data is likely to be processed in a third country for public security and law enforcement purposes;[168] and consequently, whether the Privacy Shield ensures an adequate level of protection under the GDPR.[169] The CJEU answered this question in the negative. As a result, the CJEU annulled the EU-US Privacy Shield, but upheld Standard Contractual Clauses, deeming them to provide sufficient protection.

---

[165] Commission Implementing Decision (EU) 2016/1250 of 12 July 2016 pursuant to Directive 95/46/EC of the European Parliament and of the Council on the adequacy of the protection provided by the EU-US Privacy Shield (notified under Document C(2016) 4176).

[166] The case was brought in Ireland by Max Schrems against the Irish Data Protection Commissioner. The Irish High Court referred the case to the CJEU, also asking whether the Privacy Shield ensures an adequate level of protection under Article 45 of the GDPR – see C-311/18 *Data Protection Commissioner v Facebook Ireland and Maximilian Schrems* [2020] ECJ para 160 ('*Schrems II*').

[167] *Ibid.* The CJEU was asked: (1) what level of protection applies under the Standard Contractual Clauses adopted pursuant to Article 46 of the GDPR (para 90); (2) whether the data protection authorities are required to suspend or prohibit data transfers to a third country pursuant to Standard Contractual Clauses if in their view those clauses are not or cannot be complied with in that third country and the protection of data transfers stipulated under Articles 45 and 46 of the GDPR and the EU Charter cannot be ensured (para 106); and (3) whether the Standard Contractual Clauses are valid in light of Articles 7, 8 and 47 of the EU Charter (para 122).

[168] *Ibid* para 80.

[169] *Ibid* para 160.

The decision reflects the CJEU's concerns over the US security agencies' excessive use of surveillance powers, as these fail to meet the requirements of necessity and proportionality. More specially, the decision is based on the following findings: (1) the primacy of US law enforcement requirements over those contained in the Privacy Shield, which echoes the CJEU's main objection in *Schrems I* in relation to the Safe Harbour framework;[170] (2) the lack of necessary limitations and safeguards on the powers of the authorities under US law – in particular, in view of the proportionality requirement;[171] (3) the absence of an effective remedy in the US for EU data subjects;[172] and (4) deficiencies in the Privacy Shield Ombudsman mechanism.[173] In arriving at these conclusions, the CJEU examined the use of US surveillance programs authorized on the basis of Section 702 of the FISA, in conjunction with Executive Order 12333 and Presidential Policy Directive-28 (PPD-28).[174] It first observed that Section 702 permits the Attorney General and the Director of National Intelligence to jointly authorize (following FISC approval) the surveillance of individuals who are not US citizens and who are located outside the US in order to obtain 'foreign intelligence information'. Section 702 provides the basis for, *inter alia* the PRISM and Upstream programs.[175] The CJEU then noted that Executive Order 12333 allows the NSA to access data 'in transit' to the United States via underwater cables on the floor of the Atlantic Ocean, and to collect and retain such data before it arrives in the US and becomes subject to the FISA.[176] The CJEU emphasized that the activities conducted pursuant to Executive Order 12333 are not governed by statute.[177] Finally, the Court stated that PPD-28,[178] which promised greater safeguards of foreigners' rights, merely requires that intelligence activities be 'as tailored as feasible' when it comes to the protection of non-US persons.[179] In view of these findings, the CJEU undertook to assess whether the mass processing by the US of EU citizens' personal data meets the required levels of protection

---

[170]  *Ibid* para 164.
[171]  *Ibid* paras 168–85.
[172]  *Ibid* paras 191–92.
[173]  Ibid paras 193–97.
[174]  The White House, *Presidential Policy Directive – Signals Intelligence Activities* (Policy Directive/PPD-28) (17 January 2014) ('PPD-28').
[175]  *Schrems II* (n 166) para 61.
[176]  *Ibid* para 63.
[177]  *Ibid.*
[178]  PPD-28 (n 174). Issued by the Obama administration, PPD-28 aims to limit US SIGINT operations and to ensure that in conducting intelligence gathering, the country takes account of not only its security needs, but also the privacy of people around the world.
[179]  *Ibid* para 64.

under Articles 7 (respect for private and family life) and 8 (protection of personal data) of the EU Charter. In holding that US surveillance violates these rights, the CJEU called into question the Commission's Adequacy Decision, according to which the Privacy Shield afforded adequate safeguards. To that end, the CJEU referred to Article 52(1) of the EU Charter, which provides that any limitation of Charter rights (including under Articles 7 and 8) may be made only if they meet the requirement of proportionality.[180] The CJEU noted the Commission's finding in the Privacy Shield Adequacy Decision that: 'the FISC does not authorise individual surveillance measures; rather it authorises surveillance programs (like PRISM, UPSTREAM) on the basis of annual certifications prepared by the Attorney General and the Director of National Intelligence.'[181] On these grounds, the CJEU concluded that:

> the supervisory role of the FISC is thus designed to verify whether those surveillance programmes relate to the objective of acquiring foreign intelligence information, but does not cover the issue of whether "individuals are properly targeted to acquire foreign intelligence information".[182]

It was therefore clear to the CJEU that: 'section 702 of the FISA does not indicate any limitations on the power it confers to implement surveillance programmes for the purposes of foreign intelligence or the existence of guarantees for non-US persons potentially targeted by those programmes.'[183] The CJEU also held that neither PPD-28 nor Executive Order 12333 grants data subjects actionable rights before the courts against US authorities.[184] Overall, Section 702 of the FISA, Executive Order 12333 and PPD-28 do not set out sufficient limitations on intelligence collection and, as such, do not meet the requirements set out in Article 52(1) of the EU Charter, including that of proportionality.[185] The CJEU stressed that in order to satisfy the proportionality criterion, the legal basis which permits surveillance must define the scope of the limitation on the exercise of the right concerned, and lay down clear and

---

[180] Charter of Fundamental Rights of the European Union (2012) OJ C 326/391 Art 51(1) ('EU Charter').
[181] *Schrems II* (n 166) para 179.
[182] *Ibid.*
[183] *Ibid* para 180.
[184] *Ibid* paras 181–82.
[185] *Ibid* para 185.

precise rules governing the scope and application of the measure in question, together with minimum safeguards.[186] To this end, the CJEU concluded that:

> neither Section 702 of the FISA, nor E.O. 12333, read in conjunction with PPD-28, correlates to the minimum safeguards resulting, under the EU law, from the principle of proportionality, with the consequence that the surveillance programmes based on those provisions cannot be regarded as limited to what is strictly necessary.[187]

*Schrems II* and *Big Brother Watch* are factually similar, in that they both concerned, *inter alia*, US surveillance pursuant to the PRISM and Upstream programs; yet the outcomes of these two cases could not be more different. While the CJEU considers limitless interception of and access to foreign communications data by US state intelligence agencies unacceptable, as it breaches the fundamental tenet of proportionality which must be met for such measures to be considered lawful, for the ECtHR, bulk interception programs are not axiomatically disproportionate. Quite the contrary, the ECtHR views them a 'valuable means to achieve aims pursued, particularly given the current threat level from both global terrorism and serious crime'.[188] However, following the CJEU decision in the four joint cases of *La Quadrature du Net and Privacy International*, the approaches taken by that Court and the ECtHR to the bulk collection of communications data may begin to align. In that case, the CJEU ruled that EU law precludes national legislation from requiring communications service providers to carry out the general and indiscriminate transmission or retention of traffic and location data. However, where an EU member state is facing a serious threat to national security that is genuine and present, or foreseeable, that state may derogate from the obligation to ensure the confidentiality of communications data by requiring through its legislation its general and indiscriminate retention for a period that is strictly limited and necessary, which may be extended if the threat persists. Furthermore, EU member states may also provide for the targeted retention of such data, together with the general and indiscriminate retention of IP addresses assigned to the source of communications, where this serves to combat serious crime and prevent significant threats to public security. The outcome of the joint *La Quadrature du Net* cases is underpinned by the concerns of some EU member states over the CJEU's prohibition of the general and indiscriminate retention of traffic and location data (discussed in Chapter 3 *supra*), which they contended deprives them of necessary national security tools. The common theme in all four *La Quadrature du Net* judgments is that the CJEU relied on its previous case law

---

[186] *Ibid* para 180.
[187] *Ibid* para 184.
[188] *Ibid* para 386.

– referring to, *inter alia*, the *Digital Rights Ireland* and *Tele-2/Watson* cases, together with *Schrems II* – to reinforce certain aspects of its earlier approach, in particular in relation to preventing, as a general rule, national laws from facilitating the bulk retention of traffic and location data. However, in the *La Quadrature du Net* decisions, the CJEU seems to have acquiesced to the possibility of states adopting indiscriminate data retention legislation, but only if the existence of a genuine national security threat is shown. To that end, the CJEU held that in such circumstances, EU law does not preclude recourse to an order requiring service providers to retain traffic and location data generally and indiscriminately, thus seemingly legitimizing such measures. It is in this sense that the European Courts' approaches seem, at least for the time being, to be on a similar trajectory.

## 5.   CONCLUSION

The need for greater protection of the right to privacy in the context of the surveillance of digital communications has been elevated in recent years from relative obscurity to prominence through attention and support from the UN General Assembly and various international and regional human rights courts and bodies, together with civil society. However, the emergent legal landscape pertaining to the protection of this right appears polarized, because of divergent judicial approaches to, among other matters, the grounds for justification when it comes to the bulk surveillance of foreign communications. Thus, the UN human rights apparatus maintains the conviction that indiscriminate mass surveillance is 'not permissible under international human rights law, as an individualised necessity and proportionality analysis would not be possible in the context of such measures'.[189] A similar stance has been taken in the Inter-American legal system, while the CJEU has again confirmed its antagonism to NSA surveillance through the tapping of underwater cables as being disproportionate. Having said that, following its decision in the *La Quadrature du Net* cases, the CJEU now allows EU member states, under tightly circumscribed conditions, to put in place measures for indiscriminate data retention if they can demonstrate the existence of a genuine and serious threat to national security. This approach may signal a closer alignment between the CJEU and the ECtHR, at least as far as the acceptability of the retention and analysis of communications data is concerned. However, the ECtHR appears to have gone further by embracing the mass surveillance of foreign communications in light of a number of Western governments having updated or modernized their domestic laws, thus in effect normalizing this practice. To this end, it laid

---

[189]   A/HRC/39/29 (n 72) para 17.

down differing procedural standards, depending on whether the surveillance is targeted or bulk. In the latter context, the ECtHR finds no application for the requirement of reasonable suspicion, which continues to apply only in case of targeted surveillance. Further, it seems that for the ECtHR, bulk interception programs are not categorically disproportionate; while prior judicial authorization is preferable, but not indispensable. This means that the ECtHR may focus its scrutiny in future cases not on whether the practice of mass surveillance violates Article 8 obligations *per se,* but rather on how the process itself is conducted – in other words, whether it meets the set procedural standards. However, whether these become embedded legal standards remains to be seen in light of the pending appeals of both the *Big Brother Watch* and *Centrum För Rättvisa* decisions to the Grand Chamber of the ECtHR.

# 7. International law and the future of mass surveillance

## 1. INTRODUCTION

The previous chapters of this book attested to the international legal landscape pertaining to the protection of the right to privacy appearing fragmented – comprising disparate standards and outdated privacy rules. The situation is exacerbated by states' increasing appetite for ubiquitous bulk surveillance of foreign and domestic communications alike; while its regulation through a legally binding surveillance treaty seems unlikely to be achieved in the near future. This is because, despite numerous calls from the UN organizations and human rights institutions demanding that limits be placed on these practices, there is no consensus to date on how to bring them into line with human rights law, despite the fact that the need for specific, modern rules regulating digital surveillance is undeniable.

With this in mind, this chapter aims to identify, discuss and evaluate possible international legal solutions to the challenges that these activities pose, focusing on three options: (1) an international or regional legally binding treaty; (2) the development of non-legally binding cyber norms; and (3) bilateral agreements.

The chapter discusses these matters in the following sections. Section 2 engages with numerous endeavours made since the late 1990s to set out the 'rules of the road' for state behaviour in the context of cyber security.[1] This section considers these efforts by outlining the cyber-geopolitical rivalries among the major cyber powers, broadly termed 'the West' and 'the East'. Section 3 rationalizes the failed proposals for a cyber security agreement

---

[1] The issue of responsible state behaviour in the context of international peace and security was raised by Russia in 1998, when it called for an international dialogue under the auspices of the United Nations – see UN General Assembly (UNGA), 'Letter Dated 23 September 1998 for the Permanent Representatives of the Russian Federation to the United Nations Addressed to the Secretary-General' (23 September 1998) UN Doc A/C.1/53/3.

(the Draft Codes of Conduct for Information Security 2011[2] and 2015),[3] and appraises the approaches taken to human rights concerns within that discourse. It also outlines two unsuccessful attempts at a specific cyber surveillance treaty at the regional and international levels: the CoE's Intelligence Codex ('Intelligence Codex')[4] and the Legal Instrument on Government-Led Surveillance and Privacy ('Legal Instrument'),[5] evaluating the reasons for their rejection. Section 4 then considers the role that voluntary, non-legally binding cyber norms may play in protecting the right to privacy in the cyber domain. To this end, it first outlines the work of the United Nations Group of Government Experts on Developments in the Field of Information and Telecommunications in the Context of International Security (UN GGE). Specific attention is paid to the GGE 2015 report,[6] which set out 11 norms for responsible state behaviour, focusing on Recommendation 13(e) and its interpretation made by the United Nations Office for Disarmament Affairs (UNODA) Commentary on Voluntary, Non-Binding Norms for Responsible State Behaviour in the Use of Information and Communications Technology ('UNODA Commentary').[7] Finally, section 5 highlights a number of bilateral commitments in the sphere of cyber espionage, with section 6 concluding the discussion.

---

[2]    UNGA, 'Letter Dated 12 September 2011 for the Permanent Representatives of China, the Russian Federation, Tajikistan and Uzbekistan to the United Nations Addressed to the Secretary General' (12 September 2011) UN Doc A/66/359 ('SCO Code of Conduct 2011').

[3]    UNGA, 'Letter Dated 9 January 2015 for the Permanent Representatives of China, Kazakhstan, Kyrgyzstan, the Russian Federation, Tajikistan and Uzbekistan to the United Nations Addressed to the Secretary General' (9 January 2015) UN Doc A/69/723 ('SCO Code of Conduct 2015').

[4]    CoE, Committee on Legal Affairs and Human Rights, 'Mass Surveillance. Draft Resolution' (2015) AS/Jur 2 ('CoE Mass Surveillance Resolution').

[5]    Office of the High Commissioner for Human Rights, UN Special Rapporteur on the Right to Privacy, 'Draft Legal Instrument on Government-led Surveillance and Privacy' (10 January 2018) ('Legal Instrument').

[6]    UNGA, 'Group of Governmental Experts on Developments in the Field of Information and Telecommunications in the Context of International Security' (22 July 2015) UN Doc A/70/174 ('GGE 2015'). See also UN Open-Ended Working Group on Developments in the Field of Information and Telecommunications in the Context of International Security (OEWG), 'Second "Pre-Draft" of the Report of the OEWG on Developments in the Field of Information and Telecommunications in the Context of International Security' (27 May 2020) ('OEWG Revised Pre-Draft Report'), https://front.un-arm.org/wp-content/uploads/2020/05/200527-oewg-ict-revised-pre-draft.pdf.

[7]    UN Office for Disarmament Affairs, *Voluntary, Non-binding Norms for Responsible State Behaviour in the Use of Information and Communications Technology. A Commentary* (UN Office for Disarmament Affairs, 2017) ('UNODA Commentary').

## 2.    REGULATION OF STATES' ACTIVITIES IN CYBERSPACE

### 2.1    Cyber Security Dimensions

With increased recognition of the importance of globally interconnected electronic communications, together with the economic wealth this helps to create and the political stakes involved – not to mention the threats derived from hostile cyber operations – the international community has become engrossed in the debate regarding the future of cyberspace and the challenges posed to national security. Threats of cyber attack[8] attributed to the ease and relatively low cost of inflicting harm on the functionality of computer-operated physical infrastructure by a variety of actors (eg, hackers, ideologically motivated individuals, states, criminal and terrorist organizations) expose the vulnerabilities of most nations, even those with superior military power.[9] Although extreme scenarios of cyber conflict have not yet materialized,[10] several countries have been subjected to cyber attacks, of which other nations were suspected of being the instigators.[11] One of the earliest examples is the June 1982 gas pipeline explosion in Siberia, as a result of an alleged logic bomb installed in the computer system by the US Central Intelligence Agency.[12] Other instances of high-profile and well-documented cyber operations include the 2007 denial of service attacks on Estonia;[13] the release of the Stuxnext worm in 2010 in Iran's industrial infrastructure, for the alleged purpose of sabotaging the Natanz uranium facility;[14] and North Korea's purported hack of Sony Pictures demanding the withdrawal from public release of comedy *The Interview*.[15] There are other reported cases in which cyber operations have been used in connection with and in aid of military campaigns or armed conflicts, such as against Georgia in 2008.[16] More recent disturbing reminders of states' belligerence include the July 2020 attempt to steal the UK's Covid-19 vaccine from

---

[8]    For a definition of 'cyber attack', see Michael N Schmitt (ed), *Tallinn Manual 2.0 on the International Law Applicable to Cyber Operations* (Cambridge University Press, 2017), Rule 92, 415 (*'Tallinn Manual 2.0'*); Marco Roscini, *Cyber Operations and the Use of Force in International Law* (Oxford University Press, 2014) 17 ('Roscini').

[9]    *Ibid* 2.

[10]    Thomas Rid, *Cyberwar Will Not Take Place* (C Hurt & Co Publishers, 2013).

[11]    Roscini (n 8) 4.

[12]    *Ibid.*

[13]    *Ibid.*

[14]    *Ibid* 6.

[15]    Oliver Laughland, 'FBI Director Stands by Claim that North Korea was Source of Sony Cyber Attack', *The Guardian* (7 January 2015).

[16]    Roscini (n 8).

a number of research facilities, attributed by the UK government to Russia's APT29 group; and the December 2020 SolarWinds security breach against numerous US governmental department networks and 18 000 private users, also allegedly perpetrated by the Russians.[17]

To respond to such hostile actions, most states have developed a national cyber security strategy – that is, 'a plan of actions designed to improve the security and resilience of national infrastructure and services'.[18] These documents represent a high-level, top-down approach to cyber security, which establishes a range of national objectives and priorities that should be achieved within a specific timeframe;[19] and as policy tools, have been adopted by most countries worldwide.[20] Equally, however, states have recognized that challenges to cyber security cannot be adequately dealt with by any single nation acting alone, as cyberspace extends far beyond the domain of internal affairs of a single country.[21] To this end, most governments acknowledge that fundamental to peace, security and political stability is achieving a commitment to the governance of this domain, which involves respect for international law. As a result, multinational cooperation has long been underway focused on the handling of cyber security issues, dictated by nations' broad consensus that cyber threats are serious, growing and destabilizing.[22] These concerns eventually led to the commencement of deeper regulatory discussions, through the establishment of the UN GGE process, to examine various risks in cyberspace and how to cooperatively address them. A number of international organizations have become increasingly involved in cyber security matters too,

---

[17]   See Deborah Haynes, 'Coronavirus: Russian Cyber Spies Attempting to Steal Vaccine Research from Britain, US and Canada', *Sky News* (17 July 2020); see Herb Lin, 'Reflections on the SolarWinds Breach' *Lawfare* (22 December 2020), www.lawfareblog.com/reflections-solarwinds-breach. Allegedly, the security breach of SolarWinds – a US company that monitors the computer networks of businesses and government departments – was perpetrated by the Russians, compromising 18 000 SolarWinds customers and a variety of government agencies, including the Departments of Treasury, State, Commerce, Energy (including the National Nuclear Security Administration) and Homeland Security.

[18]   EU Agency for Cybersecurity, 'National Cybersecurity Strategies' (2005–20).

[19]   *Ibid.*

[20]   For an overview of national security and defence strategies, see NATO Cooperative Cyber Defence Centre of Excellence (CCDCOE), 'Strategy and Governance', listing 82 countries with such documents in place – https://ccdcoe.org/library/strategy-and-governance/.

[21]   Kubo Mačák, 'From Cyber Norms to Cyber Rules: Re-engaging States as Law Makers' (2017) 30(4) *Leiden Journal of International Law*, 877–99 ('Mačák').

[22]   Nazli Choucri and Daniel Goldsmith, 'Lost in Cyberspace: Harnessing the Internet, International Relations and Global Security' (2012) 68(2) *Bulletin of the Atomic Scientists.*

including the Organization for the Security and Cooperation in Europe, which in its 2010 Astana Commemorative Declaration recognized cyber threats as among 'emerging trans-national threats'.[23] In 2008 NATO established the Cooperative Cyber Defence Centre of Excellence (CCDCOE), accredited with the full status of an international military organization, which in 2010 issued its New Strategic Concept, thus acknowledging the damage that can be inflicted as a result of cyber attacks.[24]

One of the crucial aspects of this international engagement is states' broad consensus that international law – in particular, the UN Charter – applies to cyberspace.[25] As yet, however, there is no all-encompassing international legal framework that regulates states' behaviour to ensure that international peace and stability are maintained. There are, however, a number of regional treaties that provide a patchwork of regulations for cyberspace activities. Among them are the 1992 Constitution of the International Telecommunications Union;[26] the Council of Europe (CoE) 2001 Convention on Cybercrime (the Budapest Convention);[27] the CoE Convention for the Protection of Individuals with Regard to Automatic Processing of Personal Data as modernized by the Protocol amending the Convention for the Protection of Individuals with Regard to Automatic Processing of Personal Data (Convention 108);[28] the 2009 Shanghai Cooperation Organization's (SCO) Information Security Agreement

---

[23]  *Ibid.*

[24]  NATO, *Active Engagement, Modern Defence. Strategic Concept for the Defence and Security of the Members of the North Atlantic Treaty Organization,* adopted by the Heads of State and Government at the NATO Summit in Lisbon (19–20 November 2010).

[25]  UNGA, Group of Government Experts on Developments in the Field of Information and Telecommunications in the Context of International Security (24 June 2013) UN Doc A/68/98 ('GGE 2013'); GGE 2015 (n 6). See also OEWG Revised Pre-Draft Report (n 6) 5, according to which 'existing obligations under international law, in particular the Charter of the United Nations in its entirety, are applicable to State use of ICTs'.

[26]  Constitution of the International Telecommunications Union, 1825 UNTS 143 (1992).

[27]  CoE, Convention on Cybercrime (March 2002) 41 ILM 282.

[28]  Convention for the Protection of Individuals with Regard to the Automatic Processing of Personal Data (28 January 1981) CETS 108, as modernized by the Protocol amending the Convention for the Protection of Individuals with Regard to Automatic Processing of Personal Data (10 October 2018) CETS No 223.

(the Yekaterinburg Agreement);[29] and the African Union Convention on Cyber Security and Personal Data Protection.[30]

The reason for the lack of a multilateral agreement is often explained by, *inter alia*, the general reluctance of states to codify the applicable legal standards,[31] with a number of governments postulating that the rules of *lex lata* are adequate to regulate their conduct in this domain. Thus, a number of unsuccessful attempts have been made since 1996, when France put forward a plan for such a treaty, titled the Charter for International Cooperation on the Internet.[32] Subsequent endeavours also failed, with the SCO submitting to the UN General Assembly (UNGA) two Codes of Conduct for Information Security in 2011 and 2015.[33] These latter proposals were presented as sets of voluntary rules to regulate states' use of ICT. Nevertheless, they were perceived by some governments as an invitation to negotiate a potential multi-national convention to stop the proliferation of information weapons and were thus received with scepticism and subsequently rejected.[34] This unwillingness to agree on a legally binding instrument is to a large extent underpinned by the political and ideological rivalries of the major 'cyber powers', coalesced in opposing 'camps', represented by the US and liberal democracies at one end of the spectrum (hereinafter broadly termed 'the West'); and China, Russia and other like-minded states at the other end (hereinafter, 'the East'). Judging from their[35] official attitudes to cyber security, outlined below, it soon becomes

---

[29]    Agreement between the Governments of the Member States of the Shanghai Cooperation Organization on Cooperation in the Field of International Information Security (16 June 2009) ('Yekaterinburg Agreement').

[30]    African Union Convention on Cyber Security and Personal Data Protection (2014) EX.CL/846(XXV).

[31]    See, for example, Kristine Eichensehr, 'The Cyber-Law of Nations' (2015) 103 *Georgetown Law Journal*, 317; Mačák (n 21); Onna Hathaway *et al*, 'The Law of Cyber Attack' (2012) 100 *California Law Review*, 817.

[32]    Mačák *ibid.*

[33]    SCO Code of Conduct 2011 (n 2); SCO Code of Conduct 2015 (n 3).

[34]    Liisi Adamson, 'International Law and International Cyber Norms. A Continuum?' in Dennis Broeders and Bibi van den Berg (eds), *Governing Cyberspace. Behaviour, Power, and Diplomacy* (Rowman and Littlefield Publishing Group, 2020) 19–43, 21 ('Adamson').

[35]    Although the position of the individual states within these groups may be nuanced (as is the case with China and Russia, and indeed within the broader SCO, where some differences have been observed), their overall policy stance is sufficiently aligned to represent convergence in the strategic thinking pertaining to the vision of cyberspace governance. Thus, China and Russia are said to present a united front to the world, largely aimed at countering US hegemony in cyberspace – see Dennis Broeders, Liisi Adamson and Rogier Creemers, 'Coalition of the Unwilling? Chinese and Russian Perspectives on Cyberspace', *The Hague Program for Cyber Norms Policy Brief* (1 October 2019).

apparent why efforts to reach a legally binding multilateral treaty on matters relating to cyber security have failed and are unlikely to succeed in the foreseeable future. It must also be noted that the desirability of such an instrument to regulate states' offensive use of cyber technologies is in doubt, as the existing international law regimes – such as *jus ad bellum* and *jus in bello* – are seen by some states and in academia[36] to be sufficiently flexible to regulate cyber operations. Nevertheless, this overview of the political debate in the context of cyber security not only serves as an illustration of the deeply rooted political divide, but also attests to the fact that states have historically paid scant attention to human rights protection within this discourse. This tendency continues unchanged today. To demonstrate these points, the next section outlines the cyber policy perspectives of the US and the UK, and compares them with those of Russia and China.

## 2.2    Cyber Security Approaches of the West

### 2.2.1    The US

The US has been described as the 'only one' cyber superpower in the world[37] and since 1999 has been prolific in its production of official documents on cyber security matters.[38] The US attitude to cyberspace generally and to the

---

[36]    See OEWG Revised Re-Draft Report (n 6) 5, where it was proposed that the 'existing international law, complemented by the voluntary, non-legally binding norms that reflect consensus among States, is currently sufficient for addressing State use of ICTs … efforts should focus on reaching common understanding on how the already agreed normative framework applies through the development of additional guidance, and can be operationalized through enhancing implementation by all States'. See also Roscini (n 8) 287. Professor Roscini observed that: 'we still have to fully understand the realities and potentialities of cyber capabilities as the developments of these technologies occur at such a speed that any treaty would potentially be outdated the day after it has been opened for signature. Existing rules are capable of adequately regulating the phenomenon and of limiting the conduct of states in cyber context: let us start by correctly identifying and applying them.'

[37]    Kenneth Geers, 'Pandemonium: Nation States, National Security and the Internet' (2014) 1(1) *The Tallinn Papers* (NATO CCDCOE Publications on Strategic Cyber Security).

[38]    These include, *inter alia*, US Department of Defense (DoD), *An Assessment of International Legal Issues in Information Operations* (May 1999); US Department of the Air Force, *Cornerstones of Information Warfare* (17 April 1997); US Chairman of the Joint Chiefs of Staff, *The National Military Strategy for Cyberspace Operations* (December 2006); US Air Force, *Cyberspace Operations Air Force Doctrine Document 3-12* (15 July 2010); US DoD, *Strategy for Operating in Cyberspace* (July 2011); the White House, *Information Operations, Joint Publication 3-13* (27 November 2012); and more recently, the White House, *National Cyber Strategy of the United States of America* (September 2018) ('Cyber Strategy 2018'); US DoD, *Cyber Strategy* (2018);

Internet in particular is broadly representative of that held by other states comprising the Five Eyes alliance, and can be encapsulated in one phrase: 'Internet freedom.' This notion was first introduced by the former Secretary of State Hilary Clinton in her speech of that title in 2010.[39] Secretary Clinton called cyberspace a 'global networked commons' and remarked, *inter alia*, that the US 'stands for a single internet, where all humanity has equal access to knowledge and ideas'.[40] These views were subsequently echoed by the Obama administration in its seminal 2011 International Strategy for Cyberspace: Prosperity, Security and Openness in a Networked World ('International Strategy 2011').[41] The Strategy sought to establish that country's normative perspective of cyberspace as a global political space and to that end, stated that the US government's main goal is to:

> work internationally to promote an open, interoperable, secure and reliable informa-tion and communications infrastructure that supports international trade and com-merce, strengthens international security and fosters free expression and innovation. To achieve that goal, [the administration] will build and sustain an environment in which norms of responsible behavior guide States' actions, sustain partnerships and support the rule of law in cyberspace.[42]

The International Strategy 2011 continues to be representative of the US view on cyberspace, as it laid down the foundations for that country's plans pertaining to its future. At the forefront of this vision is that cyberspace is to be governed by the rule of law domestically and internationally.[43] This concept the Strategy defines as 'a civil order in which fidelity to laws safeguards people and interests; brings stability to global markets; and holds malevolent actors to account internationally'.[44] The stability to which the International Strategy 2011 refers should be achieved through norms of behaviour[45] or, as the document puts it, 'an environment of expectations that ground foreign and defense policies and guide international partnerships'.[46] At the core of

---

and the White House, *National Strategy to Secure 5G of the United States of America* (March 2020).

[39] Hilary Rodham Clinton, 'Remarks on Internet Freedom' (2010) US Department of State ('Clinton').

[40] *Ibid.*

[41] The White House, *International Strategy for Cyberspace: Prosperity, Security and Openness in a Networked World* (2011) ('International Strategy 2011').

[42] *Ibid* 8.

[43] *Ibid* 3 and 5.

[44] *Ibid* 5.

[45] *Ibid* 9. Norms, unlike international law rules, are not legally binding on states. For more discussion in relation to cyber norms, see section 4.

[46] *Ibid.*

international cyberspace policy is the commitment to fundamental freedoms (freedom of expression and association; and freedom to receive and impart information and ideas through any medium and regardless of frontiers),[47] privacy, the free flow of information,[48] respect for property, protection from crime and the right of self-defence.[49] Preserving global network functionality and improving cyber security features strongly, in addition to ensuring that in future, cyberspace is globally interoperable, with stable networks and reliable access. The Strategy's vision regarding its future governance is unequivocally based on the multi-stakeholder model[50] and continues to be so to this day. This method of management has no hierarchy and consists of governments, private companies and non-governmental organizations drawing representatives from public interest advocacy groups, business associations and other parties, who all participate in intergovernmental policy deliberations.[51]

A key role in this management of the Internet is played by a private entity based in the US, the Internet Corporation for Assigned Names and Numbers (ICANN). The company, operated through a licence issued by the US Department of Commerce,[52] has as its main role the allocation and assignment of the unique identifiers for the Internet, including global domain names (forming a system referred to as the Domain Name System).[53] It enables users to communicate with each other and therefore forms an indispensable part of the functioning of the Internet. ICANN's main attribute is that it promulgates and works through a so-called 'bottom-up' process. This allows the government, the private sector, civil society and the technical community to develop incrementally and work together to set Internet policies. There is no doubt that this approach has enabled incredible technological innovation and the expansion of this facility worldwide. Nevertheless, ICANN's stewardship and its continued success in keeping the Internet 'open' have been achieved with

---

[47]   *Ibid.*

[48]   *Ibid* 5.

[49]   *Ibid* 10.

[50]   *Ibid.*

[51]   Milton Muller, *Networks and States: The Global Politics of Internet Governance* (The MIT Press, 2010) 8.

[52]   ICANN, 'Affirmation of Commitments by the United States Department of Commerce and the Internet Corporation for Assigned Names and Numbers' (30 September 2009).

[53]   ICANN '[c]oordinates the allocation and assignment of names in the root zone of the Domain Name System ("DNS") [together with] … the development and implementation of policies concerning the registration of second-level domain names in generic top-level domains' – see Article 1 of ICANN's Bylaws for Internet Corporation for Assigned Names and Numbers. A California Nonprofit Public-Benefit Corporation (28 November 2019).

the sponsorship of the US government,[54] which according to some critics has led to the US practically monopolizing the global communications industry, since ICANN has not offered a viable mechanism for other national or regional interests to be represented at a governmental level.[55] Indeed, through ICANN, the US has successfully established a governance regime dominated by itself and by non-state actors.[56] This the US government has attained by privatizing and internationalizing key policymaking functions, while retaining, until 2016, considerable authority for itself through ICANN and the Department of Commerce, together with asserting 'policy authority' over the Domain Name System's root and reserving the right to review and approve any changes to the root zone file proposed by ICANN.[57] For years, the relationship between ICANN and the US government sent a message to the rest of the world that the US is withholding the Internet from conventional international governance processes, thereby strengthening the position of already entrenched US-based enterprises in the lucrative global Internet market.[58] Criticisms of ICANN's domineering role, coupled with the lack of transparency and accountability, were repeatedly voiced in particular by the countries that would prefer to see the UN in charge of the Web. In 2011, they were joined in this vision by the Obama administration.[59] As a result, in 2016 the US Department of Commerce ceded its power over the Domain Name System, ending almost 20 years of control by handing over a crucial part of the Internet's governance to the global Internet community.[60]

The US vision in relation to the future stewardship of cyberspace inevitably encompasses the role that international law will play therein; but according to the International Strategy 2011, this does not involve the devising of any spe-

---

[54]   Geoff Huston, 'ICANN, the ITU and WSIS and Internet Governance – Part I' (2004) APNIC, www.apnic.net/community/ecosystem/igf/articles/icann-wsis-part-i/.

[55]   Geoff Huston, 'ICANN, the ITU and WSIS and Internet Governance – Part II' (2004) APNIC, www.apnic.net/community/ecosystem/igf/articles/icann-wsis-part-ii ('Huston').

[56]   Milton Mueller, John Mathiason and Hans Kein, 'The Internet and the Global Governance: Principles and Norms for a New Regime' (2007) 13 *Global Governance*, 237–54.

[57]   *Ibid* 240.

[58]   Huston (n 55).

[59]   Ian Shapira, 'Obama Administration Joins Critics of US Non-profit Group that Oversees Internet', *The Washington Post* (28 February 2011).

[60]   ICANN, 'Stewardship of IANA Functions Transitions to Global Internet Community as Contract with US Government Ends' (1 October 2016), www.icann.org/news/announcement-2016-10-01-en.

cific legally binding rules, but rather an incremental process facilitated through the use of voluntary norms. To this end, the document professes that:

> The development of norms for State conduct in cyberspace does not require a rein-vention of customary international law, nor does it render existing international norms obsolete. Long-standing international norms guiding State behavior – in times of peace and conflict – also apply in cyberspace. Nonetheless, unique attrib-utes of networked technology require additional work to clarify how these norms apply and what additional understandings might be necessary to supplement them. We will continue to work internationally to forge consensus regarding how norms of behavior apply to cyberspace, with the understanding that an important first step in such efforts is applying the broad expectations of peaceful and just interstate conduct to cyberspace.[61]

The ideological thrust of the International Strategy 2011 can therefore be sum-marized as an attempt to marry the protection of national security interests in cyberspace with the United States' core commitments to fundamental freedom of expression and association, privacy and free flow of information through close international cooperation and consensus building based on the develop-ment of non-legally binding norms. It also illustrates the reluctance to commit to a multilateral treaty or to contribute to the articulation of cyber-specific customary law rules; while Internet governance is to remain to be conducted on the basis of multi-stakeholder processes. This policy stance endures and has been reiterated in a number of subsequent documents, including the 2011 US Department of Defense Cyberspace Policy Report;[62] the 2015 US Law of War Manual 2015, as supplemented by its 2016 version;[63] and more recently the US Department of Homeland Security Cybersecurity Strategy 2018[64] and the 2018 National Cyber Strategy.[65] The latter policy statement reinforces the role of non-legally binding norms and capacity-building measures,[66] seeing the role of the US as to promote:

> a framework of responsible State behavior in cyberspace built upon international law, adherence to voluntary non-legally binding norms of responsible state behavior that apply during peacetime and the consideration of practical confidence building

---

[61]   International Strategy 2011 (n 41) 9.
[62]   US DoD, *Department of Defense Cyberspace Policy Report: A Report to Congress Pursuant to the National Defense Authorization Act for the Fiscal Year 2011* (November 2011) section 934, 78.
[63]   US DoD, Office of the General Counsel, *Law of War Manual* (2016).
[64]   US Department of Homeland Security, *Cybersecurity Strategy* (15 May 2018).
[65]   Cyber Strategy 2018 (n 38).
[66]   *Ibid* part III, 20.

measures to reduce the risk of conflict stemming from malicious cyber activities ...[67]

## 2.2.2    The UK

The UK's 2011 Cyber Security Strategy (2011 Strategy)[68] by and large reflected the international cyber policy themes of its ally, the US. The country's vision for cyber security expressed in that document was:

> for the UK to drive huge economic and social value from a vibrant, resilient and secure cyberspace, where our actions, guided by our core values of liberty, fairness, transparency and the rule of law, enhance prosperity, national security and a strong society.[69]

To achieve these goals, the 2011 Strategy acknowledged the need to seek partnerships with other countries to improve the UK's defence, in view of the fact that the Internet is fundamentally transnational and dependent on infrastructure not entirely based on that country's territory. References were made to the role and protection of human rights – in particular, the right to privacy – in the context of pursuing cyber security policies that enhance individual and collective security. To achieve these goals, the Strategy urged everyone – that is, the private sector, individuals and government – to work together.[70] This proved challenging, and to that end the subsequent UK National Cyber Security Strategy 2016–2021[71] (Cyber Strategy 2016–2021) recognized that the approach taken in the 2011 Strategy had 'not achieved the scale and pace of change required to stay ahead of the fast moving threat'.[72] As a consequence, the UK government's vision for 2021 is that 'the UK is secure and resilient to cyber threats, prosperous and confident in the digital world'.[73] In order to realize these objectives, the government has pledged to work to defend against cyber threats, deter all forms of aggression in cyberspace and develop an innovative cyber security industry.[74] The Cyber Strategy 2016–2021 reiterated the need for international action and 'investment in partnerships that shape the global evolution of cyberspace in a manner that advances [the UK's]

---

[67]    *Ibid.*
[68]    UK HM Government, *UK Cyber Security Strategy, Protecting and Promoting the UK in the Digital World* (November 2011).
[69]    *Ibid* 8.
[70]    *Ibid.*
[71]    UK HM Government, *National Cyber Security Strategy 2016–2021* (2016).
[72]    *Ibid* para 1.3, 7.
[73]    *Ibid* para 1.4, 7.
[74]    *Ibid* para 1.5, 7.

wider economic and security interests'.[75] Among the objectives stipulated in the document is the 'safeguard[ing] of the long term future of a free, open, peaceful and secure cyberspace, driving economic growth and underpinning the UK's national security'.[76] This is envisaged to be achieved through, *inter alia*, the UK's continued championship of the multi-stakeholder model of Internet governance and opposition to data localization.[77] These aims rest on strengthening and embedding a common understanding of responsible state behaviour in cyberspace; building on the consensus that international law applies in cyberspace; continuing to promote the agreement of voluntary, non-binding norms; and supporting the development and implementation of confidence-building measures.[78] The Cyber Strategy 2016–2021 also recognizes that international cooperation on cyber issues has become an essential part of the wider global economic and security debate, which nevertheless lacks a single agreed vision,[79] including on matters pertaining to human rights protection. Importantly, the Strategy stated that:

> The UK and its allies have been successful in ensuring some elements of the rules-based international system are in place: there has been agreement that international law applies in cyberspace; that human rights apply online as they do offline; and a broad consensus that the multi-stakeholder approach is the best way to manage the complexities of governing the Internet. However, with a growing divide over how to address the common challenge of reconciling national security with individual rights and freedoms, any global consensus remains fragile.[80]

In short, the US and UK policy perspectives regarding the role of international law in cyberspace, cyber security and Internet governance are sufficiently aligned to be summarized as comprising six principal characteristics: (1) the continued promotion of the Internet as an open environment, where information can flow unimpeded among jurisdictions; (2) a model of governance based on the multi-stakeholder process; (3) a broad agreement that international law applies to cyberspace, and that the existing rules can adequately address any challenges to peace and security; (4) a consensus that the same human rights that apply offline also apply online; (5) a lack of interest in the development of a hard law multilateral cyber security treaty; and (6) a belief that any additional rules should be developed through voluntary, non-legally binding norms and confidence-building measures.

---

[75] *Ibid* para 1.6, 7.
[76] *Ibid* para 8.3, 61.
[77] *Ibid.*
[78] *Ibid* para 8.4, 61.
[79] *Ibid* para 8.1, 61.
[80] *Ibid* para 8.2, 61.

## 2.3    Cyber Security Approaches of the East

### 2.3.1    Russia

By contrast, the non-Western states seem to be taking a rather different view on a broad spectrum of fundamental issues, including the definition of 'cyberspace', cyber security policies and the overall approach to its future governance.

Thus, while Western governments tend to use the term 'cyberspace', Russian and Chinese sources (the latter discussed *infra*) have traditionally referred to this domain as the 'information space', defined as 'the sphere of activity connected with the formation, creation, conversion, transfer, use and storage of information infrastructure and information itself'.[81] The term 'information space' features in such documents as the Basic Principles for State Policy of the Russian Federation in the Field of International Information Security to 2020;[82] the 2011 Draft Convention on International Information on Security (2011 Draft Convention);[83] and the Draft International Code of Conduct for Information Security 2011.

Russia's basic stance on matters relating to cyber security can be gleaned from the 2011 Draft Convention, an official government document released at an international meeting of high-ranking officials responsible for security matters in Yekaterinburg. It considers 'information security' as the 'protection of [Russia's] national interests in the information sphere defined by the totality of balanced interests of the individual, society and the State'.[84] The Draft Convention contains 23 issues of concern to Russia in that environment, a number of which run counter to the views pertaining to the use and governance of the Internet championed by Western states. The fundamental points of divergence are that Russia perceives the free flow of information as a threat. This is reflected in the Draft Convention's Article 4, which lists the 'main threats to international peace and security in the information sphere', including:

> The manipulation of the flow of information in the information space of other governments, disinformation, or the concealment of information with the goal of

---

[81]    *Ibid.*
[82]    The Government of the Russian Federation, *Basic Principles for State Policy of the Russian Federation in the Field of International Information Security to 2020* (2020).
[83]    The Government of the Russian Federation, *Draft Convention on International Information Security* (28 October 2011) ('2011 Draft Convention').
[84]    Ministry of the Foreign Affairs of the Russian Federation, 'National Security Concept of the Russian Federation' (2000).

adversely affecting the psychological or spiritual state of society, or eroding traditional cultural, moral, ethical and aesthetic values.[85]

Conversely, the US and the UK strongly advocate for the free flow of information, as evidenced by the US International Strategy 2011, which pledges that the US will 'prioritize openness and innovation on the internet', in contrast to governments that 'place arbitrary restrictions on the free flow of information or use it to suppress dissent or opposition activities'.[86] The UK is in broad consensus with this view. For example, in 2011 the then Foreign Secretary William Hague remarked during the London International Conference on Cyberspace that 'cyberspace remains open to innovation and the free flow of ideas, information and expression'.[87]

Another bone of contention is Russia's perception of information technologies as 'Western weapons', which could potentially challenge state sovereignty by causing social and political instability. The associated concept of 'Internet sovereignty' – a dogmatic policy that favours the authority of the nation state over Internet users[88] – percolates throughout the 2011 Draft Convention and stands in direct opposition to the US/UK ideal of Internet freedom. A good illustration of how deeply divided the views of the opposing sides are is Article 5(5) of the 2011 Draft Convention, which asserts that:

> Each State party has the right to make sovereign norms and govern its information space according to its national laws. Its sovereignty and laws apply to the information infrastructure located in the territory of the State party or otherwise falling under its jurisdiction. The State parties must strive to harmonize national legislation, the differences whereof must not create barriers on the road to a reliable and secure information space.[89]

Some US officials have been particularly critical of the quest for national control over all Internet resources within states' physical borders and the associated concept of the application of local legislation therein,[90] including

---

[85]  2011 Draft Convention (n 83) Art 4(8).
[86]  International Strategy 2011 (n 41) 21.
[87]  William Hague, 'Chair Statement' (2 November 2011), www.fco.gov.uk/en/news/latest-news/?view=PeressS&id=68566382.
[88]  Min Jiang, 'Internet Sovereignty – A New Paradigm of Internet Governance' in Margaret Haerners and Lynn M Zott (eds), *Internet Censorship* (Greenhaven Press, 2014) 25.
[89]  2011 Draft Convention (n 83) Art 5.
[90]  Keir Giles, 'Russia's Public Stance on Cyberspace Issues' (NATO CCDCOE Tallinn Publications, 2012).

Mrs Clinton, who in her speech of December 2011 stated that countries such as Russia wish to:

> Empower each individual government to make their own rules for the internet that not only undermine human rights and the free flow of information but also the interoperability of the network. In effect, the governments pushing this agenda want to create national barriers in cyberspace. This approach would be disastrous for internet freedom.[91]

### 2.3.2    China

China has the largest population in the world, with 721 million Internet users and has become increasingly dependent on various cyber assets.[92] With this increased reliance, the Chinese authorities place growing emphasis on cyber security measures.[93] In similar vein to the Russians, the Chinese also used the phrase 'information space', rather than 'cyberspace',[94] and perceive this as a space where:

> people [may] acquire and process data ... a new place to communicate with people and activities, [being] the integration of all the world's communications networks, databases and information, forming a "landscape" huge, interconnected, with different ethnic and racial characteristics of the interaction, which is a three-dimensional space.[95]

Thus, the Chinese perceive cyberspace as the landscape for communicating with all the world's population, which includes human information processing and the cognitive space.[96] Consequently, they regard the 'information space'

---

[91]    Clinton (n 39).
[92]    Mikk Raud, 'China and Cyber: Attitudes, Strategies, Organization' (NATO CCDCOE, 2016) ('Raud').
[93]    *Ibid* 5.
[94]    HB Wasuo, 'Information Space' (Shanghai: Translation Publishing House 2000) in Keir Giles and Willian Hagestad II, 'Divided by Common Language: Cyber Definitions in Chinese, Russian and English' (2013) 5th International Conference on Cyber Conflict 2013, NATO CCDCOE ('Giles and Hagestad II).
[95]    Giles and Hagestad II, *ibid* 7. This terminology no longer features in the more recent policy documents, such as the 2016 National Cyber Security Strategy, which instead adopts the term 'cyberspace' and defines it at para 1 as 'composed of the Internet, telecommunications networks, computer systems, automatized control systems, digital equipment and the applications, services and data they carry' – see People's Republic of China, *National Cybersecurity Strategy* (27 December 2016) ('PRC Cybersecurity Strategy 2016').
[96]    Giles and Hagestad II (n 94).

and 'information security' holistically – unlike Western governments, which tend to approach cyberspace and cyber security separately.[97]

The Chinese domestic cybersecurity strategy is set out in, *inter alia*, the National Cybersecurity Strategy 2016.[98] The 2016 Cybersecurity Law of the People's Republic of China (Cybersecurity Law 2016)[99] also plays a significant role in meeting these goals. Generally, the Chinese understand matters relating to cyber activities as being strongly integrated within the fabric of society and do not separate them from the general flow of governance. Uncontrolled information is perceived as a threat to the regime and ever since the Internet became publicly available, the question has not been whether to control it, but how to do so. As a result, the Chinese vision of the Internet is premised on real-time censorship by means of the Great Firewall, which sharply contrasts with the West's idea of 'Internet freedom'.

The main cyber security related policy goals and national strategies were first published in 2003 (in the so-called Document 27) by the State Network and Information Security Coordination Small Group.[100] However, since 2006, all of China's information security policies can be linked to the 15-year grand strategy for future innovation, the National Strategy 2006–20, issued by the State Council.[101] This instrument is widely perceived as a cornerstone of China's overall standardization policy and includes the protection of the Internet against harmful activities directed against, or having the effect of undermining, national security or commercial, social and individual interests.[102] To achieve these ends, a state must be able to defend itself and society; compete fairly and productively in the national and global economic order; and preserve the social norms, privacy and security of the individual citizen.[103] In contrast to the Western approach, the Chinese regime places particularly strong emphasis on the challenges posed by cyber activities that threaten existing domestic social and political norms or values, such as the dissemination of false rumours, as well as the sovereignty of the nation state.[104] It is in this context that the major ideological differences lie. Thus, the Chinese

---

[97] *Ibid.*

[98] PRC Cybersecurity Strategy 2016 (n 95).

[99] Cybersecurity Law of the People's Republic of China 2016 ('Cybersecurity Law 2016').

[100] Raud (n 92) 11. This was issued in *Document 27: Options for Strengthening Information Security Assurance Work* (2003).

[101] The State Council, the People's Republic of China, *The National Programme for the Development of Science and Technology in the Medium and Long Term 2006–2020.*

[102] Michael D Swaine, 'Chinese Views on Cyber Security in Foreign Relations' (30 July 2013) 42 *China Leadership Monitor* ('Swaine').

[103] *Ibid.*

[104] *Ibid.*

authorities call for the establishment of a sovereign 'virtual territory' on the Internet, termed 'cyber sovereignty',[105] advocating the need for the government to identify the boundaries of such a territory to protect it against cyber threats.[106] In this sense, the Chinese approach to both cyber security and the administration of the Internet is distinctly state centric. This can be gleaned from the National Strategy,[107] which has made security and the protection of information technology a national priority. The State Council's focus is on all information technologies, suppliers and infrastructure, civilian and military alike, including the People's Liberation Army.[108] It is a top-down, proactive and holistic governmental approach, aimed at protecting commercial enterprises and governmental entities by giving detailed instructions to civilians and government leaders as to how to protect information networks and on the importance this plays in the State Council's overall plan.[109] The recognition that the 'strategic significance of the internet lies in the fact that it has become an effective tool that transgresses national boundaries, communicates information worldwide and influences international and domestic affairs'[110] reinforces the long-standing Chinese concerns with social disorder and therefore the need for a strong supervisory state to uphold societal norms and preserve social harmony.[111] The idea of 'Internet freedom', whereby information flows unrestricted, is viewed with suspicion. Rather, the ideological thrust of China's cyber security is encapsulated in the quest for the 'defense and expansion of socialist ideology and culture', whereby the Internet in China must reflect socialist 'cyber culture' and resist 'ideological infiltration and political instigation'.[112] Furthermore, the Chinese see the US dominance and *de facto* control over Internet technologies and cyber infrastructure as unfair, representing a source of instability and potential danger for the global cyber system.[113] This to some extent is reflected in the National Strategy, which supports 'techno-nationalism' by calling on China not to obtain from abroad any 'core technologies in key fields that affect the lifeblood of the national economy and

---

[105] For example, Zhong Sheng, 'Fill in 'Regulation Blank' in Cyberspace', *People's Daily* (9 July 2013).

[106] Swaine (n 102).

[107] Gu Fa, 'State Council Vigorously Promotes the Development of Information Technology and to Effectively Protect the Information Security' (2012), www.gov.cn/zwgk/2012-07/17/content_2184979.htm in Giles and Hagestard II (n 94).

[108] *Ibid.*

[109] *Ibid.*

[110] *Liberation Army Daily,* 'Experts Discuss Prospects of 'Cyber Defence' and National Defence' (4 January 2011).

[111] Swaine (n 102).

[112] *Ibid.*

[113] *Ibid.*

national security', including next-generation Internet technologies, digitally controlled machine tools and high-resolution Earth observation systems.[114]

The State Council's subsequently issued 2012 New Policy Opinion (NPO)[115] by and large reflects these themes. However, unlike the previous documents, the NPO links developments in information security with people's economic and social improvement.[116] The instrument comprehensively covers the majority of the essential areas of cyber security and indicates the main weaknesses in China's information security model, pointing out the increased vulnerabilities resulting from the growing dependence on the Internet.[117] Moreover, it reflects the Chinese government's sensitivity about foreign information systems and belief that technology that originates from the West is equipped with Trojan horses and loopholes to steal China's national secrets and prevent its economic upsurge.[118] As a result of these concerns, not only are the development and supply of high-quality home-grown products encouraged,[119] but heavy controls have also been imposed on the information security industry, deterring foreign investors – especially from the US – from seeking business opportunities in that country.

This is reflected in the 2016 Cybersecurity Law, which took effect on 1 June 2017 and reinforces China's aim to protect 'cyberspace sovereignty'[120] by placing a focus on the protection of critical information infrastructure.[121] The Cybersecurity Law provides the Chinese government with sweeping authority to regulate and monitor Internet services.[122] It is said to be the first fundamental law exclusively centred on network security protection in that

---

[114]   Raud (n 92) 12.
[115]   The State Council Information Office, New Policy Opinion (2012), http://politics.gmw.cn./2012-07/17/content_4571519.htm. The title of the State Council's 2012 NPO has been translated as: 'The State Council vigorously promotes informatization development and offers several options on conscientiously protecting information security.'
[116]   Raud (n 92) 14.
[117]   *Ibid.*
[118]   PRC Cybersecurity Strategy 2016 (n 95) para 2.
[119]   *Ibid* para 6.
[120]   See Cybersecurity Law 2016 (n 99) Art 1.
[121]   It has been observed that critical information infrastructure, which is not defined in the Cybersecurity Law 2016, may include any services needed for public communication and information, power, transportation, finance and public services, as well as any infrastructure that could endanger national security, welfare, 'popular livelihood' or the public interest if destroyed or hacked (9 July 2013) – see Chris Mirasola, 'Understanding China's Cybersecurity Law', *Lawfare* (8 November 2016), www.lawfareblog.com/understanding-chinas-cybersecurity-law.
[122]   *Ibid.*

country,[123] underpinned by three fundamental principles: (1) cooperation with authorities;[124] (2) data localization;[125] and (3) restrictions on key network products.[126] The Cybersecurity Law predominantly serves to increase the Chinese government's ability to control domestic Internet activity, thus impacting on multinational businesses and Internet companies operating in that country, which are subject to a broad, yet poorly defined array of regulations and potential punishments. The legislation could therefore be perceived as an indication of the direction that China has been pursuing for some time now – that is, towards the Internet and the technology sector being heavily regulated by the Chinese government, with Western companies such as Google and Facebook having been blocked behind the Great Firewall. To this end, the Cybersecurity Law has been described as a manifestation of China's hostility towards foreign technologies, which goes hand in glove with the broader policy of censorship of Internet content, as it extends to the monitoring of infrastructure, which has implications for technical standards and network interoperability.[127]

By 2014, the Chinese government's prioritization of information security has led to the establishment of the Central Leading Small Group for Internet Security and Informatization, a new body chaired by President Xi Jinping.[128] This policy formulation and implementation unit is said to manage Internet-related issues, including security concerns and Internet censorship. The President explained the necessity for establishing this body, stating that: 'no internet safety means no national security and no informatization means no modernization.'[129] Subsequently, he also proclaimed that Internet security and information management are 'two wings of one bird, two wheels on one car'.[130] This approach to cyber security encapsulates the need to improve the security of the domestic Internet infrastructure, to reinforce the move towards indigenous innovation detailed in the State's Council's 15-year plan and to

---

Emily Xu, 'China's Cyber Security Law – More Stringent Regulations for Network Security', *Lexology* (8 November 2016), www.lexology.com/library/detail .aspx?g=5ed61c4f-6dbc-450b-b812-1b1d94edb1da.
Cybersecurity Law 2016 (n 99) Art 9.
*Ibid* Art 50.
*Ibid* Art 3.
Hogan Lovells, 'China Passes Controversial Cyber Security Law' (11 November 2016), www.hoganlovells.com/en/publications/china-passes-controversial-cyber-secu rity-law.
Raud (n 92) 15.
Shannon Tiezzi, 'Xi Jinping Leads China's New Internet Security Group', *The Diplomat* (28 February 2014).
Raud (n 92).

position China as a leading actor on the global stage by promoting its role in Internet governance.[131]

The National Cybersecurity Strategy of 2016 follows this policy thrust by envisaging China's development of its cyber territory, reflecting that country's culture and values underpinned by a socialist ideology.[132] However, it also testifies to the government's acknowledgement that cyberspace is open and borderless. This environment, being replete with security threats, requires international cooperation.[133] To this end, the Strategy recognizes the need to 'strengthen international cyber security dialogue and cooperation and to promote the reform of the global Internet governance system'.[134] It supports the role of the UN and advocates the adherence by all countries to the principles laid down by the UN Charter concerning the threat and use of armed force and the promotion of peace and security in cyberspace.[135] It also insists that the cyber domain must be governed according to the rule of law, while privacy and intellectual property rights must be protected.[136] Most importantly, however – and in contrast to the US stance on this issue – the Strategy not only subscribes to the formulation of international norms for cyberspace that are 'universally recognized by all sides', but also advocates the need for an 'international treaty on anti-terrorism in cyberspace'.[137]

The domestic policy underpinnings outlined above are reflected in the stance that China takes towards the issue of cyberspace governance. Termed 'multilateralism' and embraced by Russia and other like-minded nations, this theoretical antithesis of multi-stakeholderism sees the stewardship of this domain through the same prism as that applied to the domestic policies of those countries.[138] This necessarily entails the adoption of a centralized, top-down and state centric approach, with decisively prescribed roles for national governments, which is administered through a UN forum – preferably the International Telecommunications Union (ITU).[139]

---

[131]  *Ibid.*
[132]  PRC Cybersecurity Strategy 2016 (n 95) para 4.
[133]  *Ibid* para 8(g).
[134]  *Ibid.*
[135]  *Ibid.*
[136]  *Ibid* para 3.
[137]  *Ibid* para 8(g).
[138]  See Lu Wei, 'Cyber Sovereignty Must Rule Global Internet', *World Post* (15 December 2014). Reportedly, Lu Wei, the head of the Cyberspace Administration of China, has embraced multilateral governance, stating that 'with regard to the cyberspace governance the US advocates "multi-stakeholder" while China believes in "multilateral"'.
[139]  A number of attempts have been made to increase the ITU's role in Internet governance, including the World Summit on the Information Society two-phase process

In summary, the East's position regarding cyber policies can be encapsulated in four key points: (1) a distrust in the Internet as a medium for the free
flow of information; (2) a belief that it is the role of the government to take
control and safeguard domestic cyberspace and create a 'virtual territory',
thus promulgating cyber sovereignty; (3) the regulation of state behaviour in
cyberspace through an international, legally binding treaty; and (4) a multilateral model of cyberspace governance with greater involvement of the UN
institutions, such as the ITU.

## 2.4    The Divergent Approaches to Cyber Security and Internet Governance – an Overview

The international community has recognized the need to develop common
minimum standards for the governance of cyberspace and has reached
a broad-brush consensus that international law applies to that domain.
However, for over two decades, the international dialogue in relation to how
the rules of *lex lata* apply, the maintenance of peace and security and broader
governance issues has been plagued by political disagreements. The points
of divergence in the strategic thinking between the West and the East can be
outlined as comprising four fundamental aspects: (1) Internet freedom versus
Internet sovereignty; (2) domestic policy based on centralized, state centric
government command and control by the Chinese and Russian authorities
versus the decentralized, self-governing approach of a variety of stakeholders
upheld by the US and its allies; (3) multi-stakeholder versus multilateral governance of cyberspace; and (4) the regulation of state behaviour through the
development of non-legally binding norms versus the development of a legally
binding multilateral treaty and/or customary law rules.

On these bases, it could be said that the Western and Eastern approaches
to cyberspace and cyber security have historically differed and to date do not
sufficiently align. For these reasons, the development of legally binding rules
in the near future seems unlikely, whether to ensure peace and security in that
domain or to address state surveillance activities, since both are perceived as
undesirable. To illustrate this status quo, the next section will discuss four failed

---

(Geneva 2003 and Tunis 2005), and the 2012 ITU World Conference on International
Telecommunications held in Dubai. At that event, the ITU introduced an amended
version of the International Telecommunication Regulations (ITRs), updating the previous convention, which sought to involve the ITU more closely in the running of the
Internet. However, with only 89 out of 151 states adopting the new ITRs, the process
was perceived as a failure to secure the ITU a future role in the development and management of the Internet – see, for example, David Post, 'Stand Down! UN "Takeover of
the Internet" Postponed Indefinitely', *The Washington Post* (7 November 2014).

attempts at agreeing legally binding rules for cyberspace pertaining to security and surveillance issues, made since 2011, namely the Russian-championed Draft Codes of Conduct 2011 and 2015; the CoE Intelligence Codex 2015; and the UN Draft Legal Instrument on Government-led Surveillance 2018.

## 3. (FAILED) ATTEMPTS TO AGREE LEGALLY BINDING RULES FOR CYBERSPACE

### 3.1 SCO Draft Codes of Conduct for Information Security

In the context of cyber security, two attempts at the deliberate regulation of ICT were made, with the SCO initially submitting to the UNGA in 2011 a Draft Code of Conduct for Information Security (Draft Code of Conduct 2011). This Code did not secure global support and was redrafted and resubmitted in 2015 (Draft Code of Conduct 2015), but again to no avail. Both of these instruments were sponsored by Russia, which since the 1990s has made a number of attempts to assert itself as a key player in international peace and security policy planning. It was also the first country to link international law and information security in the context of international peace and security, when in 1998 it tabled at the UNGA's First Committee the Resolution on developments in the field of information and telecommunications in the context of international security (Resolution 53/70).[140] The issues of international regulation of ICT to prevent possible future conflicts among nations raised by that Resolution were subsequently echoed in both Draft Codes of Conduct. Their overriding aim was to identify the rights and responsibilities of states in the information space. Although not drafted as a treaty, the Draft Codes have nevertheless been described as a first step towards the development of a universal document under the auspices of the UN aimed at providing comprehensive information security.[141]

### 3.1.1 SCO Draft Code of Conduct for Information Security 2011
Prior to submitting the first Draft Code of Conduct in 2011 to the UNGA, the SCO adopted its precursor, the 2009 Yekaterinburg Agreement, which focused on determining the main threats and modes of cooperation for SCO members,

---

[140] UNGA Resolution, 'Developments in the Field of Information and Telecommunications in the Context of International Security' (4 December 1998) UN Doc A/RES/53/70 ('A/Res/53/70').

[141] The Embassy of the Russian Federation in the UK, 'International Code of Conduct for Information Security' (26 October 2011).

including in relation to the threats to 'international information security'.[142] The Draft Code resembled, and to at least some extent reflected, the SCO's Internet governance agenda. The Code called on states to voluntarily subscribe to its pledges, *inter alia*: (1) to comply with the UN Charter by emphasizing respect for sovereignty, territorial integrity, human rights and fundamental freedoms; (2) not to use ICT for hostile activities and aggression, and not to proliferate information weapons or related technologies; (3) to cooperate in combating criminal and terrorist activities that use ICT; (4) to promote the establishment of a democratic and multilateral Internet management system; and (5) to promote the 'important role of the United Nations in formulating international norms'.[143] The document failed to garner global support, as it contained a number of controversial issues. First, it was perceived as a first step towards the establishment of new rules governing cyberspace and the use of ICT, which was opposed by the US and its allies, as they believe that existing international law is sufficient and thus that new rules could stifle technological development and growth.[144] Second, the Code advocated a multilateral system for Internet governance, largely to counter the US dominance of the Internet. Unsurprisingly, this idea did not gain much traction, being inconsistent with the US-championed multi-stakeholder model for the stewardship of cyberspace. The US unequivocally disagreed with multilateral policy, stating at the 67th Sessions of the UNGA that the Draft Code presented 'an alternative view' that sought to establish an international justification for government control over Internet resources and to strengthen governmental power over the Internet by invoking multilateral governance that would replace the multi-stakeholder model, in which all users have a voice, with top-down control and regulation by states.[145] Third, the Code placed emphasis on the principle of territorial sovereignty as means of wielding sovereign control in cyberspace. This too was strongly opposed the US and its partner states, which viewed this as legitimizing censorship and state domination of the Internet, thus potentially stifling freedom of expression and association, and representing a possibility for suppressing free speech through government control of content for political purposes. It was also felt that the proposed Code would 'legitimize the view that the right to freedom of expression can be limited by national laws and cul-

---

[142] See 2011 Draft Convention (n 83) Art 2, listing six threats to 'international information security'.

[143] SCO Code of Conduct 2011 (n 2) paras (a)–(c), (g) and (j).

[144] See James A Lewis, 'Liberty, Equality, Connectivity: Transatlantic Cybersecurity Norms' (2014) Centre for Strategic and International Studies.

[145] Statement by Delegation of the United States of America, 'Other Disarmament Issues and International Security Segment of Thematic Debate on the First Committee of the Sixty-seventh Session of the United Nations' (2 November 2012).

tural proclivities, thereby undermining that right, as described in the Universal Declaration of Human Rights'.[146] Significantly, to the US and likeminded states, the 2011 Code represented an attempt to 'replace existing international law that governs uses of force and relations among States in armed conflict with new, unclear and ill-defined rules and concepts'.[147] Finally, the Code used the phrase 'information space', rather than 'cyberspace', and sought 'to reaffirm all States' rights and responsibilities to protect, in accordance with relevant laws and regulations, their information space and critical information infrastructure from threats, disturbance, attack and sabotage'.[148]

### 3.1.2    SCO Draft Code of Conduct for Information Security 2015

Following the rejection of the original text, the Code's amended version was resubmitted to the UNGA in 2015, with an accompanying letter stating that the document had been 'revised taking into full consideration the comments and suggestions from all parties'.[149] Some of the new Code's provisions, however, remained practically unchanged. For example, it restated the same vision that the SCO countries share regarding state control of cyberspace governance, reiterating the proposed 'establishment of multilateral, transparent and democratic international Internet governance mechanisms, which ensure an equitable distribution of resources, facilitate access for all and ensure the stable and secure functioning of the Internet'.[150] This stipulation, the Western governments felt, once again attempted to side-line the multi-stakeholder model of Internet governance. As one commentator noted, it also confirmed that: 'SCO member States' views on internet governance have not shifted and are not intended as any accommodation to the advocates of the multistakeholder governance model.'[151] Furthermore, the 2015 Code, like its predecessor, referred to the 'information space' and reaffirmed the rights and responsibilities of all

---

[146]    *Ibid.*

[147]    *Ibid.* Interestingly, the US Delegation's statement alleged that: 'one of the primary sponsors of the draft *Code* has stated repeatedly that long-standing provisions of international law, including elements of *jus ad bellum* and *jus in bello* that would provide a legal framework for the way that States could use force in cyberspace, have no applicability.'

[148]    SCO Code of Conduct 2011 (n 2) para (e).

[149]    UNGA, 'Letter Dated 9 January 2015 from the Permanent Representatives of China, Kazakhstan, Kyrgyzstan, the Russian Federation, Tajikistan and Uzbekistan to the UN Addressed to the Secretary General' (13 January 2015) UN Doc A/69/732 1.

[150]    *Ibid* para 8.

[151]    Kristen Eichensehr, 'International Cyber Governance: Engagement Without Agreement?' (2015) *Just Security*, http://justsecurity.org/19599/international-cyber -governance-engagement-agreement/.

states to protect it from threats, interferences, attack and sabotage.[152] It also emphasized state sovereignty and territoriality in the digital sphere above all else, and was replete with national security and regime stability rhetoric. For example, it made a stronger reference to nations' equal rights than its predecessor by emphasizing that: 'All States must play the same role in, and carry equal responsibility for, international governance of the Internet, its security, continuity and stability of operation and its development.'[153] This was further underpinned by a call to 'prevent other States from exploiting their dominant position' in ICT, including resources, critical infrastructure, core technologies, goods, services and networks.[154] For these reasons, and since the revised Code did not include major changes, it is unsurprising that it was once again rejected, in effect merely reinforcing the ideological differences among the international community in reaching a new consensus on the development of new rules to regulate state behaviour in cyberspace.[155]

### 3.1.3   SCO Draft Codes of Conduct and Human Rights Protection

Both the 2011 and the 2015 Draft Codes of Conduct were dominated by the oratory of state sovereignty, territoriality, national security, non-intervention in internal affairs and regime stability in the digital space, but paying scant attention to states' responsibilities for the protection of human rights and fundamental freedoms. Having said that, the 2015 Draft Code did encourage states to respect human rights, but the main focus was placed on freedom of expression set out in Article 19 of the International Covenant on Civil and Political Rights 1966 (ICCPR). To that end, the Code introduced a new pledge, calling on states to:

> recognize that the rights of an individual in the offline environment must also be protected in the online environment; to fully respect rights and freedoms in the information space, including the right and freedom to seek, receive and impart information, taking into account the fact that the International Covenant on Civil and Political Rights (article 19) attaches to that right special duties and responsibilities. It may therefore be subject to certain restrictions, but these shall only be such as are provided by law and are necessary:
> (a)   for respect of the rights or reputations of others;
> (b)   for the protection of national security or of public order (*ordre public*), or of public health or morals.[156]

---

[152]   SCO Code of Conduct 2015 (n 3) para 6.
[153]   *Ibid* para 8.
[154]   *Ibid* para 5.
[155]   Henry Rõigas, 'An Updated Draft of the Code Distributed in the United Nations – What's New?' (10 February 2015) NATO CCDCOE.
[156]   *Ibid* para 7.

A rather controversial aspect of this proposed undertaking is that although (unlike in the original Code) an express reference was made to the ICCPR, this was strictly confined to its Article 19, with conspicuous emphasis placed on the restrictions available to states with regard to this right. This seems to reflect the SCO states' belief in their right to exercise control over any digital content within their territories and at their discretion.[157] Notable by its absence is a reference to the right to privacy under Article of the 17 of the ICCPR. This is rather surprising, bearing in mind that privacy has featured very prominently on the UN agenda since the 2013 Edward Snowden disclosures and before the redrafted Code was resubmitted to the UNGA – that is, two years after the allegations regarding the National Security Agency's (NSA) surveillance first came to the fore. This can be interpreted as an unwillingness of the SCO countries to confront state cyber surveillance/privacy issues, and their general interest in regulating Internet content at the expense of calling the international community to protect and respect other related rights, including that of privacy. It may also mean that addressing surveillance through such avenues would curtail their own surveillance practices at home and abroad, which they might be unwilling to contemplate.

In conclusion, it could be said that the protracted history of the two SCO Draft Codes of Conduct attests to the multitude of security, political and ideological differences of the global cyber powers in their diplomatic endeavours to identify the rights and responsibilities of states in cyberspace. As far as individuals' privacy is concerned, it is quite obvious that – at least in the context of these two instruments, being decisively state centric and security orientated – neither government-led surveillance nor the protection of individuals' privacy was of major concern.

Since the cyber security discourse does not seem to be an effective avenue to pursue the regulation of states' mass surveillance, the question that arises is whether there are other available means (outside of the development of customary law rules) that could be pursued in order to bring these practices in line with states' international law obligations. This question has been addressed by the CoE and the UN Special Rapporteur on the right to privacy, as discussed below.

---

[157] Sarah McKune, 'An Analysis of the International Code of Conduct for Information Society', *The Citizen Lab*, (29 September 2015) https://citizenlab.org/2015/09/international-code-of-conduct/.

## 3.2    CoE Intelligence Codex 2015

In response to the Snowden disclosures, the CoE specifically confronted the issue of regulation of cyber espionage among its 47 member states and in 2015 proposed a non-spy treaty, called the Intelligence Codex – a project which to date has remained unsuccessful. This does not necessarily mean that achieving reduced surveillance will always be impossible at a regional or international level. Nevertheless, this failed attempt illustrates how difficult it is to secure political support for subjecting states' intelligence activities to a set of internationally legally binding standards.

The Parliamentary Assembly of the Council of Europe (PACE), in its 2015 Resolution 2045, among other solutions to stop violations of human rights, urged its member and observer states to adopt the Intelligence Codex – a binding multilateral European treaty that would regulate the activities of intelligence agencies for the purposes of the fight against terrorism and organized crime.[158] The need for this legal framework on the national and international plain was explained by PACE as important to rebuild trust not only among transatlantic partners and CoE member states, but also between citizens and their governments.[159] Furthermore, it was recognized that surveillance practices endanger other human rights enumerated in the European Convention on Human Rights (ECHR), which are the cornerstone of democracy, including Article 10 (freedom of information and expression); Article 6 (right to a fair trial); and Article 9 (freedom of religion). The PACE explanatory memorandum that accompanied the proposed instrument summarized these concerns, stating that:

> The political problems caused by 'spying on friends' and the possible collusion between intelligence services for the circumvention of national restrictions show the need for States to come up with a generally accepted 'codex' for intelligence agencies that would put an end to unfettered mass surveillance and confine surveillance practices to what is strictly needed for legitimate security purposes.[160]

To achieve these aims, the CoE proposed that such a codex:

> would lay down precisely what is allowed and what is prohibited between allies and partners; it would clarify what intelligence agencies can do, how they can co-operate and how allies should refrain from spying on each other ... it would be a signal that

---

[158]  CoE Mass Surveillance Resolution (n 4).

[159]  *Ibid* para 13.

[160]  CoE, Committee on Legal Affairs and Human Rights, 'Mass Surveillance. Explanatory Memorandum by Mr Pieter Omtzigt, Rapporteur' (26 January 2015) ('CoE Mass Surveillance Memorandum').

governments are willing to provide some degree of transparency in the conduct of their surveillance programmes and guarantee citizens' rights to privacy to the extent possible.[161]

The Codex is premised on four basic rules for governing cooperation among the intelligence agencies. First, any form of mutual political, economic espionage must be prohibited without exception.[162] Second, any intelligence activity on the territory of another CoE member state may be carried out only with that country's approval and within a statutory framework – that is, for a specific reason relating to the prevention of crime or terrorism.[163] Third, the tracking, analysis and storage of mass data are strictly prohibited if that data is from non-suspected individuals from a friendly state. Only information pertaining to legitimately targeted individuals may be collected on an exceptional basis for specific purposes; while any data that is stored, but not needed for these ends must be immediately destroyed.[164] The Codex also proposed that the intelligence agencies be banned from forcing telecommunications and Internet companies to grant them unfettered access to their massive databases of personal data without a court order.[165] Importantly, CoE Resolution 2045 specified that: 'the codex should include a mutual engagement to apply the same rules to the surveillance of partner states' nationals and residents as those applied to the surveillance of their own nationals and residents, and to share data obtained through lawful surveillance measures solely for the purposes for which they were collected.'[166] Finally, the instrument was to adopt the safeguards devised by the European Court of Human Rights (ECtHR) for surveillance.[167]

The Codex represents the first concrete scheme of this kind and without a doubt is a positive development, as at the very least it recognizes the dangers of global surveillance and takes proactive steps to address them. In principle, it stipulates that any form of political, economic or diplomatic espionage, as well as mass surveillance, should be prohibited in law. This, however, has proved to be a lofty aim. Viewed from a realistic perspective of international relations, it could be said that the proposed treaty's prospects of ever being endorsed by the CoE member states do not appear to be very promising. Thus far, there has been little reaction[168] from the CoE states to it. The reasons for such an unwel-

---

[161] *Ibid.*
[162] *Ibid* para 116.
[163] *Ibid.*
[164] *Ibid.*
[165] *Ibid.*
[166] CoE, Mass Surveillance Resolution (n 4) para 19.5.
[167] *CoE Mass* Surveillance Memorandum (n 160) para 97, 80.
[168] Matthijs Koot, 'Dutch Government Rejects Idea of No-Spy Agreements Between European Countries', *Matthijs R. Kott's Notebook* (13 March 2015), https://blog

coming response are numerous, but seem to boil down to three fundamental aspects. First, as noted in Chapter 2, states have historically shied away from subjecting their espionage activities to regulation under international law. It comes as no surprise, therefore, that the Codex's suggested prohibition on 'the exercise of mutual political, economic espionage' has been rejected as unrealistic.[169] Signals intelligence (SIGINT) collection is not subject to specific control by international law, being subsumed within the broader concept of peacetime espionage. It is a tool widely used by states to protect their own core national security interests, usually deployed to facilitate such fundamental aspects of statecraft as the gathering of evidence of hostile intent or a planned terrorist attack originating from abroad.[170] In addition, governments are very secretive about their own espionage capabilities. Therefore, discussing ways and means to limit espionage conducted against other nations without revealing certain information about their own abilities in this field means not only publicly admitting to their engagement, but also losing an advantage over other states.[171] Related to this is the fact that surveillance is becoming a truly universal practice, because states are unwilling to give other states the advantage of amassing large volumes of digital intelligence, thus giving them a monopoly over such data. To do so could lead to a political or diplomatic advantage over those states which do not have the same proficiency, ultimately resulting in security concerns. This 'surveillance arms race' encourages nations to continually expand their surveillance proficiency to prevent a state, or a group of states, from monopolizing surveillance data. Second, SIGINT collection abroad for political gains used to be predominantly focused on the acquisition of information on the decision making of foreign governments and various state entities, in order to provide support for the spying state's own policy direction, and was thus relatively constrained in scope. The collection of vast amounts of information on private individuals abroad was limited and was also costly. Consequently, public pressure to curtail espionage was minimal until recently, as this was not seen to affect the average citizen abroad.[172] This has changed dramatically in recent years, as the targets of surveillance now comprise entire populations, thus emerging as a permanent feature in states' SIGINT operations. Although, as a result of this shift, the calls from civil society to curtail mass surveillance have intensified, especially following the

---

.cyberwar.nl/2015/03/dutch-minister-of-the-interior-rejects-eu-pace-proposal-omtzigt
-of-anti-spy-treaty-between-european-countries/.

[169]  *Ibid.*

[170]  Ashley Deeks, 'An International Legal Framework for Surveillance' (2015) 55 *Virginia Journal of International Law*, 292–367.

[171]  *Ibid.*

[172]  *Ibid.*

2013 Snowden revelations, they seem to have had scant impact. A case in point is the legislation for bulk powers in such countries as the UK and France, where – despite civic disquiet – draconian surveillance laws have been adopted.[173] In addition, following the ECtHR decisions in *Centrum För Rättvisa v Sweden* and *Big Brother Watch v UK*, at least in the ECtHR jurisprudence, bulk surveillance and intelligence sharing seem to have acquired a new legitimacy, making the Codex's calls for the cessation of unfettered surveillance and collusion for circumvention difficult to reconcile and 'sell' to the CoE countries. Finally, as the Codex is regional in scope, even if it is revived and relaunched, it is unlikely to be of interest to such countries as the US, Russia, China and Israel, as it could potentially curtail their present and future activities in the area of intelligence collection. To date, these nations have resisted placing legal constraint of espionage beyond their own borders and without their support, any attempt at the regulation of mass surveillance seems futile.

Nevertheless, the treaty's rejection by the European states does not mean that the endeavour to set out some basic legal parameters in relation to how these practices are to be conducted should be abandoned altogether. Another such proposal was made three years after the CoE introduced the Intelligence Codex by the UN Special Rapporteur on the right to privacy, and is discussed next.

### 3.3 UN Draft Legal Instrument on Government-Led Surveillance and Privacy

#### 3.3.1 Legal Instrument – rationale for the treaty
The Special Rapporteur on the right to privacy, Professor Joseph Cannataci, presented the Draft Legal Instrument on Government-led Surveillance and Privacy[174] to the UN Human Rights Council in 2018. The draft treaty is intended as a separate source of legal obligations that are binding on nations

---

[173] See Hugh Schofield, 'Surveillance Law Prompts Unease in France', *BBC News* (4 May 2015); Rory Cellan-Jones, 'Snoopers Law Creates Security Nightmare', *BBC News* (29 November 2016).

[174] Legal Instrument (n 5). The Legal Instrument is the result of meetings and exchanges between the EU-founded MAPPING project (Managing Alternatives for Privacy, Property and Internet Governance) and several categories of stakeholders involved in the development and use of digital technologies, including global technology companies, experts with experience of working with civil society, law enforcement, intelligence services, academics and other members of the multi-stakeholder community shaping the Internet and the transition to the digital age – see Legal Instrument, 'Introduction'.

if they so choose,[175] specifically aimed at protecting the privacy of individuals against arbitrary interference with this right through both mass and targeted surveillance by law enforcement, security and other publicly mandated services. The instrument is solely concerned with limiting state surveillance[176] in cyberspace, and its purpose has been stated as giving 'clear and detailed guidelines for the area of government-led or organized surveillance using electronic means'.[177] In this sense alone, the Legal Instrument can be distinguished from the earlier mechanisms proposed at the UN level – that is, the SCO Draft Codes of Conduct of 2011 and 2015. First, it specifically deals with domestic and foreign electronic surveillance, setting out a number of limitations on how this may be carried out. By contrast, the Draft Codes of Conduct sponsored by Russia and issued by the SCO sought to identify nations' rights and responsibilities in the information space by, *inter alia*, calling on them not to use ICT for hostile activities and aggression, and to cooperate in combating criminal and terrorist activities that use ICT.[178] For these reasons, the Draft Codes are distinctly state centric – issued by states and directed at the global community of nations, advising them of their respective rights and duties, thus with a pronounced horizontal effect. Conversely, the Legal Instrument, developed under the auspices of the UN human rights mandate, is chiefly concerned with the

---

[175] *Ibid.* The Commentary to Article 1 explains that the term 'legal instrument' is 'an interim one and is capable of being substituted by the term "Recommendation" or "Directive" or "Treaty" or "Convention" depending on the binding force that parties may wish to accord the instrument. It is intended that this draft legal instrument is capable of being used in part or in whole by regional intergovernmental organizations such as the European Union (EU) or the Council of Europe (CoE) or indeed even at the global level by the UN'.

[176] *Ibid.* Article 2(1) defines 'surveillance' as 'any monitoring, collecting, observing or listening by a state or on its behalf or at its order to persons, their movements, their conversations or other activities or communications including metadata and/or the recording of the monitoring, observation and listening activities'. The Commentary to Article 2 states that this term 'includes all forms of bulk acquisition of personal data, all forms of mass surveillance and targeted surveillance'. The bulk acquisition of personal data includes activities conducted under the UK Investigatory Powers Act 2016 – that is, the bulk interception of communications, bulk equipment interference, the acquisition of bulk communication data from service providers and bulk personal datasets.

[177] *Ibid* part I 'Introduction'; (a) 'Background'.

[178] The SCO Draft Code 2011 (n 2) encouraged states to pledge '[n]ot to use information and communications technologies, including networks, to carry out hostile activities or acts of aggression, pose threats to international peace and security or proliferate information weapons or related technologies'; the SCO Draft Code 2015 (n 3) provides that states must not 'use information and communications technologies and information and communications networks to carry out activities which run counter to the task of maintaining international peace and security'.

protection of fundamental rights[179] and thus places the individual at its centre. It is directed at states, but *vis-à-vis* their responsibilities towards persons, rather than other states, and in that sense it also has a vertical effect. This means that government agencies must refrain from infringing individuals' rights when conducting online surveillance, both domestic and foreign. In addition, the draft treaty places a positive duty on states, as it obliges them to take proactive steps to give effect to the rights set out therein to protect and promote those rights domestically and internationally, thus fostering 'an environment, which enables their citizens to develop their personalities freely and positively'.[180] Furthermore, and perhaps most significantly, it also recognizes the need for a new global consensus among states on the impact of digital technologies in carrying out surveillance and the detrimental effect this has 'on the dignity of humans, regardless of their race, colour, gender, language, religion, political or other opinion, national or social origin, citizenship, birth or other status (including age)'.[181]

The launch of this initiative was dictated by a number of factors. First, it was recognized that existing privacy standards and guidance are not sufficient and consequently, as the document notes:

> the protection of human rights by States in the Digital Age must also be outlined in a more detailed and comprehensive way [and] one of the means for such protection of human rights is through a comprehensive and innovative [Legal Instrument] on governmental surveillance, which would assist in establishing safeguards without borders and effective legal remedies across borders.[182]

Second, the need for the treaty is a result of the acknowledgement that, thus far, efforts to establish rules on states' behaviour in cyberspace have been solely underpinned by cybersecurity concerns, with little attention paid to human rights protection. Special Rapporteur Cannataci made explicit reference to this policy agenda in his 2018 statement to the Human Rights Council when, introducing the Legal Instrument, he observed that:

> some Member States have to date insisted on excluding privacy as a priority consideration when discussing cybersecurity. Moreover, a number of powerful States appear allergic to anything which in any way could constrain their ability to carry

---

[179] See Legal Instrument (n 5). The Commentary to Article 1 states that 'the legal instrument is drafted to tackle [surveillance carried out by using or manipulating electronic devices] from a perspective which has international human rights protection and human dignity at its centre'.

[180] *Ibid* 'Preamble'.

[181] *Ibid.*

[182] *Ibid* 'Introduction'.

out surveillance free from ... adequate levels of proportionality, necessity, oversight and accountability.[183]

These concerns, together with the need for a set of principles and model provisions for their integration into national laws, serve as a rationale for such an instrument being put forward. To this end, Professor Cannataci explained that:

> [It] is my strong view that an instrument of some form is necessary, whether as soft law in the form of a recommendation or possibly more appropriately, as an international multilateral treaty. The latter solution would go some way towards creating a clear and comprehensive legal framework on privacy and surveillance in cyberspace which would operationalize the respect of the right to privacy, domestically and across borders.[184]

### 3.3.2    Legal Instrument – key features

The Legal Instrument is comprised of a preamble and 17 articles, each accompanied by a commentary, thus setting out a detailed, yet comprehensive legal framework restricting state sponsored surveillance. Among some of its features are provisions stipulating basic requirements that governments must meet,[185] general principles that they must adhere to when using surveillance systems,[186] together with an individual's rights to notification that he or she has been the target of government surveillance.[187] Five aspects of the document are particularly worthy of note, some of which provide innovative solutions to the problem of mass surveillance.

---

[183] Office of the High Commissioner for Human Rights, Statement by Mr Joseph Cannataci, Special Rapporteur on the Right to Privacy, Geneva (6 March 2018).

[184] *Ibid.*

[185] Legal Instrument (n 5) Art 3. Article 3(1)–(3) provides, *inter alia*, that surveillance (whether domestic, foreign, civil or military) may be conducted only by law enforcement, security and intelligence services or an officially mandated entity tasked by a specific law, which must be publicly available and meet the standards of clarity and precision, and aim to prevent any real danger; to prevent, detect, investigate or prosecute crime; and/or to increase public safety and protect state security.

[186] *Ibid* Article 4 stipulates that surveillance systems must be authorized by law prior to their use, which must, *inter alia*, (1) identify the purposes and situations where the surveillance system is to be used; (2) define the category of serious crime and/or threats for which the surveillance system is to be used; and (3) stipulate that the surveillance system must not be used by the state agency unless a reasonable suspicion exists that a serious crime and/or threat may be committed.

[187] *Ibid* Article 8 – individuals have a right to know that they have been the target of state surveillance (whether directly or indirectly), unless an independent authority has adjudicated that the disclosure would prejudice the operation of law enforcement.

First, the treaty concerns the rights of all persons within the given state's jurisdiction, not only its citizens.[188] Thus, the document adopts the view that the protection of human rights (including privacy) is not territorially limited, but extends beyond state borders. To this end, it provides that all surveillance must be on the basis of domestic law, which shall:

> demand from the authority to justify that each single measure envisaged is strictly necessary and proportionate for the obtaining of vital intelligence in an individual operation as well as considering the overall impact of this and such measures on the right to privacy of individuals irrespective of whether the individual is a citizen or resident of that State.[189]

The Legal Instrument thus addresses one of the central questions in the current international human rights law discourse pertaining to the extent of the human rights obligations of states in the digital context, by stipulating their obligation to respect and protect those rights not only within their territory, but also within their jurisdiction. This is a welcome development, as it reinforces the approach to human rights protection based on equality and non-discrimination, reiterating the founding principles of the International Bill of Rights.

The explicit recognition and referencing of these core human rights values are the Legal Instrument's second notable feature. To this end, the Preamble explains that: 'all human rights are rooted in human dignity. Human dignity must be protected, respected and promoted using a holistic approach.'[190] Accordingly, the document addresses the challenges that state surveillance presents from the perspective of the universality of international human rights protection, acknowledging human dignity as its core value and the role that privacy plays in ensuring this, irrespective of nationality or any technical considerations, such as the nature of communications. This basic premise is underpinned by three fundamental requirements – namely that all surveillance measures (domestic and foreign alike) must be necessary, proportionate[191] and based on reasonable suspicion.[192] The document explains that 'necessity' refers to the specific end or purpose of a measure, which not only must be prescribed by law, but also must itself be the result of a legitimate legislative process.[193]

---

[188] *Ibid* Art 1 Commentary.

[189] *Ibid* Art 4(e).

[190] *Ibid* 'Preamble' para 4.

[191] *Ibid* Article 3(3) – 'any law regulating surveillance shall aim at the prevention of a real danger and/or the prevention, detection, investigation and prosecution of crime and/or for increasing public safety and/or protecting State security. The surveillance itself must be necessary and proportionate and the least intrusive means shall be used'.

[192] *Ibid* Art 3(b) and Art 4(1)(c).

[193] *Ibid* 'Preamble'.

The draft treaty further states that: 'typically necessity is a purpose that is legitimate in a society which is based on values such as human rights, rule of law and democracy.'[194] 'Proportionality' is defined through a three-stage test, necessitating the measure's assessment first from the perspective of it being potentially capable of realizing the aim; then being the least intrusive means to do so; and finally being legitimate (ie, with regard to its impact on the overall situation and particularly on other human rights infringed during the process of surveillance).[195]

Third, the Legal Instrument prohibits surveillance – whether domestic or foreign, civil or military – except where conducted by law enforcement, security or another publicly mandated authority (such as tax, revenue, customs and anti-corruption services), thus forbidding it by any entity, whose existence is secret.[196] To this end, the draft treaty introduces a new mechanism for privacy protection. It proposes that these specifically assigned organizations may engage in surveillance only on the basis of laws which provide adequate protection,[197] comprising five interrelated safeguards: (1) legislative oversight; (2) a pre-authorization authority (*ex-ante* oversight); (3) an independent operational oversight authority (*ex-post* oversight); (4) an inter-institutional whistle-blower mechanism; and (5) the presentation and publication of separate reports by the legislative oversight, the independent pre-authorisation and independent operation oversight authority.[198] The amalgam of these provisions are the first omnibus means of rights protection of this kind, as these measures are 'supposed to reinforce each other and thus represent a complete system'.[199] This approach is to a large extent motivated by the lack of appropriate mass surveillance procedural safeguards in many countries, which has been and continues to be of concern to the UN human rights bodies and mandate holders. In that sense, it not only is envisaged as a harmonizing measure, which could ensure a degree of uniformity among those states that choose to adopt this standard into their legal systems, but also offers more stringent guarantees against abuse of power for those states with modernized surveillance legislation already in place, if they decide to adopt the treaty.

Fourth, the Legal Instrument introduces the International Data Access Warrant (IDAW),[200] a novel and unique feature which requires surveillance

---

[194]   *Ibid.*
[195]   *Ibid.*
[196]   *Ibid* Art 3(1) and (5).
[197]   *Ibid* Art 3(6).
[198]   *Ibid* Art 3(6) (a)–(e), Commentary.
[199]   *Ibid.*
[200]   *Ibid* Article 3(8) – 'Any surveillance activity must only be carried out for concretely defined specific and legitimate purposes and in response to a concrete and legit-

authorization to be obtained from a new body, termed the International Data Access Authority (IDAA).[201] This organization is mandated to grant a warrant to a law enforcement or security agency if there is a multiple jurisdictional dimension – that is, where the personal data is located in the territory of another treaty state. This proposal is a result of the recognition that states must not 'assert extra-territorial jurisdiction over data or persons in contravention of relevant treaties and principles of international mutual assistance'.[202] The Legal Instrument thus attempts to create a 'privacy friendly one-stop shop for the [law enforcement and security services] to apply for the IDAW, which could greatly reduce costs and delays in data transfers at both the domestic and international level'.[203] This supranational mechanism is envisaged by the Legal Instrument to serve a twofold purpose. It aims to simultaneously protect individuals' rights and to facilitate cross-border access to data by law enforcement authorities, prosecutors and intelligence services in the context of criminal proceedings, thus providing a pragmatic solution which recognizes and responds to the needs of these agencies for timely access to such data. In that sense, the proposal offers a solution to the problems highlighted in, *inter alia, Re Warrant to Search a Certain Email Account Controlled and Maintained by Microsoft Corporation (Microsoft Ireland)*.[204] It concerned

---

imate need ... all surveillance, domestic and foreign, shall be carried out only provided that a relative warrant is obtained ex-ante from a regional or national pre-Authorisation Agency in the case of persons or data located within the regional or national jurisdiction, or that an International Data Access Warrant (IDAW) is obtained from the International Data Access Commission (IDAC) as created in terms of Article 15 of this legal instrument, or provided that a valid legal request is obtained ex-ante under a legal framework for cross-border requests that includes the relevant regional or national government authorities.'

[201] *Ibid* Article 15(1) proposes the establishment by contracting states of an 'International Data Access Authority with the purpose of protecting personal data, privacy, freedom of expression and other fundamental human rights while facilitating the timely exchange of personal data across borders as may be required for the legitimate purposes of law enforcement agencies, intelligence and security services'. Article 2 states that the IDAA shall comprise four further organs, namely (1) the Surveillance Legal Instrument Consultative Committee; (2) the International Data Access Commission; (3) the International Committee of Human Rights Defenders; and (4) the International Data Access Tribunal.

[202] *Ibid* Art 4(4)(a).

[203] *Ibid* Art 15 Commentary.

[204] *Re Warrant to Search a Certain Email Account: Controlled and Maintained by Microsoft Corporation*, 15 F Supp 3d 466 (SDNY 2014). See also *R (on the application of KBR, Inc) v Director of the Serious Fraud Office* UKSC 2018/0215. The UK Supreme Court held that the UK Serious Fraud Office (SFO) lacked statutory authority to compel a US company to disclose overseas data under threat of criminal sanction. Generally, the SFO is empowered to issue a notice pursuant to s 2(3) of the Criminal

a search order made by the US Department of Defense under the US Stored Communications Act 1986 that sought to compel Microsoft's Irish subsidiary to disclose the content of emails held on the company's servers for the purposes of a criminal investigation. Generally, states are not allowed to exercise their enforcement jurisdiction on the territory of another state, as doing so may be treated as a breach of international law, particularly the principles of territorial sovereignty and non-intervention. To avoid such problems, countries cooperate in the investigation or prosecution of criminal offences on the basis of bilateral agreements known as mutual legal assistance treaties (MLATs).[205] Such collaboration typically involves the service of documents; searches and seizures; restraint and confiscation of the proceeds of crime; the provision of telephone interception material; and facilitation of the taking of evidence from witnesses. Although described as legally robust,[206] the procedure for seeking this type of assistance abroad is long and cumbersome, as it entails bureaucratic administrative and legal processes in each country and the duplication of paperwork. This has become a particularly acute problem when seeking to gain access to digital data located on servers abroad, where time is of the essence to obtain evidence that would facilitate the prosecution of serious crime. The *Microsoft Ireland* case brought both of these issues into sharp focus, ultimately reiterating that states are prohibited from applying their domestic laws extraterritorially, thus circumventing the MLATs. The subsequent enactment of the CLOUD Act 2018 in the US has undermined the outcome of this case,[207] but it nevertheless highlights the operational needs of law enforcement when their pursuit of a successful conviction is hindered by the rigidity of the formal

---

Justice Act 1987 requesting information from those under investigation, but the SC ruled in that case that s 2(3) did not confer on the SFO power to unilaterally compel a foreign company to produce documents held abroad on pain of a criminal penalty.

[205] The UK Home Office defines 'mutual legal assistance' as 'a method of cooperation between states for obtaining assistance in the investigation or prosecution of criminal offences. MLA is generally used for obtaining material that cannot be obtained on a police cooperation basis, particularly enquiries that require coercive means. Requests are made by a formal international Letter of Request (LOR). In civil law jurisdictions these are also referred to as "Commission Rogatoire". This assistance is usually requested by courts or prosecutors and is also referred to as "judicial cooperation"' – see UK Home Office, 'Guidance. Mutual Legal Assistance'.

[206] Gail Kent, 'The Mutual Legal Assistance Problem Explained', The Center for Internet and Society (23 February 2015).

[207] Clarifying Lawful Overseas of Data Act 2018 (CLOUD Act) (23 March 2018) Pub L 115–41. Amending the Stored Communications Act, the CLOUD Act expressly allows US law enforcement through a warrant, subpoena or court order to access data located outside the US, as long as the information sought is relevant and material to an ongoing criminal investigation. The powers under the Act apply to any provider of an electronic communications, or computing service that is subject to US jurisdiction.

processes of the MLATs – in particular, when access to data held in a foreign jurisdiction is denied. For these reasons, an important innovation introduced by the Legal Instrument is the establishment of a means for transborder access to personal data set out in its Article 15, which attempts to bring the mutual legal assistance mechanisms in line with the demands of modern investigatory methods. The provision empowers the IDAA to facilitate the timely exchange of personal data across borders when that is required for a legitimate law enforcement/security purpose,[208] by issuing an IDAW. The commentary to Article 15 explains this, stating that:

> In a world where personal data is increasingly held by private companies in data centres which are established in accordance with rules dictated by technical and financial expediency, it would also become much simpler for a company to handle a request for personal data coming from a law enforcement or national security or intelligence agency located outside a particular jurisdiction: if a company is presented with an IDAW it can rest assured that such a warrant was issued in full protection of human rights and authorised by the law of the State where its data centres are located – which would presumably be a party to this legal instrument.[209]

The Legal Instrument thus recognizes the challenges posed by having to pursue the formal MLAT channels where a need to access digital data located abroad arises and as a result creates a more flexible transnational system that concurrently aims to answer the needs of the intelligence community and ensure greater privacy safeguards.

Lastly, but equally importantly, the Legal Instrument emphasizes the need for 'reasonable suspicion' that a serious crime may be committed, as a procedural criterion for granting surveillance authorization, in relation to all forms of surveillance, domestic and foreign alike.[210] The draft treaty makes specific reference to the *Zakharov* case, which explains why the threshold of 'reasonable suspicion' features prominently throughout the document's text. Admittedly, the inclusion of this requirement pre-dates the *Big Brother Watch* judgment, which as discussed in Chapter 6 *supra* only applies in the context of domestic surveillance of communications. However, bearing in mind the Legal Instrument's distinctly universalist outlook, it is doubtful that the outcome in that case would have influenced its drafters to follow suit and prescribe different standards of protection for bulk and targeted surveillance. In setting out the same benchmark of protection, the Legal Instrument therefore not only upholds the principle of non-discrimination and equality of treatment, but also echoes the more stringent privacy protection standards set by the Court of

---

[208] Legal Instrument (n 5) Art 15(1).
[209] *Ibid* Art 15 Commentary.
[210] *Ibid* Art 4(1)(c).

Justice of the European Union's (CJEU) jurisprudence,[211] which is fundamentally antagonistic towards the bulk collection and retention of data within the EU. This has been unequivocally stated in the Legal Instrument's commentary, which makes clear that there must be an actual request for surveillance; a certain level of suspicion; impartial and effective oversight of the activities; authorization by judicial warrants; and no bulk collection of information.[212] Consequently, the proposed treaty forbids any surveillance measures that are carried out without a particular purpose or objective, and conducted only for the mere collection of information or its potential future use without any concrete threat.[213] It requires that reasonable suspicion be present against the target of the surveillance, rather than simply a reasonable suspicion that exists generally.[214] It further stipulates that when deciding whether such a suspicion exists, state authorities must demonstrate that the specific anticipated surveillance will yield evidence of a crime or help to mitigate that threat.[215] By contrast, it will be recalled that in the *Big Brother Watch* decision, the ECtHR recognized the value of bulk interception of foreign communications for counter-terrorism purposes and held that reasonable suspicion is not an appropriate procedural standard for this type of surveillance.

### 3.3.3    Legal Instrument – the prospects of success

In light of the above overview of some of its key aspects, it is regrettable that the Legal Instrument met with a hostile reception from a number of states, including Brazil, Germany, the US and China. At the Human Rights Council meeting on 6 March 2018, Brazil, also speaking on behalf of Germany, dismissed the proposed convention as 'unnecessary', stating that 'international law provides a clear, universally applicable framework to support and protect the right to privacy'.[216] Asked why Germany would not adopt an international legally binding treaty on surveillance and privacy, Niels Annen, the Minister

---

[211] In *Tele-2/Watson* the CJEU stated that: 'while the effectiveness of the fight against serious crime, in particular organised crime and terrorism, may depend to a great extent on the use of modern investigation techniques, such an objective of general interest, however fundamental it may be, cannot in itself justify that national legislation providing for the general and indiscriminate retention of all traffic and location data should be considered to be necessary for the purposes of that fight' – see C-203/15 and C-698/15 *Tele2 Sverige AB v Post- och telestyrelsen and Secretary of State for Home Departments v Tom Watson and Others* para 103 ('*Tele-2/Watson*').

[212] Legal Instrument (n 5) Art 4(1) Commentary.

[213] *Ibid* Art 3(8) and Art 3(8) Commentary.

[214] *Ibid* Art 3 Commentary.

[215] *Ibid* Art 4 Commentary.

[216] Stefan Talmon, 'No Need for Legal Instrument on Electronic Surveillance and Privacy', *German Practice in International Law* (5 June 2018).

of State at the Federal Foreign Office, stated that 'the Federal Government does not see any gap in international law in this area', adding that the government was not aware of any country prepared to accede to such a treaty.[217] Similarly, strong rebuttal of the draft was made by the US, whose rejection was justified not only on the basis of 'each country's surveillance framework [being] complex and different', but also because such an instrument 'could be disruptive, with unforeseen consequences for public safety and privacy'.[218] Reiterating this view, China further pointed out that a treaty-making process oversteps the boundaries of the Special Rapporteur's mandate.[219]

This repudiation represents a major setback for privacy protection and, as in the case of the CoE Intelligence Codex, serves both as a reminder and confirmation that states are not prepared to subject their surveillance activities to a set of legally binding rules – be it at a regional or international level – as this would potentially significantly impair their intelligence-gathering capabilities. While at this stage it is difficult to predict with certainty what the future of such legally binding measures may be, another option that could be pursued to limit mass surveillance is through states' adoption of the provisions of the Legal Instrument as non-legally binding guidelines and/or the development of non-legally binding norms for state surveillance.

The process of formulating such norms for cyberspace has been underway for the past two decades; but as the following discussion demonstrates, this endeavour is distinctly security orientated, state centric and protracted – although some consideration has been given to the protection of online privacy in the context of states' use of ICT through the development of voluntary standards.

## 4. UN GGE PROCESS – CYBER NORMS AND CONFIDENCE-BUILDING MEASURES

### 4.1 UN GGE Process – General

Highly sceptical of agreeing to a multilateral treaty for cyberspace, the major cyber powers have for a number of years engaged in the process of identifying the 'rules of the road' and promoting responsible state behaviour in cyberspace through broadly shared cyber norms. Unlike international law rules, these mechanisms are not legally binding on states and consequently provide a

---

[217] *Ibid.*
[218] Monika Ermert, 'UN Rapporteur for Privacy Rebuffed on Surveillance Oversight Negotiations', *Intellectual Property Watch* (7 March 2018).
[219] *Ibid.*

'certain flexibility', allowing states to 'coalesce around a particular principle or value, without compromising their official legal position'.[220] In the context of information technologies and their impact on international stability, the value and the importance that cyber norms play have been explained in the following terms:

> Voluntary, non-legally binding norms of responsible State behaviour can reduce risks to international peace, security and stability. Accordingly, norms do not seek to limit or prohibit action that is otherwise consistent with international law. Norms reflect the expectations of the international community, set standards for responsible State behaviour and allow the international community to assess the activities and intentions of States. Norms can help to prevent conflict in the ICT environment and contribute to its peaceful use to enable the full realization of ICTs to increase global social and economic development.[221]

As previously noted, the discussions on the actual and potential threats that states' use of ICT may cause to international peace and security have been underway since 1998, in the UN First Committee under the Russian initiative.[222] In 1999 the UNGA adopted Resolution 53/70,[223] which recognized the

---

[220] Cedric Sabbah, 'Pressing Pause: A new Approach for International Cybersecurity Norm Development (NATO CCDCOE Publications Tallinn, 2018) 263–81, 266.

[221] GGE 2015 (n 6) para 10. See also the OEWG Revised Pre-Draft Report, stating that 'voluntary, non-binding norms reflect the expectations of the international community and set standards regarding the acceptable and unacceptable behaviour of States in their use of ICTs. They play an important role in increasing predictability and reducing risks of misperceptions, thus contributing to the prevention of conflict. Norms do not replace or alter States' obligations under international law, which are binding, but rather provide additional specific guidance on what constitutes responsible State behaviour in the use of ICTs... Alongside international law, voluntary non-binding norms complement confidence-building and capacity-building measures and related efforts to promote an open, secure, stable, accessible and peaceful ICT environment'; OEWG Revised Pre-Draft Report (n 6) 7.

[222] See the following UNGA Resolutions: 'Developments in the Field of Information and Telecommunications in the Context of International Security', UN Doc A/Res/53/70 (4 December 1998); UN Doc A/Res/54/49 (1 December 1999); UN Doc A/Res 55/28 (20 November 2000); UN Doc A/Res/56/19 (29 November 2001); UN Doc 57/53 (22 November 2002); UN Doc A/Res/58/32 (8 December 2003); UN Doc A/Res/59/61 (3 December 2004); UN Doc A/Res/60/45 (8 December 2005); UN Doc A/Res/61/54 (6 December 2006); (UN Doc A/Res/62/17 (5 December 2007); UN Doc A/Res/63/37 (2 December 2008); UN Doc A/Res/64/25 (2 December 2009); UN Doc A/Res/65/41 (8 December 2010); UN Doc A/Res/66/24 (2 December 2011); UN Doc A/Res/67/27 (3 December 2012); UN Doc A/Res/68/243 (27 December 2013); UN Doc A/Res/69/28 (2 December 2014); UN Doc A/Res/70/237 (23 December 2015); UN Doc A/Res/71/28 (9 December 2016).

[223] *Ibid* A/Res/53/70 (n 140).

possible detrimental effects of the use of information technologies, including the potential destabilization of international security. This widely supported initiative paved the way three years later for the establishment of a group of government experts (GGE), tasked with considering 'existing and potential threats in the field of information security, as well as possible measures to limit the threat emerging in this field'.[224] The established system of the UN GGE has resulted in five GGE processes[225] and the adoption of three consensus reports in 2010,[226] 2013[227] and 2015.[228] The focus of the GGE discussions has been on two inter-related themes: (1) existing and emerging threats, norms, confidence and capacity-building measures;[229] and (2) international law pertaining to states' use of ICT in the context of the UN Charter's provisions on sovereignty and non-intervention, the peaceful settlement of disputes and self-defence.[230] Other areas under consideration included international humanitarian law; international human rights law; principles derived from sovereignty, such as due diligence and aspects of the customary international law of states' responsibility for internationally wrongful acts; matters of attribution; and self-help measures (retorsion and countermeasures).[231]

A notable feature of the 2010 consensus report[232] is that it served as a precursor to further the GGE's diplomatic efforts by recognizing the lack of a shared understanding pertaining to states' use of ICT. It recommended, *inter alia*, that a dialogue be undertaken among states to discuss norms to reduce collective

[224] *Ibid* A/Res/57/53 (n 222), para 4.

[225] These were held in 2004–05, 2009–10, 2012–13, 2014–15 and 2016–17.

[226] UNGA, 'Group of Government Experts on Developments in the Field of Information and Telecommunications in the Context of International Security' (30 July 2010) UN Doc A/65/201 ('GGE 2010').

[227] GGE 2013 (n 25).

[228] GGE 2015 (n 6).

[229] 'Confidence-building measures' are 'actions and procedures undertaken within the context of policy, legal and/or institutional framework(s) for the purpose of enhancing openness and transparency, assuring mutual understanding and reducing misunderstandings, threats and tensions among States' – see Ram S Jakhu, 'Transparency and Confidence-Building Measures for Space Security' in Ajey Lele (ed), *Decoding the International Code of Conduct for Outer Space Activities* (Pentagon Security International, 2012) 35; see also UNGA, 'Special Report of the Disarmament Commission to the General Assembly at its Third Special Session Devoted to Disarmament' (28 May 2006) UN Doc A/S-15/3.

[230] UN, 'International Law in the Consensus Reports of the United Nations Groups of Government Experts', Background paper prepared for the UN Open-Ended Working Group on Developments in the Field of Information and Telecommunications in the context of International Security (2020), www.un.org/disarmament/wp-content/uploads/2020/01/background-paper-on-international-law-in-the-gges.pdf.

[231] *Ibid.*

[232] GGE 2010 (226) para 1.

risk and protect critical domestic and international infrastructure,[233] together with confidence-building measures to 'address the implications of State use of ICTs, including exchanges of national views on the use of ICTs in conflict'.[234]

The idea of cyber norms gained traction with the US, the UK and their allies; and in 2013 another consensus report was issued, which for the first time established the principle that international law applies to cyberspace, affirming that: 'international law and in particular the Charter of the United Nations is applicable and is essential to maintaining peace and stability and promoting an open, secure, peaceful and accessible ICT environment.'[235] More specifically, in relation to the existing international law rules, the report avowed the principle of state sovereignty, stating that: 'State sovereignty and international norms and principles that flow from sovereignty apply to State conduct of ICT-related activities, and to their jurisdiction over ICT infrastructure within their territory.'[236] Furthermore, the document acknowledged the role of international human rights law, stating that: 'State efforts to address the security of ICTs must go hand-in-hand with respect for human rights and fundamental freedoms set forth in the Universal Declaration of Human Rights and other international instruments.'[237]

The third successful conclusion of the GGE process was the 2015 session, which resulted in a consensus report containing three distinct parts: (1) rules and principles of responsible behaviour of states;[238] (2) confidence-building measures;[239] and (3) clarification of how international law applies to the use of ICT.[240] This textual compartmentalization thus makes an explicit distinction between binding international law and non-legally binding norms for cyberspace. In that sense, the report recognizes the role played by norms, rules and principles as a means of reducing risks to international peace, security and stability. Being consensual, it represents to date the most detailed elaboration of standards, which the GGE encapsulated in 11 recommendations.[241] As explained in the UNODA Commentary, the normative value of these recommendations rests in their 'being accepted by the international community as standards of responsible State behaviour in uses of ICTs and implemented at

---

[233]   *Ibid* para 18(i).
[234]   *Ibid* para 18(ii).
[235]   GGE 2013 (n 25) para 19.
[236]   *Ibid* para 20.
[237]   *Ibid* para 21.
[238]   GGE 2015 (n 6) paras 9–15.
[239]   *Ibid* paras 16-19.
[240]   *Ibid* paras 24-29.
[241]   *Ibid* para 13(a)–(k).

the national, regional and international levels'.[242] To this end, the UNODA Commentary notes that:

> All recommendations in the 2015 report can be read as serving the purpose of filling in the gaps in existing instruments and practices. It is less relevant whether such gaps are mitigated in international or national law, or whether their implementation occurs by binding or non-binding instruments. What is essential is that States pay attention to the issues shared and raised by experts with relatively diverse views and preferences as to the development of information society and maintaining an open, free, secure and peaceful cyberspace.[243]

In the context of human rights, the GGE agreed on a broad spectrum of principles, which are set out in Recommendation 13(e), discussed next.

**4.2      UN GGE 2015 – Recommendation 13(e)**

The inclusion of this Recommendation in the GGE 2015 report was the result of both states' prior addressing of the relationship between human rights and the use of ICT within the UNGA's First Committee[244] and the increased attention paid at that time to the protection of human rights, in particular as the result of the Snowden leaks.[245]

---

[242]   *Ibid* 6.

[243]   *Ibid* 7.

[244]   See, for example, Developments in the Field of Information and Telecommunications in the Context of International Security, Report of the Secretary General (17 September 2003) UN Doc A/58/373 (Russian Federation at 10 and Ukraine at 15–17).

[245]   See Statement by HE Dilma Rousseff, President of the Federative Republic of Brazil at the Opening of the General Debate of the 68th Session of the UNGA (24 September 2013) ('Dilma Rousseff's Statement)'. At the opening of the UNGA's 68th Session on 24 September 2013, the then President of Brazil, Dilma Rousseff, condemned cyber surveillance activities as 'grave violations of human rights and civil liberties'. Outside of the UN-led initiatives, Recommendation 13(e) was preceded by a number of multi-stakeholder intergovernmental, private industry and civil society efforts, including (1) the Multi-stakeholder Statement from the Global Multi-Stakeholder Meeting on the Future of Internet Governance ('NETmundial') in April 2014, which expressly acknowledged the need for human rights to underpin Internet governance – see Global Multistakeholder Meeting on the Future of Internet Governance, 'NETmundial Multistakeholder Statement' (24 April 2014); and (2) the issuance by the Organization for Economic Co-operation and Development (OECD) of a set of guidelines governing the protection of privacy and transborder flow of personal data – see OECD, *Guidelines Governing the Protection of Privacy and Transborder Flows of Personal Data, Recommendation of the Council Concerning Guidelines Governing the Protection of Transborder Flows of Personal Data*, C(80)58/FINAL as amended on 11 July 2013 by C(2013)79 ('OECD *Guidelines*').

The GGE 2015 report progressed from the previous broad-brush consensus whereby states must respect international human rights and fundamental freedoms to reach a more detailed agreement set out in Recommendation 13(e), which provides that:

> States, in ensuring the secure use of the ITCs, should respect Human Rights Council resolutions 20/8 and 26/13 on the promotion, protection and enjoyment of human rights on the Internet, as well as General Assembly resolutions 68/167 and 69/166 on the right to privacy in the digital age, to guarantee full respect for human rights, including the right to freedom of expression.[246]

The purpose of the Recommendation is for nations to ensure that the means they employ to address the malicious use of ICT (eg, cyber attacks on critical infrastructure, vulnerabilities in the supply chain, cyber terrorism and cybercrime) by both state and non-state actors are in accordance with human rights as stipulated in the four resolutions enumerated therein.[247] Consequently, in addressing matters concerning the relationship between human rights and ICT, states must adhere to a number of stipulations set out in these resolutions, such as: (1) ensuring respect for and the protection of the right to privacy, including in the context of digital communications, and taking measures to put an end to violations of this right, together with creating conditions to prevent such infringements;[248] (2) reviewing procedures, practices and legislation concerning the surveillance of communications, their interception and the collection of personal data, including mass surveillance, interception and collection, with a view to upholding the right to privacy;[249] (3) establishing or maintaining existing independent, effective, adequately resourced and impartial judicial, administrative and/or parliamentary domestic oversight mechanisms capable of ensuring transparency and accountability for state surveillance of communications, their interception and the collection of personal data;[250] and (4) providing individuals whose right to privacy has been violated by unlawful and arbitrary surveillance with access to an effective remedy, consistent with international human rights obligations.[251]

---

[246] GGE 2015 (n 6) para 13(e).

[247] Barrie Sander, 'Recommendation 13(e)' in UNODA *Commentary* (n 7), 95-168, 98 ('Sander').

[248] UNGA Resolution, 'The Right to Privacy in the Digital Age' (21 January 2014) UN Doc A/Res/68/167, para 1 and 4(a)–(b) ('A/Res/68/167'); UNGA Resolution, 'The Right to Privacy in the Digital Age' (10 February 2015) A/Res/69/166 para 1 and 4(a) ('A/Res/ 69/166').

[249] A/Res/68/167 *ibid* para 4(c); A/Res/69/166 *ibid* para 4 (c).

[250] A/Res/68/167 *ibid* para 4(d); A/Res/69/166 *ibid* para 4 (d).

[251] A/Res/69/166 *ibid* para 4 (e).

While agreeing and reiterating these standards, Recommendation 13(e) does not detail exactly how in practice states must ensure the secure use of ICT that guarantees full respect for human rights. This task has been undertaken by the UNODA Commentary, which seeks to provide general guidance to states on how best to implement the voluntary norms proposed in the GGE 2015 report, including those introduced in Recommendation 13(e).[252] In contributing such guidance, the Commentary draws on the interpretation of the right to privacy by, *inter alia*, the treaty bodies, courts, experts, civil society groups and scholars, and situates Recommendation 13(e) within the framework of international human rights law.[253] This allows for the identification of appropriate suggestions for responsible state behaviour in relation to, among other matters, circumscribing the scope of application of the international human rights referenced within this norm – in particular, in relation to states' extraterritorial obligations and to the conduct of surveillance,[254] addressed next.

**4.2.1 Scope of application of international human rights**
According to the UNODA Commentary's guidance, in their implementation of Recommendation 13(e), states are under a negative obligation to respect human rights and a positive duty to protect them.[255] They must satisfy these negative and positive duties in relation to both persons within their territory and those located in territories under their effective control.[256] In reiterating the view taken by most human rights courts and bodies that states' extraterritorial jurisdiction in the cyber context is not territorially confined, the Commentary provides that 'control' in the context of negative obligations should be understood to mean not only physical control, but also control over individuals' rights.[257] However, in terms of states' positive obligations, it is still under dispute whether states must protect the rights of individuals under their power and effective control. In any case, the Commentary asserts that states will generally need effective control over a territory in order to comply with their positive obligations in practice.[258]

---

[252] Sander (n 247) para 24, 112.
[253] *Ibid* para 12, 104.
[254] *Ibid* para 25, 112–13. Other areas that the Commentary to Recommendation 13(e) elaborated on are data protection; encryption and anonymity; access to online content; and access to Internet infrastructure.
[255] *Ibid* para 101 (A), 158.
[256] *Ibid* 159.
[257] *Ibid.*
[258] *Ibid.*

**4.2.2    State Surveillance**

The Commentary's guidance in relation to surveillance programs advises that states should ensure that the design and implementation of such measures are in line with their human rights obligations, particularly the right to privacy.[259] The Commentary recognizes that the interception of both content and metadata constitutes an interference with the right to privacy of communications; as does the mere existence of legislation which allows a system for the secret monitoring of communications. States are thus under a duty to ensure that interference with an individual's privacy through surveillance practices has a basis in domestic law, which must possess the following characteristics: (1) be accessible to the public, providing individuals with an adequate indication of the circumstances and conditions on which public authorities are empowered to resort to surveillance measures, and identifying the scope of the state's discretion in the exercise of these powers; (2) identify the nature of offences that may give rise to an interception order; put forward a definition of the categories of people liable to be subject to surveillance; and specify the limit on their duration, the procedures to be followed for examining, using and storing the data obtained, the precautions to be taken when communicating the data to other parties and the circumstances in which it must be erased or destroyed; (3) set out effective procedural safeguards, including effective, adequately resourced institutional arrangements, in the form of either independent prior authorization and/or subsequent independent review of the surveillance measures; (4) give access to an effective remedy for the victims of privacy violations; (5) conform with the non-discrimination principle, meaning that the same protection and safeguards must be afforded to nationals, non-nationals and those outside the state's jurisdiction; and (6) ensure that intelligence sharing arrangements are conducted pursuant to a publicly accessible legal framework that complies with these safeguards.[260] Any interference with the right to privacy must be justified on the basis of a legitimate aim, including such grounds as national security; public safety or the economic wellbeing of the country; the prevention of disorder or crime; or the protection of health or morals, or the rights and freedoms of others.[261] In addition, interference though surveillance must satisfy the requirements of necessity and proportionality in achieving its legitimate aim. To this end, and reflecting the *Zakharov* criteria, the Commentary requires that the competent entity which authorizes the surveillance be independent and capable of verifying the existence of a reasonable suspicion against the person concerned – in particular, whether

---

[259]  *Ibid.*
[260]  *Ibid* para 101(B), 159–61.
[261]  *Ibid.*

there are factual indications for suspecting that person of planning, committing or having committed criminal acts or acts endangering national security.[262] Furthermore, the interception authorization (eg, a warrant) must clearly identify a specific person or premises to be placed under surveillance, a requirement which can be satisfied through providing names, addresses, telephone numbers or other relevant information.[263] Crucially, the Commentary asserts that states should avoid the following: (1) 'mass or bulk surveillance programmes that permit public authorities to have access on a generalized bases to the content of electronic communications'; (2) 'mandatory third party retention programmes that require Internet service providers to store metadata about their customers' communications and location for subsequent law enforcement and intelligence agency access'; and (3) 'data sharing arrangements between law enforcement agencies, intelligence bodies and other State organs that lack use limitations'.[264]

In summary, the GGE 2015 report set out numerous norms to help prevent conflict and contribute to the peaceful use of ICT, but did not provide detailed guidance to states as to their content or application. The UNODA Commentary focused on 'putting the flesh on the bone' by elaborating on the substance of those norms and provided suggestions to states pertaining to their implementation. In particular, the interpretation of Recommendation 13(e) focused on the responsibilities of states to respect and protect human rights in ensuring the secure use of ICT, including on such matters as their extraterritorial obligations and procedural standards for conducting surveillance. Above all, the Commentary advises nations against the use of mass or bulk surveillance.

### 4.3 UN GGE 2017 and Beyond

The task of agreeing further details on how the norms enumerated in the GGE 2015 report can be applied by states and engaging with the issues as to how international law applies to states' use of ICT was left to the subsequent 2017 GGE. Having failed to reach a consensus, the 2017 GGE did not produce a report. The considerable speculation that followed as to the reasons for this failure seems to boil down to fundamental political disagreements that resurrected the old rivalries between the Western and Eastern powers. In short, the US and the UK wished to expand discussions pertaining to the rules on cyber operations in the context of the laws on the use of force; while Russia and China focused their diplomatic efforts on preventing cyber-based

---

[262] *Ibid* 162.
[263] *Ibid.*
[264] *Ibid.*

conflict, rather than agreeing on standards relating to situations that ought not to be allowed to occur in the first place,[265] such as possible responses to the use of force. The main bone of contention was the applicability of the right to self-defence under Article 51 of the UN Charter, international humanitarian law and the use of countermeasures in the context of cyber operations. In particular, in relation to the right to self-defence as a response to armed attacks by cyber means, Russia, China and Cuba voiced their opposition, declaring that this could be the first step towards transforming this domain into a realm of endless conflict.[266] They argued that introducing this right would establish a legal basis for the emergence of hostile cyber operations of unprecedented intensity and impact, thus 'legitimising cyber war'.[267] With that being the main concern, the position expressed by the Chinese representatives was that the right to self-defence does not align with China's cyber security strategy, which prioritizes peace, followed by sovereignty and only then security.[268] Similarly, according to Cuba, an agreement on Article 51 of the UN Charter would inevitably turn cyberspace into a theatre of military operations; while Russia's position[269] was that the use of force in both cyberspace and real space is absolutely inadmissible. Consequently, an agreement as to how the existing international law rules apply in the cyber context remains, at least for the time being, elusive. In the words of one commentator, this is:

> not just because of yawning technical capacity divides and the unknown difficulties of attribution of state behaviour in cyberspace, but also because the principal questions of the international cyber security discourse are far from settled politically. Importantly, different proposals for new binding and non-binding norms are often premised on controversial arguments and beliefs about issues of international cyber security, their causes and trends.[270]

---

[265] Alex Grigsby, 'The End of Cyber Norms' (2017) 59(6) *Survival*, 109–122.

[266] Ann Väljataga, 'Back to Square One? The Fifth UN GGE Fails to Submit a Conclusive Report at the UN General Assembly', NATO CCDCOE, https://ccdcoe.org/incyder-articles/back-to-square-one-the-fifth-un-gge-fails-to-submit-a-conclusive-report-at-the-un-general-assembly/.

[267] *Ibid.*

[268] *Ibid.*

[269] *Ibid.* This stance was explained on German pro-Kremlin news site *Russkoe Pole* by the special representative of the Russian President for international cooperation in the field of information security and envoy to the Russian Foreign Ministry, Andrei Krutskikh.

[270] Eneken Tikk and Mika Kerttunen, 'The Alleged Demise of the UN GGE. An Autopsy and a Eulogy' (Cyber Policy Institute, 2017) 5.

## 4.4    UN GGE Cyber Norm Setting – an Evaluation

Since 2004, five GGEs have studied the threats posed by the use of ICT in the context of international security and how they should be addressed, with each group building on the work of its predecessor. Three of these groups have agreed on a substantive report. In particular, the GGE 2015 document has been recognized as the 'most remarkable achievement', as it represents the joint efforts of experts from different countries – often with opposing views on the preferred role and functions of ICT, globally and nationally – to agree a set of recommendations which they believe would contribute to the improvement of international security.[271] In recognition of this, the UNGA adopted the GGE 2015 report by consensus in Resolution 70/237, which 'calls upon Member States to be guided in their use of information and communication technologies by the 2015 report of the Group of Government Experts'.[272]

The 11 Recommendations for cyber norms to a large extent reflect the existing international law, but have been set out in general terms. The process of their further elaboration, left to the 2016–17 GGE, stalled because of strategic and political differences among the GGE's members. This indicates that, despite a broad consensus that cyberspace and related activities need regulation, the agreement of non-legally binding standards is proving as difficult as coming to the negotiating table to discuss cyber-specific legislation. This is partly on account of different understandings of what norms are, their role and their utility.[273] In addition, assuming that international law rules 'are expressions of norms that international community accepts [and] States conform their behaviour to laws because of the wider acceptance of the underlying norms',[274] it becomes apparent why accepting such norms can be seen as setting a dangerous precedent. One illustration of this is the reluctance of some states during the 2016–17 GGE to agree to the acceptability of self-defence in the cyber context – perhaps seen as a tacit agreement to the legitimization of the use of force, which may eventually harden to become binding treaty or customary law rule. This approach can also explain states' lack of agreement to flesh out exactly how the obligations to respect and protect human rights and fundamental freedoms set out in Recommendation 13(e) apply to their activi-

---

[271]  *Ibid* 2.

[272]  UNGA Resolution, 'Developments in the Field of Information and Telecommunications in the Context of International Security' (30 December 2015) UN Doc A/Res/70/237 para 2(a).

[273]  For a useful discussion on norms, see Liisi Adamson, 'International Law and International Cyber Norms. A Continuum?' in Broeders and van den Berg (n 34) 26–27.

[274]  *Ibid.*

ties in cyberspace, as this may adversely impact on their intelligence-gathering activities and prove a bridge too far. Having said that, both the GGE and the SCO processes framed their proposed norms from the outset as voluntary and non-legally binding. As such, their aim is to encourage socially and morally responsible behaviour, thus influencing nations by circumscribing what is and what is not acceptable. However, unlike treaty and customary law, the breach of voluntary standards of behaviour does not trigger state responsibility and sanction mechanisms, such as self-defence, or countermeasures. Nevertheless, and despite their non-legally binding nature, one advantage of norms is that they do provide guidance and a set of goals; while non-compliance may be met with political, rather than legal consequences, such as economic and diplomatic responses from other states.

The deeply embedded political and ideological divisions, the general distrust and the increase in offensive cyber activities not only led to the halting of diplomatic efforts, with the 2017 GGE unable to produce a consensus report, but also subsequently bifurcated cyber diplomatic efforts. Thus, in 2018 both Russia and the US submitted resolutions to the UNGA with an aim to pursue their policy goals under separate diplomatic mandates. To this end, the Russian-sponsored Resolution[275] integrated the content of the GGE 2015 report and established an Open-Ended Working Group (OEWG), whose purpose is to continue to further develop the rules, norms and principles of responsible state behaviour and the methods for their implementation; introduce changes (should they be necessary); and propose new rules.[276] The establishment of the OEWG, which commenced its work in 2019, is a new development that the Russian delegation insists is open to all states. In that sense, it is perceived as a rival process to the UN GGE – which, following the 2017 fiasco, was purportedly rejected by the Russian delegation as 'the practice of club agreements that should be sent to the annals of history'.[277] The parallel US-led Resolution[278] reaffirmed the UN GGE and proposed the establishment of a new GGE 2019 to continue to study norms, confidence and capacity-building measures, together

---

[275] UNGA, Developments in the Field of Information and Telecommunications in the Context of International Security (29 October 2018) UN Doc A/C1/73/L27/Rev1.

[276] *Ibid* para 5. The OEWG Revised Pre-Draft Report stipulates that: (1) international law – in particular, the UN Charter – is applicable to states' use of ICT; and (2) voluntary, non-legally binding norms and confidence and capacity -building measures play an important role in the prevention of conflict – see OEWG Revised Pre-Draft Report (n 6) 5–11.

[277] See Xymena Kurkowska, 'What Does Russia Want in Cyber Diplomacy?' in Broeders and van Den Berg (n 34) 85–105.

[278] UNGA, Advancing Responsible State Behaviour in Cyberspace in the Context of International Security (8 October 2018) UN Doc A/C1/73/L37.

with how international law applies to cyberspace.[279] As a result, two competing diplomatic tracks have been created, which has arguably further complicated the process of arriving at mutually and conceptually agreeable standards for responsible state behaviour in cyberspace. While it would be unwise to speculate at this stage on what the outcome of these rival systems may be in the future, the splintering of cyber diplomatic efforts seems to have confirmed that the development of non-legally binding norms and/or a cyber surveillance *lex specialis* has moved further away.

## 5.   BILATERAL AGREEMENTS

For a number of years, states' cyber diplomacy has also been concerned with building bilateral relationships with other nations. Such engagements or collaborations among smaller groups of countries provide valuable opportunities to share views, identify areas of agreement, address different opinions and develop cooperation.[280] More specifically, the advantage of such arrangements is that states may find it easier to make a reciprocal commitment on matters that are of particular concern to them, rather than making a pledge on a broad range of issues.

A case in point is norm development in the area of restraining cyber industrial espionage. Thus, a specific voluntary pledge – stating that 'no country should conduct or support ICT-enabled theft of intellectual property, including trade secrets, or other confidential business information with the intent of providing competitive advantage to companies or commercial sector' – was made by the Group of 7 (G7) in its 2016 Principles and Actions in Cyber[281] and in the 2017 G7 Lucca Declaration.[282] Another example of such a commitment is the US-Sino 2015 economic cyber espionage agreement concluded between the then US President, Barack Obama, and the Chinese leader Xi Jinping. The

---

[279]   *Ibid* para 3.

[280]   For example the US-Russia agreement of June 2013 – an agreement to reduce the risk of conflict in cyberspace through real time communications about incidents of national security concerns – see Ellen Nakashima, 'U.S. and Russia Sign Pact to Create Communication Link on Cyber Security', *The Washington Post* (17 June 2013); Russia-China agreement of May 2015 – a non-aggression agreement to refrain from cyber attacks against each other and to jointly respond to technologies that may have a destabilizing effect on political and socio-economic life or interfere with internal affairs of the state – see Andrew Roth, 'Russia and China Sign Cooperation Pact', *The New York Times* (8 May 2015).

[281]   United Nations Institute for Disarmament Research (UNIDIR) Cyber Policy Portal, Group of 7, G7 Principles and Actions in Cyber (27 May 2016).

[282]   UNIDIR Cyber Policy Portal, Group of 7, G7 Declaration on Responsible State Behaviour in Cyberspace (G7 Lucca Declaration) (11 April 2017).

accord is aimed at the reciprocal curtailment of commercial cyber spying, committing both countries' governments not to knowingly conduct or support the cyber-enabled theft of intellectual property.[283] The agreement was reached chiefly as a result of US concerns at the prolific 'digital theft' of US intellectual property, which the US attributes to China,[284] and marked a significant step towards the establishment of voluntary norms in this area. A notable aspect of the process was that the US and China agreed that a distinction be made between economic cyber espionage and political cyber espionage, to which the Chinese government reluctantly acquiesced. This classification was put forward by the US, which maintains that cyber intelligence gathering and the collection of information about economic and financial matters for the purposes of benefiting national security are routine intelligence activities and not acts of cyber economic espionage.[285] By contrast, the Chinese government has not only traditionally denied engaging in intellectual property theft to gain a commercial advantage, but also considered a distinction that specifically prohibits only economic cyber espionage to be unjustifiable, especially in light of the US-led cyber surveillance exposed by the Snowden leaks. In this sense, President Xi's agreement that the Chinese government would cease to engage in or knowingly support the theft of intellectual property in order to provide a competitive advantage to Chinese private companies represents China's concession that there exists a type of cyber espionage distinct from national security espionage. However, the Chinese government may have been motivated to accept this distinction and enter into the agreement due to fears that China could face US-imposed sanctions or tariffs on its products.[286] In the years that followed, a number of allegations were made regarding China's failure to adhere to the Obama-Xi arrangement.[287] If these reports are correct, what transpires from the perspective of norm setting is that bilateral commit-

---

[283]   The White House, *Fact Sheet: President Xi Jinping's State Visit to the United States* (25 September 2015).

[284]   Tim Stevens, 'Economic Cyber-Espionage and the China-US Relationship', *The Asia Dialogue* (4 June 2018), https://theasiadialogue.com/2018/06/04/economic-cyberespionage-and-the-china-u-s-relationship/. For general discussion regarding cyber espionage against the US, see Chapter 2 *supra*.

[285]   *Ibid.*

[286]   Justin Lynch, 'What Happens When the US-China Cyber Agreement Isn't Working', *Fifth Domain* (11 November 2018), www.fifthdomain.com/international/2018/11/12/what-happens-when-the-us-china-cyber-agreement-isnt-working/.

[287]   *Ibid.* For example, NSA senior adviser Rob Joyce stated, during the Cybersecurity Summit in Aspen on 8 November 2018, that 'we have certainly seen [China's] behaviour erode over the past year and we are very concerned'; see also Andy Greenberg, 'China Tests the Limits of its US Hacking Truce', *Wired* (31 October 2017), www.wired.com/story/china-tests-limits-of-us-hacking-truce/.

ments are relatively easy to make, but equally easy to break. Nevertheless, they also suggest that states are more willing to come to the negotiating table to address a concrete need, and this in turn contributes towards the development of norms.

To summarize, norms and confidence-building measures have the undoubted benefit of opening an international dialogue about matters on which nations find it difficult to reach a legally binding agreement. They are not regarded as a substitute for treaties, but are perceived as standalone measures that have normative value or as supplementary mechanisms to other legally binding and non-legally binding measures. Two developments are particularly important for cyber diplomacy. First, in the context of the impact of the use of ICT on the protection of human rights, states are guided to adhere to their duty to protect and respect the right to privacy and conduct surveillance in light of the obligations set out and developed by the international human rights organs, as reiterated in Recommendation 13(e) of the UN GGE 2015. Second, an attempt has been made to prevent, or at least reduce, the theft of intellectual property through a bilateral commitment between the US and China, underpinned by these countries' agreement to distinguish between two categories of cyber espionage, namely economic and political.

## 6.    CONCLUSION

The process of limiting mass cyber surveillance is most likely to be incremental, facilitated by careful diplomacy and the development of non-legally binding norms and confidence-building measures. There are no 'quick fixes'.

The historical thumbnail sketch outlining the reasons for the failed attempts to reach acceptance of the SCO's Draft Codes of Conduct submitted to the UNGA in 2011 and 2015 illustrates the deeply embedded geopolitical struggles between the opposing ideologies and visions for cyberspace. The fundamental differences between the Western and Eastern approaches pertaining to the stewardship of this domain at least to some extent explain the current stalemate in relation to the negotiation of a multilateral legally binding convention, further fuelled by the distrust generated by the 2013 Snowden disclosures. In addition, the normative focus of the SCO proposals is firmly on maintaining security and stability; the protection of individuals' rights was peripheral at best. In the context of state sponsored cyber surveillance, attempts to secure an agreement on a legally binding treaty at the regional and international levels with the main purpose of protecting human rights were made in 2015 and 2018; but these efforts too have failed to secure states' support. This suggests that, despite the heightened prominence given to the right to privacy in the years that followed the Snowden revelations at the UN and in a number of regional forums, states simply lack the commitment to regulate the working methods of intelligence and law enforcement agencies by means of a hard law instrument.

That being the case, reduced surveillance could be achieved incrementally through non-legally binding voluntary norms and confidence-building measures. The intergovernmental process to arrive at a consensus in relation to how international law applies to cyber activities and to develop such a mechanism was facilitated by the UN and undertaken through consecutive UN GGE meetings between 2004 and 2017. In this regard, the GGE 2015 report setting out Recommendation 13(e) provides valuable guidance on the use of surveillance programs and advises nations on how these can be made compatible with the international human rights frameworks. Another positive development in this area is the commitment of several individual states to curtail their cyber espionage activities, in particular relating to the theft of intellectual property. To this end, the 2015 US-Sino agreement to limit the theft of intellectual property is of note. From a semantic point of view, the concession made by the Chinese government that cyber economic espionage can be distinguished from other forms of cyber spying is also an important step forward, as it signals states' adoption of a more nuanced approach to the issue of cyber espionage and how to address it.

Whether the diplomatic efforts outlined above will help in the further development of norms and/or legally binding rules pertaining to cyber surveillance on a global, regional or bilateral level is hard to predict; but efforts to do so must continue.

# 8. Conclusion to *State Sponsored Cyber Surveillance*

The first two decades of the twenty-first century marked the process of an almost irreversible erosion of privacy, both as a social norm and as a legal right, which to a large extent has been facilitated by states' surveillance of digital communications. Cyber surveillance is a state's indiscriminate monitoring and capture of digital communications, comprising their content and metadata, with the aim of identifying future rather than investigating known threats; and includes all forms of bulk acquisition methods, such as bulk interception of communications, bulk equipment interference and compiling bulk personal datasets.

Ever since the 2013 Edward Snowden disclosures, it has become apparent that these activities have grown into a 'massive surveillance industrial complex'[1] and are used by democracies and autocracies alike. With the strategic utility perceived in terms of anticipating enemy actions, supressing rival states and guarding against the growing threat of terrorism, mass surveillance is viewed by all regimes as politically necessary. However, the preponderance of this practice, enabled by ever-increasing technological innovations, raises significant questions in relation to the impact that this has on the rights of individuals, society *sensu lato* and, more broadly, international law. In consequence, the surrounding political and legal debate centres on such matters as its necessity and what it protects, the impact on democracy, the rule of law and fundamental freedoms. In terms of international law, it presents a number of challenges. These include possible violations of territorial sovereignty and non-intervention. In addition, it raises the question of the effectiveness of international human rights legislation, both in terms of individuals' protection and its relevance, which has been and continues to be significantly undermined by the global surveillance race, fuelled by exponential changes in bulk acquisition patterns and techniques.

From international law perspective, surveillance has traditionally been viewed as a type of signals intelligence collection and as such it is doctrinally classified as falling within states' espionage activities. This stance is often

---

[1] Council of Europe (CoE), Committee on Legal Affairs and Human Rights, *Mass Surveillance. Draft Resolution* (2015) AS/Jur 2 ('CoE Mass Surveillance Resolution').

undertaken in relation to mass cyber surveillance. This book has queried this view and argued that, due to the nature, scale and targets involved, international law should distinguish among different types of cyber intelligence operations. That being the case, it is proposed that mass cyber surveillance falls within a *sui generis* category. The book has aimed to explore the impact it has specifically on international human rights law, with a narrow focus on the individual's right to privacy of communications. To that end, the overriding theme of this work has been to ascertain first, how this law applies to state sponsored cyber surveillance; and second, whether the existing treaty regime is adequate to meet the challenges posed by the ubiquity of this state practice. Alternatively, it considered whether, in addition to the *lex lata*, there is a need to develop a privacy/surveillance *lex specialis* at the international level to regulate the operational methods of intelligence and law enforcement agencies.

It is submitted that, assessed against an international human rights framework pertaining to the right to privacy of communications, mass cyber surveillance *prima facie* constitutes an interference with this right and its justification is challenging on necessity and proportionality grounds, which likely makes it unlawful. Furthermore, on the basis of the research undertaken for the purposes of this book, it is argued that the international human rights conventions and their interpretations are inadequate to solve the current and future problems posed by these measures and address the now almost irreversible erosion of privacy – mostly due to their general, outdated and fragmented nature. Put another way, the existing international human rights law pertaining to the right to privacy of communications is rather feeble, as it has not been designed to address mass surveillance and to keep up with the changes in global surveillance technologies and schemes. This is because the treaties that enshrined this right were adopted well before the Internet came to dominate nearly every aspect of human activity, and therefore lack specific rules that are designed to ensure the adequate protection of this right in the cyber context. Equally, the study has shown that the manner in which the international human rights courts and bodies interpret these rules and apply them to mass cyber surveillance lacks uniformity and cohesion. To this end, the book demonstrates that the current jurisprudence often presents conflicting and inconsistent legal standards when it comes to the application of the principles set out in Article 17 of the International Covenant on Civil and Political Rights (ICCPR), Article 8 of the European Convention on Human Rights (ECHR) and Article 11 of the American Convention on Human Rights (ACHR). This is evident in relation to such issues as the varied stance that the international judicial organs take regarding the asymmetric privacy protection of domestic surveillance laws; the meaning of 'interference' with the protected right; how the criterion of 'legitimate aim' should be circumscribed; the problem of proportionality; and matters relating to the oversight and transparency of surveillance, to name but a few. In addition, the extraterritorial application of these treaties in the context of states' mass surveillance has not been directly addressed by the court, leaving the powerful cyber nations such as the US to argue that the ICCPR does not apply outside their territories. For these reasons, the basic tenet of this book is that in order to counteract the threat to fundamental human rights, including privacy, states' digital surveillance practices must be regulated by a set of bespoke, internationally agreed principles, preferably in the form of a universal, legally binding treaty. Such an instrument should define the circumstances in which and how surveillance may be conducted, by prescribing procedural safeguards that adhere to the requirements of proportionality, transparency and oversight – a cyber surveillance *lex specialis*.

The book's starting point to support the need for such a framework was to argue that cyber surveillance has evolved to form a separate category of states' intelligence operations. Indeed, one of the fundamental thesis of this work is that in order to attempt any regulation of these undertakings, cyber espionage and cyber surveillance should doctrinally be treated as disparate categories. This formed the kernel of the discussion in Chapter 2, where it was contended that the focus of states' intelligence gathering, fuelled by the rhetoric of the 'war on terror',[2] has shifted since the 9/11 attacks on the US from military intelligence collection and/or that pertaining to government activities to the interception of communications of often entire civilian populations. Having analysed current state practice, the chapter categorized cyber intelligence activities to comprise three types: (1) cyber espionage, both for political ends (including electoral interference, but only through doxing) and for economic gains; (2) cyber surveillance; and (3) foreign cyber electoral interference, consisting of cyber tampering with a state's election infrastructure; and information operations, encompassing malinformation and disinformation. Further, it distinguished two categories of mass cyber surveillance: (1) targeted surveillance – that is, the covert interception and collection of communications content and metadata based on a suspicion against a particular target; and (2) mass surveillance, being the indiscriminate monitoring and capture of large volumes of communications content and metadata, without suspicion against a particular individual or group. In relation to cyber electoral interference, the chapter observed that this new phenomenon goes to the very heart of the founding principles of egalitarian societies – namely the making of free democratic choices – and likely engages international law, in particular the

---

2    The 'war on terror' was a phrase used by the then US President George W Bush following the 9/11 attacks and recognized in the US National Strategy for Combating Terrorism first published in 2003 – see US White House, 'President Discusses War on Terror' (5 September 2006), https://georgewbush-whitehouse.archives.gov/news/releases/2006/09/20060905-4.html.

principles of territorial sovereignty and non-intervention. In dogmatic terms, only one aspect of cyber electoral interference – that is, doxing operations – falls within states' cyber spying and, as with other forms of deleterious cyber activities (including political and economic cyber espionage), requires attribution to the state to trigger its responsibility for internationally wrongful acts. This is notoriously difficult to establish, especially since the identity of the entity behind the activity is often unknown – for example, when it is conducted by a non-state organ or a proxy. Thus, in order to hold a state accountable (or give the victim state the right to resort to countermeasures), it must be shown that the act in question can be attributed to the state, both factually and legally. These aspects present evidential problems, in particular in relation to the burden and standard of proof required. Although to date the International Court of Justice has not addressed these issues, the arguments put forward, according to which the burden rests on the claimant state to show, on the basis of convincing evidence or its preponderance, that the cyber operation has been conducted by the respondent state, seem sound. In the context of mass cyber surveillance programs, such as PRISM and Tempora, the problems with attribution appear less complex, as a number of official admissions have been made in relation to the use of these surveillance methods. They have also been carried out by state organs (the National Security Agency (NSA) and Government Communications Headquarters (GCHQ)) pursuant to domestic legislation, and in this sense may potentially trigger responsibility for, *inter alia*, breach of the principles of territorial sovereignty and non-intervention.

International law applies to low-level cyber activities, but does not regulate them directly. There is, however, a patchwork of norms comprising general principles and specialist regimes, which to some extent limit these practices. Thus far, states have failed to reach an agreement as to how these rules relate to cyber operations below the use of force threshold. This creates uncertainty – an example of which is the lack of agreement as to whether the principle of territorial sovereignty applies to various remote cyber operations, with France and the UK taking opposing views on this matter. Such unresolved issues create ambiguity in relation to both ascertaining how states may conduct cyber activities within the legal parameters and their lawful response to adverse cyber exploits by other states. Given the propensity of these practices in the future, it is necessary to have a clear articulation of the legal boundaries within the existing international law paradigm as to how international law relates to a broad spectrum of cyber operations. This process is now underway, with numerous states putting forward their vision as to how international law rules and general principles apply in cyberspace, but this does not diminish the need for the development of the specialist regimes – in particular dealing with the protection of states' democratic processes and the harmonization of the working methods of the intelligence community in the digital sphere.

Such instruments are essential to the maintenance of international peace and security, together with the safeguarding of the rule of law and human rights.

The taxonomy of cyber intelligence operations set out in Chapter 2 led then to a discussion in Chapter 3 which focused specifically on states' targeted and mass surveillance activities, viewed through the prism of an individual's legal recourse against states' privacy violations. To this end, the chapter engaged with the concept of privacy as a basic human need and as a necessary component for the functioning of any society. It considered the complex and multifaceted nature of this right, noting that it does not fit easily into an all-encompassing definition. This to a certain extent is also reflected in the difficulties of pigeonholing privacy into a neat legal category, which have been recognized by most international human rights courts and bodies. Notwithstanding this apparent obstacle at defining privacy as a monolithic right, conceiving of it as a bundle of inter-related concepts is probably its great advantage. This is because its 'fuzzy' boundaries and obfuscated nature facilitate the debate as to its contours for contemporary society and thus help to engage with the taxing issue as to how to circumscribe it for the purposes of updating its legal parameters to fit the demands of the digital age. The first steps in this regard have been undertaken, with the international community recognizing that the right to privacy applies online as much as offline. This has been confirmed by the UN General Assembly (UNGA) (Resolutions 68/167 and 69/166 on the right to privacy in the digital age) and by the Human Rights Council (Resolutions 20/8 and 26/13 on the promotion and enjoyment of human rights on the Internet). This 'normative equivalence paradigm' served as a basic premise in Chapter 3 for an enquiry into the sources of this right in relation to its possible violation online. The presiding question therein was whether individuals have a right to seek protection against states' arbitrary interference based solely on treaty law, or whether there is another source of this right, derived from customary international law. In order to engage with this question, the chapter positioned its scrutiny within the traditional doctrine used to establish customary international law rules, namely the two-stage test set out under Article 38(1)(b) of the Statute of the International Court of Justice 1946, which demands the existence of general state practice and *opinio juris* for the formation of a customary rule. The chapter first considered the current developments in this field through an examination of a representative sample of states' legislative efforts aimed at protecting privacy/data privacy and found that there is a general practice in this regard, primarily evidenced through legislative activism. However, when placed in the context of how these rights are protected in practice, it soon transpires that there is no uniformity of approach, as the legal recourse against states' arbitrary interference is replete with disparate rules and remedies. In addition, the surveillance context within which these legal safeguards exist often counterbalances any protective effects envisaged by the privacy/data protection laws. This situation was recognized and aptly summarized by *Boundaries of Law*, a 2017 global survey examining states' surveillance, according to which 'the discrepancy between continuing government surveillance practices and the relevant international human rights and the rule of law standards is breath-taking'.[3] Chapter 3 also identified the ease with which states are prepared to compromise this right in the face of a global pandemic (Covid-19), in particular through attempts to install far-reaching surveillance mechanisms (eg, mobile phone tracing apps). The crisis has arguably created a global semi-permanent state of quasi-emergency, consequently allowing states to devise new means of monitoring their citizens, with a realistic possibility of these becoming a permanent feature of governments' surveillance apparatus. A case in point is the UK's plan, unveiled in September 2020, to introduce online identification cards for British citizens, with a variety of functions, including to prove their 'disease status'.[4] Having concluded that there is a lack of uniformity and consistency in state practice, Chapter 3 then discussed whether the protection of online privacy constitutes *opinio juris* – that is, states' general belief that this is a legally binding obligation. The answer to this part of the test must necessarily be in the negative. First, on the domestic level, the conclusion reached is that these rights are guaranteed in principle, but not respected in practice. On the international level, the chapter considered the UNGA Resolutions on the right to privacy (in particular Resolutions 68/167 and 69/166), where the international community united not only to condemn mass surveillance, but also to affirm the right to privacy online. Through analysing their content and the method of their adoption, the chapter concluded, however, that these instruments cannot be viewed as a clear articulation of *opinio juris*, but rather as a contribution to the future development of a customary law rule for online privacy. Furthermore, although the UN mechanism for human rights protection evidences a consistent commitment to safeguarding this principle in the digital sphere, this seems to be counteracted by the practice of domestic courts in some of the most influential states in the cyber domain, including the US and the UK, which appear unwilling to pronounce these practices as unlawful. This is exacerbated by the recent bifurcation in the European Court of Human Rights (ECtHR) jurisprudence pertaining to privacy's procedural safeguards, with the Court approving weaker protection standards in relation to the interception of foreign communications compared with their domestic counterparts.

---

[3]     Douwe Korff, Ben Wagner, Julia Powles, Renata Avila and Ulf Buermeyer, *Boundaries of Law: Exploring Transparency, Accountability and Oversight of Government Surveillance Regimes* (University of Cambridge Faculty of Law, 2013) 11.

[4]     George Grylls, 'Digital "ID Cards" Lead to Dominic Cummings Data Revolution', *The Times* (2 September 2020).

These factors, taken together, indicate that at this stage it cannot be said that there is a sufficiently uniform and consistent state practice and clear evidence of *opinio juris* to categorically state that online privacy is a customary law rule. Rather, it is an emergent one. It follows that from the perspective of international law, its only source is treaty law. Consequently, individuals whose privacy has been infringed may first bring their complaint in their domestic courts and then, having exhausted all available remedies, seek recourse through the relevant international or regional judicial forums.

The first matter to be determined in the context of treaty-based privacy protection is the extent of states' human rights obligations in relation to cyber surveillance, conducted both within states' borders and extraterritorially. This is a particularly probing question, as a number of states regard the extent of their duties differently, depending on the nature or locality of communications, thereby raising issues of discrimination and equality of treatment, together with seeking to limit their responsibility in relation to their extraterritorial interception and collection methods. This formed the background of the enquiry in Chapter 4. Having first engaged with the principles of non-discrimination and equality of treatment, the chapter concluded that it is indefensible for states to continue with an asymmetric approach to privacy protection when legislating for powers of surveillance, used for the interception of digital communications. This is because, although states may in principle provide for different treatment of nationals and aliens, this is permissible only if the measure in question pursues a legitimate aim and there is a reasonable relationship of proportionality between the aims sought and the means employed. Two domestic surveillance regimes – namely those of the US and the UK – were taken into consideration to illustrate that although the first criterion may be satisfied (ie, that the means deployed are for genuine national security ends), it is doubtful whether they meet the requirement of proportionality and for this reason they are likely to be discriminatory in nature. The chapter highlighted the fact that although most UN treaty bodies attest to this, the ECtHR takes a different view. First, in the *Big Brother Watch v UK*[5] case, the Court concluded that the allegations of discrimination based on Article 14 read together with Article 8 of the ECHR were unfounded, as the different treatment in question (ie, based on Section 8(4) of the Regulation of Investigatory Powers Act 2000 providing lower standards of protection for external communications) related to geographical location and not the claimants' nationality and therefore did not meet

---

[5] *Big Brother Watch and Others v the United Kingdom* App no 58170/13; *Bureau of Investigative Journalism and Alice Ross v the United Kingdom* App no 62322/14; *10 Human Rights Organizations and Others v the United Kingdom* App no 24960/15 (12 October 2018) ('*Big Brother Watch*').

the Article 14 criteria. Second, the ECtHR decided that domestic legislation providing lower safeguards for foreign bulk surveillance of communications falls within states' wide margin of discretion. In addition, the ECtHR rejected the submission for applying the same procedural safeguards (based on reasonable suspicion) to domestic and foreign surveillance alike, justifying this on the basis that the inclusion of such a criterion would defeat the very purpose of bulk surveillance. However, even if specific methods of surveillance have not been recognized by the ECtHR as discriminatory, the same cannot be said of the principle of equality before the law and its equal protection enshrined in Article 26 of the ICCPR. Consequently, arguments that reject this viewpoint to privacy protection in the age of surveillance are unconvincing. Despite the ECtHR's recent endorsement of the operational value of mass surveillance in the *Big Brother Watch* and *Centrum För Rättvisa v Sweden*[6] cases, its utility has been doubted by, *inter alia*, the UN mandate holders, US government agencies and industry experts.[7] In addition, the technical design of the way in which communications travel is such as to make it difficult or impossible in practice to distinguish between communications along nationality/location lines. This presents additional opportunities for so-called 'incidental collection', whereby domestic communications are intercepted using the procedural and oversight safeguards applicable to foreign/overseas communications. For these reasons alone, continued differential treatment of individuals based on the nationality/ nature of digital communications is unjustifiable. Consequently, this chapter supported the contention that all national surveillance laws legislating for foreign data acquisition ought to adopt the same standards, safeguards and oversight mechanisms – namely those compliant with human rights obligations for domestic surveillance.

Chapter 4 then discussed the related issue of the ambit of treaty protection in the context of states' extraterritorial surveillance. Since at present, it seems that online privacy is not an established customary law rule and no specific international law treaty regulating cyber surveillance exists, the issue of whether foreigners who are not located within the territory of the intercepting state can bring a claim based on a specific human rights treaty has proved particularly vexatious. This is because some nations (principally the US) have traditionally read their human rights obligations restrictively. Applying a literal approach to

---

[6]     *Centrum För Rättvisa v Sweden* App no 35252/08 (19 June 2018) ('*Centrum För Rättvisa*').
[7]     See, for example, Office of the UN High Commissioner for Human Rights, 'The Right to Privacy in the Digital Age. Report of the United Nations High Commissioner for Human Rights' (30 June 2014) UN Doc A/HRC/27/37; see also Michelle Cayford and Wolter Pieters, 'The Effectiveness of Surveillance Technology: What Intelligence Officials Are Saying' (2018) 34(2) *The Information Society* 88–103.

the interpretation of the ICCPR's jurisdictional clause, the US has maintained that in order to rely on the provisions of this treaty, an individual has to be both within that state's territory and subject to its jurisdiction. This is a difficult requirement to satisfy when applied in the context of that country's mass surveillance pursuant to Section 702 of the Foreign Intelligence Surveillance Act 1978 (FISA) (as amended) and Executive Order 12333. The more expansive view – namely that an individual benefits from the treaty's protection when he or she is either within a state's territory or subject to its jurisdiction – has been accepted by most UN treaty bodies and is also considered as applicable in the cyber domain. It follows that although jurisdiction is primarily territorial, states will be accountable for their human rights violations if it is shown that an individual was within the effective control of the state concerned (on the basis of either the spatial or the personal model). That this device is not suitable to apply in the context of the surveillance of digital communications has been recognized by the UN human rights mandate holders and intensely debated in academia. Although the courts have not yet directly arrived at an appropriate test, the 'control over individuals' rights' concept seems to have gained some traction. According to this approach, a state may be held accountable for its human rights violations in respect of all persons over whose rights it exercises power or effective control. To this end, two judicial pronouncements are of note which might influence future international jurisprudence on this point: the first is the dictum of the German Constitutional Court in the 2020 *1 B v R*[8] case; while the second is the Inter-American Court of Human Rights' (IACtHR) 2018 *Advisory Opinion on the Environment and Human Rights*[9]. Thus, in *1 B v R* the German Constitutional Court held that that country's state services are bound by the provisions of its Constitution to respect the right to privacy when conducting communications surveillance in relation not only to their own nationals, but also to foreigners in other countries, irrespective of whether the surveillance is conducted from within Germany or from abroad. The IACtHR's *Advisory Opinion on the Environment and Human Rights* represents a pioneering new method of holding states accountable for human rights violations in the context of transboundary pollution of the environment that has a detrimental impact on individuals' human rights outside of the polluting state's territory. The IACtHR conceived of the term 'jurisdiction' to mean any situation in which a state exercises authority over a person or subjects a person

---

[8]   *1 B v R 2835/17* (Judgment 19 May 2020) ('*1 B v R*').
[9]   *State Obligations in Relation to the Environment in the Context of the Protection and Guarantee of the Rights to Life and to Personal Integrity: Interpretation and Scope of Articles 1(1) and 2 of the American Convention on Human Rights,* Advisory Opinion OC-23/17 Inter-American Court of Human Rights (15 November 2017) ('*Advisory Opinion on the Environment and Human Rights*').

to its 'effective control', whether within or outside of its territory. Thus articulated, this conceptualization of the term aligns with the trends in the current
jurisprudence of the other international human rights courts and bodies – that
is, the test based on 'effective control over individuals' rights'. However, the
IACtHR's interpretation expands this doctrine, as it advances that a state may
be found responsible for actions or omissions emanating from its territory,
which it was under a duty to prevent, when these cause a cross-border effect,
impacting adversely on the human rights of individuals located abroad. The
chapter applied this principle by analogy to states' mass cyber surveillance. It
proposed that legal responsibility might be triggered when a state has effective
control over the activities in question conducted from its territory – namely
the mass interception and collection of data – that cause an unjustifiable interference with the right to privacy of communications of individuals outside its
borders and, being in a position to prevent such an interference, fails to do so.

Despite the fact that the human rights courts have not yet directly and in
detail examined jurisdictional clauses in light of extraterritorial cyber surveillance, numerous cases concerning state surveillance legislation have been
reviewed by the Human Rights Committee (HRC), together with a number of
claims brought before the European Courts (the ECtHR and the Court of Justice
of the European Union (CJEU)) – the latter analysing the right to privacy and
data protection in the context of the mass surveillance programs of the NSA
and GCHQ, data retention and data transfers from the EU to third countries.
All judicial organs adopt a similar stance to ascertaining whether a violation of
privacy rights has occurred. This is based on a two-stage test, where it is first
considered whether a particular state measure amounts to an interference; if
so, the second aspect of the Courts' enquiry is whether that interference can be
justified. Chapter 5 addressed the first part of this equation. Having outlined
a variety of interests that are subsumed within the right to privacy protected
under treaty law, it focused on the meaning of 'interference' with the privacy
of digital communications. The chapter identified that all the international
courts and bodies under review agree that interference with the protected right
occurs where legislation exists that allows for secret surveillance measures and
where data is intercepted and retained. However, the chapter also considered
the uncertainties pertaining to numerous key areas relating to the meaning of
'interference', namely: (1) the operation of mass surveillance programs *per se*;
(2) the collection of metadata; (3) intelligence-sharing arrangements; and (4)
the capture of data without it first being analysed, by a human or a machine.
Thus, all the examined human rights courts and mandate holders agree that the
collection of metadata as well as the content of communications is regarded
in law as an interference. Furthermore, intelligence-sharing arrangements also
seem to fall within a spectrum of activities that may amount to the said intrusion. For this practice not to amount to a violation of privacy rights, it must

be justified, meaning that it has to be conducted on the basis of the prescribed legal grounds; the data must be collected for a legitimate aim and not used for other purposes; and the practice must be necessary and proportionate. As to whether interference with privacy occurs when the data is collected or when it is examined, the HRC and the European Courts hold the former view – interference takes place irrespective of whether the collected data is analysed. This perspective is, however, at variance with that expressed by the US, the UK and in the *Tallinn Manual 2.0*[10] on this matter. The Manual's experts considered a scenario in which a state merely collects communications without them being scrutinized by a human, a machine or a combination of both. The majority view is that the right to privacy is not implicated until such time as the state accesses the content of communications or processes personal data found in them.[11] This thus suggests that states' acquisition of vast troves of data could potentially have no legal restraints and constitute interference only further along the intelligence cycle. This view, when compared with the stance taken by the relevant international human rights institutions on the issue, is at the very least controversial.

An issue closely related to this is that of legal standing. In accordance with the ECtHR jurisprudence, the mere existence of secret surveillance legislation allows the Court to review its compatibility with the ECHR standards – a principle reiterated in *Zakharov v Russia*.[12] This means that the ECtHR will hear an allegation of a violation of Article 8 where an individual shows a likelihood of being affected by the measure in question. In other words, he or she need not produce evidence of being actually subjected to surveillance, but may bring the case for the Court's consideration *in abstracto*. The task of the Court is then to determine whether the manner of the application of the law and practice in question to the applicant gave raise to violation of the Convention's rights. This approach contrasts with that taken by the US courts and in the *Tallinn Manual 2.0* outlined above, where it seems that interference occurs only at the point of the collected data being analysed. Such an interpretation means that the victim of surveillance will be denied the right to bring a claim, unless he or she can demonstrate both that he or she was its target and that the data gathered was in fact analysed. This varied understanding of 'interference', together with the disparity of legal thresholds in relation to legal standing, provides differing standards pertaining to the availability of effective remedies, with the ECtHR

---

[10]   Michael N Schmitt (ed), *Tallinn Manual 2.0 on the International Law Applicable to Cyber Operations* (Cambridge University Press, 2017) ('*Tallinn Manual 2.0*').
[11]   *Ibid*, Rule 35 para 9, 190.
[12]   *Roman Zakharov v Russia* [GC] App no 47143/06 (4 December 2015).

adopting a more permissive attitude to the question of the 'victim status'.[13] Finally, as for the question of whether the operation of mass surveillance programs amounts to a violation of the right to privacy, the Courts' views are also polarized. Thus, both the ECtHR and the German Constitutional Court, in the cases specifically concerning extraterritorial state surveillance,[14] confirmed that having such programs in place/conducting strategic surveillance does not *per se* amount to a violation of privacy. Quite the contrary, the view they expressed is that these surveillance tools serve a legitimate aim and are within states' margin of discretion. However, they may constitute an interference, which can amount to an infringement of the right to privacy if that interference is not justified (ie, if it does not fulfil the minimum procedural requirements set out in *Weber v Germany*). This approach seems to conflict with that adopted at the UN level and by both the CJEU and the IACtHR, which maintain an altogether higher standard, holding that mass surveillance compromises the very essence of the right to respect for private life, as it is inherently disproportionate.

Having discussed the meaning of 'interference' with the privacy of digital communications, Chapter 6 then engaged with the issue of whether the use of mass surveillance programs can be justified by applying the test adopted by all three judicial organs – the HRC, the ECtHR and the IACtHR. Accordingly, a state will not be held liable for interference with the right to privacy where the surveillance: (1) is in accordance with the law; (2) pursues a legitimate aim; and (3) is necessary and proportionate to achieving that aim. To satisfy the first criterion, the surveillance has to be conducted pursuant to a domestic legal basis, which must be accessible, clear and foreseeable to the public. Although governments routinely engage in domestic and extraterritorial cyber surveillance, only the former tends to be conducted pursuant to a legal framework, which (apart from in a handful of exceptions) is often outdated; while the basis for conducting foreign surveillance is frequently secretive and unclear (a case in point is the US Executive Order 12333). Furthermore, the benchmark of 'in accordance with the law' requires that the laws be foreseeable – that is, that they comport a degree of predictability in relation to when governments may resort to surveillance. The ECtHR jurisprudence has long recognized that states do have a degree of discretion in this regard, but that this must not be expressed in a way that confers unfettered power on the executive. Consequently, the Court devised six minimum standards (the *Weber* criteria)

---

[13]    CoE, European Convention for the Protection of Human Rights and Fundamental Freedoms amended by Protocols Nos 11 and 14 (4 November 1950) (ECHR) Art 34; *Zakharov ibid*, *Big Brother Watch* (n 5).

[14]    *1 B v R* (n 8); *Centrum För Rättvisa* (n 6); *Big Brother Watch* (n 5).

that surveillance laws must meet to be compatible with Article 8 of the ECHR. The ECtHR has further enhanced these requirements, and in *Zakharov v Russia* introduced an additional safeguard of 'reasonable suspicion' applicable to domestic bulk surveillance. As a result, any organization authorizing the interception of domestic communications must verify that a sufficient factual indication exists that a person or a group that is to be placed under surveillance is suspected of involvement in conduct that endangers national security. However, the same requirement does not pertain to bulk interception of foreign communications as the ECtHR in *Big Brother Watch* did not consider this to be a relevant criterion. Consequently (at least until the appeal judgment is delivered by the Grant Chamber), the legal benchmark appears to have been bifurcated. To this end, according to the rules relating to domestic surveillance, the authorizing body must satisfy the 'reasonable suspicion' test, together with the *Weber* criteria. By contrast, in cases pertaining to the bulk interception of foreign communications, the authorization may be issued provided the *Weber* conditions alone have been met. This approach does not seem to align easily with that of the UN and the inter-American human rights bodies, which view such differentiation in standards as nothing short of incompatible with the principle of non-discrimination and equal treatment set out in Article 26 of the ICCPR. To this end, the operation of mass surveillance programs to intercept communications in other jurisdiction lacks the necessary degree of accessibility and foreseeability, as foreigners located abroad simply do not know that they might be subject to foreign interception. Having highlighted this disparity, the chapter then discussed the second ground for justifying the interference with the right to privacy – that is, legitimate aim. It concluded that although this may not have caused much of an issue for the ECtHR, as in both the *Big Brother Watch* and *Centrum För Rattvisa* decisions the Court recognized that bulk interception is a valuable means to achieve the legitimate aim of fighting terrorism or serious crime, this is not the case for the HRC and the IACtHR. Both of these adjudicating bodies hold that the justification of ubiquitous surveillance on a broad 'national security' basis opens up the possibility for abuse and therefore have called on states to ensure a closer adjustment between the use of surveillance powers and the needs that they are meant to protect – that is, the surveillance must be tailored to a specific legitimate aim.

Equally split is the opinion of the UN treaty bodies/the IACtHR/the CJEU and that of the ECtHR when it comes to assessing the third and final part of the test – that is, the necessity and proportionality of mass surveillance. Thus, while the Office of the High Commissioner on Human Rights considers that bulk surveillance programs may be deemed arbitrary for being neither necessary nor proportionate (on account of the sheer volume of collected and retained data), the ECtHR has a different view. First, the Court recognized that the operation of such programs falls within states' discretion. Second, it held that their use is not automatically disproportionate, as it represents a valuable means of fighting global terrorism and cross-border crime; while the alternative methods to bulk interception, including targeted surveillance and the use of human sources, are insufficient substitutes for bulk powers. This is in sharp contrast with the approach of other judicial organs, such as the CJEU, who have also been confronted with this issue in such cases as *Schrems I*[15] and *Schrems II*.[16] In the latter case, the Court invalidated the Privacy Shield Framework as a means of conducting private data transfers between the US and the EU, having considered US surveillance pursuant to Section 702 of the FISA, Executive Order 12333 and Presidential Policy Directive-28. Among other considerations, the CJEU based the annulment of the scheme on the finding that the US's mass processing of EU citizens' personal data violates the right to privacy and data protection under the EU Charter, as the powers conferred by Section 702 of the FISA do not meet the requirements of proportionality, being practically limitless. Having said that, following the CJEU decision in the four joined cases of *La Quadrature du Net and Privacy International*,[17] the CJEU may be signalling the closing of a conceptual gap between its own jurisprudence and that of the ECtHR. This is because in those cases, the Court confirmed that in exceptional circumstances, EU member states facing a serious threat to national security that is genuine and present or foreseeable may derogate from the obligation to ensure the confidentiality of communications data by requiring through legislation its general and indiscriminate retention for a limited period.

The post-Snowden enthusiasm for curtailing mass cyber surveillance has significantly subsided since the initial disclosures in 2013, leaving the issue 'swept under the carpet', with states exhibiting little willingness to establish internationally binding rules to regulate these practices. This book has shown that there are conflicting global standards pertaining to the legality of mass cyber surveillance in the jurisprudence of the leading human rights courts and bodies, although the approach of the ECtHR and the CJEU may begin to converge. Having said that, a number of unanswered questions remain, including: (1) how exactly are states' obligations triggered when conducting foreign surveillance? (2) What amounts to interference with privacy in the digital age? (3) Is mass surveillance unlawful *per se* or it is fundamentally compatible with

---

[15]   C-362/14 *Maximilian Schrems v Data Protection Commissioner* [2015] ECJ para 87 ('*Schrems I*').
[16]   C-311/18 *Data Protection Commissioner v Facebook Ireland and Maximilian Schrems* [2020] ECJ para 160 ('*Schrems II*').
[17]   C-623-17 *Privacy International*, C-511/18 *La Quadrature du Net and Others*, C-512/18 *French Data Network and Others* and C-520/18 *Ordre des Barreaux Francophones et Germanophone and Others* (6 October 2020).

human rights treaties and as such, may be lawfully conducted if it meets the required procedures? (4) If so, what are these procedures? It therefore comes as no surprise that in 2018, the UN Special Rapporteur for the right to privacy, Professor Cannataci, proposed a Draft Legal Instrument on Government-Led Surveillance and Privacy to help states and the multi-stakeholder community shaping the Internet to protect, respect and promote human dignity. The Legal Instrument was one of the options under consideration for the international law regulation of mass cyber surveillance in Chapter 7. The motivation behind putting this document forward was the recognition that the global impact and constantly evolving nature of surveillance technologies demand specific measures, general guidance being no longer sufficient. Consequently, the protection of human rights by states in the digital age must be stipulated in a more detailed and comprehensive way. The Legal Instrument thus potentially represents a unique and innovative draft treaty specifically on governmental surveillance, which could assist in 'establishing safeguards without borders and effective legal remedies across borders'.[18] It sets out in detail basic requirements for these practices, making no distinction between domestic and foreign surveillance, thus stipulating that the requirement of 'reasonable suspicion' and the necessity/proportionality criteria are equally applicable in both scenarios. Among its other features are a mechanism for transborder access to personal data via International Data Access Warrants and the right to notification. However, as with the previous attempt at treaty making for the regulation of state intelligence activities (that is, the Council of Europe non-spy Intelligence Codex), this proposal was met with a frosty reception from a number of governments, testifying to the fact that any articulation of legally binding standards is futile unless it secures their interest and political support. This has historically been and remains lacking. Having provided a thumbnail sketch pertaining to the well-entrenched rivalries of the cyber powers over the governance of cyberspace in the context of cyber security, the chapter discussed the reasons as to why the efforts to achieve a treaty to regulate the offensive use of cyber technologies have been equally protracted. Furthermore, it accentuated the fact that the protection of human rights, including individuals' privacy, has not played a significant role within that discourse. It also highlighted the scepticism as to the need for such a treaty. To this end, some states – including the US and Israel[19] – remain cautious when it comes

---

[18] Office of the High Commissioner for Human Rights, UN Special Rapporteur on the Right to Privacy, 'Draft Legal Instrument on Government-led Surveillance and Privacy' (10 January 2018), Introduction ('Legal Instrument').

[19] See The White House, *International Strategy for Cyberspace: Prosperity, Security and Openness in a Networked World* (2011) 9; Roy Schöndorf, 'Israel's Perspective on Key Legal and Practical Issues Concerning the Application of International Law

to the development of additional rules regulating cyber operations; a view shared by some scholars,[20] who doubt the urgent necessity for and the utility of such an instrument, as the existing rules of *jus at bellum* and *jus in bello* are adequate to meet the challenges to international peace and security posed by such activities. The same cannot, however, be said of cyber surveillance and its impact on human rights. Having said that, the need for such a legal framework does not mean that states will adopt it. Based on their behavioural patterns, states' consistent rejection of treaties regulating intelligence operations can be explained on the basis of, *inter alia*: (1) the fact that they regard cyber surveillance as a key component in their decision making in international relations; (2) their unwillingness to expose information relating to their technical capabilities; and (3) the fact that such an instrument could potentially stifle states' future use of the technologies of surveillance and thus hinder the early detection of cyber attacks, including on critical infrastructure.

Notwithstanding the lack of interest in a legally binding instrument for cyber operations, the international community did reach a broad-brush agreement that international law, including the UN Charter, applies in cyberspace. This was followed by the process of closer collaboration through a sequence of United Nations Group of Government Experts on Developments in the Field of Information and Telecommunications in the Context of International Security (UN GGE) consultations, with the main objectives of not only agreeing how international law applies to the use of ICT, but also identifying a non-legally binding set of norms for responsible state behaviour and confidence-building measures. In particular, the GGE 2015 consensus report resulted in 11 recommendations, including Recommendation 13(e), urging states to respect

---

to Cyber Operations', transcript of the Keynote Speech Delivered by Israeli Deputy Attorney General (International Law), Dr Roy Schöndorf on 8 December 2020 at the US Naval War College's Event on 'Disruptive Technologies and International Law' (9 December 2020), www.ejiltalk.org/israels-perspective-on-key-legal-and-practical -issues-concerning-the-application-of-international-law-to-cyber-operations/. Israel's position is that an 'extra layer of caution must be exercised in determining how exactly international law rules apply to cyber operations, and in evaluating whether and how additional rules should be developed'; see also UN Open-Ended Working Group on Developments in the Field of Information and Telecommunications in the Context of International Security (OEWG), 'Second "Pre-Draft" of the Report of the OEWG on Developments in the Field of Information and Telecommunications in the Context of International Security' (27 May 2020) ('OEWG Revised Pre-Draft Report'), https:// front.un-arm.org/wp-content/uploads/2020/05/200527-oewg-ict-revised-pre-draft.pdf. The consensus presented in the report is that existing international law, complemented by the voluntary non-legally binding norms, is currently sufficient to address states' use of ICT – see OEWG Revised Pre-Draft Report, para 31, 5.

  [20]   See Marco Roscini, *Cyber Operations and the Use of Force in International Law* (Oxford University Press, 2014) 287.

the standards set out in Human Rights Council Resolutions 20/8 and 26/13 on the promotion, protection and enjoyment of human rights on the Internet and UNGA Resolutions 68/167 and 69/166 on the right to privacy in the digital age. However, any hopes for further elaboration as to exactly how Recommendation 13(e) and the remaining norms are to be applied to states' use of ICT were soon dashed when in 2017 the GGE, consisting of 25 government experts, failed to come to an agreement. This resulted in the splitting of the process, with Russia and like-minded states coalescing within the newly established Open-Ended Working Group on Developments in ICTs in the Context of International Security. The US and its allies have continued with the GGE agenda by establishing a new group to study norms, confidence-building measures and how international law applies to cyberspace. It would perhaps not be an overstatement to venture that this splintering may result in two rival diplomatic efforts within the UN. For the time being, therefore, the conclusion that must be reached is that the prospect of putting into place an international or regional set of legally binding standards to regulate state surveillance is elusive. However, states have agreed and laid down non-legally binding norms for responsible behaviour, taking into account their human rights obligations in the use of ICT, which in time may crystallize to form a set of customary international law rules, provided the necessary requirements are met. Additionally, a number of bilateral arrangements have been undertaken to restrain economic cyber espionage, including the US-China 2015 accord pertaining to the theft of intellectual property. Similarly, the G7 has issued a political statement calling on states not to conduct or support ICT-enabled cyber economic espionage. Although these are non-legally binding pronouncements, they do contribute towards the international community's greater cooperation in this sphere.

This book began by positioning the discussion within the security/privacy trade-off. It seems appropriate to end its deliberations on this note by quoting the observations of the UN Legal Instrument's drafters, who emphasized the need for fundamental rights to be promoted in the context of states' intelligence gathering operations through cyber means observing that: 'rather than a trade-off between rights, ways should be sought to strengthen them collectively and to ultimately promote human dignity. Hence, it is necessary to provide both privacy and security rather than one or the other.'[21]

The mass surveillance of digital communications is a reality. The question for human rights defenders and privacy advocates is no longer whether this is lawful *per se*, but how states are to conduct it to discharge their human rights obligations, in particular in relation to privacy protection. The private sector's insatiable appetite for data, facilitated by the use of the Internet of Things, arti-

---

[21]   Legal Instrument (n 18) Art 1, Commentary para 2.

ficial intelligence, Big Data analytics and post quantum cryptography, coupled with governments' continued interception and collection of vast quantities of communications, means that for future generations, the right to privacy will inevitably take on an entirely different meaning to that ascribed to it by the founding fathers of the International Bill of Rights. Chapter 1 of this book framed these security-privacy-surveillance issues as a paradox and proposed that it be addressed in terms of cost-benefit analysis. For democratic societies, whose leaders will continue to be voter dependent, the question in conducting this examination must be: how much surveillance is enough to be of benefit to them, their nation and their position within the international arena, and at what cost?

# Index